20ᵗʰ CENTURY DESIGN

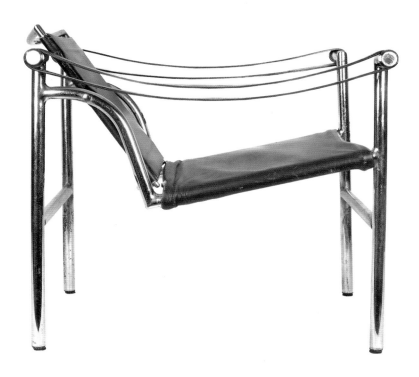

20TH CENTURY DESIGN

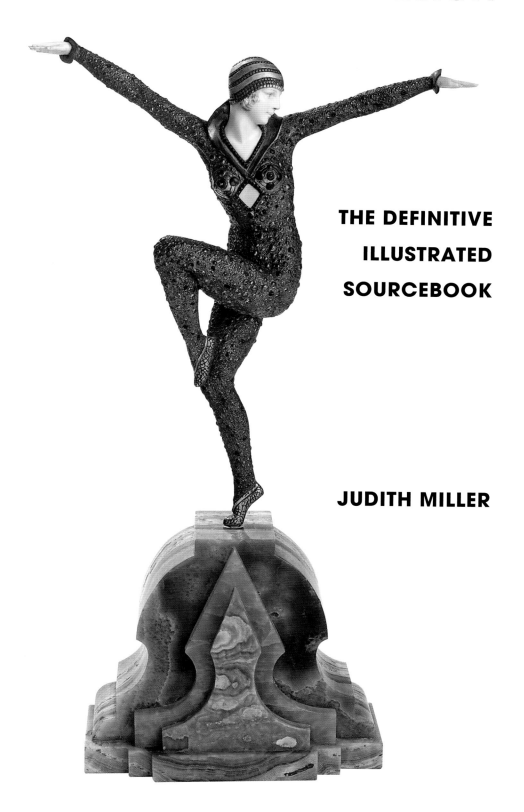

THE DEFINITIVE
ILLUSTRATED
SOURCEBOOK

JUDITH MILLER

MILLER'S

MILLER'S 20TH CENTURY DESIGN
by Judith Miller

First published in Great Britain in 2009 by Miller's
a division of Mitchell Beazley,
imprints of Octopus Publishing Group Ltd,
2-4 Heron Quays, London, E14 4JP.
An Hachette Livre Company
www.millersonline.com

Distributed in the U.S. and Canada by Octopus Books USA:
c/o Hachette Book Group USA,
237 Park Avenue, New York, NY 10017
www.octopusbooksusa.com

ISBN 978 1 84533 516 8

A CIP record of this book is available from the British Library.

Set in Sabon and Univers
Printed and bound in China by Toppan Printing Company
Colour reproduction by United Graphics Pte Ltd, Singapore

Publishing Manager: Julie Brooke
Design: Tim Foster
Editor: Davida Saunders
Copy Editor: Alison Wormleighton
Digital Asset Co-ordinator: Katy Armstrong
Picture Research Manager: Giulia Hetherington
Picture Researcher: Maria Gibbs
Index: Isobel McLean
Production Manager: Lucy Carter

Value codes
Throughout this book the value codes used at the end of each caption
correspond to the approximate value of the item. These are broad price
ranges and should only be seen as a guide to the value of the piece, as
prices for antiques vary depending on the condition of the item, geographical location, and market trends.

A	under $75	S	$15,000-20,000
B	$75-150	T	$20,000-25,000
C	$150-300	U	$25,000-30,000
D	$300-450	V	$30,000-35,000
E	$450-600	W	$30,000-45,000
F	$600-750	X	$45,000-60,000
G	$750-1,000	Y	$60,000-75,000
H	$1,000-1,500	Z	$75,000-90,000
I	$1,500-2,000	AA	$90,000-100,000
J	$2,000-3,000	BB	$100,000-120,000
K	$3,000-4,500	CC	$120,000-135,000
L	$4,500-6,000	DD	$135,000-150,000
M	$6,000-7,500	EE	$150,000-225,000
N	$7,500-9,000	FF	$225,000-300,000
O	$9,000-10,500	GG	$300,000-375,000
P	$10,500-12,000	HH	$375,000-450,000
Q	$12,000-13,500	II	$450,000 and over
R	$13,500-15,000	NPA	No Price available

Contents

ART DECO

MID CENTURY MODERNISM

POSTMODERNISM TO CONTEMPORARY

Foreword

The designers of the 20th century fervently believed that design was an instrument for improving the quality of man's life. He has been regarded as a saviour by some, by others as a revolutionary subversive. The designer has also had to re-define his own role in society, most vitally in his relationship with the machine. It is against this background that my own fascination with the development of design in the 20th century, encompassing some of the biggest questions we face, has become an over-riding passion.

The roots of 20th century design are firmly lodged in the industrial chaos of the 19th century. The flurry of revivalist styles that dominated the design of the mid to late 19th century lost all sense of design cohesiveness. Design lost out to the intoxicating clash of styles – often represented on the same piece. All encouraged by soulless machine-made production.

It was against this background that the voices of William Morris and John Ruskin resonated for a return to the golden age when artist-craftsmen created furnishings that were handcrafted with honest appreciation of the natural qualities of the materials. It was a romantic notion of a medieval period as a golden era of honest craftsmanship which was appreciated by intellectuals and designers. Morris's Arts and Crafts battle cry "Have nothing in your houses that you do not know to be useful or believe to be beautiful" had a resonance with people who felt sated with over-decoration. Utility was fundamental to the design of everything from furniture to ceramics, from textiles to silver. Interiors had to be carefully designed so that every element made up a harmonious whole. Although the British movement had at its centre a largely socialist philosophy, due to the insistence of the rejection of the machine and the importance of the individual, the objects produced were expensive and the movement was regarded as elitist. In America, with designers such as Elbert Hubbard and Gustav Stickley and others, the concept was further developed by the acceptance of the machine as subservient to the designer – the designer had to forge an alliance with the machine. This allowed the movement to reach a much wider audience. Ceramics, in particular, reached a large and receptive public.

Functionalism dominated the early years of the 20th century in many countries. Radical writings fanned the first shoots of the modern movement. In 1905, in their seminal work "The Work-Programme of the Wiener Werkstatte", Josef Hoffmann and Koloman Moser wrote "We wish to create an inner relationship linking public, designer and worker and we want to produce good and simple articles of everyday use. Our guiding principle is function, utility our first condition, and our strength must lie in good proportions and the proper treatment of material".

After World War One Walter Gropius and his fellow luminaries in institutions including the Bauhaus, integrated honest design with

An Axel Salto for Royal Copenhagen hemispherical bowl, with lobes, covered in a tortoiseshell glaze.
1935 2.25in (14.5cm) high L

A design for a "modern" house by Joseph Maria Olbrich from an album dated 1901-14. A founder of the Vienna Secession he also established the artists' colony at Darmstadt in Germany.
19.25in (49.5cm) high M

A 'Lattenstuhl TI 1A' chair, designed by Marcel Breuer, for Bauhaus Weimar.
1924 37.25in (94.5cm) high V

new industrial means of production. The 'enfant terrible' of French design was the architect Charles Edouard Jeanneret, known as Le Corbusier. His idea that 'The house was a machine for living in' upset 1920s French society's sensibilities and appreciation of luxury.

At the same time the Art Deco style influenced every area of design from trains, liners and cars, skyscrapers and cinemas, silverware and jewelry, make-up and fashion, furniture and domestic appliances, posters and book design. From the opening of Tutankhamun's tomb, to the music of the Jazz Age, to the influence of African Art, the 1920s and 1930s revelled in 'weapons of mass communication' as these styles 'flew' round the globe. Bevis Hillier reviewing the style of the era wrote in 1968 that Art Deco was "an assertively modern style… a Classical style in that like Neoclassicism but unlike Rococo or Art Nouveau, it ran to symmetry rather than asymmetry, and to the rectilinear rather than the curvilinear: it responds to the demands of the machine and of new materials…(and) the requirements of mass production".

After World War Two there was a slow economic recovery, particularly in Europe. But a new breed of designer was once again excited by the possibilities of an enthusiastic consumer class and new materials available. Designers such as Charles and Ray Eames in the United States said their mission was "getting the most of the best to the greatest number of people for the least amount of money". It was fully realized that the new designers encouraged onto the Italian glass-making island of Murano had to have a good working relationship with the glass blower, just as the architect or furniture designer had to work with the engineer. The

A Goldscheider pottery Art Deco figure. c1930 9in (22.5cm) high G

design has to work. And the finished item had to be perceived by the consumer as good value.

The fun and promiscuity of postmodern design was initially revitalising but can become tiresome. Poor quality factory replicas can dull our senses. And what happens when designers become celebrities and brands? The history of 20th century design tells us that a new wave of designers will challenge the computer-crazed fads. Once again they will not only innovate but will try to impose a pleasing order.

And from a personal viewpoint I feel that the fascinating twists and turns of design throughout the century can be interpreted from the words of some design luminaries; from the exponent of extreme simplicity Ludwig Mies van der Rohe's "Less is more" to the architect/engineer's Richard Buckminster Fuller's goal of "More for Less" to the postmodern visionary Robert Venturi's "Less is a Bore". The 20th century offers it all. From the late 19th century flowing curves of Art Nouveau and the romantic handcrafted designs of the Arts and Crafts movement, to the global excitement of Art Deco, to the wanton excesses of the postmodernism, the designers of the 20th century strove to invent, excite, confront, educate, stimulate, beautify. I trust this book does just that.

Judith Miller

A Maurice Calka/Leleu-Deshay rare 'Boomerang' desk of biomorphic form in orange fiberglass, its four drawers with circular recessed pulls. One of only 35 made. It was designed with a matching chair.
1969 70in (178cm) wide O

Frank Gehry for Vitra 'Little Beaver' laminated cardboard chair and ottoman. Marked with brass tag, numbered 54/100.
1987 Chair 33in (85cm) wide M

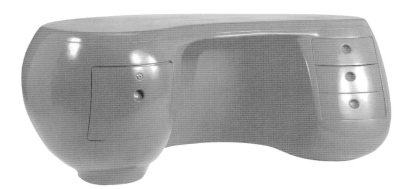

"All recognized styles are more or less discredited by the sad misuse which they have undergone at the hands of our own generation and the preceeding one ... The old styles simply do not apply to us, and we have to disregard them." Russell Sturgis

The Birth of Modernism

The imposing entrance to the atelier of the Darmstadt Artists´ Colony in Germany is flanked by Ludwig Habich´s sculptures of Adam and Eve. Two bronze Victory goddesses by Rudolf Bosselt are suspended above the door and harmonize with Joseph Maria Olbrich´s golden wall decorations. The building, called the Ernst-Ludwig-Haus, was designed by Olbrich, and was used by the colony from 1899 to 1914. Today it is a museum.

The Birth of Modernism

From about the mid-19th century in the West, historical revival styles were the height of fashion in furniture and the decorative arts. Period designs from Classical antiquity to late 18th-century Neo-classicism were reinvented and sometimes combined in an eclectic expression of nostalgia for bygone ages. Often they were mass-produced for the burgeoning middle-class market using newly pioneered methods. This resulted in an excess of ornament, which sacrificed purity of style for virtuosic statements of grandeur and conservative, morally grounded principles. For the newly rich, it satisfied the longing for legitimacy that the style patrons of old enjoyed, without the bourgeoisie having to risk too much in the name of experimentation and audacity.

SEEDS OF CHANGE

Toward the latter part of the century, however, newly creative forces were emerging, which looked forward again to innovation and originality in design. This was partly in response to a growing weariness with seemingly endless reworkings of the past in countless decorative permutations. Some prominent personalities appeared at the forefront of these movements. They responded to a new and fast-developing age, in which old preconceptions were being swept away and new ideas promulgated ever more quickly.

Cataclysmic events affecting Europe such as the Crimean War and economic disruption were leading many to question the old order. New scientific discoveries and technological advances increasingly contributed to an interest in looking forward. The tendency to dwell in the past was seen as being rooted in outmoded and invalid ideology. By the end of the 19th century,

19TH CENTURY PORCELAIN

This porcelain ewer, created at the Meissen factory in the late 19th century, was based on a design by 18th-century Meissen modeller J.J. Kändler, and harked back to the factory's Baroque origins. The shape of the ewer is graceful and elegant, with a fragile beauty. The overall effect, however, is severely compromised by the excessive overlaid decoration, which almost obscures the elegant form. The riot of painted color further detracts from the underlying simple aesthetics of the piece. Three-dimensional winged putti crawl over the handle and body, along with Neptune and sea creatures, and thick marine motifs are plastered around the base in a 19th-century interpretation of the Meissen factory's traditional virtues of lightness and symmetry.

A large late 19th century Meissen porcelain maritime ewer, with shell-form spout.
26in (66cm) high O

the developed Western world was truly witnessing the birth of modernism, not only in social and technological terms, but reflected, and often heralded, by achievement in the arts.

The result was the germination of distinct artistic movements in Europe and North America. In Britain and the United States, the Arts and Crafts movement advocated the rejection of mass production and revivalism, and a return to simplicity and craftsmanship. On the Continent, centers such as Vienna and Darmstadt saw the birth of national schools of thought driving toward new artistic styles. These movements evolved into what we today call modernism, and eventually into Art Deco, the first truly international and democratic style.

Peruvian designs inspired Christopher Dresser to design a bridge-spouted earthenware pitcher with streaked and dribbled glaze for Ault and Co.
c1893 NPA

TIMELINE

1842 German-Austrian Michael Thonet patents his method for steam-bending wood.

1876 Christopher Dresser visits Japan and is inspired by the arts and crafts he sees there.

1897 Viennese Secession founded by a group of artists including Joseph Maria Olbrich, Josef Hoffmann, Koloman Moser, and Gustav Klimt.

1899 Darmstadt Artists Colony founded by Ernst Ludwig, Grand Duke of Hesse on the lines of a concept developed by the Austrian architect and designer Josef Maria Olbrich.

1900 Charles Rennie Mackintosh and the Glasgow Four exhibit at the Viennese Secession exhibition to much acclaim.

CHRISTOPHER DRESSER

The great centers of industry produced innovators in the arts such as the Glaswegian, Christopher Dresser, Britain's first independent industrial designer. A botanist, he was inspired by plants and their structures, which he believed to be geometrically balanced.

Dresser stressed the importance of abstracting the essence of design to its most basic linear form, but as a true Victorian he also took inspiration from a wide range of sources. He was influenced by foreign aesthetics, such as those from the civilizations of Egypt, Persia, Mexico and Morocco. However, the most powerful influence on his work came from Japan, where he traveled in 1876–7. He was a major contributor to the Aesthetic movement which advocated art for art's sake.

Influential in both Britain and the United States, Dresser's books provided instruction and examples for students and designers on topics such as color theory, ornamentation, and interior decorating. He established principles based on truth, beauty, and power: truth criticizing the imitation of materials, beauty describing a sense of timeless perfection in design, and power implying strength, energy, and force in ornament, achieved through knowledge. Believing that truth was founded in science and that art reflected beauty, he pursued a radically scientific approach to art and design.

CHARLES ROHLFS

In the United States, the cabinet-maker and designer Charles Rohlfs specialized in elaborately pierced and carved oak furniture in a new take on the Gothic style. In 1901 he established a small workshop in Buffalo, New York, where he created custom-built solid oak pieces inspired by the English Arts and Crafts style, with exposed joinery and stylized abstract ornament.

His unusual designs combine a variety of influences – Gothic, Moorish, and Scandinavian among them – yet they remain decidedly unique. Of solid construction in oak with a rich, dark patina, his one-of-a-kind pieces are typically elongated and are enriched by hand-carved fretwork, Gothic ornament, and sinuous, Art Nouveau-inspired motifs. Elaborate cut-out designs featuring Gothic lettering and brass embellishments such as nail heads are recurring decorative hallmarks. He described his style as having "the spirit of today blended with the poetry of the medieval ages".

Rohlfs and Dresser attracted international admirers. Designers such as William Morris and Louis Comfort Tiffany were influenced by Dresser, while Rohlfs was an inspiration in particular for Gustav Stickley. These design reformers spread their ideas through their publications and lectures; their works spoke for themselves.

CHARLES ROHLFS HALL CHAIR

This oak hall chair is a complete departure from the mass-produced and cluttered furniture of the period. Individually crafted, it is a fascinating study in simplicity of line reduced to bare essentials, punctuated by a minimal cutout and some curving lines in the chair back. While looking far back to Celtic/Nordic motifs, it also looks ahead to further refinements in functionality, foreshadowing the works of Frank Lloyd Wright. Iconic for the period in its rejection of excess and overstatement, it is an early and true expression of modernism.

The chair back is of very simple form. The plain, square uprights and pierced panel are the only decoration.

Geometrically cut brackets reinforce the uprights where they meet the saddle seat. The design is echoed in the shape of the apron of the chair.

The uprights extend below the seat to meet the stretcher.

The plain square section legs add to the simplicity of the design.

Charles Rohlfs hall chair. 1901 54.75in (139cm) high U

1903 Wiener Werkstätte founded by Josef Hoffmann, Koloman Moser, Gustav Klimt and Otto Wagner, with the aim of bringing good design to the middle classes.

1905 Work begins on the Wiener Werkstätte's greatest achievement, the Palais Stoclet in Brussels.

1907 Landmark exhibition of Cubist paintings by Pablo Picasso and Georges Braque opens in Paris. Wiener Werkstätte begins work on the Cabaret Fledermaus.

1907 Deutscher Werkbund founded by Hermann Muthesius, Peter Behrens, Josef Maria Olbrich, and Richard Riemerschmid among others.

1909 The Italian artist Filippo Marinetti launches Futurism with the declaration "Art [...] can be nothing but violence, cruelty, and injustice."

1911 Frank Lloyd Wright completes the Robie House. Designed as "the cornerstone of modern architecture" it is to inspire an architectural revolution.

The Arts and Crafts Movement

Inspired by John Ruskin and William Morris, the Arts and Crafts movement, which emerged in England in the late 19th century, galvanized the decorative arts. The idea that everyday household objects could be beautiful and well made as well as functional touched the imagination of artists and craftsmen who lamented the Victorian taste for clutter and the proliferation of cheap, mass-produced wares.

Looking to strengthen the relationship between art and craftsmanship, William Morris and his followers turned for inspiration to the medieval guild system. The cornerstone of the Arts and Crafts ideology was the determination to bring back to life what had been sacrificed in the name of progress and industrialization – traditional, time-honored craft techniques along with the prestige and dignity of the artisan. Followers believed the increasing dependence on the machine to meet the demands of a burgeoning middle class had resulted in a decline in the quality of life.

ANTIDOTE TO VICTORIAN EXCESS

On the other hand, objects created with an eye to simplicity, good materials, and hand-craftsmanship were the perfect antidote to excess, forging a path to a pure, more authentic existence. Furniture had clear, simple lines and depended on its construction and the inherent beauty of the wood for decorative effect. Nature was a source of inspiration and motifs inspired by flowers, foliage, and animals gave shape to wall hangings, vases, and silver buckles.

The philosophy championed by William Morris made its way to the Continent, where the style was interpreted in a variety of ways. In France artists such as Léon Jallot highlighted the belief in hand-

A Morris and Company tapestry designed by John Henry Dearle, woven in wool and mohair by John Martin and William Sleath.
1892 184.5in (461cm) wide FF

craftsmanship and natural motifs, while in Austria and Germany the style developed by Richard Riemerschmid and Josef Hoffman took up the geometric outlines that were central to the designs of Ernest Gimson and Charles Rennie Mackintosh.

Across the Atlantic, Morris's visionary principles were warmly embraced and adapted to create a unique incarnation of the Arts and Crafts style. What separated the American version from its British counterpart was a willingness to remain open to the tantalizing potential proffered by the machine. Entrepreneurs in the United States included Elbert Hubbard at his Roycroft community, the Stickley family, and Charles Rohlfs. Their mission was to bring the new style within reach of the middle classes by using carefully controled methods of mass production.

Eventually the standard promoted by Morris and his disciples in England proved too costly for the very audience it sought to impress. Yet it had a profound impact, and was seminal to the development of Modernism in the decades ahead.

Naturalistic tooled and applied leaves and a feathered matte green glaze decorate a Grueby Kendrick vase by Wilhemina Post.
c1900 12in (30.5cm) high V

Dirk van Erp used traditional handtools to make table lamps such as this example, which has a hammered copper milk-can base and copper and mica shade.
c1912 24.5in (61cm) high EE

GUSTAV STICKLEY MORRIS CHAIR

Gustav Stickley's visit to Europe in 1898 convinced him that his own company should create household furniture in the Arts and Crafts style, inspired by the designs of William Morris. With its vertical side splats, through-tenon jointed stretchers, and flat arms supported at the front by short corbels – construction features that are incorporated into the design – and leather-upholstered cushions, this adjustable reclining armchair stands out as a Mission-style interpretation of an original design by Philip Webb for William Morris, c.1910.

The leather cushions add a touch of comfort to an otherwise austere design.

The rich, dark patina finish was achieved not by stain but by applying chemicals that reacted with the wood – an aging technique that is a hallmark of Stickley furniture.

Made by hand from quartered oak, the heavy, solid form and geometric lines of the chair are typical of Morris-inspired designs.

The chair has a drop-in spring seat.

A Gustav Stickley flat-arm Morris chair, no. 332. c1910 32in (81.5cm) wide R

Decoration is provided by the vertical side splats, through-tenon jointed stretchers, and the short corbels which support the arms at the front.

THE BIRTH OF MODERNISM

The Vienna Secession and Charles Rennie Mackintosh

As the sinuous and flamboyant form of Art Nouveau that had developed in France and Belgium began to lose its luster, it was the simple geometric interpretation of the style created by designers from Germany, Austria, and Scotland that endured, challenging the whims of fashion and laying the foundations for Art Deco and modernism.

The Arts and Crafts style that flourished in the decorative arts across Britain in the late 19th century was equaled by an influential design movement based in Glasgow and pioneered by the visionary architect and prize-winning designer Charles Rennie Mackintosh. Influenced by the Japanese aesthetic highlighting simple forms, natural materials, and texture, light and shadow rather than pattern and ornament, Mackintosh's designs comprised bold, geometric lines and minimal decoration. Any decorative motifs that were used were so strongly stylized they became almost abstract, such as the Glasgow rose. Mackintosh championed the idea that architecture, interior decoration, and furnishings should be practical, functional, and form a unified, cohesive whole.

Across continental Europe there was much admiration for the rectilinear style promoted by the "Glasgow Four" –

Mackintosh, his wife Margaret MacDonald, her sister Frances MacDonald, and Frances's husband Herbert MacNair, all of whom were associated with the Glasgow School of Art. The "Glasgow style" exerted enormous influence across the globe but especially found favor in Germany and Austria. The sophisticated, fresh designs captured the imagination of artisans who shared his enthusiasm for spare, streamlined shapes decorated with sharp-edged, elongated rectangles, triangles, and squares.

THE VIENNA SECESSION

In Vienna in 1897 a group of these artists and architects – including Joseph Maria Olbrich, Josef Hoffmann, Koloman Moser, and Gustav Klimt – broke away from the established arts organization, the conservative Künstlerhaus, and formed an organization they called the Wiener

Künstlerische Kostüme · Porzellane · Fotogr. Porträts · Buchgewerbe.

DEUTSCHE KUNST UND DEKORATION

VERLAG ALEX KOCH DARMSTADT

V. JAHRG. HEFT 8.   MAI 1902.   EINZELPREIS M. 2.50.

The Glasgow Four were an influence on German and Austrian designers. Margaret Macdonald Mackintosh designed this handbill poster for Deutsche Kunst und Dekoration. It features typical Glasgow School decoration including a stylized bird and flowers.
c1902 11.25in (28.5cm) high M

Pulled glass strands show the typical geometric designs of Josef Hoffmann. This vase, with "syrius optical" decoration, was made by Johann Lötz.
c1900 7.4in (18.5 cm) high O

A striped and flecked glass vase with brass rim and handles, by Antoinette Krasnik, made by Johann Lötz.
c1903 9.5in (24cm) high P

Josef Hoffmann's geometric silver basket has a clear glass insert. The arched handle echoes its circular shape.
1905 5.75in (14.5 cm) high K

Sezession, or Vienna Secession. Aiming to elevate the status of the applied arts to that of fine art, the Secession rejected the prevailing taste for historicism in favor of a fresh approach that celebrated the geometry found in the natural world.

The Secession's ideals were similar to those of some of the leading British Arts and Crafts designers as well as the Glasgow Four. More than the British themselves, they recognized that Charles Rennie Mackintosh and his followers were breathing a gust of fresh air into the home by emphasizing light and space.

POINTING THE WAY

The refinement and imagination of Mackintosh's contribution to the Scottish section of the Eighth Secessionist Exhibition in 1900 in Vienna caused a sensation and confirmed his place in the pantheon of highly influential designers working in the "New Art".

The Secessionists were inspired by Mackintosh's bold rectilinear shapes and stylized geometric motifs. As a result, they ignored the curvilinear Art Nouveau aesthetic championed in France and Belgium and instead began producing designs in linear and geometric forms that reflected the influence of the innovative Scot.

The Secessionists were to forge a path of artistic creation in the decorative arts that would lead to the foundation in 1903 of the Wiener Werkstätte (Vienna Workshop) by Josef Hoffmann and Koloman Moser, which was loosely based on C.R. Ashbee's cooperative Guild of Handicraft in Britain. After World War I it would point the way toward the linear Art Deco style of the 1920s and 1930s and ultimately to the new radical aesthetic known as Modernism.

By bravely choosing to reject the conventional Victorian fashion and interpret the taste for Art Nouveau in new and highly imaginative ways, Charles Rennie Mackintosh and the Secessionists dedicated themselves to creating clean and livable spaces. Their furniture and decorative objects embodied the simplicity, crisp geometric lines, and barely-there decoration that in time were to underpin the ideology of the Modern movement and the distinctive flair of Art Deco interiors.

CHARLES RENNIE MACKINTOSH CHAIR

The simple shapes that make up the components of this chair are hallmarks of furniture by Charles Rennie Mackintosh. Constructed of ebonized sycamore, the chair has sparse decoration of clean, rectilinear forms comprised of squares and rectangles, with the geometric trellis back resembling a stylized tree. Designed in collaboration with the decorator George Walton in 1904 for one of Miss Kate Cranston's chain of tearooms in Glasgow, it is a splendid example of furniture that was created by Mackintosh to function as an integral part of a unified decorative scheme – a pioneering program for buildings and interiors that was widely celebrated not only in continental Europe but across the Atlantic as well.

The decoration on the chair back is limited to a grid created by lengths of wood. The effect is that of a stylized tree.

While the ebonized finish on the wood is not uncommon for Mackintosh furniture, much of it was painted white, or in pale, pastel colors to complement his light, airy interiors.

The geometric pattern continues down to the stretchers.

An ebonized sycamore chair, designed by Charles Rennie Mackintosh for Hous'hill, Nitshill, Glasgow.
1904 28in (71.7cm) high BB

FURNITURE GALLERY

Furniture made by craftsmen working in the artistic traditions of the early 20th century was often handmade. The ideals of the movements they were part of influenced every element of the design. The decorative vocabulary included geometric and rectilinear details, naturalistic motifs and the use of joints and other parts of the construction as decoration.

Henry van der Velde used organic carving around the apron, along the legs and feet of this walnut occasional table.
c1916 27.25in (69cm) high K

Decorative brass legs support mahogany tiers on this Richard Müller, Dresden, table.
1902 29.5in (74.5cm) high M

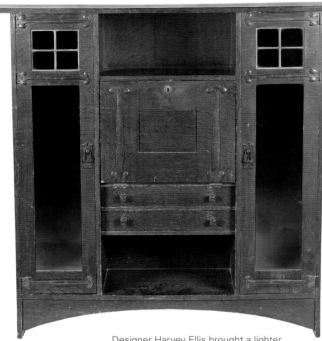

Arched stretchers, stylized hoof feet and a marble top embellish an oak bedside table by Henry van der Velde.
1897-98 15.75in (40cm) wide H

Designer Harvey Ellis brought a lighter, more sophisticated look to Gustav Stickley's furniture. This desk/bookcase is decorated with leaded glass panels.
c1903 56in (142.25cm) wide BB

Diagonal side supports and undulating arms and top rail feature on a Richard Riemerschmid, stained oak armchair.
1899 30.2in (98 cm) high R

The shape of the arched top rail is echoed in the curve of the back of this walnut armchair by Bruno Paul.
c1901 30.75in (78cm) high M

Dark and light stained mahogany veneers are arranged in a geometric pattern on a German display cabinet by J. Groschkus. The rectilinear design is echoed by vertical panes of glass at the tops of the doors.
c1904 39.25in (100cm) K

GREENE AND GREENE CABINET

Brothers Charles Sumner Greene and Henry Mather Greene started an architectural firm in Pasadena, CA, in 1893. By the early 20th century they were also designing furniture, stained glass and metalware. Their work is uniquely Californian but in the tradition of the American Arts and Crafts movement. It incorporates European, Japanese and Native American influences. The brothers are best known for designing the Gamble House in Pasadena.

The standing architectural cabinet was the personal property of Charles Sumner Greene, who was the firm's chief designer, 1894–1922.

It was created by Swedish émigré master woodworkers Peter and John Hall. Working with the Halls allowed the Greenes to refine their furniture designs.

The handles are inlaid with iridescent glass squares.

The cabinet was handmade from fumed Honduras planked mahogany.

The cabinet retains its original fumed finish.

Greene and Greene architectural cabinet. **1907-1911 57.5in (146cm) wide GG**

Rectilinear decoration is enhanced by ebonized balls on the chairs Josef Hoffmann designed for the Wiener Werkstätte's Kabaret Fledermaus in Vienna. **1905 29in (73.5cm) high M**

The curved back of Frank Lloyd Wright's dining chair is offset by vertical struts. **1937 32in (81cm) high NPA**

Paneling and long corbels under the wide armrests are the embellishments on this L. & J. G. Stickley prairie settle. **84.5in (214.5cm) long U**

Josef Hoffmann's hallmark geometric decoration features on this nest of four tables manufactured by J. & J. Kohn. **c1905 Largest 30in (76cm) high M**

The Wiener Werkstätte

The Wiener Werkstätte ("Vienna Workshop") was founded in 1903 by the architect Josef Hoffmann and the designer Koloman Moser. But while in Britain, Ashbee's Guild looked back to the medieval guild system for inspiration, Hoffmann and Moser's design cooperative was a forward-looking collection of workshops. It became internationally renowned as a center for progressive design in metalwork, leatherwork, ceramics, jewelry and furniture. Members believed useful wares could also be beautiful.

Stylized designs were promoted by the Wiener Werkstätte, including posters created for the group. 1925 12.5in (32cm) high K

By 1905 many of the celebrated artists, architects, and designers who had established themselves in Vienna as the independent Vienna Secession in 1897 – among them the painter Gustav Klimt and the architect Otto Wagner – had joined Hoffmann and Moser at the Wiener Werkstätte. In the following years this brash, innovative enterprise welcomed other distinguished creative minds to the fold, including Otto Prütscher, Michael Powolny, Oskar Kokoschka, Dagobert Peche, and Carl Otto Czeschka. The group came to dominate the decorative arts scene in Vienna.

BEAUTY IN EVERYDAY OBJECTS

Central to the philosophy of the Wiener Werkstätte was the idea that useful and functional household wares could also be aesthetically pleasing. Why shouldn't utilitarian, everyday objects made for the middle classes – lamps and vases, tables and chairs, cabinets and cupboards – be beautifully designed and finely crafted with an eye to quality materials? By 1905 the group had more than a hundred workers, of whom 37 were master craftsmen who were given their own individual marks. The high level of technical expertise was celebrated by periodicals such as "Deutsche Kunst und Dekoration".

MATERIALS AND WORKMANSHIP

The artists, designers, and craftsmen of the Wiener Werkstätte sought to elevate the decorative arts to the status of fine art. With the avowed aim of approving only

Elegant, tapered uprights and stylized brass rose motifs inlaid into the arms and backrests provide minimal, geometric decoration on a Hans Christiansen mahogany armchair.
c1910 28.5in (71cm) high M

Rectilinear decoration follows the shape of a brass table centerpiece designed by Josef Hoffmann. The coupe was hammered and chased to create the design and has twisted ribbon handles.
1925-1931 7.75in (20cm) high V

items of originality and beauty, they created simple, imaginative and distinctive designs for furniture, metalwork, glass, ceramics, textiles, leatherwork, jewelry and even graphic arts and the theater.

The Werkstätte chairs, cabinets, lamps, and pins were made by hand and characteristically featured clean lines with simple geometric decoration. The earliest Werkstätte pieces had the most limited decoration, with designs becoming less severe after 1905. Stylized floral motifs inspired by local folk art, or neat patterns of spheres, circles or the "Hoffmann square" were typical.

Pieces were often subtly embellished with luxurious materials. Exotic timbers such as rosewood, maple, or mahogany might be decorated with mother-of-pearl and ivory marquetry inlays, copper or silver mounts, plated nickel drawer pulls, or rich leather upholstery punctuated with brass tacks. Pearls and amber, lapis lazuli, or onyx cabochons in vivid hues enriched silver pendants and pins as well as pewter candlesticks. A picture frame or clock might feature decorative motifs of stylized flowers highlighted by richly colored enamels.

WORKING WITH MACHINERY

Although the Wiener Werkstätte spurned what they considered to be second-rate mass-produced wares, they did not reject the possibilities offered by working with machinery. Indeed, the machine ultimately held sway in the quest to create functional, high-quality furniture, metalware, and graphics to decorate the interior of a middle class dwelling.

Like progressive workshops in Germany, England, and the United States, the artists and designers at the Wiener Werkstätte eventually came to recognize that the ideal world put forth by Morris, Ashbee, and their followers, in which everyone would have access to superbly constructed handcrafted furniture and decorative objects, could not be sustained in any practical and affordable way. They reasoned – with no little success – that the machine could be their friend when carefully controled, to produce elegant, refined, and functional designs in quality materials.

RICHARD RIEMERSCHMID CUPBOARD

In the pantheon of creative talents working in the Arts and Crafts style, the versatile and prolific German architect and designer Richard Riemerschmid stands out from his contemporaries. A founder of the Munich Werkstätten für Kunst im Handwerk (the United Workshops for Art and Handicraft) which encouraged designers and manufacturers to work together for the benefit of the common man, he was also a co-founder of the Deutscher Werkbund. He created elegant, abstract designs that owed a debt to historical sources, the Arts and Crafts movement, and the more subtle, sinuous versions of Art Nouveau.

This stained-oak cupboard boasting a pair of glazed panel doors above an overhanging shelf is a fine example of Riemerschmid's affinity for clean, straight lines enhanced by soft, subtle curves.

The simple, straightforward construction from modest materials is enhanced with nickel-plated decorative ornament in the form of barely-there drawer pulls and structural features such as strap hinges.

Stained-oak cupboard by Richard Riemerschmid. c1905 80.25in (204cm) high K

Darmstadt and the Deutscher Werkbund

By the late 19th century a host of German artists' guilds had been established that sought to embrace the latest developments in decorative arts. Once they had finally rejected stifling historicism, designers in Germany became enthusiastically committed to the Modern style. Many pioneering centers for the "New Art" were set up – including the celebrated artists' colony at Darmstadt and the Deutscher Werkbund in Munich. In their designs the natural world appeared abstract and more structured than it had in the past.

Artists' communities thrived across Germany, from Berlin to Stuttgart, Weimar and Dessau, Hamburg and Frankfurt. Also flourishing during the last decades of the 19th century was a modern, innovative style known as Jugendstil ("Youth style"). Named after the popular journal "Die Jugend" ("Youth"), which promoted it, the style was associated with the Vienna Secession (see p.16) and an angular version of Art Nouveau.

The more curvilinear style of Art Nouveau owes much of its success in Germany to Henry van de Velde (see below), and a range of gifted German artists including Richard Riemerschmid, Peter Behrens, and Franz von Stuck.

DARMSTADT ARTISTS' COLONY

Among the most notable of the German artists' guilds was the one founded at Darmstadt in 1899 by Ernst Ludwig, Grand Duke of Hesse. In large part a visionary concept developed by the Austrian architect and designer Josef Maria Olbrich, the Darmstadt Artists' Colony introduced a number of innovations. These included public buildings and private dwellings designed, built, and furnished by a medley of gifted artists.

At the Mathildenhöhe in Darmstadt, one of the most celebrated examples of the "New Art" proved to be the house created by the architect and designer Peter Behrens as his own residence, in which the

Tapering conical pewter decanter with peacock feather decoration by Albin Muller for Metallwaren Fabrik Eduard Hueck.
1903-04 14in (35.5cm) high H

Stylized leaves decorate a bulbous vase and cover by Henry van de Velde, made by R. Merkelbach.
c1902 13.5in (34.5cm) high S

HENRY VAN DE VELDE

Influenced by French Art Nouveau and the Secessionists, the Antwerp-born designer Henry van de Velde believed that art should respond to organic form. In 1892 he abandoned painting to pursue design. His house near Brussels – Bloemenwerf, where furniture, carpets, and wall coverings created a harmonious whole – brought him international acclaim. Although his functional and elegantly simple designs were widely admired across Europe, he reached the apogee of his career in Germany, setting up shop in Berlin. There he designed furniture, porcelain, silver, jewelry, and textiles. A founding member of the Deutscher Werkbund, Van de Velde eventually resigned his post. He cited the demise of quality that was brought about by greater emphasis on the machine at the expense of the artist.

Minimal decoration typifies the oak chairs designed by Richard Riemerschmid at Darmstadt.
c1905 35.75in (91cm) high L

PATRIZ HUBER CABINET
Partly carved with sinuous, curving lines, this polished cupboard in lemon mahogany is by Patriz Huber, a member of the influential artists' colony at Darmstadt. The top features faceted glazing and shelves on each side, and it is embellished with inlaid geometric patterns of flower buds and foliage rendered in sumptuous and colorful exotic woods. Other Art Nouveau touches include copper mountings and decorative details such as the gently bending copper key fitting highlighted with simple embossed foliate designs.

Cabinet designed by Patriz Huber
c1901 50.25in (128cm) wide Z

The cabinet features facetted glazing which is bordered by strips of copper.

The doors are embellished with an embossed pattern of peacock feathers. The wood has been stained black and then polished.

The copper hinges and escutcheons to the doors on the base echo the decoration of the upper part.

architecture, decoration, and furniture were a unified whole. He designed it in 1901 as part of the first Mathildenhöhe exhibition, whereby the houses built by the artists themselves were the exhibits.

Darmstadt's progressive community of artists – including Olbrich, Behrens, Patriz Huber, Hans Christiansen, and Paul Bürck – turned their backs on the flowing, sinuous thread typical of the French Art Nouveau style. Instead, they aimed to bring a more structural and abstract interpretation of the natural world to decorative wares.

Olbrich, for example, designed and produced furniture with restrained rectilinear forms. It had clean, geometric lines and little ornamentation save the occasional embellishment of leather. Behrens, who designed furniture with the machine in mind, created well-proportioned and simple shapes that largely depended on the quality of the timber used. Although Patriz Huber was active for only a few years, owing to his premature death, his talents extended from furniture and interiors to designs for glass, silver, jewelry, carpets, textiles, and books.

THE DEUTSCHER WERKBUND
In the late 19th century, Munich was another important center for creativity and innovation in architecture and design. Following his appointment in 1896 to the German embassy in London, the architect, philosopher, and journalist Hermann Muthesius found himself captivated by the Arts and Crafts vision. On his return to Germany, his enthusiasm for a new style based on clear, clean-cut forms led to the establishment in Munich of the Deutscher Werkbund ("German work federation") in 1907. This company of artists, architects, and designers – whose founding members included Hermann Muthesius, Peter Behrens, Richard Riemerschmid, and Josef Maria Olbrich – celebrated and promoted the fundamental principles that lay at the heart of modernism: the union of innovative design and high-quality, machine-produced, decorative, and useful furniture and household wares. Members made their voices heard by publishing books and magazine articles, giving lectures, and mounting exhibitions as far afield as the United States. However, the alliance proved to be short-lived, as the demand for practical, affordable products in the wake of World War I ultimately won out over the distinctive and creative path to imaginative design – standardization became the order of the day.

Germany had cultivated a myriad of noteworthy ideas that led to some of the key ground-breaking artistic developments of the modern era. However, Hitler did not trust the non-Germans who took part in the movement, and his rise to power in 1933 presaged the end of Germany's pre-eminence as a champion for modernism. It was left to other countries to step into the breach, where the broad assortment of Modern styles was eventually explored.

CERAMICS GALLERY

Having rejected both the mania for historical revivals and the romance of French Art Nouveau, ceramics designers from movements such as the Wiener Werkstätte and the Darmstadt Artists' Colony were free to experiment with geometric and naturalistic forms and decoration. The results vary widely but all have one thing in common – the aim to give consumers new, better designed items for their homes.

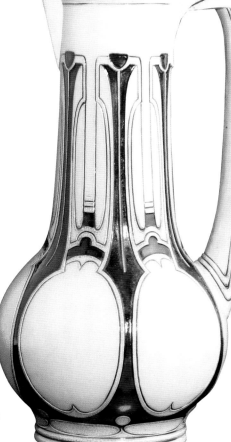

Raised green and black glaze tendrils envelop a ball-shaped vase designed by J. K. Liehm. The vase is marked "Kunst Keramik".
1912 5.75in (14cm) high C

Stylized, dynamic whiplash curves decorate the rim of a porcelain plate, from the van de Velde service designed by Henry van de Velde for Meissen.
1903 10.75in (27cm) diam I

Streaky glazes highlight the flared rim and applied shoulder decoration on this vase designed by Henry van de Velde for Merkelbach & Wick.
c1902 10.4in (26 cm) high O

Incised then glazed repeating geometric patterns decorate a tankard with pewter lid by Patriz Huber.
c1905 5in (13cm) high E

A vertical geometric pattern is repeated on a stoneware ewer designed by Peter Behrens for Simon Gerz.
13in (33cm) high F

JUTTA SIKA COFFEE POT

Austrian designer Jutta Sika was trained by Koloman Moser, one of the founders of Wiener Werkstätte, who encouraged his pupils to work with ceramic factories. Sika reaped the benefits of those connections and became one of several prolific female designers working for Wiener Werkstätte, during an era in which the contribution of women artists was rarely recognized within artistic movements. One of the companies she worked for was the Josef Bock porcelain company in Vienna.

The cover and handle are pierced with holes to aid opening and pouring.

The holes are echoed in the red circular design which has been applied to the body.

The shape and decoration of the coffee pot look fresh and modern over 100 years since they were designed.

A Jutta Sika coffee pot made for the Jos. Bock porcelain company.
1900-1905 7in (18cm) high H

Oval vase with four applied ovals designed by Henry van de Velde and shown at 1904 St Louis World's Fair.
c1903 7in (18cm) high U

Classical inspired decoration embellishes a footed vase by Dagobert Peche, made by Gmundner Keramik.
c1912 7in (17.5cm) high L

Bands of flowers and leaves enhance a jar by Albin Müller for Villeroy & Boch.
c1912 18.5in (46cm) high L

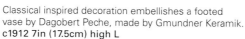

Frank Lloyd Wright (1867–1959)

Without question the most influential, prolific, and forward-looking American architect and designer promoting the Arts and Crafts movement in the United States was Frank Lloyd Wright. As a founding member in 1897 of the Chicago Arts and Crafts Society, Wright revolutionized architecture and design by creating innovative integrated interiors and furnishings for the offices, churches, schools, hotels, and houses that he designed throughout his long and celebrated career.

Frank Lloyd Wright's admiration for Japanese and Mission furniture was to inform his pioneering decorative schemes as an architect and interior designer. So, too, did his training as a draughtsman for the distinguished American architect Louis Sullivan.

Wright's vision was of an organic and integrated architectural whole – the structure, interior, and exterior of his buildings were all interrelated, and frequently with custom-made furniture. Central to this integration was his love of horizontal lines and geometric shapes, reflected in hundreds of simple yet sophisticated rectilinear designs, including his own house in Oak Park, Chicago, Illinois. Fundamental to his practice of organic architecture was the relationship of a building to the surrounding landscape – for example, houses in wooded areas relied on local timber for construction and furnishings.

From his monumental commercial commissions such as the Solomon R. Guggenheim Museum in New York City, to the spectacular Fallingwater house near Pittsburgh, or the modest and practical middle-class Usonian dwellings, Wright devised his highly original organic architectural creations with a keen eye for detail. Furniture and carpets, windows and doors, light fixtures and other features were conceived as an integrated whole. He was one of the first of a new breed of architects to design and supply custom-made, purpose-built furniture and fittings that functioned as intrinsic components of a harmonious design. Decorative ornament was simple but elegant, favoring abstract or geometric interpretations of organic forms – flowers and foliage, circles, and squares – that highlight his passion for Japanese design.

Wright embraced innovative building materials such as precast concrete blocks and glass bricks, plus zinc rather than

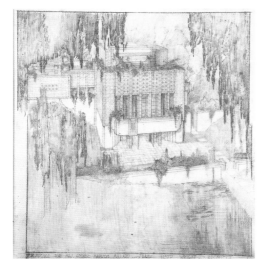

A Frank Lloyd Wright pencil and colored pencil drawing for the Millard residence in Pasadena, California. The Millard House, designed by Wright in 1923, was the first of four concrete-block homes he designed in the Los Angeles area.

Rectilinear designs feature in much of Frank Lloyd Wright's work. This hall chair has a tall spindled back.
46.5in (118cm) high S

traditional lead for the divider bars of his leaded-light windows. His imaginative use of Pyrex glass tubing as an important design feature in Wisconsin's Johnson Wax Headquarters met with great acclaim. Glass figured prominently in Wright's building designs throughout his career, as it conformed to his philosophy of organic architecture. By stringing panes of glass along whole walls, he made possible the interaction and viewing of the landscape while still protected from the elements.

From 1900 to 1917, Wright created designs for his famous "Prairie Houses" – so-called because they were believed to complement the land surrounding Chicago. The low-built houses using rustic materials – where open-plan was used for the first time – have shallow sloping roofs, clean skylines, suppressed chimneys, overhangs, and terraces. Wright's Prairie Houses used themed, coordinated design elements, often

based on plant forms that are repeated in windows, carpets, and other fittings. His most celebrated glass is in the Prairie Style, with intricate windows ornamented with simple geometric patterns.

The Westcott House (1907–1908) in Springfield, Ohio, remains one of the most distinguished examples of his innovative Prairie Style dwellings. Some elements in its design also reflect his enthusiasm for Japanese architecture.

Wright's year-long stay in Europe beginning in 1910 saw 100 lithographs of his designs published in collaboration with Ernst Wasmuth. Known as the Wasmuth Portfolio, the two-volume folio brought the first major exposure of Wright's work to Europe. Throughout his long and distinguished career, the remarkable legacy of buildings created by Frank Lloyd Wright played a key role in the birth of modernism, and continue to resonate today.

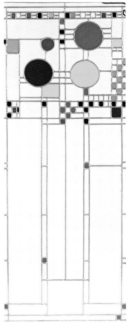

The two-storey living room of the Storer House in Los Angeles features Mayan-inspired decoration which also decorates the exterior. It was built in 1923 using concrete textile blocks, many molded with Mayan designs.

Geometric patterns feature on this leaded glass window, designed by Frank Lloyd Wright after those he created for the Coonley Playhouse in Riverside, Illinois, which are considered some of his finest glass designs.
54.75in (139cm) high J

METALWARE GALLERY

Embossed decoration was used to great effect by designers working at the turn of the 20th century. From Arts & Crafts to the Wiener Werkstätte and on to the Darmstadt Artists' Colony it proved to be an effective way of decorating metalwares for the home. Designs tended to be geometric in inspiration, sometimes combined with naturalistic themes.

Embossed floral motifs contrast with the angular handle on the lid of a Joseph-Maria Olbrich covered pewter and glass butter dish, made by Eduard Hueck.
c1902 8in (20cm) diam M

Circles, diagonal lines and triangles combine in a Marianne Brandt silver plated napkin holder, produced by Ruppelwerk.
c1930 5in (13cm) high F

Four embossed geometric motifs are the sparse decoration on a pewter plate designed by Hans Christiansen and made by Ludwig Lichtinger, Munich.
c1903 10.5in (27cm) high L

Simple relief decoration and facetted sides created a streamlined appearance on a beak-lipped pewter wine jug designed by Joseph Maria Olbrich and made by Eduard Hueck.
1901 13.5in (34cm) high M

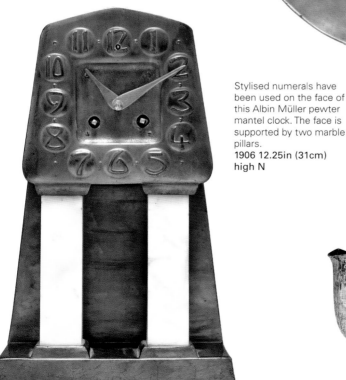

Stylised numerals have been used on the face of this Albin Müller pewter mantel clock. The face is supported by two marble pillars.
1906 12.25in (31cm) high N

Hammered brass kettle with wicker handle designed by Peter Behrens.
c1909 7.25in (18.5cm) high F

JAN EISENLOEFFEL TEA SERVICE
The work of Dutch metalworker, Jan (Johannes Wigbold) Eisenloeffel is considered avant-garde for its purity of form and functionalist aesthetic. His work was much admired at the 1900 World Exposition in Paris. Influences from Munich to Japan contributed to his native Dutch "Neue stile", and his sleek and practical metalware made an important contribution to Dutch modernism.

The decoration accentuates the austere, masculine forms.

Eisenloeffel emphasised the construction of his pieces, sometimes using features such as joints as a form of simple decoration.

A Jan Eisenloeffel brass, wicker and glass tea service for J.K.C. Sneltjes, Haarlem.
c1905 tray 12in (30cm) diam J

This enameled metal and Bakelite desk lamp by Marianne Brandt and Hin Bredendieck has a simple, functional design.
c1928 17in (43cm) high F

Flat relief ribbon decoration, and tapering, leaf motifs decorate this pair of pewter candlesticks designed by Joseph-Maria Olbrich for Eduard Hueck.
c1902 14.5in (36cm) high R

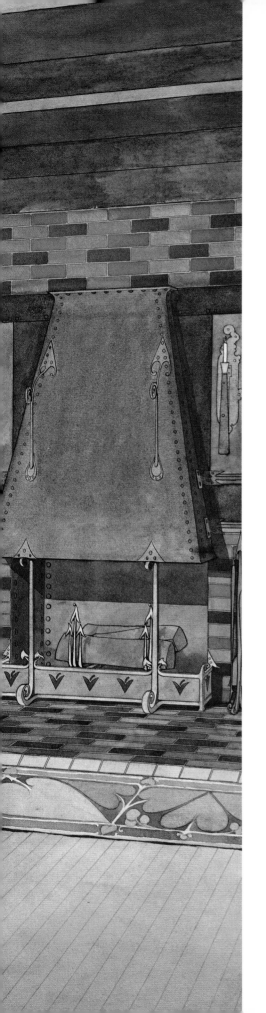

"If you want a golden rule that will fit everything, this is it: have nothing in your houses that you do not know to be useful or believe to be beautiful."
William Morris

The Craft Movement

Furniture which features parts of its construction as decoration, hand-wrought metalware, painted walls and patterned floor coverings decorated the room in Will Bradley's 'Drawing for a Library' created in 1901.

The Craft Movement

Throughout the 20th century artists continued to work in the craft tradition, taking their inspiration from a diverse ramge of sources. Although not affected by trends in design, their work does reflect current themes and contemporary concerns. Two World Wars, ever-changing technology, urbanization, and the advent of the nuclear age inevitably drew artists back to an ethos of craftsmanship and human scale. At the same time, designers continued to push the boundaries of creativity and innovation.

THE CRAFT MOVEMENT IN BRITAIN

The Arts and Crafts movement, pioneered by William Morris and John Ruskin, originated in Britain in the last decades of the 19th century. It played a key role in the return to well-designed, functional furniture and decorative objects in humble indigenous materials – a reaction against the rampant historicism that had for too many years dictated interior design. Among those who took up the baton for change were the members of the enterprizing Cotswold School, a group of craftsmen based in central England. They created clean-lined, handcrafted furniture that exploited the natural color and grain of local woods.

The craft ideology soon made its way to the United States, and can be seen in the furniture designed by Gustav Stickley, Frank Lloyd Wright, and the Roycrofters, among others. This furniture, along with the ceramics by Ohio's Rookwood Pottery, William Grueby in Boston, and the eccentric but highly original George Ohr in Biloxi, Mississippi, established a high standard for well-made household furnishings.

The rise of facism in Europe meant that a number of talented artisans left their home countries for the safer havens of Britain and the United States. The arrival in Britain in the late 1930s of the Viennese ceramicist Lucie Rie and her German-born collaborator Hans Coper had an enormous influence on the development of artistic studio pottery which had been inspired by Bernard Leach and Shoji Hamada. So, too, did the emigration to California of the Austrian ceramic

The Pennsylvania town of New Hope became home to a colony of craftsmen. 'The Bridge at New Hope' by Harry Leith-Ross, oil on canvas.
20in (50cm) wide AA

designers, Otto and Gertrud Natzler. Before long for these two innovative potters had taken their place alongside other visionary American art potters such as Beatrice Wood and Maija Grotell.

THE NEW HOPE SCHOOL

By the middle of the 20th century, a number of craftsmen had taken up residence in the art colony of New Hope, Pennsylvania. This aptly named town had initially attracted painters in the early 20th century, and some became known as the Pennsylvania Impressionists. A few decades later, furniture designers, silversmiths, ceramicists, and other artists followed. They established studios and workshops dedicated to the production of well-designed furnishings and decorative objects celebrating the role of the craftsman and looking back for inspiration to the Arts and Crafts ideal.

Bernard Leach inspired studio potters. A Bernard Leach flat-sided stoneware bottle painted with stylized pattern in rust on a matte gray quadrant.
7.75in (19.5cm) high M

TIMELINE

1853 Japan is forced to re-open its ports after decades of isolation.

1856 Theodore Deck opens a faience studio in Paris and begins to experiment with Islamic, and later Chinese, styles.

1880 Rookwood Pottery opens in Cincinnati, Ohio.

1881 William Morris opens a workshop at Merton Abbey Mills in South London.

1884 Art Workers Guild founded in London to promote communication between artists and craftspeople.

1897 The first Arts and Crafts exhibition is held in Boston.

Luminaries such as George Nakashima, Philip Lloyd Powell, and Paul Evans contributed to the extraordinary artistic output of the New Hope community, raising furniture design to the status of fine art. Their highly original wares championed art over functionality.

FORM STOPS FOLLOWING FUNCTION

The central principles that initially underpinned the Arts and Crafts philosophy, that form should follow function, began to become less important in the 1960s. Instead the aesthetic and artistic properties of furniture, ceramics, glass, and other materials began to be favored over their usefulness.

Perhaps no thread of the decorative arts demonstrates this rejection of function over design more than the development of studio glass. The technological innovations of Harvey Littleton and Dominick Labino in Toledo, Ohio, in the 1960s – developing small kilns and glass that could be worked in them – would ultimately resonate around the world.

By the end of the 20th century, the craft ideals championed by innovators such as William Morris, Bernard Leach, George Nakashima, and Harvey Littleton and Dominick Labino had come full circle. Dale Chihuly's sculptural glass shapes decorated with woven patterns inspired by Navajo textile designs, the "Funk" ceramics developed from a new white-clay mix by Robert Arneson at the Davis campus of the University of California, the revolutionary furniture designed by Milan's Memphis group , and the Crafts Revival furniture promoted by John Makepeace and Wendell Castle. These are but a few of the countless forward-looking artist-designers who again and again have pushed the boundaries of conventional styles in an effort to create aesthetically pleasing pieces that hold form in higher esteem than function.

GEORGE NAKASHIMA TABLE

George Nakashima's tables were created from a single piece of wood. A "slice" was cut from a tree trunk. The top surface was polished while the edges were left in their natural shapes – these are known as "free edges". Rather than reject logs that had flaws, he used them as part of the design. This created an organic, natural shape.

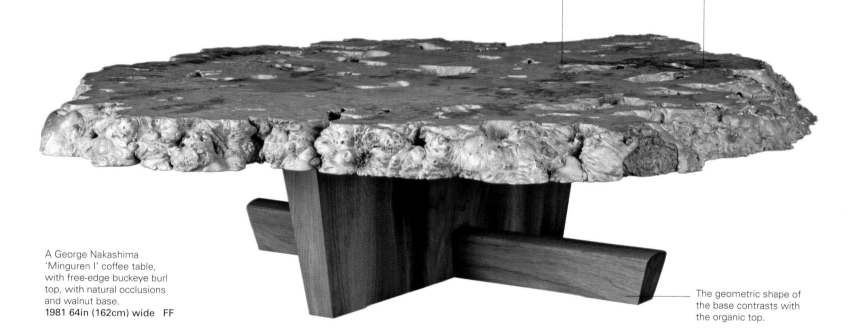

Natural burls in the wood were left to form the decoration.

The "free edge", freeform top is made from a single piece of wood.

A George Nakashima 'Minguren I' coffee table, with free-edge buckeye burl top, with natural occlusions and walnut base.
1981 64in (162cm) wide   FF

The geometric shape of the base contrasts with the organic top.

1901 Gustav Stickley launches The Craftsman magazine.

1920 Bernard Leach founds the St Ives Pottery.

1943 George Nakashima is released from internment and moves to New Hope.

1955 Paul Evans moves to New Hope and opens a studio there.

1959 Peter Voulkos joins the University of California at Berkley and establishes an art pottery department.

1971 Pilchuck Glass School is co-founded by Dale Chihuly.

Mission Furniture

By the late 19th century the Arts and Crafts philosophy championed by William Morris and John Ruskin had crossed the Atlantic. The first American Arts and Crafts Exhibition, held in Boston in 1897, showcased the work of talented British designers, inaugurating an Arts and Crafts movement that was to flourish across the United States during the first quarter of the 20th century. Mission furniture became the hallmark of the style.

OLD MISSIONS

MISSION SANTA BARBARA ·1786·

Southern Pacific

The Spanish Missions were a popular tourist destination as well as an inspiration to designers and architects. Southern Pacific poster by Maurice Logan, advertizing the missions in Santa Barbara, California.
23.25in (59cm) high C

SIMPLE AND UNADORNED

The American furniture known as Mission, Mission-style, or Mission Oak is said to have been named after the simple furnishings of the early Spanish missions of California. Having grown in popularity following the 1901 Pan-American Exposition, held in Buffalo, New York, Mission furniture became associated with the burgeoning Arts and Crafts style. It was simple, solid, sturdy, and unadorned.

The leading designer in this style was Gustav Stickley, who set up a workshop, United Craftsmen, in Eastwood, New York, in 1898. One of the first to marry Arts and Crafts design with American vernacular styles such as Shaker, he set new standards in design. He launched a periodical, *The Craftsman*, in 1901, to promote his furniture and Arts and Crafts aims.

Three basic principles governed the furniture's design: form should follow function, the materials should be well-suited to the design, and applied decoration

should be spare. Stickley's workshop produced well-made, comfortable furniture, mainly in solid oak. Stickley employed a combination of hand-craftsmanship and mechanization, and construction features such as pins, pegs, chamfered boards, and mortise-and-tenon joints were incorporated into the decorative design. Both his workshop and his magazine closed in 1916.

Mission furniture, ceramics, and household items in beaten copper were designed and produced by the Roycrofters, a community of craftworkers in East Aurora, New York. Founded in 1895 by the writer Elbert Hubbard, the Roycroft community was based on the Arts and Crafts principles of William Morris.

Gustav Stickley's brothers Leopold and John George set up their own company L. & J.G. Stickley. Their designs included this A Prairie rocker (no. 409).
32in (81.5cm) high L

WHARTON ESHERICK (1887-1970)

Wharton Esherick is often called the "Dean of American Craftsmen" by his peers. He began creating furniture influenced by the Arts and Crafts movement in the late 1920s. By the 1930s, however, he had begun to apply the principles of sculpture to his furniture. His angular forms show the influence of German Expressionism, though soon even these forms gave way to the free-form curvilinear shapes of Modernism. Esherick's sculptural yet functional forms combine furniture with high art. He saw himself as an artist rather than a craftsman, claiming: "it takes a sculptor to know how to sculpt."

A sculptural Wharton Esherick carved cherry music stand, on three legs.
1962 44in (112cm) high BB

LIMBERT LAMP TABLE

The company established in 1894 by Charles Limbert, near Grand Rapids, Michigan, made solid oak tables, chairs, and cabinets. These pieces were decorated with cut-out patterns of hearts or squares and echoed the style promoted by Britain's Charles Rennie Mackintosh and the Glasgow School. Limbert, who was an expert on European furniture, always described his designs as Arts and Crafts, rather than Mission.

The table top overhangs the base of the table. It is supported by geometric corbels which form part of the decoration.

Limbert used oak for many of his designs.

A Limbert Oval lamp table, with canted cut-out sides and rectangular lower shelf.
45in (114.5cm) wide M

The panel shelf and splayed legs are typical of Limbert's tables.

The geometric cut outs in the legs create a light and airy feel to the solid wood.

The British Craft Tradition

Faced with the dehumanizing effects of industrialization and conformity of mass production, some British furniture designers championed the aims of the Arts and Crafts movement. These cabinetmakers embraced the use of indigenous woods, worked with traditional tools and promoted quality craftsmanship. They also had a discerning eye for decorative detail.

In the late 19th century, a group of furniture designers and craftsmen, inspired by the teachings of William Morris, left the cities to establish workshops in the English countryside. One of the most popular destinations for these artisans was the Cotswolds, an area of the county of Gloucestershire known for its rolling limestone hills and wooded valleys.

THE COTSWOLD SCHOOL

The architect and designer Ernest Gimson was among the first to leave behind the urban way of life, moving from London to Pinbury Manor, near Cirencester in 1893. He was joined in this enterprise by a number of like-minded craftsmen, including the brothers Ernest and Sidney Barnsley, the Dutch immigrant Peter Waals, and Gordon Russell. The aim was to keep alive the tradition of designing furniture with an eye to tradition and quality craftsmanship.

They also planned to grow their own food and set up a furniture-making workshop. Their distinct school of design has become known as Cotswold School. In 1902 they moved to Daneway House in Sapperton. By then the architect C.R. Ashbee's influential Guild of Handicraft was based in nearby Chipping Campden.

Choosing the natural color and grain of local timbers, including elm, ebony, ash, oak, and fruitwood, the furniture designers of the Cotswold School produced elegant yet simple, clean-lined furniture. Construction details such as dovetails and the wooden pins that joined the timbers were left exposed as decorative features. A concerted effort was made to celebrate the production of quality pieces by hand.

However, some of the craftsmen made furniture which was embellished in other ways. Handcrafted tables, chairs, sideboards, dressing tables, desks, and

A Cotswolds School Arts & Crafts oak compendium, includes chest of drawers, bookcase and wardrobe, retailed by Heal's.
79in (197.5cm) high E

ROBERT "MOUSEMAN" THOMPSON (1876-1955)

The celebrated Yorkshire furniture craftsman Robert Thompson, who began his career as an apprentice in his father's joinery, had by 1895 assumed the directorship of the family business in Kilburn, Yorkshire. There he produced sturdy, handcrafted furniture that looked for inspiration to traditional 17th-century designs as well as to the medieval carvings he has seen and admired at the nearby cathedrals of York and Ripon. His rural workshop, which by the 1930s employed 30 workers and which remains in existence today, created country furniture in solid English oak. Based on time-honored designs – occasionally incorporating wrought iron and leather – it used traditional tools and

methods of manufacture. For example, the surfaces of the wood tend to be uneven and rippled – an effect created by using an adze. From the beginning, the furniture produced by Robert "Mouseman" Thompson has featured a carved mouse signature, which was registered as a trademark in the 1930s.

A Robert 'Mouseman' Thompson oak monk's chair, with two carved heads on the rail.
1936 31.75in (80.5cm) high O

SIDNEY BARNSLEY DINING TABLE

Sidney Barnsley, and his brother Ernest, were born in Birmingham and trained as architects. They worked for Ernest Gimson at his workshop at Pinbury Mill in the Cotswolds from 1893, making furniture while continuing their architectural work. The brothers used local, oak, ash, elm and fruitwoods to make simple, elegant pieces with subtle carved and inlaid decoration. Sidney Barnsley handmade all his furniture . After Gimson's death in 1919 he continued working as an architect.

The three boards that make up the top of the table are joined by wooden inserts. These form the decoration of the table top.

The edges of the table top and the legs are decorated with chip carving.

Barnsley used local woods such as oak for his furniture designs.

An oak rectangular dining table, by Sidney Barnsley made for the architect Robert Weir Schultz. c1905 84in (213.5cm) wide X

The square chamfered legs are joined by hay rake and wishbone stretchers.

cabinets created in simple, geometric forms and rendered in English oak were lavishly decorated with inlays of holly, ivory, silver, pearl, abalone shell, and fruitwood.

Ironically, the handmade Arts and Crafts furniture – which looked back to traditional methods of craftsmanship with the aim of making well-designed, quality furniture available to everyone – became too expensive for all but the very wealthy. Unlike their American cousins, British artisans had been reluctant to take advantage of the new technology. For example, the sharp, austere furniture created by the artist-craftsman Sidney Barnsley was constructed by his own hand.

USING MACHINES

The advances in furniture making machinery were embraced by a host of innovative craftsmen. They recognized the benefits afforded by improvements in industrial technology which made possible the mass production of well-designed, well-crafted, and affordable furniture for the middle classes. At the forefront of the effort in England to match quality carpentry and joinery with the machine was the designer and manufacturer Gordon Russell.

The outbreak of World War One in 1914 brought the demise of the Cotswold community, as designers, craft-workers, and artisans were lost to the war. Younger members were called up for war service, and older craftsmen focused on the production of goods to aid the war effort.

George Nakashima (1905-90)

A father of the American Craft Movement, the Japanese American architect and craftsman George Nakashima enjoyed a distinguished career. He created highly original designs that explore the intrinsic beauty and expressive qualities of wood. He said: "My relationship to furniture and contruction is basically my dialog with a tree, with a complete and psychic empathy." Nakashima used traditional techniques and regarded himself as a woodworker rather than a designer. He believed his furniture gave a second life to the trees.

Born in Spokane, Washington to Japanese parents, George Nakashima – trained as an architect. Having earned a Master's degree from the Massachusetts Institute of Technology, he traveled in 1931 to France and then to North Africa before settling in Japan. There he joined the company of American architect Antonin Raymond, an innovative designer who was working with Frank Lloyd Wright to develop the Imperial Hotel in Tokyo. While there, Nakashima became fascinated by the Mingei (Japanese Folk Art) movement which was gaining popularity and called for a return to traditional techniques and craftsmanship.

In 1937, while employed by Raymond on the construction of a dormitory at an ashram in Pondicherry, India, he designed his first furniture: simple, teak pieces.

Returning to the USA in 1941, Nakashima settled in Seattle, where he worked as an architect and made furniture part time. During World War Two his family was interned at Idaho's Camp Minidoka. Here he met a traditional Japanese carpenter, Gentaro Hikogawa, who taught him how to construct furniture using time-honored Japanese skills and traditional hand tools. Nakishima practiced his carpentry with imagination, zen-like self-control and quiet serenity and with an eye to creating well-designed, flawlessly constructed pieces of furniture.

Nakashima's signature woodworking designs are his large-scale free-form tables with tops made from a single piece of wood. These tables – frequently rendered in walnut, which was his favored timber – boast smooth top surfaces but unfinished edges that follow the natural shape of the wood, combining his love of organic forms with precise and painstaking craftsmanship.

He famously used butterfly joints to reinforce natural splits in the wood so as to allow them to remain exposed, emphasizing the individuality of the piece.

Nakashima was released from the camp in 1943, with the help of Raymond, on the understanding he lived on Raymond's farm at New Hope, Pennsylvania. There, officially, he took care of the chickens. However, he soon began making furniture using scraps of wood. His home and studio were constructed

A George Nakashima walnut conoid bench, with spindle back.
98in (249cm) wide W0

from stones collected from the fields.

His highly accomplished furniture designs exploited the intrinsic beauty and figure of the natural timber and married function with the Japanese aesthetic of tranquillity and contemplation.

As well as private commissions, Nakashima developed furniture designs for companies including Knoll and Widdicomb-Mueller. However, working with these corporations he was unable to control every stage of creation, something that was of great importance to him.

PHILIP LLOYD POWELL (1919-2008)

Philip Lloyd Powell took up furniture design at the urging of George Nakashima, his neighbor in New Hope, and established a showroom there in 1953. Powell created highly original and sophisticated furniture that relied on masterful carving in an array of luminous timbers and a play of textures for much of its appeal. His curving organic shapes looked to nature for inspiration. Powell's reputation as one of the most accomplished furniture craftsman of his generation was cemented by his elegant and highly prized wooden cabinets that boasted interiors lined with luxurious materials. In the mid-1950s Powell shared his studio with Paul Evans (see p.40) and together they created a variety of imaginative designs for furniture and decorative accessories. The two men also shared a showroom where they sold their own designs alongside other modern furniture and accessories.

A Phillip Lloyd Powell walnut 'New Hope' chair, with woven seat support, cushion missing.
28in (71cm) high V

GEORGE NAKASHIMA FURNITURE

A George Nakashima burl and rosewood floor lamp with a tall drum-form shade.
62in (157.5cm) high S

A George Nakashima conoid cushion chair, in American black walnut with hickory spindles and leather webbing.
1964 33.5in (86cm) high U

A George Nakashima English walnut single-pedestal desk, with freeform, free-edge top incorporating four rosewood butterfly keys.
78in (198cm) wide CC

A George Nakashima walnut wall-hanging cabinet, with two sliding doors lined in pandanus cloth.
72in (183cm) wide U

Paul Evans (1931-87)

Paul Evans designed monumental furniture with sculptured metal decoration that defied the 1950s and 1960s trend for sleek, modern design. Using materials such as bronze, aluminum and copper on wooden bases, Evans never hesitated to marry the unique skills afforded by hand-craftsmanship with the latest technological innovations. A sculptor and entrepreneur, Evans believed that it was possible to make a profit from handmade furniture. At the beginning of the 21st century his unique furniture found a new audience which delighted in his bold designs.

The studio furniture movement owes a great debt to the highly skilled American artist Paul Evans. His trailblazing designs for tables, sofas, chairs and cabinets have gained the status of hard-wearing, practical and useful works of art.

Having studied both sculpture and jewelry design at the School for American Crafters in Rochester, New York and at Michigan's Cranbrook Academy of Art, he held the post of Artist in Residence as a silversmith at the working history museum of Sturbridge Village near Springfield,

Massachusetts. In 1951 he visited the furniture designer Philip Lloyd Powell's store in New Hope, Pennsylvania, where he was intrigued and later inspired by the pieces on sale there. Four years later Evans abandoned his calling as a silversmith and settled in New Hope, where he began making furniture. He sold his work through Powell's store and eventually the two men began to collaborate on designs.

Together Evans and Powell produced unique and highly unusual pieces that often fused a host of disparate materials together:

metal, stone, wood and glass, for example, with the occasional addition of gold or silver to highlight a design. Color also played an important role, with the metalwork often vividly painted.

In around 1958 Evans began to make copper chests with embellished doors, later adding cabinets with fronts of sculpted steel. These consisted of a wood base onto which he would mark the design using chalk. The craftsmen working for him then created the decoration to his specification. Evans' bold, dramatic and unconventional

The geometric elements of this Paul Evans steel sculpture-front room divider are covered in treated paint in reds, greens and purples with gold-leaf accents.
1967 96in wide Y

designs for his molded sculptural metal furniture were unique. His work includes a highly original series of tables and wall-mounted cabinets that were initially constructed from looped metal screens described as 'fish scales'. Evans went on to create sharp geometric furniture designs in welded steel.

His 'Sculpted Bronze' tables – a host of unusual pedestal shapes such as cubes, arches, serpentines and stalagmites were rendered in copper, bronze, pewter and welded aluminum known as argente – which were topped with sleek surfaces of glass, slate or wood.

In 1961 Evans started to work on a range of furniture for Directional Furniture. The range was launched in 1964 with unique pieces as well as several series of manufactured furniture lines, such as the Argente series, the Sculpted Bronze series, and the popular Cityscape series.

The first collection for Directional Furniture included pieces by Powell, but he left New Hope in 1964 to travel, leaving Evans to focus on the business of creating furniture collections. Directional wanted innovative ideas rather than the mass-produced designs favored by competitors such as Knoll and Hermann Miller. The company advertized Evans' work as follows: "Every piece is made by hand. One piece at a time. Every piece is finished by hand. One piece at a time. And every piece is supervized every step of the way by the artist who conceived it – Paul Evans." The design which proved to be his best- and longest-selling range for Directional Furniture was the bronze Disc bar – a large, abstract-decorated disc that was wall-mounted. Its pair of doors opened to reveal a bar.

By the mid-1970s Evans employed 88 people and sent 300-400 pieces of furniture to New York every week. The relationship with Directional Furniture ended in 1980. The following year Evans opened a showroom in New York from which he continued to sell his own work. He retired in 1987.

Evans' partnership with Directional Furniture was instrumental in bringing the taste for imaginative and original furniture design, coupled with quality construction, to a broad and appreciative audience.

PAUL EVANS FURNITURE

A rare 'Sculpted Bronze Cat' cabinet, by Paul Evans.
c1972 17in (43cm) wide W

A Paul Evans welded and wrought steel fountain sculpture, abstract floral and geometric elements.
c1956-57 43.25in (82cm) high X

A Paul Evans sculpted and painted steel cocktail table, with plate glass top.
1973 36in (91.5cm) wide V

A Paul Evans sculpted bronze chair with orange crushed velvet upholstery.
31.75in (80.5cm) high U

A Paul Evans steel patchwork sculpture.
1964 76in (193cm) high BB

Custom-designed wall-hanging cabinet by Paul Evans, in sculpted bronze and rosewood, with three interior shelves.
1970 139in (353cm) long W

Early American Craft Ceramics

The ideals of hand-craftsmanship that were advanced by the Arts and Crafts movement inspired many to create ceramics. In the United States, artist potters, ceramic studios, and some factories produced imaginative and highly original pottery that honored the aesthetic based on simple, functional, and well-made wares. They used local clays and experimental glazes to create a wide range of innovative artistic ceramic wares.

Across the United States the last two decades of the 19th century witnessed the development of an art pottery industry, and by 1900 more than 200 companies – ranging from modest studio ventures to large kiln works – were producing wares. Their aim was to make innovative, well-crafted handmade earthenware vessels that were both decorative and useful.

Tucked away in Biloxi, Mississippi, in the studio and kiln that he built himself, George Ohr (see p.44-45) most successfully achieved the Arts and Crafts ideal of individual craftsmanship, digging his own clay and molding, firing, and decorating his objects himself. At the opposite end of the spectrum, the commercially successful Rookwood Pottery (est. 1880) in Cincinnati, Ohio, built up a workshop boasting a team of talented artists and

highly skilled technicians who produced hand-carved wares of the highest standard in the Arts and Crafts style. By the 1920s it had around 200 employees.

DISTINCTIVE GLAZES

American studio potteries created innovative designs and developed distinctive glazes, often inspired by nature. At his Boston manufactory, William Grueby covered hand-thrown earthenware vessels in organic shapes with thick, opaque, matt glazes in a palette that celebrated the luminous green and yellow tones found in the foliage of trees and flowers. The reputation of the commercial Fulper Pottery (est. 1814) in New Jersey, which began making art pottery c1900, was strengthened considerably by its experiments with a variety of glazing techniques for its art

An embossed design featuring geese and covered in matte mustard glaze against a textured moss and mustard ground were used on this Van Briggle vase. 1902 6.5in (16.5cm) high V

An unusual combination of blue, cat's eye and mahogany glazes cover this three-handled Fulper baluster vase.
6.5in (16.5cm) high F

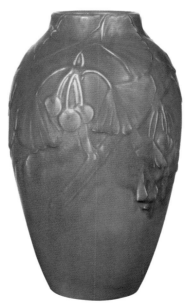

Branches of ginkgo leaves and berries in relief under a green and yellow matt glaze feature on this Rookwood carved matte ovoid vase by Kataro Shiriyamadani.
1905 10.5in (26.5cm) high Q

An oak stand frames this Owens Mission baluster vase, cold-painted with dark brown matte drips on a dark green ground.
11.5in (29.25cm) high L

ceramics, resulting in dazzling metallic, matt, gloss, and crystalline glazes in rich, muted colors. On a larger scale, the influential Rookwood Pottery developed a number of sophisticated glazes, including the 'Vellum' matt glaze, the 'Tiger Eye' crystalline glaze highlighted by flecks of gold, and its popular 'Standard' glaze.

INSPIRATION FOR DECORATION

The handmade ceramics produced in the United States adopted a number of decorative schemes and ornamental patterns that were also used in Europe. Among these are a many designs inspired by nature, such as the stylized embossed flower blossoms and leaf patterns seen on the molded vases at the Van Briggle Pottery (est. 1899) in Colorado.

Imaginative flower and plant forms were rendered in relief on hand-painted wares produced at Ohio's Roseville Pottery (est. 1890) during the tenure as art director of the renowned British potter Frederick Hurten Rhead. Rhead also conceived the bestselling, vibrantly colored line of dinnerware known as 'Fiesta ware', as well as some of the tooled and applied leaves that enhance many Grueby vessels.

The naturalistic art of Japan was another key influence. Some Fulper vessels were cast in Japanese shapes. The Newcomb Pottery (est. 1895) in New Orleans used Japanese-influenced Arts and Crafts designs and also looked to the flora and fauna native to the American South – such as cotton plants and waterfowl – for inspiration.

Alongside motifs reminiscent of the bayou, other decorative themes for art pottery remain uniquely American. These include Native American designs at Clifton and the plaques and vases from Rookwood featuring realistic, highly detailed portraits of American statesmen, historical figures, and Native Americans by artists including Grace Young.

The Arts and Crafts ideology was fulfilled by the many potteries that thrived across the United States during the first decades of the 20th century. Talented designers and craftsmen experimented with a variety of richly colored glazes and innovative shapes to produced high-quality wares that would influence ceramic design for generations.

FREDERICK RHEAD SANTA BARBARA VASE

Frederick Hurten Rhead was born in England and trained as a potter. In 1902 he immigrated to the US where he worked for the Avon Faïence Company and the Weller, Roseville, Jervis, University City, and Arequipa Potteries. By the time he reached the Arequipa Pottery in California he was creating the best work of his career. In 1913 he started his own pottery in Santa Barbara, covering his wares with the innovative glazes he had developed. The business was not a success and closed in 1917.

The incised design is unusual, squeezebag decoration is more common.

The stylized design reflects Rhead's interpretation of the California landscape, the lean, tall trees with a canopy of foliage are set against a midnight blue sky with the ocean and clouds beyond.

The vase and decoration are perfectly executed.

A Rhead Santa Barbara vase.
c1915 11.25in (28.5cm) high II

George Ohr (1857-1918)

Although the eccentric American ceramicist George Ohr – the self-styled "Mad Potter of Biloxi" – achieved little commercial success during his lifetime, he nonetheless created some of the most original and highly decorative pottery. His work embraced the aesthetic ideals that lay at the heart of the Arts and Crafts movement. Displaying a technical skill that remains unrivaled today, his pottery was as individualistic as he was.

A virtuoso potter, the flamboyant and colorful George Ohr created one-of-a-kind ceramic vessels from the small studio he established in 1883 in his hometown of Biloxi, Mississippi. He called the more than 10,000 wafer-thin, hand-thrown decorative wares that he created during his colorful career his "mud babies", displaying them to a curious and mystified public at his shop called Pot-Ohr-E.

Ohr began potting in 1879 when Joseph Mayer, a family friend invited him to move from Biloxi to New Orleans to learn the craft. Until that point the little-educated Ohr, had had a number of short-term jobs. After about two years he went traveling across the United States, visiting as many potteries as he could. In 1882 he returned to New Orleans, working for the William

Virgin Pottery and, possibly, for Meyer. The following year he returned to Biloxi and used his savings to build a pottery.

Using a wheel and wood-burning kiln that he built himself, Ohr achieved his vision of creating exceptional, one-of-a-kind pottery. He made every piece by hand, believing that each one should stand on its own as a distinctive, well-constructed design. "No two alike" was his mantra. He used local clay that he dug himself and hauled to his studio in a wheelbarrow.

Most of his work was fashioned in red earthenware. He manipulated the clay by pinching, folding, crushing, twisting, and pressing it into fantastic and unusual forms. These tortured, forceful shapes were complemented by his handmade mix of rich, lustrous, mottled and speckled glazes

A George Ohr vase, deep in-body twist, covered in several glazes as a glaze test.
3.5in (9cm) high U

BISQUE WARES

By 1900 George Ohr had abandoned his enthusiasm for the luminous, shimmering glazes that highlighted his sculptural ceramic shapes in favor of unglazed bisque ware. He believed that the absence of any glaze allowed the form to be more clearly perceived. He claimed: "God put no color in souls, and I'll put no color on my pottery." He shaped the unglazed bisque pottery by twisting, pressing, and pinching it into asymmetrical and expressionistic sculptural shapes. Without the color and shine supplied by the glaze, the fired clay shows the intricate twists and folds Ohr created in his thin-walled vessels.

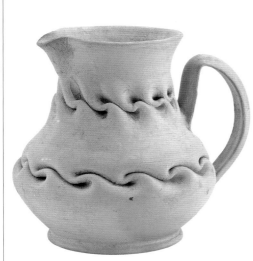

A pitcher of bisque clay, by George Ohr with two deep in-body twists and a ribbon handle.
6in (15cm) high Q

A George Ohr vase, with ribbon handles, covered in mottled gun-metal and amber glaze, with raspberry and green flashes. 8.25in (21cm) high W

George Ohr in his Biloxi workshop. Potential buyers were often thrown out of the shop before they were able to make a purchase.

in a rainbow of hues. They ranged from the deep green and brown to red, blue, golden bronze, orange, black, and purple.

The genius of George Ohr can be measured by the extraordinary and imaginative ceramic designs created in the aftermath of the devastating fire that swept though his workshop (and much of Biloxi) in the autumn of 1894, destroying most of his inventory as well as seriously damaging his building and kiln. In keeping with his rebellious spirit, Ohr kept the blackened pots covered with charcoal shards and called them his "burnt babies".

Although Ohr had a remarkable output, producing practical and ornamental ware, and despite receiving a silver medal at the 1904 St. Louis World's Fair, he was generally unappreciated during his lifetime, and sold relatively few pieces. In 1900 he set aside a box of work and addressed it to the Smithsonian Institution, with the inscription, "I am the potter who was".

Ohr closed his studio in 1907, leaving a remarkable legacy of ceramic wares. While not necessarily in tune with the American South of the early 1900s, his work is among the most brilliantly conceived, imaginatively designed, and highly prized pottery to emerge from the American Arts and Crafts movement. In a final twist to Ohr's remarkable story, his personal collection of more than 6,000 pieces – packed in barrels in the family attic as an inheritance for his children – was not recovered from storage until 1972. The collection was sold to a New Jersey antique dealer who slowly sold the pieces to a growing number of collectors. Today Ohr's work fetches high prices – including a record $84,000 paid for a vase in 2006.

A George Ohr teapot with exaggerated snake-like spout, covered in a spectacular white, red, and pink glaze sponged on an amber ground.
12.5in (31.75cm) long X

British Studio Ceramics

In Britain the reaction against the overly embellished machine-made ceramics popular in the late 19th century gathered apace. A band of creative artisans, inspired by William Morris, established art potteries. Later, handcrafted traditional pottery from China and Japan was extremely influential on pioneering studio potters such as Bernard Leach.

A Martin Brothers stoneware bird jar and cover, by Robert Wallace Martin, glazed in shades of blue, brown and ocher with distinctive green, on ebonized wood base.
8.5in (21.5cm) high S

FANTASTIC CREATURES

The distinctive and highly original sculptural salt-glazed stoneware produced by the four Martin Brothers – first at their pottery in Fulham and then at Southall, Middlesex after 1877 – represents the transition from excessively decorated Victorian ceramics to 20th century studio pottery in England. Each brother made a significant contribution to the Martin enterprise. Walter, for example, was responsible for throwing pottery shapes, creating incised decoration and developing colored glazes. Robert Wallace Martin, who had trained as a sculptor, took inspiration from the Neo-Gothic imagery he had observed while working as a stone carver at the Houses of Parliament in London. Edwin Bruce Martin, who had worked like his brother Walter at Doulton's of Lambeth, was a thrower and decorator. Charles Douglas Martin was the business manager.

The Martin brothers were celebrated for their eccentric, fanciful and imaginative designs featuring a whimsical menagerie of finely modeled birds and parrots, toads, fish, hedgehogs, armadillos and salamanders that frequently boasted grinning or sneering human characteristics, and a bizarre range of menacing goblins and mythological dragons. These decorated an array of vases, water jugs, tobacco jars and punch bowls that were covered with mottled 'orange peel' glazes in a subdued palette of browns, greens, blues, cream and gray which served to highlight the realistic impressed and incised surface decoration. The pottery closed in 1914.

RUSKIN'S IDEOLOGY

In keeping with their Arts and Crafts ideals, the art pottery established in Smethwick in 1898 as the Birmingham Tile and Pottery Works by William Howson Taylor and his father, was renamed Ruskin in 1904 after the 19th century writer and critic John Ruskin. Howson Taylor held similar ideological beliefs to Ruskin.

Ruskin pottery was celebrated for the production of high quality wares with a stunning array of sumptuous, brightly-colored glazes. The glazes were developed by Howson Taylor and inspired by oriental techniques. The vases, bowls and other ceramic wares produced in small numbers by the factory were expensive, largely due to the many firings in the kiln the glazes required. As a result of its limited output the factory fell victim to the Depression and in December of 1933 it was forced to close.

FATHER OF STUDIO POTTERY

A Bernard Leach stoneware bottle painted with brown fish on a white ground.
12in (30cm) high Q

A Ruskin pottery high-fired stoneware vase with lavender over silver-gray, liver-red speckled with turquoise glaze.
1908 6in (15cm) high L

SHOJI HAMADA BOTTLE

Shoji Hamada was born in Tokyo and studied ceramics at Tokyo Institute of Technology under Kawai Kanijiro. With Bernard Leach, co-founded the St Ives Pottery in 1920. He has been called the 'archetypal Oriental potter'. He was a gifted thrower and his pottery was fired in Japanese-style wood-fired kilns. It often features contrasting glazed and unglazed surfaces. The vigorous decoration is usually applied using the austere glazes which are typical of Japanese *mingei* wares. Hamada used shapes that were typical of wares from Japan and China.

The square bottle shape is a traditional Japanese form.

Hamada often used areas of contrasting glaze to decorate his work.

The glazes was poured onto the clay using a ladle, resulting in drips and runs.

A Shoji Hamada faceted bottle, with ladle-pour design.
1960s 7.5in (19cm) high N

Considered by many to be the 'father of British studio pottery', Bernard Leach was born in Hong Kong where his father was a colonial judge. He studied art in London before settling in Japan in 1909. There he studied ceramics and, in 1919, made friends with the potter Shoji Hamada. Returning to St Ives in Cornwall in 1920, Leach and Hamada set up a studio where they created handmade pottery inspired by traditional Japanese, Chinese and Korean ceramics combined with Western techniques such as slipware and salt glazed wares.

Fired in a Japanese-type, wood burning kiln, Leach and Hamada's utilitarian stoneware pots, bowls, vases and bottles were distinguished by spare decoration and contrasting areas of glazes and unglazed surfaces using a variety of glazing techniques. Together they made ceramics which were a collaboration between imaginative design, skilled craft techniques, art and philosophy.

By 1923 their collaboration had come to an end, and Hamada returned to Japan where he settled in the town of Mashiko. It is now a pottery center of world renown and he is celebrated as a major figure of the *mingei* folk art movement. In 1955 the Japanese government named him a "Living National Treasure".

In the early years of the St Ives Pottery, many people considered Leach's work to lack refinement. However, when he published his handbook for potters, *A Potter's Book*, in 1940 the public began to re-evaluate his pottery.

The influence of Bernard Leach can be seen in the work of many other potters. The first of the many apprentice potters at the Leach pottery, Michael Cardew, emerged as a champion of the studio ceramics movement. Like Leach, he believed that functional handmade pottery lay at the heart of the philosophy behind the studio ceramics movement. Cardew used the slipware technique to decorate his broad array of pitchers and chargers. The decoration of his pots shows the fluidity and immediacy of his technique.

Lucie Rie (1902-95)

Born in Vienna, the studio potter Lucie Rie arrived in Britain in the late 1930s. She established a workshop in London where she produced restrained wares. Rie experimented with many different glazes which she used to decorate her austere, delicate, angular elegant pots, some decorated with incised decoration. Her carefully applied glazes are evidence of her deep technical knowledge. She is considered to be one of the most important British potters of the 20th century.

Having studied pottery under Josef Hoffmann and Michael Powolny at the Vienna *Kunstgewerbeschule* – a school of Arts and Crafts associated with the *Wiener Werkstatte*, Lucie Rie set up her first studio in Vienna in 1925. Born Lucie Gomperz, she exhibited at the Paris International Exhibition that year, but by 1938 she had been forced to flee Austria. She moved to London where, at her studio near Hyde Park, she made handcrafted art pottery whch showed great imagination.

During and after World War Two she earned money by making buttons and jewelry for couture dress designers. She employed a number of fellow emigrés to help her and in 1946 Rie hired the young Hans Coper to help her fire the buttons. Although he had no experience in making ceramics and harbored ambitions to learn sculpture, Rie encouraged Coper's aspirations. She introduced him to the potter Herbert Matthews, gave him lessons on the finer points of creating wheel-thrown pots. Coper was rewarded with the offer to become a partner in Rie's studio. He remained there until 1958, and they were friends until his death.

Together Rie and Coper designed and manufactured the Lucie Rie Pottery's standard lines, which included tea and coffee services, cruet sets, and salad bowls. The wares were angular and thin-walled, with dark brown or white glazes and, sometimes, sgraffito – fine, scratched, linear decoration. They were sold in upmarket stores such as Heal's in London. Both Rie and Coper pursued their individual work when they could.

Renowned for her experiments with innovative glazes, Rie's austere pottery wares are simply decorated, such as finely inscribed parallel lines inlaid with delicate hues or vivid glazes that have been mottled or banded together to achieve an effect of

A Lucie Rie mottled brown porcelain pedestal bowl, the flared rim with pink blue and green bands.
c1979 7.5in (18.5cm) diam N

great depth, or surface textures. She once said: "To make pottery is an adventure to me, every new work is a new beginning. Indeed I shall never cease to be a pupil. There seems to the casual onlooker little variety in ceramic shapes and designs. But to the lover of pottery there is an endless variety of the most exciting kind. And there is nothing sensational about it only a silent grandeur and quietness." She added: "I do not attempt to be original or different. Something which to describe I am not clever enough moves me to do what I do."

Rie had a highly original vision for modern domestic pottery that continues to be a trailblazer of modern ceramic design.

HANS COPER (1920-81)

Born in Germany, Hans Coper fled to Britain in 1939, joining the workshop of Lucie Rie and collaborating on her domestic pottery. Coper forged his own individual path for studio ceramic design, creating distinctive and unusual shapes with spare decoration highlighted with a range of intense colors. The deep shades of ocher and metallic black he used were devised by applying oxides to the pale, finely textured surface of unglazed clay. Coper produced bold, idiosyncratic forms.

A Hans Coper 'Spade' stoneware vase, the body picked out with a matt manganese glaze.
c1965-70 8.5in (21.5cm) high P

LUCIE RIE CERAMICS

A photograph of Lucie Rie's hands at the potter's wheel.

A Lucie Rie porcelain vase with flaring rim, covered with a bronze glaze and with blue and incised pinstripe rim and shoulder.
7.5in (19cm) high U

A Lucie Rie stoneware vase, of shouldered form with narrow neck and flared rim with dark brown edge, otherwise pale bluey-oatmeal tones.
10in (25.5cm) high M

A porcelain bowl by Lucie Rie, the white ground decorated at the rim with a bronze band and brown dribbled glaze.
5.75in (14.5cm) diam R

Later American Studio Ceramics

The American studio ceramic movement continued to build upon the principles of craft and simplicity that had marked the output of the Arts and Crafts potteries. New participants, including immigrants from Europe, contributed their skills and helped to teach and inspire a new generation of potters during the middle years of the century.

Painted Shakespearian scenes decorate a large four-sided faience vase by Henry Varnum Poor. 1932 14.5in (37cm) high Q

MAMA OF DADA

Among the visionary art potters of the early 20th century was the San Francisco-born artist, studio potter and sometime actress Beatrice Wood. In the years following World War One she collaborated with the legendary artists Marcel Duchamp and Henri-Pierre Roche. Together they realized a common vision by publishing the avant-garde journal *The Blind Man*, which gave voice to the Dada art movement in New York City. Later in life Wood was dubbed the 'Mama of Dada'.

Returning to California in the 1940s, Wood enrolled in ceramics classes and, inspired, she dedicated over fifty years to creating imaginative art pottery. Her work shows diverse influences, including folk art, ethnic jewelry and Modernism. She developed sculptural vessels featuring the rough pitted surfaces characteristic of an innovative technique of luster – or 'volcanic' – glazing in a range of earth tones and bright colors. She explained: "most potters, they go in for earth tones and subdued things, and I like color."

A Scheier footed floor vase, embossed with faces, masks and bodies covered in a volcanic bronzed glaze against shaded matte turquoise. 1966 22.5in (56cm) high T

BRIGHT BLUE GLAZES

Born in Finland, the award winning American studio ceramicist and teacher Maija Grotell trained as a painter and sculptor in Helsinki before turning her talents to the study of pottery guided by the celebrated ceramicist and painter Alfred William Finch. Finch was a founder of "Les XX", a group of 20 Belgian artists who rebelled against the prevailing artistic standards, rules, and traditions.

Grotell's distinctive large size wheel-thrown ceramic vessels are decorated with a palette of colored slips and glazes – including a range of luminous bright blues, made from copper oxide, that were brushed onto the surface of the pot.

In 1927 Grotell moved to the United States and enrolled at New York State's College of Ceramics at Alfred University. By the early 1930s her success as a studio potter led her to take up a variety of posts at prestigious institutions, including tenure of nearly thirty years at the Cranbrook Academy of Art in Michigan, where she numbered among her students the future luminaries Richard Devore, John Glick, Suzanne Stephenson and Toshiko Takaezu.

SOPHISTICATED SHAPES

Other talented studio potters included Otto and Gertrud Natzler. Trained as a textile designer in Vienna, Otto Natzler was introduced to pottery by his wife. After fleeing the Nazi encroachment on Austria in the late 1930s they moved to Los Angeles with a potter's wheel and a small kiln. They earned a living by teaching pottery – among their students was Beatrice Wood – while in their spare time they made imaginative and original ceramic designs.

Gertrud's fascination with the medium of clay is reflected in her vases and useful wares in elegant and sophisticated shapes that unite form and decoration. Her husband once said: "Gertrud had a feeling

A faience faceted vase painted with potters at the wheel, by Maija Grotell. 7.5in (19cm) high O

NATZLER BULBOUS VASE

Husband-and-wife team, Otto and Gertrud Natzler, spent over three decades working together in southern California. They moved to the US from Vienna in 1937, the year after winning a silver medal at the World Exposition in Paris. They divided the work between them: Gertrud worked the wheel, producing many bowls and vases, while Otto formulated the glazes and fired the pots, creating their unique style. Each piece can be recognized by a crystalline or volcanic glaze, which often combines colors of deep blue, purple and green.

The bulbous vase has a cupped rim.

Gertrud's graceful, balanced and well-proportioned pieces suited the style of the time.

This is a superior example of the Natzlers's blue-green striated volcanic glaze. Otto experimented to create the pock-marked glaze, where layers of color bubble up to the surface.

The walls are paper-thin.

A monumental Natzler bulbous vase.
17.5in (44.5cm) high X

for form right from the very beginning." Many of her designs reflect the Art Nouveau vocabulary as filtered through the Vienna Secessionist Movement – stylized and restrained organic forms and decoration that look to the natural world for inspiration. Otto concentrated on kiln techniques. Natzler wares owe much of their originality to the more than 1,000 individual glaze recipes developed by Otto. Among the most celebrated are his multi-layered 'crater' and 'lava' glazes, a shimmering crystalline glaze and a textural

'hare-fur' glaze. He explained: "Anything you do is a craft until you master it. And if you really master it and add to this craft, invent maybe something new, give it another turn, it may become an art." The enduring partnership resulted in some of the most original and imaginative designs for art pottery to emerge from the modern ceramic movement, and many of their students went on to become enormously successful. Following Gertrud's death in 1971, Otto carried on creating ceramics, among them handmade slab compositions.

Other talented American artisans who created well-made, innovative studio ceramics in the United States were the architect, painter, sculptor and self-taught potter Kansas-born Henry Varnum Poor – widely admired for his hand-painted vases and chargers using the decorative sgrafitto technique – and the gifted couple Edwin and Mary Scheier, whose distinctive thrown and sculptural ceramics celebrate their interest in both human and animal forms, with decoration frequently featuring symbols for life, birth and rebirth.

THE CRAFT MOVEMENT

CERAMICS GALLERY

Innovative shapes and glazes typify the work of craft potters. Many looked to Japan and China for inspiration, while others revisited ancient potting techniques and developed innovative ways to use them. The result is a plethora of shapes, colors and styles of decoration.

A marbleized glaze on yellow ground decorated this ceramic pocket vase, by Jacqueline Poncelet.
8in (20.5cm) diam K

Mottled glazes with a copper luster cover this large wheel-thrown vase by Maija Grotell.
10in (25.5cm) wide P

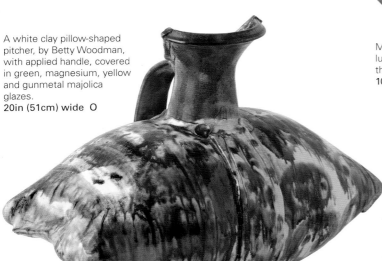

A white clay pillow-shaped pitcher, by Betty Woodman, with applied handle, covered in green, magnesium, yellow and gunmetal majolica glazes.
20in (51cm) wide O

Colorful glazes decorate a Hui Ka Kwong earthenware charger.
1968 13in (33cm) diam H

A Jim Malone stoneware bottle with brushed slip and painted decoration.
11in (28cm) high E

An earthenware vessel by Ralph Bacerra, carved and pierced with abstract and geometric patterns, the exterior covered in volcanic uranium glaze, the top in turquoise and black majolica glaze.
1998 20in (51cm) wide T

A large stoneware 'Saalal' vessel, by Claude Conover.
18.5in (49.5cm) high T

RICHARD DEVORE

Richard DeVore was born in Ohio and studied at the Cranbrook Academy of Art, where he later become head of the ceramics department. In 1987, DeVore was installed as a fellow of the American Craft Council. He is known for simple vessels (most often low bowls or tall vessels). These are typically colored and textured to resemble bone, weathered skin or rough earth, and have irregular rims and hidden interior spaces, tapering to a rounded or flat base.

The vase has an asymmetrical rim and 'torn' edges.

It is hard to say whether it is a utilitarian piece or sculpture.

It is covered with a crackled light brown glaze.

A Richard DeVore ovoid vase.
13.75in (35cm) wide P

A flaring stoneware vessel, by Richard DeVore, 'Untitled no. 1024', with a dead-matte gray interior.
12.75in (32.5cm) wide O

A large faceted sculptural ceramic pitcher, by Alison Britton, decorated with abstract brush strokes.
1982 10.5in (26.5cm) high G

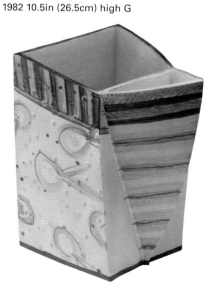

Three 'Unfolding Vases' by Takeshi Yasuda.
17.75in (45cm) high L each

A glazed stoneware moonpot, by Toshiko Takaezu.
1982 10.5in (26.5cm) high T

Early Studio Glass

Until the 1950s glass production was mostly confined to industrial factories which were home to large furnaces, teams of glassblowers and machinery. But that was to change in the following decade when the pioneering work of a handful of visionary glass makers, including Harvey Littleton and Dominick Labino, gave birth to the Studio Glass Movement.

An extremely rare Mdina Glass 'Crizzle Stone' vase, designed and made by Michael Harris.
c1971 7.25in (18cm) high L

TAKING GLASS FROM FACTORIES

The contemporary glass-blowing movement was born in 1962 at the Toledo Museum of Art in Ohio when two workshops were held by ceramics instructor Harvey Littleton and chemist Dominick Labino. Their aim was to prove that artists could blow glass individually in a studio, rather than in factories. The pair began experimenting by melting glass in a small furnace. At first they made simple, experimental vases and bowls.

The son of a glass scientist at the Corning works in New York where he had apprenticed, Littleton was inspired to consider glass as a means of pure artistic expression. Although as a ceramicist he had little practical experience his idea was that "glass should be a medium for the individual artist". He first put his idea forward in 1959 at a conference of American craftsmen at Lake George.

Littleton was able to realize it with the help of Pennsylvania-born Dominick Labino, a chemist with the Johns-Manville Fiber Glass Corporation.

Labino established a studio on his farm in Ohio, a sizable space where he could bring to fruition his dream of freehand blowing with molten glass. For Littleton he developed a metal – or glass recipe – with a low melting point and a small furnace that could be used in a studio. This development proved to be a turning point for the making of glass objects as individual and innovative artistic creations, as glass artisans were no longer dependant on large industrial factories to realize their visions.

Together Littleton and Labino created unique works of art from molten glass, with Labino specializing in objects featuring subtle color effects and Littleton devising abstract sculptural pieces. Littleton also taught the new techniques at an offshoot of

the first fine art glass program at Wisconsin's University at Madison, where over the years he trained many contemporary glass artists including the pioneer Martin Lipofsky, Fritz Dreisbach, Dale Chihuly and Sam Herman.

AN INTERNATIONAL MOVEMENT

During the 1960s the Studio Glass Movement gathered momentum, traveling across the Atlantic to Europe. In Britain, glassmakers including Pauline Solven, Annette Meach, Steven Newell, Jiri Suhajek, and Michael Harris became the first generation of artists who were able to experiment with glass.

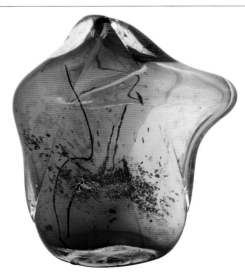

A Sam Herman glass 'Torso' sculpture.
8in (20cm) high F

Sam Herman in his studio working on a piece of blown glass, seen attached to the pontil rod.

SAM HERMAN

Sam Herman was one of Harvey Littleton's first students. Born in Mexico, Herman now lives in London and Mallorca. He was head of the glass department at the Royal College of Art for several years. He taught his students to work directly with molten glass, beginning the Studio Glass movement in Britain. In 1969 he co-founded the Glasshouse, in London, the first glass studio of its kind in the country. In 1974 he set up Australia's first hot glass studio at the Jam Factory in Adelaide. He has also been a consultant to Belgium's Cristalleries Val Saint Lambert.

DOMINICK LABINO
Recognized as the Father of the Studio Glass Movement, Dominick Labino developed the technologies needed for small furnace glassmaking. He introduced new methods, such as color fusing. Some of his early, experimental works represent breakthroughs in the glass making process; others just a step on the road. Labino also helped to develop the fiberglass that was used within NASA's Space Shuttles.

Early pieces of Labino's glass are often experimental in nature and forms are still rudimentary. Variations in the thickness of the glass create graduated color.

This elegant vase is decorated with applied swirling prunts.

A deep ruby red studio-glass vase designed and made by Dominick Labino. 1973 6.25in (16cm) high L

Born in Derbyshire, Michael Harris studied glass design at the Stourbridge College of Technology and Art, an area at the historic center of British glass making. However, as glass was factory-made at this time, Harris did not have the opportunity to work directly with molten glass, although he did learn engraving and other cold-working skills.

Harris went on to study Industrial Glass Design at London's Royal College of Art. There he met research fellow Sam Herman, freshly arrived from Wisconsin and keen to share the small-furnace technology he had helped to develop. Beginning in 1966, Harris worked closely with Herman, learning further how to work the molten glass and, crucially, how to incorporate different colors. It was the beginning of the Studio Glass movement in Britain.

While at the Royal College of Art, Harris produced the highly successful Calypto pattern for Chance Brothers, of Birmingham in 1959. From 1963-65 he visited a glassworks in Slovenia. Following the trip he began to experiment with textural surface patterns on glass, using such materials as bark and mesh to create the molds.

INDEPENDENT GLASS MAKING

Harris saw the inherent commercial possibilities for an artist to make their own glass, not just to decorate blanks made by others or direct glassblowers to create their designs. The next step was to set up on his own, somewhere with no pre-conceived ideas about how glass should be made. In late 1967, Harris left England to start a new life. He founded a glass studio on the

Mediterranean island of Malta, building a highly successful business exporting his distinctive Mdina glass around the world. Returning to Britain in 1972, he founded a studio on the Isle of Wight, which continues to make hand-blown glass today.

For the early studio glassmakers, venues such as The Glasshouse (see Sam Herman box opposite) provided the ideal starting point for setting up a studio. Herman said he wanted to "to establish a workshop that would act as a halfway house between college and the real world, and of creating a life in glass away from the industry." Its first members were graduates from the Royal College of Art but over the years it also trained apprentices and other students. The Glasshouse closed in 1998, having made an exceptional contribution to British studio glass.

Later Studio Glass

In the 1960s and 1970s the Studio Glass Movement gathered increasing momentum in the United States as well as in Britain and across Europe, attracting a number of progressive glass designers, many of whom are still active today. They built on the skills of their predecessors to create innovative, technically advanced glass works of art.

ADVANCED TECHNIQUES

While the first generation of Studio Glass artists continued to develop their skills, a second generation of students built on their experience, improving techniques and production processes. They created more complicated, more sophisticated and more challenging glass which began to attract interest from museums and collectors who were fascinated by the way glass had been transformed into an artistic medium rather than a craft.

During the 1970s, the opening of glass schools introduced an increasing number of people to the possibility of working with glass. In 1971 Dale Chihuly (see p266), John Hauberg and Anne Gould Hauberg opened the influential Pilchuck Glass Center near Seattle in the United States. It has dominated the development of studio glass ever since.

By the 1980s artists were exploring social and narrative issues in their glass. It was being combined with other media such as wood and metal. Also, traditional hot glass-working techniques such as pate de verre were being explored. The result was technically assured, confident works that soon achieved fine-art status.

A sculpture by Marvin Lipofsky, 'California Loop Series #3', which combines glass, flocking and electroformed copper.
1969 17in (43cm) long U

ARTISITC EXPRESSION

The American Studio Glass Movement owes a debt to the celebrated glassmaking pioneer Marvin Lipofsky, who was encouraged to pursue glass studies with the trailblazing Harvey Littleton at the University of Wisconsin. Lipofsky believed glass should be liberated from its role as the material of choice for functional and useful wares. Lipofsky recognized glass as a viable instrument for independent artistic expression, and he spread this gospel to a host of future studio glass artisans when he took up a post as a design instructor at the prestigious Berkeley branch of the University of California.

Lipofsky's signature "bubbles" of glass and his 'Great American Food Series', inspired by 1970s pop culture, are among his most widely admired designs. During his distinguished career he also inaugurated a glass program at the California College of Crafts as well as helping to establish the Glass Art Society.

One of Lipofsky's Berkeley students, Richard Marquis, traveled to Murano where he learnt the glassblowing techniques used by the craftsmen at Venini. He has taught these skills to artists across the world, and used them in his own works.

Marquis was not the first American to work at Venini. That honor went to

Three sections of colored glass make up Thomas Stearns' 'A doppio incalmo' vase for Venini.
1962 4.25in (11cm) high NPA

Red and black glass fibers were used to create this "filet-de-verre" bowl by Mary Ann "Toots" Zynsky.
1980-90 9.25in (23.5cm) diam O

Thomas Stearns who was at the Murano glassworks from 1959 to 1961. A student at the Cranbrook Academy, his ground-breaking designs and won the "best of show" award at the 1962 Venice Bienalle. However, the award was rescinded when the judges discovered he was an American. His sculptural glass was too challenging to put into mass production and so today is very rare.

INTERNATIONAL APPEAL

Like many studio glass pioneers, Peter Layton began his career as a student of ceramics. Born in Prague – for centuries the center of Bohemian glass production – Layton was seduced by what he considered to be the magic of working in molten glass and he set about teaching himself to master glassmaking techniques. His imaginative free-blown decorative glass designs feature organic sculptural shapes. They reflect his enthusiasm for the natural world and display his talent for wedding color, pattern and form. At Layton's London glassblowing studio, considered to be one of the most important glass workshops and places of leraning in Europe, Layton and his team are dedicated to creating and displaying one-of-a kind contemporary art glass that enjoys an international reputation for originality and innovation.

Having studied with the eminent glass artist Dale Chihuly at the Rhode Island School of Design, Mary Ann 'Toots' Zynsky is among a cluster of innovative and influential American studio glass craftsmen working today. She was also one of the founding artists of the Pilchuck Glass School. In 1980, Zynsky helped to found and develop the second New York Experimental Glass Workshop, which is now called UrbanGlass. While she was there she advanced her work with hand pulled glass threads, working on ways to fuse them separately as well as to combine them with blown forms. Eventually, with a colleague, she designed a thread pulling machine which enabled her to produce larger quantities of longer and finer thread. This allowed her to work in as many colors as she wanted and she was also able to make pieces that were entirely comprised of thousands of glass threads. She calls this innovative technique "filet-de-verre".

RICHARD MARQUIS GLASS TEAPOT

Arizona born Richard Marquis helped to lead the way in the 1960s Studio Glass movement. He travelled to Venice in 1969, where he worked at the Venini glassworks. There, he absorbed many Venetian glass-making skills and soon began to combine these with his imaginative aesthetic to create glass that demonstrates his sense of humor. His pieces were often in functional forms, such as teapots and bottles, yet each is decidedly non-functional – such as this glass teapot. Today Marquis works in comparative isolation, producing pieces that make light of convention and often comment on consumerism.

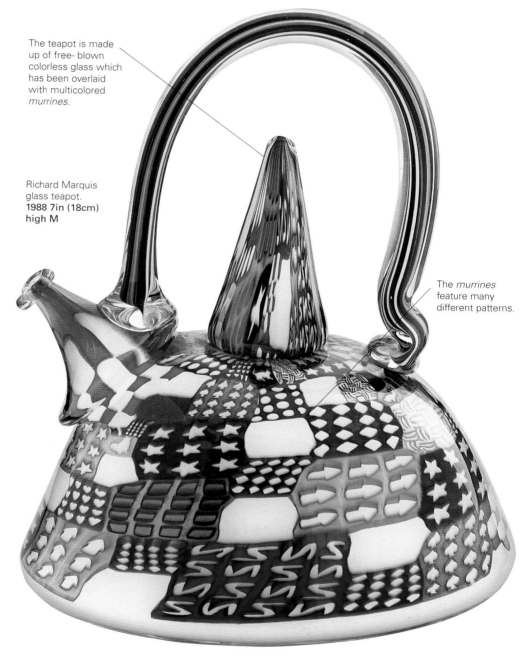

The teapot is made up of free-blown colorless glass which has been overlaid with multicolored *murrines*.

Richard Marquis glass teapot. 1988 7in (18cm) high M

The *murrines* feature many different patterns.

"Form follows function – that has been misunderstood. Form and function should be one, joined in a spiritual union." Frank Lloyd Wright

The Modern Movement

The Bauhaus Director's house at Dessau, was designed by Walter Gropius and was his home from 1925-1928. Gropius aimed to put the principles of efficient construction into practice by building the house, and those he designed for the masters, using simple, industrially prefabricated building blocks. The result is a house built of different sized cubes.

The Modern Movement

The modern movement was inspired by the belief that a new era was beginning, and that this new world required good-quality, functional design. Ornament was unnecessary and distracting: form should be derived from function and from the new mechanical processes available. Maintaining that technology and machine production were there to be exploited for the common good, Modernism was often allied with left wing social and political beliefs. Both believed that art and design could transform society.

CHALLENGE TO TRADITIONALISM

Early believers included members of the Deutscher Werkbund, which was founded in 1907, and Austrian architect Adolf Loos, who published his famous text 'Ornament and Crime' a year later. However, it was after 1918 that Modernism really started to take hold. World War One was a major turning point for modernists. It was like no previous war – the cataclysmic and senseless slaughter and the mechanized destructive force of the new "machine age" changed the perception of a whole generation.

At the same time, it was perhaps inevitable that people would question the cultural values that had initially caused the war and the caused the most radical cultural shift for centuries. Modernism likewise rejected traditional manufacturing methods and materials, embracing the new.

As well as psychological scarring, survivors had to deal with the economic ruin of their countries and mass homelessness. Consequently Modernist furniture placed considerable emphasis on lowering production costs and producing lightweight furniture that could be moved easily out of temporary housing and into a proper home.

Many significant advances were made in Germany: the country that had been hit hardest by the war. The Bauhaus school – arguably the powerhouse of early Modernism – opened in Weimar in 1919. Led by Walter Gropius, the Bauhaus aimed to put Modernist ideals into practice and introduce unity to the arts. The resulting design style, epitomized by Wilhelm Wagenfeld's glass and nickel Bauhaus lamp, was mimicked all over the world.

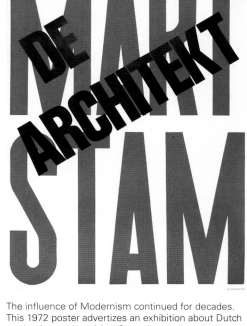

The influence of Modernism continued for decades. This 1972 poster advertizes an exhibition about Dutch modernist architect Mart Stam. It was designed by a father of modern Dutch graphism Paul Schuitema.

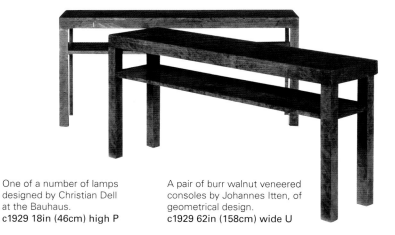

One of a number of lamps designed by Christian Dell at the Bauhaus.
c1929 18in (46cm) high P

A pair of burr walnut veneered consoles by Johannes Itten, of geometrical design.
c1929 62in (158cm) wide U

TIMELINE

1917 The de Stijl movement is founded in the Netherlands. The Russian Revolution leads to the overthrow of the Tsar.

1919 The Bauhaus is founded in Weimar, Germany. Its first director is Walter Gropius.

1923-4 Nikolai Suetin works at Russia's State Porcelain factory

1924 Gerrit Rietveld designs The Schroeder House in Utrecht. The building is created from a series of abstract planes.

1925 Le Corbusier at creates his Pavillon de L'Esprit Nouveau at the Exposition des Arts Décoratifs et Industriels Modernes in Paris.

AN INTERNATIONAL STYLE

Increased national and international travel, and improved telephone communication made it easy for designers to keep track of developments that were being made elsewhere. Marcel Breuer first experimented with tubular steel at the Bauhaus in 1925 and it soon became one of the signature materials of Modernism in many countries across the world. The Dutch De Stijl movement found common ground with the German Bauhaus.

The term "International Style", or "International Modern", referring to a Modernist style of architecture, became part of design vocabulary, though there were variations to the style from country to country: in Scandinavia, for example, wood was often used rather than steel.

By 1930, Modernism was an accepted facet of life in most developed countries and flourished alongside Art Deco. The idea of urbanized populations housed in purpose-built homes had become so acceptable to the masses that Modernism had become a recognisable design style. It was based on abstract, rectilinear geometry, industrial production techniques and modern industrial materials, such as chrome, steel, glass. Eye-catching graphics and advertizing filtered down from Modernist art, especially through poster design. Form and function were still vitally important and by producing these simple, practical forms, the Modernists achieved better standardisation, which allowed greater efficiency in production and materials.

Unfortunately, the economic turmoil continued. In 1926 Britain was rocked by the General Strike and three years later the Wall Street crash began the Great Depression in the United States. The mid-1930s became a time of poverty and disillusionment for many people. Extremist political parties, such as the National Socialist Party of Germany, promised the necessary changes. When the Nazi party eventually rose to power in 1933, the Bauhaus was forced to close, and its most notable designers and artists fled to Britain and the United States.

The head rest serves to emphasize the sleek, modern design.

LE CORBUSIER, CHARLOTTE PERRIAND, PIERRE JEANNERET 'B306' CHAISE LONGUE
In 1928 Le Corbusier, born Charles-Edouard Jeanneret, and his collaborators Charlotte Perriand and Pierre Jeanneret, set out to develop three chairs with chrome-plated tubular steel bases for architectural projects they were working on: one was to be designed "for conversation", one "for relaxation", and the third for sleeping. The 'B306' chaise longue fulfilled the sleeping requirement.

The recliner was inspired by 18th century day-beds but is more sculpture than furniture.

A Le Corbusier, Charlotte Perriand and Pierre Jeanneret B306 chaise longue.
1928 64in (160cm) long L

The upholstery is covered with black leather and supported by rubber stretchers.

1926 Mart Stam designs a tubular steel cantilever chair. Mies van der Rohe and Marcel Breuer are working on similar forms.

1925-6 The Bauhaus moves from Weimar to Dessau.

1929 Ludwig Mies van der Rohe completes the German Pavilion at the Exposición Internacional in Barcelona.

1929-33 Alvar Aalto designs and builds the Paimio sanitorium and creates a range of furniture and fittings for it.

1934 Frank Lloyd Wright completes Fallingwater, which is hailed as his architectural masterpiece.

1939-40 MoMA's Organic Design in Home Furnishing includes a plywood chair by Eero Saarinen and Charles Eames.

Gerrit Rietveld (1888-1964)

The De Stijl movement and the architect and designer Gerrit Thomas Rietveld are synonymous in the language of design, even though Rietveld was not the founder of De Stijl. His famous 'Red Blue' chair was one of the first pieces of furniture inspired by the new machine aesthetic and was arguably the most influential chair of the 20th century. The chair encapsulated the De Stijl philosophy which was to ignore natural form and color in favor of a limited palette and a reliance on horizontal and vertical lines.

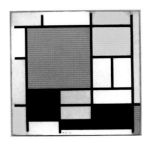

"Composition with red, yellow, blue and black" by the Dutch painter Pieter Cornelis 'Piet' Mondrian. His work inspired the members of the De Stijl group.

Born in Utrecht, Gerrit Rietveld worked with his father as a cabinet-maker from the age of 11, later taking architecture classes and starting his own workshop in 1916. The De Stijl movement was founded a year later by the Dutch painter, writer, and designer Theo van Doesburg.

The title De Stijl was derived from the Dutch for "The Style", the name given to a journal published by Dutch artists who found themselves segregated from the art world as a result of the Netherlands' neutrality in World War One. Dutch artists were unable to leave the country after 1914; the Dutch painter Mondrian, for example, had been visiting from Paris and was unable to return to France after the outbreak of war. The artists published the journal *De Stijl* as a manifesto for their revolutionary utopian ideal of creating a new and universal art. The movement was also known as Neo-plasticism.

DE STIJL COLORS AND FORMS

Rietveld designed the 'Red Blue' chair in 1917–18. It was originally made in a natural wood finish – only later did he paint it in the signature colors of the De Stijl movement, which he officially joined in 1919. A principal member of the group was Piet Mondrian, who proposed ignoring natural form and color. De Stijl advocated no less than pure abstraction based on a palette of red, yellow, and blue along with black, white, and gray, composed within the highly simplified boundaries of horizontal and vertical "directions". The movement sought to make each element within a design independent of the other parts.

The phrase De Stijl also has a secondary meaning in Dutch: "a post, jamb, or

The Schroeder House in Utrecht was designed by Rietveld as a Modernist model of abstract planes. The house is built of wood, concrete and metal and was conceived as a complete project with Rietveld designing the furnishings.

Gerrit Rietveld's 'Red Blue' chair was designed to conform to the strict design code of the de Stijl group. This reproduction follows the same principles.
1917-18 34in (86.5cm) high E

support". This is certainly applicable in the structure of the 'Red Blue' chair, which consists of a framework of 13 rails, set at right angles and supporting the four boards that comprise the back, seat, and two arms. The layering and lack of intersection exemplify the strict design vocabulary of the group.

The architectural equivalent of the 'Red Blue' chair was the Schröder House in Utrecht, which Rietveld designed in 1923–4. The only building completely conceived according to De Stijl principles, it is often described as a "three-dimensional realization of a Mondrian painting". This description is also sometimes used for the "Red Blue" chair.

The character of De Stijl started to change in the early 1920s, and in 1924 Mondrian split from the group over van Doesburg's proposal that the diagonal line was more important than the horizontal and the vertical. With van Doesburg's death in 1931 the De Stijl movement lost its figurehead and its impetus. The group had never existed as a close-knit community of artists. Surprisingly, Rietveld never even met Mondrian – they only communicated by letter.

NEW DEPARTURES

Rietveld continued to design, and in 1932–4 the classic 'Zig-Zag' chair was added to his catalogue of ground-breaking designs. Many saw it as a response to van Doesburg's earlier call for the use of oblique lines, the very reason for Mondrian's departure. Rietveld's 'Crate' chair of 1934 was so basic that it looked like it was fabricated from old crates. An obvious response to the Depression, it was later labeled as one of the earliest forms of "Poor Art".

Rietveld's legacy is solid, but it was rooted in a philosophy outside of normal comfort zones, rather like his "uncomfortable" chairs. With the 'Red Blue' chair, he had abandoned all notions of traditional comfort and made a chair that kept the sitter mentally aware and awake. The "Steltman" chair of 1963 was a classic re-interpretation of his earlier work and the last design before his death. As he once said, "We must remember that sit is a verb too."

GERRIT RIETVELD FURNITURE

Angular armrests enhance the geometric air of an upholstered oak easy chair by Gerrit Rietveld for De Toekomst.
1952 24.25in (61.5cm) wide M

Primary colors and geometric shapes are assembled in a Gerrit Rietveld wood side table.
25.5in (cm) high F

Diagonals, horizontals and verticals join in a reproduction of Gerrit Rietveld's 'Zig-Zag' chair.
1934 E

Gerrit Rietveld crate chair, made up of 18 rectangular sections of stained pine.
c1934 K

The Bauhaus

The avant-garde German school of industrial design known as the Bauhaus, which operated from 1919 to 1933, had a major influence on modernist architecture and design, especially furniture design. One of its early aims was the unification of architecture, art, craft, and technology, to produce designs suitable for mass production. It emphasized the importance of simplified forms, standardization, functionality, and cooperative work.

The influence of the Bauhaus continues. This poster advertizes a German Bauhaus exhibition in 1968. It was designed by Herbert Bayer, a former Bauhaus student who went on to be the school's director of printing and advertizing.

Following the defeat of Germany in World War One and the abolition of its monarchy, the new Weimar Republic promised liberalism and an end to the censorship of the old regime. The suppression of experimentation in the arts was over and the innovators in society were at last free to pursue their ideals.

THE NEW SCHOOL AT WEIMAR

The Bauhaus ("Building School") was founded in 1919 by Walter Gropius. As a former employee of Peter Behrens, Gropius had absorbed the burgeoning philosophy of modernism, and the Bauhaus offered a platform to pursue this. He continued his private architecture practice with Adolf

Meyer while he was at the school. The school's reputation as an architectural innovator was largely based on their output rather than that of the students. Despite the intention that the school would include architecture on its syllabus, a specialist department did not open until 1927.

Within the fertile environment he created, Gropius and his distinguished faculty taught mass-production techniques and the use of innovative materials. Industrial ideals were applied to everyday objects. The concept of interior walls as supportive elements was made redundant by the ever-improving structural advances of steel and concrete. Gropius exploited these with great fervor, pioneering the form

Architecture became an important part of the Bauhaus' curriculum. This study for a building, by Naum Slytzky, dates from the Weimar Bauhaus.
1920/21 14in (35.5cm) high V

Innovative design is the hallmark of the Bauhaus' output. This table lamp, by Christian Dell, rotates in all directions.
1920s 17in (43cm) high K

The Bauhaus' students studied all aspects of design. Bauhaus telephone, manufactured by Fuld & Co. of Frankfurt.
1929 5.25in (13.5cm) high N

of construction that was to become a symbol of the modernist movement and known as the International Style.

The Bauhaus went through three periods corresponding to one of its three directors: Walter Gropius (from 1919 to 1928); Hannes Meyer (from 1928 to 1930); and Ludwig Mies van der Rohe (from 1930 to 1933). These periods of change, along with a move to Dessau in 1925, were disruptive for the school. Despite the assertion that the Bauhaus was apolitical, it seemed unable to escape the various political wrangles of the period.

Gropius had attracted an illustrious faculty of tutors including Paul Klee, Wassily Kandinsky, Marcel Breuer, and László Moholy-Nagy. Gropius designed the Bauhaus Dessau building, which is in the International Style, and unified the objectives of the school in art, craft, and technology. Product design was of paramount importance, be it graphics, textiles, furniture, or ceramics.

NEW DIRECTORSHIPS

Under the directorship of Hannes Meyer, the style of Bauhaus architecture became heavily functional. Meyer was popular with prospective clients for providing accurate and well-costed breakdowns of potential builds. In 1929 the school made its first profit from his approach, but Meyer was an ardent Communist and his outspoken nature compromised the existence of the school with the philosophy of Nazism. He had also alienated key people such as Marcel Breuer, who subsequently resigned. When Mies van der Rohe replaced him as director, in 1930, supporters of Meyer were banned from the school.

The Nazis were critical of the Bauhaus, labeling it "un-German". Despite the similarities with later Nazi architecture and design, it was deliberately portrayed as subversive and a hotbed of Communism, making Mies van der Rohe's position untenable. The school closed in April 1933 after a final year in Berlin.

The impact of the Bauhaus upon modern thinking is beyond question and almost beyond measure. The spread of the International Style and of modernist ideals is largely down to the Bauhaus and its innovative designers, many of whom fled

MARCEL BREUER 'B3' CHAIR
The 'B3', known as the 'Wassily' club chair, was designed in 1925 when it was among the first pieces of furniture constructed from tubular steel. It was designed by Hungarian architect and designer Marcel Breuer and is reputed to have been inspired by the curved metal handlebars on his bicycle. The frame consists of nine pieces of metal tube that are screwed together to give the appearance of a single, continuous length and create a framework which supports the weight of the sitter. The original seat, back and armrests were five fabric slings, but later versions substitute thick leather.

The chair showed the design possibilities of tubular metal which was a revolutionary material at the time. Early versions were nickel, rather than chrome, plated.

It was nicknamed 'Wassily' after the abstract painter Wassily Kandinsky who was at the Bauhaus at the time and admired the chair's design.

A 'Wassily' 'B3' chrome-plated and leather armchair, designed by Marcel Breuer.
c1925 31in (78.75cm) wide E

abroad as the Nazi government took hold. Its influence is proved by iconic Machine Age pieces such as classic door furniture by Gropius, a stylish table lamp by Christian Bell, and the 'B3' ('Wassily') chair by Breuer, industrial design began to be considered a positive force. The prototype of the 'B3' was of welded construction but was soon replaced by a nickel-plated version with bolted connections. Produced by the Berlin-based Standard-Möbel

Lengyel & Co., the chair was the first of a series of standardized tubular steel furniture designed by Breuer that strongly mirrored the Bauhaus ideal of highly functional, well-costed, mass-produced modular designs.

Gropius, who wanted no barriers between the structural and decorative arts, said, "We want an architecture adapted to our world of machines, radios, and fast cars" – and the Bauhaus delivered.

Walter Gropius (1883-1969)

Walter Gropius heads the line-up of the masters of modern architecture. The founder of the highly influential Bauhaus school in Germany in 1919, he pioneered the modern movement through his teaching and his innovative buildings. As well as the new architecture, he promoted modern, forward-thinking designs which were suitable for mass production. Having fled Nazi Germany in 1934, he promoted Bauhaus ideals abroad, first in England and then in the United States, where he became a naturalized citizen.

Born in Berlin, Walter Gropius followed in his father's footsteps and became an architect. Like several of his peers, he worked for the firm of Peter Behrens. Mies van der Rohe and Le Corbusier also benefited from the tutelage of Behrens, co-founder in 1907 of the Deutscher Werkbund. Behrens's work in 1907 with the German electrical company AEG on the creation of their corporate identity earned him the accolade of the "world's first industrial designer", and his influence on the young Gropius was significant.

After leaving Behrens, Gropius formed an architectural practice in Berlin with his friend Adolf Meyer. Their joint design in 1910 for the facade of the Fagus Factory in Alfeld-an-der-Leine is regarded as a seminal modernist work of the period. The floor-to-ceiling glass windows with no obvious structural supports give the building a noticeable lightness, and the play between the vertical and horizontal lines of the facade enhances this etherealizing effect.

With the advent of World War I, Gropius was called up as a reservist, almost losing his life on the Western Front. After the war, he was recommended to succeed Henry Van de Velde, who, owing to his Belgian origins, was not deemed suitable to continue as master of the Grand-Ducal Saxon School of Arts and Crafts, in Weimar. Gropius amalgamated it with the School of Fine Arts to form the Bauhaus. He designed everything from the buildings to the door furniture, including the now iconic lever door handles designed in collaboration with Gareth Steele in 1923.

Gropius resigned from the Bauhaus in 1928. Two years later, Mies van der Rohe took over, but the Nazis disliked the school, seeing it as an expression of Communism, and finally closed it down in 1933. Gropius left Germany in 1934 under the pretext of a brief visit to Britain, where he worked for Isokon. Three years later he moved to the United States. He lectured at Harvard University and collaborated with Marcel Breuer on several projects. In 1945 he founded The Architects' Collaborative (TAC) based in Cambridge, Massachusetts.

The family home that Gropius designed and built in Lincoln, Massachusetts, in 1938 blends the traditional materials of New England, such as brick, wood, and fieldstone, with the pure principles of the Bauhaus and innovative materials such as glass block and chrome. Like the master himself, his house epitomizes the philosophy and goals of the Modern movement.

Walter Gropius designed every aspect of the Bauhaus building at Weimar. The floor to ceiling windows are typical of his designs.

Students completed a *Vorkurs* or "preliminary course" which acted as an introduction to the ideas of the Bauhaus, before going on to specialize in their chosen field.

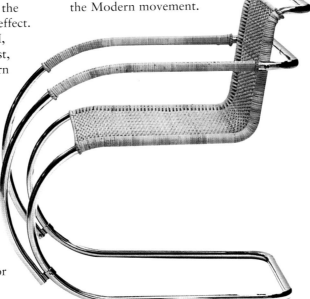

A cantilever armchair, designed by Walter Gropius while he was at the Weimar Bauhaus.
1927 31in (79cm) high J

Gropius promoted the work of the Bauhaus by furnishing his study with work by the students and teachers. The armchair and document stands are his own designs. The carpet was designed by Gertrud Arndt, who was a photographer and wife of Bauhaus master Alfred Arndt.

Ludwig Mies van der Rohe (1886-1969)

The German-born architect and designer Ludwig Mies van der Rohe was the greatest exponent of the International Style in architecture, combining simplicity – to the point of austerity – and clarity of form with fine materials and delicate detailing. His furniture was similarly functional in design while being produced in rich materials, including leather and chrome, for the luxury market. Pieces such as the 'Barcelona' chair have become modern classics.

Ludwig Mies van der Rohe was born into a traditional world. The late 19th century was a time of imperialism, with a strict social order based on the power of the aristocracy. Mies appended 'van der Rohe' to his surname (his mother's maiden name was Rohe) to lend an air of distinction. Indeed, it was undoubtedly helpful in his early career among Berlin's cultural elite.

After working in his father's stone-carving workshop, he moved to the studio of the designer Bruno Paul and then in 1908 to the studios of the influential Peter Behrens, where he worked alongside Walter Gropius and Le Corbusier. He then worked independently as an architect, despite his lack of formal training, designing traditional homes for the upper classes, but he soon began to challenge the old order. Against the background of the myriad dead of World War One and the social and political changes caused by the outcome of the war, superfluous ornamentation became a badge of dishonor among the protagonists of the new modernist movement. Their declared aim was to strip away all ornament unrelated to structure.

In 1921 Mies van der Rohe produced a radical competition design for the Friedrichstrasse Skyscraper Project – although the visionary steel and glass building was never built, it had a major impact on the architectural world. His philosophy rapidly developed: in 1927, as the director of the Deutscher Werkbund, he organized the influential Weissenhof Siedlung exhibition in Stuttgart, showcasing a prototype workers' housing estate in the International Style. However, it met with the disapproval of the German establishment, which saw it as "socialist".

Nevertheless, as a result of work by Mies van der Rohe and other architectural luminaries such as Mart Stam,

Black leather cushions on polished steel frames sum up the simplicity of Mies van der Rohe's 'Barcelona' chairs, produced by Knoll. Their clarity of line and form suited the interior of the pavilion perfectly.
31in (79cm) wide O

Le Corbusier, and Walter Gropius, the rational approach of what he called "skin and bones" architecture was manifesting itself as the new radical style. The decade culminated in two of his most iconic buildings: the German Pavilion built for the Barcelona Exhibition in 1929 and the privately commissioned Villa Tugendhat at Brno, in today's Czech Republic, which was finished in 1930. Mies van der Rohe's use of open, free-flowing spaces devoid of any superficial detail gives his buildings an air of efficiency that is perhaps too clinical for many. Yet he emphasized that "God is in the details", and his ground-breaking use of modern materials, minimal structural frameworks, and plate glass enhanced his "less is more" approach to construction. His collaboration with Lilly Reich, his companion and working partner, resulted in the iconic 'MR90' ('Barcelona') chair and table, designed for the Barcelona pavilion, and the 'MR50' ('Brno') chair, which mirrors the simplicity of its original surroundings at the Villa Tugendhat.

Mies van der Rohe admired and drew inspiration from his contemporaries, including the functional and spatial philosophies of Gerrit Rietveld and the De Stijl group, Russian Constructivism and the exterior spatial awareness of Frank Lloyd Wright. In 1930, he became the last director of the Bauhaus design school. The Nazi regime soon forced him to close it and, disillusioned with the political state of Germany and lack of possible commissions, he moved to the USA in 1937. Mies van der Rohe's initial appointment in the United States was at Chicago's Armor Institute of Technology (now known as the Illinois Institute of Technology, or ITT). His American period was highly productive, with masterpieces such as the S.R. Crown Hall for ITT, the iconic and influential Farnsworth House near Chicago, and the Seagram Building in New York. He became an American citizen in 1944.

Mies van der Rohe left the world an enduring legacy. In a 1959 interview he said: "The influence my work has on other people is based on its reasonableness. Everybody can use it without being a copyist because it's quite subjective. I think if I find something objective I will use it. It doesn't matter at all who did it."

LUDWIG MIES VAN DER ROHE FURNITURE

Polished chrome legs contrast with the wood frame and black leather upholstery on Mies van der Rohe's daybed, produced by Knoll.
79in (197.5cm) wide M

The square plate glass top of Mies van der Rohe's 'Barcelona' coffee table sits on a polished chrome base, produced by Knoll.
40in (100cm) square D

A nickel-plated frame supports a canework seat on the 'MR-10' swinging tubular steel chair by Ludwig Mies van der Rohe, made by Josef Müller, Berlin.
Late 1920s 32in (80cm) high N

Marcel Breuer (1902-81)

The Hungarian-born architect and designer Marcel Lajos Breuer is widely regarded as one of the most influential exponents of the modernist cause. His tubular steel chairs, stools, and tables, and modular unit furniture which could be mass-produced revolutionized furniture design. Defining the designer's task as that of "civilizing technology", he left an indelible architectural and design-based legacy cemented by his skilful amalgamation of art and technology.

Marcel Breuer photographed in one of his 'B3' or 'Wassily' club chairs. He designed the chair while at the Bauhaus and it is considered to be his most iconic piece of furniture.

Marcel Breuer studied at the Bauhaus in the 1920s and went on to be one of its most prolific designers. Despite being a protege of Walter Gropius, he was frustrated by the intellectual debates which inspired many of his fellow students, preferring to design "without having to philosophize before every move". He left the Bauhaus in 1924 and worked for an architect in Paris. However, a year later, when Gropius invited him to lead the cabinet-making workshop at the Bauhaus in Dessau, Breuer accepted. That year he designed the iconic tubular steel 'B3' club chair, one of the first to reveal the possibilities of this new material. It is now known as the 'Wassily' chair (see p65).

In 1927 Breuer exhibited one of the first cantilevered tubular steel chairs, his model 'B33'. The form has no back legs and so the weight of the sitter is supported by the front legs and base alone. It fascinated

Modernist designers and Breuer, Mart Stam and Ludwig Mies van der Rohe all created early examples.

In 1928 Breuer left the Bauhaus and set up an architectural practice in Berlin. He left Germany in 1931 due to the economic slump. He worked in France, Spain, Greece, Morocco and Switzerland before finally emigrating to London in 1935. There Breuer was employed by one of Britain's leading "modernizers", Jack Pritchard at Isokon. He had already patented a string of steel and aluminum chair frames but his association with Isokon pushed him in a new direction, involving experimentation with molding plywood. Breuer's 'Long Chair' of 1935–6 undoubtedly exploited some of the popularity of Alvar Aalto's earlier laminated furniture, but most of his molded plywood pieces were wooden versions of his metal designs.

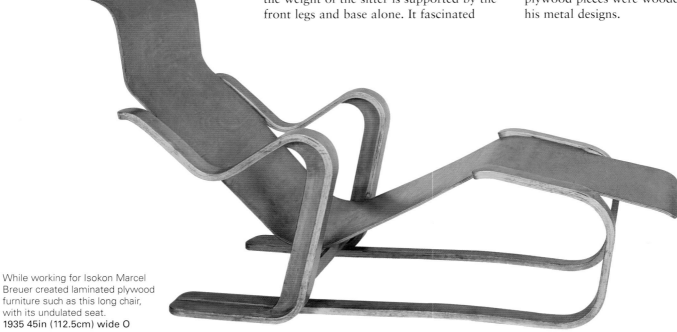

While working for Isokon Marcel Breuer created laminated plywood furniture such as this long chair, with its undulated seat.
1935 45in (112.5cm) wide O

After Breuer moved to the United States in 1937, he concentrated on architecture rather than furniture design. He worked in the architecture department at Harvard with his old colleague from the Bauhaus, Walter Gropius. At the same time, they collaborated on a series of house designs in and around the Boston area. In 1941 the men separated professionally, leaving Breuer to pursue his own architectural practice based in New York.

In 1945 we see the clarity and vision of Breuer's ideals manifested in the "binuclear" design of the Geller House, on Long Island. The initial bi-nuclear concept was to split the home into two separate zones: one for living and socializing (which he listed as "eating, sport, games, gardening, visitors (and) radio"), and the other for "concentration, work, and sleeping". Breuer explained that "The bedrooms are designed and dimensioned so that they may be used as private studies." The two wings would be separated by an entrance hall. However, rather than separate living and resting, the final design split parents and children.

The Geller House comprised a remarkably simple but effective separation of spaces under a roof characterized by its similarity to the wings of a butterfly. Some critics found this form of architectural segregation dated – however, the concept was quickly adopted as part of the modernist architectural rhetoric. Breuer's standing was further boosted in 1949 by his "House in the Garden" exhibition at New York's Museum of Modern Art which showcased his "binuclear" concept.

Despite his long list of residential commissions, Breuer designed very few public and commercial buildings before the 1950s. In 1953 this changed with a commission for the UNESCO headquarters in Paris, plus perhaps his most iconic building of the mid-1960s, the Whitney Museum of American Art, in New York City. Breuer was regarded as one of the leading exponents of the Brutalist style. However, his concrete buildings were designed with a more human approach than other Brutalists. The concrete was generally cast *in situ* which led to the texture of the wooden forms being imprinted into the surface of the blocks.

MARCEL BREUER FURNITURE

Lacquered wood arms embellish this 'B-35' armchair by Marcel Breuer. The chrome plated steel frame has a fabric seat and back.
1928 34in (85cm) long H

Nickel-plated steel frames are typical of Marcel Breuer's early furniture. This 'B5' chair has a fabric seat and back. Made by Standard Möbel Lengyel & Co., Berlin.
1926/27 32.5in (83cm) high O

A wood top and chrome plated tubular steel legs are a feature of Marcel Breuer's 'B-10' table.
c1927 26in (66cm) high M

Thonet produced some of Marcel Breuer's furniture, including this 'B-22' three-tiered occasional table.
c1928 37.5in (95cm) wide M

A cantilevered 'B-34' armchair by Marcel Breuer, produced by Thonet.
1928 33in (85cm) high G

Le Corbusier (1887-1965)

One of the titans of 20th century architecture, Charles-Edouard Jeanneret, who chose to be known as Le Corbusier, was also responsible for some of modernism's best-known furniture. In collaboration with designer Charlotte Perriand and his architect cousin Pierre Jeanneret, he created machine-age classics such as the 'Grand Confort' armchair. Free from any form of decoration these tubular steel designs exude relaxed, timeless elegance.

Le Corbusier was born Charles-Edouard Jeanneret in La Chaux-de-Fonds, Switzerland. He was apprenticed to a watchmaker at the age of 13 but gave this up to study at the local art school, with the intention of becoming a painter. However, he also studied architecture and went on to complete his first house, Villa Pallet, in 1907. He then traveled across Europe, studying for a time in Paris, and returned home in 1912 to teach and start his own practice. At the end of World War One he moved to Paris, adopted the name Le Corbusier in the early 1920s and became a naturalized Frenchman in 1930.

The luxurious thick leather upholstery and chrome plated frames of Le Corbusier's 'LC2' or 'Grand Confort' club chairs have become modern style icons.
1928 30in (76cm) wide K each

In 1922 Le Corbusier co-founded a magazine, *L'Esprit Nouveau*, where he expounded his ideals. He went on to convince the organisers of the 1925 Paris Exhibition that they should include him. The result, the *Pavillon de L'Esprit Nouveau*, was met with outrage. His building was little more than a box sparsely furnished with Thonet chairs.

Le Corbusier had his theories about furniture, writing his his 1925 publication *L'Art Décoratif d'Aujourd'hui* that there were three different types: "need", "furniture" and "human limb" pieces. He described the latter as: "Extensions of our limbs and adapted to human functions ... The human-limb object is a docile servant. A good servant is discreet and self-effacing in order to leave his master free. Certainly,

works of art are tools, beautiful tools. And long live the good taste manifested by choice, subtlety, proportion and harmony."

Le Corbusier does not appear to have produced any furniture designs before deciding to collaborate with Charlotte Perriand. Perriand is central to the story of Le Corbusier furniture. Having completed her studies at Paris' Ecole de l'Union Centrale des Arts Décoratifs, she began to realize that the materials and production methods used in engines, bicycles and automobiles might also be suitable for furnishings. After a friend suggested reading Le Corbusier's theories she realized he too might be interested in the machine-age aesthetic she had developed for her furnishings. However when she approached the legendary architect for a job he turned

LE CORBUSIER, CHARLOTTE PERRIAND AND PIERRE JEANNERET FURNITURE

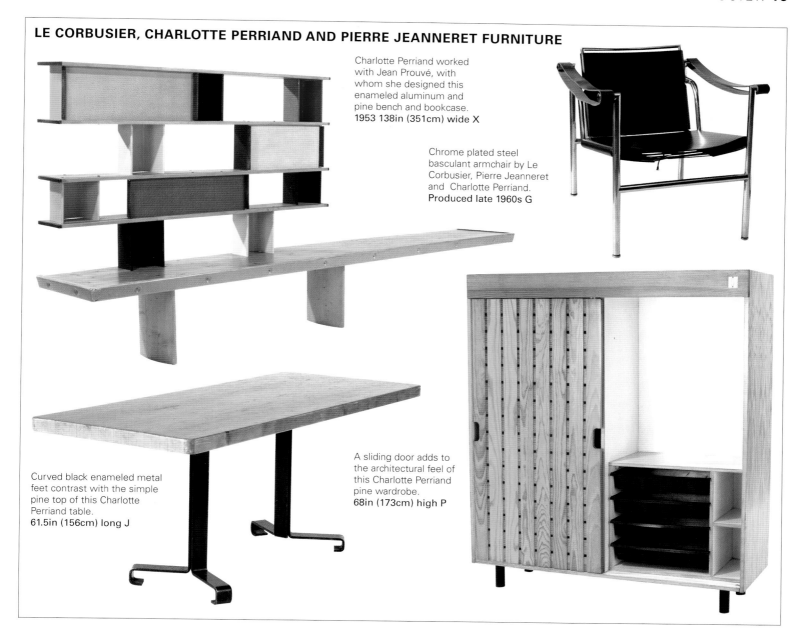

Charlotte Perriand worked with Jean Prouvé, with whom she designed this enameled aluminum and pine bench and bookcase. **1953 138in (351cm) wide X**

Chrome plated steel basculant armchair by Le Corbusier, Pierre Jeanneret and Charlotte Perriand. **Produced late 1960s G**

Curved black enameled metal feet contrast with the simple pine top of this Charlotte Perriand table. **61.5in (156cm) long J**

A sliding door adds to the architectural feel of this Charlotte Perriand pine wardrobe. **68in (173cm) high P**

her down flat with the now infamous put down "we don't embroider cushions here."

He would change his mind a few months later following a visit, with his cousin and chief associate Pierre Jeanneret, to the 1927 Salon d'Automne. At this design exhibition he admired Perriand's roof-top bar filled with audacious tubular steel furniture.

Le Corbusier, Jeanneret, and Perriand's most celebrated designs were conceived for Maison La Roche in Paris, and a garden pavilion for American clients, the Churchs, just outside the city. They created the 'B301' a sling-back chair for conversation; the boxy upholstered 'Grand Confort' or

'LC2' chair for relaxing; and the 'Cowboy' or 'B306' chaise longue for sleeping. These adorned abstract forms had tubular steel frames and hide or canvas upholstery.

"We wanted to make furniture that was accessible to everyone, mass-produced and affordable," Perriand would later recall. At the time these designs were so radical they were not successful. The designs debuted as 'Equipment for the Home' at the 1929 Salon d'Automne. The room-set devised to display them was made almost entirely from glass and metal, with concealed lights, sliding doors and modular storage units. Only the chaise longue originally had the

chrome frame and black leather upholstery, which came to epitomize modern furniture design. The 'Grand Confort' for example had a blue painted tubular steel frame.

During the 1930s, Perriand continued to supply Le Corbusier with designs. She left his studio in 1937 to work with Fernand Leger, the Modernist painter. She went on to collaborate with Le Corbusier and Jeanneret from time to time.

When Le Corbusier furniture was finally put into mass production, it was Perriand along with the Foundation Le Corbusier who ensured these designs retained as much of their original spirit as possible.

THE MODERN MOVEMENT

Eileen Gray (1878-1976)

Eileen Gray was a pioneering Modernist designer and architect and produced some of the finest minimalist interiors of the 1920s. Though barely known outside design circles before the 1970s, she is now widely recognized as one of the most innovative designers of the early 20th century. She began her career as a lacquer artist, was among the first to adopt tubular steel for furniture design and then went on to create radical, open-plan architecture.

At a time when most craftswomen chose bookbinding, weaving or jewelry making as their metier, Eileen Gray chose the obscure oriental art of lacquer-making. The Anglo-Irish designer had started to train as a painter at the Slade School of Fine Art in London, but became inspired by some Oriental lacquer pieces she discovered at a London antique-restorer.

In 1906 she moved to Paris to study this technically challenging art with a Japanese master called Sugawara. Gray took an apartment in the rue Bonaparte and, apart from a period during World War One when she returned to London, she made France her home. The intellectual and arty elite in

Paris appreciated Gray's designs and in time her work came to be seen as quintessentially French. Invited to decorate the Rue de Lota apartment of the fashion designer Suzanne Talbot, she created a sophisticated interior that was at once opulent and minimalist – a dramatic backdrop for her lacquered furniture. She lined walls with small rectangular lacquered panels – a prototype for her famous 'Block' screen. The centerpiece was her spectacular 'Pirogue' bed, a canoe-like daybed decorated with brown lacquer and silver leaf.

In 1922 she opened her own gallery under the synonym Galerie Jean Désert where she sold her lighting, lacquer screens

and abstract geometric rugs. She had her first major public showing in the Salon des Artistes Décorateurs in 1923 and attracted clients such as the fashion designer Elsa Schiaparelli.

Gray began experimenting with tubular steel, producing even more revolutionary furniture. Stripping away all references to the past, her designs anticipated 1930s Art Modern furniture. Her work has a unique clarity of line, yet is always comfortable and practical.

Though she had no formal training Gray also became increasingly interested in architecture. She collaborated on a number of projects during the 1920s and early

EILEEN GRAY FURNITURE

An abstract Eileen Gray wool area rug 'Solidadi: Nude/Torso'.
c1929 125in (312.5cm) long K

Eileen Gray's 'Transat' chair features an upholstered wooden frame.
1925-30 NPA

Perforated black metal panels make up Eileen Gray's 'Metallic Curtain' screen.
c1929 66in (168cm) high H

A chrome frame upholstered with curved leather tubes create comfort for Eileen Gray's 'Bibendum' chair.
36in (91cm) wide M

EILEEN GRAY E-1027 TABLE

Familiar to most fans of 1920s and 1930s design thanks to numerous reproductions, Eileen Gray's 'E-1027' side table is now considered a modernist masterpiece on a par with Charlotte Perriand and Le Corbusier's 'Cowboy' chaise longue. This clinically chic circular table is made from clear glass with a chrome-plated tubular steel frame. Its unusual asymmetry and emphasis on utility is typical of her independent aesthetic. The table adjusts in height by means of a sliding pole. Gray originally developed the idea for her sister who was fond of breakfast in bed. She used the 'E-1027' table in the guest bedroom at her cliff-top seaside house, also intriguingly named 'E-1027' (also referred to as the "Maison en bord de mer") near Monaco. This is a secret code for her name and that of her partner Jean Badovici: E is for Eileen, 10 for Jean (J is the 10th letter of the alphabet), 2 for B(adovici) and 7 for G(ray).

A pair of Eileen Gray 'E-1027' adjustable glass and chrome tables.
1927 24.75in (63cm) high E for the pair

1930s with her sometime lover the Romanian architect and critic Jean Badovici. Their most important building, a house at Roquebrune near Monaco, was cryptically named 'E-1027'. Built in 1924 this flat-roofed L-shaped villa is exquisitely simple, with floor-to-ceiling windows facing the sea. Most of the furniture for which Gray is now famous – including the 'Bibendum' and 'Transat' chairs – was designed for this house.

After World War Two, Gray was largely forgotten by the design and architecture establishment. In the 1970s, retrospectives in London and New York, and auction of the contents of Doucet's apartment, revealed her as an intrepid and original

Eileen Gray's record-breaking 'Dragon' chair features rounded lacquered wood arms decorated with the intertwined bodies of two dragons.
1917-1919 35.75in (91cm) high II

designer. Gray originally created her designs in limited editions for the exclusive use of wealthy patrons. In 1973 she permitted Zeev Aram to start manufacturing them on a wide scale. It has made her better known than she could possibly have dreamed in her heyday.

Collectors look for her rare original pieces or prototypes. At the Yves Saint Laurent sale in Paris in 2009 the 'Dragon' armchair that was originally in Suzanne Talbot's apartment sold for €21.9 million, a world record price for 20th century design.

THE MODERN MOVEMENT

Alvar Aalto (1898-1976)

Alvar Aalto is among the giants of design in the period before World War Two. The Finnish architect and designer softened the stark modernist aesthetic with rounded shapes and natural materials. By placing comfort above style he helped to establish the foundations of the softer approach to modern design that would prove so popular across the world in the 1950s and 1960s. Aalto is considered to be the most important Finnish architect of the 20th century.

Alvar Aalto's ultimate goal as a designer was to promote people's comfort and happiness. One of his first major projects, the Paimio Tuberculosis Sanatorium (1929-1933), was designed with the requirements of the patients and staff uppermost in his thoughts. For example he designed the floors to minimize dust accumulation and specified cheery yellow paint for the stairs.

Aalto and his wife Aino Marsio, who was his design collaborator, had been exploring designs in molded wood since they married in 1924. Aalto invented new methods for bonding veneers and molding ply as part of the design process and held numerous patents for bent plywood. In 1933 his experiments led him to design a pioneering chair especially for the Paimio Sanatorium. The chair was designed to allow the tuberculosis patients to sit in a position that enabled them to breathe easily.

Aalto's 'Paimio' chair is made from two hoops of laminated birch, which form the arms, legs, and floor runners, with a curving plywood seat in between. Its basic shape was a homage to Marcel Breuer's 'Wassily' chair – as newlyweds the Aaltos had imported some of his tubular steel chairs from Germany and used them in their home. However Aalto had come to believe wood would be warmer and more comfortable than cold angular metal.

In the early 1930s Aalto worked on the Viipuri Library in Turku, Finland. For this commission he designed a simple stackable stool made of birch plywood. He called it 'Stool 60'. When he exhibited this stool, together with other plywood designs

Bent laminated birch sides and the original tiger-skin fabric upholstery feature on Alvar Aalto's 'Tank' chair. This chair was previously known as 'Easy Chair 400'.
30.5in (77.5cm) long K

including the 'Paimio Chair', at London's Fortnum & Mason department store, they created a sensation.

What made Aalto's bent plywood furniture so innovative was that the legs were joined directly onto the seat without a supportive framework. In addition, in an era when tubular metal was a novelty, his furniture was made of a natural material and had an organic shape.

The public embraced Aalto's use of wood and his fluid designs. His work initiated a trend for furniture made from laminates and plywood. In fact Aalto's designs proved so popular that in 1935 together with his wife he set up a business called Artek to mass-manufacture a variety of plywood seating and furnishings including side tables and tea trolleys. The company is still doing so today.

Curves feature prominently in Aalto's furniture as well as on what many consider to be his most iconic design – the 'Savoy' vase. He and his wife originally created this famous piece of tableware as an entry for a design competition held by Karhula-Iittala glassworks to find pieces to exhibit at the 1937 Paris World's Fair. Its undulating form was inspired by an Eskimo woman's leather breeches. About ten of their designs were selected and shown in the pavilion Aalto also designed after winning an architectural competition. Another Aalto architectural project, the upmarket Helsinki restaurant the Savoy, placed the first major order for this design in 1937 and the vase bcame known as the 'Savoy' vase.

In 1939, Aalto was asked to plan the Finnish Pavilion at the New York World's Fair. Fellow architect and Modern pioneer Frank Lloyd Wright described the pavilion, which was inspired by the light and shadow of Finland's forests, as a "work of genius". It launched Aalto's career in the USA, where he was awarded visiting professorships and architectural commissions including a dormitory designed for the Massachusetts Institute of Technology.

Aalto's softer take on Modernism would go on to have a huge impact on American design in the years after World War Two. The organic fluidity of designs like Charles and Ray Eames' 'DAR' chair are indebted to his style.

ALVAR AALTO FURNITURE

Examples of Alvar Aalto's early work, these chests are made from birch wood. **36in (91cm) wide R for the pair**

A Modernist birch wood tea trolley, designed by Alvar Aalto for Artek, Helsinki. **c1936 35.75in (91cm) long J**

Native birch wood was used to make this circular, sunburst garden table, number '330'. **1938-39 (80cm) diam K**

A bent laminated birch and plywood armchair, model number '31', by Alvar Aalto. **1932 25.75in (65.5cm) high K**

FURNITURE GALLERY

Modernist furniture designers reveled in the possibilities of the new materials that were being developed in the years between the wars. Malleable nickel- and chrome-plated metal tubing, plywood that could be bent into ever more inventive shapes, as well as traditional wood and wicker, found their way into numerous designs.

Mart Stam created some of the first cantilever chairs. This one has a chrome-plated tubular steel frame and ebonized plywood seat.
c1930 I

A René Herbst Sandows chair, tubular steel with elasticated sprung straps, inspired by the straps used to secure parcels to a bicycle.
1928-29 32in (81cm) high N

A wicker chaise longue by Erich Dieckmann, who was apprenticed as a carpenter at the Weimar Bauhaus.
c1931 62.25in (158cm) long C

A chrome-plated steel frame lounge chair by Kem Weber for Lloyd Mfg. Co., Michigan.
c1930 34.5in (87.5cm) wide I

A stained pear wood armchair, designed by Peter Keler, upholstered with hand-woven fabric, and made at the Bauhaus Weimar.
1925 27.5in (69cm) high P

A single sheet of cut and bent birch plywood was used to create this Gerald Summers chair.
1930s 23.75in (60.5cm) wide U

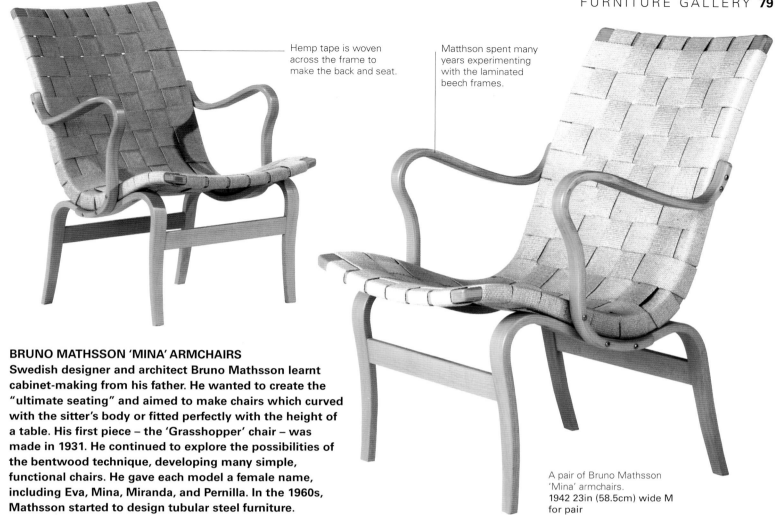

Hemp tape is woven across the frame to make the back and seat.

Matthson spent many years experimenting with the laminated beech frames.

BRUNO MATHSSON 'MINA' ARMCHAIRS
Swedish designer and architect Bruno Mathsson learnt cabinet-making from his father. He wanted to create the "ultimate seating" and aimed to make chairs which curved with the sitter's body or fitted perfectly with the height of a table. His first piece – the 'Grasshopper' chair – was made in 1931. He continued to explore the possibilities of the bentwood technique, developing many simple, functional chairs. He gave each model a female name, including Eva, Mina, Miranda, and Pernilla. In the 1960s, Mathsson started to design tubular steel furniture.

A pair of Bruno Mathsson 'Mina' armchairs.
1942 23in (58.5cm) wide M for pair

A curving stainless steel tubular frame is the base of Giuseppe Terragni's "Sant'Ellia" armchair.
1936 31in (79cm) high NPA

An ebonized wood and tubular aluminum desk by Warren McArthur.
44in (112cm) wide H

METALWARE GALLERY

Sleek shapes and futuristic forms were common themes for Modernist metalworkers. Both new and established designers and workshops took up the new trend to create decorative and practical pieces using silver and other metals.

Tea infuser designed by Christian Dell at the Bauhaus metal workshop. Silver plated brass with disk finial to handle. **1924 5in (13cm) long H**

Stacked sphere handles decorate this Mexican Sterling silver Modernist centerpiece bowl. **Late 1930s 17.5in (44.5cm) wide K**

Silver-plated brass and ebony tea pot designed by Marianne Brandt, at the Bauhaus. **c1927 6in (15cm) wide GG**

A triangular electric heater with ball finial and ball feet designed by Peter Behrens for AEG, Berlin. **1920 27.5in (69.5cm) high M**

Silver tea service designed by Philippe Wolfers, Brussels. **c1930 M**

JOHAN ROHDE PITCHER NUMBER 432
In 1906 the painter Johan Rohde met the silversmith Georg Jensen and the two men worked together for the rest of their lives. The silverware Rohde designed was so modern and restrained some pieces were not produced for many years. However, these wares fitted with Jensen's belief: "Do not follow fashion but be guided by the present if you want to stay young in the struggle."

A Georg Jensen jug, designed by Johan Rohde. c1920s 4in (10cm) high M

The bow-like handle has an ebony insert. Its shape complements that of the smooth, baluster body.

The curved, angled neck creates a harmonious whole.

The simple, streamlined shape is typical of Rohde's work.

A Georg Jensen lidded water pitcher, designed by Johan Rohde. c1920s 9.5in (24cm) high O

A Georg Jensen water jug, designed by Johan Rohde, design no. 432. c1925 8.75in (22.5cm) high N

Posters

The poster was a popular medium for the promotion of modernism. Graphic designers were at the cutting edge of various design movements. Cubism and its derivatives (such as Vorticism, Futurism, and Suprematism), De Stijl and Russian Constructivism, were all manifested in their works. The period after World War I saw an explosion of ground-breaking modernist output.

The modernist poster challenged the artistic hierarchies. Though sometimes strange and anarchic, it was undeniably "stripped down" and advanced. The Machine Age, with its abstract forms of mechanical and electrical symbolism, speed, and architectural suggestion, would soon blend with the Art Deco movement.

CHALLENGING HIERARCHIES

In Germany, prior to World War One, the design style known as Plakastil (Poster style) was championed by Lucian Bernhard and Ludwig Hohlwein. Their abstract visual language was achieved by dispensing with realism and reducing the colors and shapes to a stark simplicity.

The Austrian Herbert Bayer, who studied for four years at the Bauhaus under Wassily Kandinsky and László Moholy-Nagy, was later appointed by Walter Gropius to be the school's director of printing and advertizing. Bayer's contribution to the field of graphics was progressive and highly influential, including the development of lower-case typefaces for the Bauhaus. His 1925 sans-serif typeface "universal" (now available as Bayer Universal), consisted entirely of lower-case letters, constructed from circles and straight lines. It was contemporary with the typography of other modernist thinkers such as Kurt Schwitters. Unlike many of his peers, Bayer worked for the Nazis, which included designing a tourist brochure for the 1936 Olympic Games. However, in 1937 his work was exhibited in the infamous "Degenerate Art" exhibition, and he fled to the United States. His post-war output is exciting and distinguished, particularly his work for the visionary American industrialist Walter Paepcke.

Maria, the central character of Fritz Lang's science fiction movie 'Metropolis', is depicted as a robot in an hypnotic image of stylized realism in this poster designed by Werner Graul.
1927 27.25in (68cm) high W

Pieck plays with industrial architecture, turning the typography into an important element in his constructive building in 'Jaarbeurs Utrecht', a poster for a fair.
c1935 39.25in (98cm) high K

The stylized Ziggurat in Franz Ter Gast's poster for 'Jaarbeurs Utrecht' is treated with a modernist touch, as it emerges from a forest. The typography and the rigid layout reflect earlier Dutch design.
1920 46.25in (115.5cm) high F

VALENTINA KULAGINA POSTER

Valentina Kulagina was a graduate of Vkhutemas, the Russian equivalent of the Bauhaus. She worked for IZOGIZ (the State Art Publishing Agency) and VOKS (the All-Union Society of Cultural Relations with Abroad), receiving domestic and international commissions for posters and exhibition and book designs. In 1928 she designed parts of the Soviet Pavilion of the landmark Pressa exhibition in Cologne. Kulagina's work combines drawing with elements of the photomontage style developed by her husband, the artist Gustav Klutsis.

Valentina Kulagina produced many propaganda posters. She used visual imagery to convey the message as illiteracy was common.

The angular line and perspective add to the impersonal feel of the design and help to promote the state over the individual.

Defending the USSR, by Valentina Kulagina.
1930 35.5in (91cm) high
N

The Swiss artist Niklaus Stoecklin drew inspiration from the Bauhaus for his remarkably austere but striking 1928 poster 'Schweizerische Städtbau-Ausstellung' (Swiss City Planning Exhibit). He was part of a highly influential school of Swiss artists inspired by the Bauhaus and working in a manner later known as the International Typographic Style.

ABSTRACTION AND STYLIZATION

Charles Loupot produced highly stylized designs, such as the famous 'Stop-Fire' poster of 1930. In the 1920s, the Dutch graphic artist Paul Schuitema applied the principles of De Stijl and Constructivism to advertizing, characteristically using only black, red, and white. The use of both styles is also visible in the work of Franz Ter Gast and Henri C. Pieck in the 'Jaarbeurs Utrecht' series.

In an effort to inspire and educate its users, London Transport commissioned some of the best Modernist artists in the interwar period. These included the Cubist Edward McKnight Kauffer, the Surrealist Man Ray, and the former Bauhaus tutor László Moholy-Nagy, who arrived in Britain fleeing Nazi oppression.

Perhaps the most famous of all the London Transport posters was the Tube map itself, originally designed by the engineering draughtsman Harry Beck in 1933 and acknowledged as a design classic. Based on a circuit diagram, it stripped the network down to basics, making the system comprehensible to users. His design has been used as a template for transport maps worldwide.

Other media also benefited from the poster's dominance – its use in film promotion, for example, proved powerful and timelessly symbolic. Werner Graul, Heinz Schulz-Neudamm, and Jósef Bottlik produced modernist masterpieces for Fritz Lang's 1927 film 'Metropolis' which have become icons of poster and film history.

Textiles and Carpets

Modernist designers challenged the tradition that fabrics should feature naturalistic patterns of flowers and leaves. Instead they created repeating patterns of stylized motifs or bold, geometric designs. The trend began with the Wiener Werkstatte and the Glasgow School of Art, but the next generation of designers took it a new and exciting direction.

By the 1890s the British designer C.F.A Voysey had developed a strong personal style that rejected the more complicated aspects of Art Nouveau. Regularly contracted by manufacturers, he recognized the need to adapt textile designs to modern industrial production techniques. He was, in effect, a modern thinker. Jessie Newbery, the wife of the principle of Glasgow School of Art, taught embroidery to the students from 1894. The simplified motifs she favored can be seen in the elongated figures and geometric motifs used by her pupil Margaret MacDonald, the wife of Charles Rennie Mackintosh, in 1902. Members of the Wiener Werkstatte created textiles and carpets with linear, goemetric motifs until c1910 when folk art-inspired designs started to be made.

In 1913, the artist and art critic Roger Fry established the Omega Workshops in London. His co-directors were Duncan Grant and Vanessa Bell, fellow members of the Bloomsbury Group. Their attitude to pattern-making was based on a rejection of naturalism in favor of bold abstract design.

Fry had championed Post-Impressionism and was keen to apply the principles of Fauvism to British design. The main exponents of the movement were André Derain, Henri Matisse, and Raoul Dufy. Derain and Pablo Picasso were both clients of the Omega Workshops, and its innovative geometric designs served as a reference and influence for the modernist and Art Deco movements.

PAINTERS' CONTRIBUTIONS

When Raoul Dufy declared that "paintings have spilled from their frames and stained our dress and our walls", his credentials as a textile designer were already beyond doubt. Often credited as the father of fabric design, he witnessed an early 20th-century explosion in technology and techniques, all allied to the progressive mood that prevailed in the design world. New synthetic fabrics, chemical dyes, and printing processes had become part of the designer's armory, igniting different mediums and areas of potential creativity to express the ideals of modernism.

A large French geometric rug, tan field with brown and teal geometric design in wool with original fringe.
c1930 85in (216cm) long M

A Modernist wool rug with geometric pattern in shades of peach, brown, and gray.
77in (195.5cm) long F

A French Modernist wool rug.
1930s 76in (193cm) long M

EILEEN GRAY 'BLUE MARINE' CARPET

Of Irish birth and from a privileged family, Eileen Gray was initially constrained by the rigid social conventions of the time. With no male mentor and no affiliation to a particular movement, she remained steadfastly independent. Latterly, she is recognized as a pioneer in the Modern movement. Lifted from her former obscurity, she has been rightly reinstated as an iconic trendsetter in the International Style. Her 'Blue Marine' carpet was designed for her own house in the South of France.

Eileen Gray Blue Marine carpet.
c1929 84.5in (215cm) long M

The geometric pattern is typical of Gray's carpet designs.

The shades of blue and wavy lines are reminiscent of the sea.

FEMALE LEADERS IN THE FIELD

The weaving workshop at the Bauhaus was a female domain. This was partly a reflection of the sexism within a profession that was still deemed to be largely suited to women. But it was also an opportunity for the women to exploit new notions of equality and freedom. The development of products suited to the Bauhaus manifesto that promoted mass production did not always fit with a craft such as weaving. The idea of a Bauhaus fitted carpet was not a reality. However, the workshops produced a plethora of superb designs for fabrics, wall hangings, rugs, and blankets, particularly during the period of 1920–27 under Georg Muche, a colleague and friend of Max Ernst and Paul Klee.

Notable Bauhaus weavers include Grete Reichardt and Gertrud Arndt. Early experimentation with man-made fibers such as rayon and Cellophane were part of the Bauhaus remit, as well as wire-mesh weaving for seating. Despite the diversity of the school's output, wallpaper was one of its most profitable and successful products.

Like her Bauhaus contemporaries, Marion Dorn challenged the male system. Born in the United States, her early training and visits to Europe helped her foster good connections with masters such as Raoul Dufy. In 1923 she moved to London with Edward McKnight Kauffer, fellow designer and prominent modernist. Her abstract designs are among the best of the interwar years and include carpet commissions for major hotels and shipping lines such as the Savoy, Claridges, the Cunard Line (the *Queen Mary)*, and the Orient Line.

"There was going to be no more poverty, no more ignorance, no more disease. Art Deco reflected the confidence, vigor and optimism by using symbols of progress, speed and power." Robert McGregor

Art Deco

The entrance hall to Eltham Palace in London was designed in the style of a fashionable ocean liner with marquetry wall panels by the Swedish artist Jerk Werkmäster, a rug by Marion Dorn and sleek, streamlined furnishings. The windows and skylight flood the room with natural light. Completed in 1936, it is a showcase for the Art Deco style.

Art Deco

Art Deco was born into a changing society, and it went on to change the world. This was the first truly international design movement, encircling the globe from North and South America to New Zealand, and from China, Japan, and India to Czechoslovakia (now the Czech Republic). Modernity was the watchword of the day, and Art Nouveau's sinuous curves were rapidly replaced by geometric shapes and bold, simplified styling.

Daring, dramatic, and totally different from the Art Nouveau era that preceded it, Art Deco was a phrase that derived from the name of the 1925 Paris Exhibition: *L'Exposition Internationale des Arts Décoratifs et Industriels Modernes*. Yet it was not popularly described as Art Deco until the late 1960s, when the writer Bevis Hillier coined the term following the 1966 retrospective exhibition *Les Années "25"*, which was held at the Musée des Arts Décoratifs in Paris.

Geometric shapes in contrasting colors bring Art Deco modernism to a design for a stamp.

AFTERMATH OF THE WAR

The 1920s and 1930s saw seismic shifts in the political and economic landscapes. The horrors of World War I had brought hardship and shortages which led to a desire for progress – and it was progress that ultimately drove Art Deco design.

During the war years, industries around the world had to develop innovative mass-production techniques in the fields of manufacturing, medicine, and transportation. The materials – plywood, reinforced concrete, Perspex (Plexiglas), Bakelite, and Galalith (Erinoid), to name a few – that evolved from this experimentation led to new products for the mass markets that were opening up globally. During the 1930s, electrical goods such as refrigerators and vacuum cleaners started to become available for worldwide consumption, although only the wealthy could afford them.

Women were enjoying their first taste of real freedom, and manufacturers saw an opportunity catering for their new lifestyles. The war had brought women emancipation, liberation, and independence: they were now used to being employed outside the home and it was even acceptable for them to smoke and drink in public.

Flapper girls wore sleeveless dresses and plunging necklines, bobbed "garconne" ("little boy") haircuts, and armfuls of exotic bangles. This was the Jazz Age and men and women wanted to enjoy life – they read F. Scott Fitzgerald's *The Great Gatsby*, published in 1925, danced to the Charleston, and drank cocktails until dawn in fashionable bars filled with chrome tables and chairs or lined with exotic paneling.

EXALTING SPEED

Speed and movement were the crucial driving forces behind Art Deco's sensational motifs. Sleek, streamlined shapes appeared on every conceivable object – from clocks to cars and locomotives, and from dress clips to a complete town in the case of Napier, New Zealand. In the US in particular, streamlining became an important influence on the trend.

Aeronautical designers had discovered that streamlining meant less drag, which in turn equaled greater speed, and this understanding of the mechanics of flight inspired Art Deco design concepts throughout the 1920s and 1930s.

Charles Lindberg flew solo nonstop across the Atlantic in 1927. This remarkable achievement was followed by the take-off of the Douglas DC-3 airliner, which was in operation by 1935. Over 21,000 DC-3s were subsequently made. The success of this, and similar, airplanes helped to popularize the possibility of air travel for many people.

Trains, too, were traveling at ever-higher speeds. In 1938 Sir Nigel Gresley, the chief mechanical engineer of the London and North Eastern Railway (LNER), designed the 4468 *Mallard* locomotive, which reached a speed of 126mph (203kph). It still holds the record for the fastest steam locomotive in the world.

The Chrysler Airflow automobile was introduced in 1934. This super-modern car, with its long, thrusting bonnet, was the first full-size production car to use streamlining to reduce air resistance.

Stylized geometric renderings of New York skyscrapers and nightclubs, create an exuberant decoration for Cowan's "Jazz Bowl". Officially called 'New Year's Eve in New York City', the bowl was designed by Viktor Schreckengost.
1931 14in (35.5cm) wide X

DEMETRE CHIPARUS 'BAL COSTUMÉ'

Demêtre Chiparus was one of the leading sculptors of his day, creating many works in a fashionable combination of bronze and ivory. He was often inspired by dancers and the costumes worn by this couple, who are depicted at a fancy dress party, suggest that they were inspired by the 1911 Ballet Russes production of *Petrouchka,* **in which Vaslav Nijinsky wore a similar outfit to the male figure. Owning a figure such as this would have indicated the sophisticated taste and wealth of the owner.**

Carving the ivory to create such fine and naturalistic detail took great skill – one careless slip and many days' work would be lost.

Chiparus designed this group in two sizes, of which this is the larger.

The bronze "clothing" has been sculpted to suggest movement as the couple dance – they appear to have been frozen in a moment of the dance.

The woman's exotic, Eastern costume would have been considered daring at the time, even when worn to a party.

A patinated bronze and ivory 'Bal Costumé' figure group, by Demêtre Chiparus.
c1925 19.25in (49cm) high X

The shape of the Chrysler Airflow was ahead of its time, and the public – struggling under the weight of the worldwide depression that had begun with the Wall Street Crash of 24 October 1929 – did not respond to it as fully as had been anticipated, and it was taken out of production in 1937.

The Cord 810 car, with its low, sleek lines, wrapround radiator grille, and teardrop-shaped mudguards, made its powerful entrance in 1936. But it too had disappeared by 1937, squeezed out of the marketplace by the big boys of the automobile industry.

The fascination with speed is perhaps best exemplified by Malcolm Campbell. In 1924 the English racing enthusiast and journalist broke the land speed record at 146.16mph (235.22kph) at Pendine Sands, Wales, in a 350HP V12 Sunbeam, which he called *Blue Bird*. He set his final land-speed record at Bonneville Salt Flats in Utah in 1935, becoming the first person to drive a car at over 300mph – his fastest speed was 301.337mph (484.955kph).

THE SHIP OF LIGHT

Travel by ocean liner epitomized Art Deco at its most luxurious. The largest of the ocean-going ships, the *Normandie*, which completed her maiden voyage in 1935, was redolent of opulence from bow to stern. Longer than the height of the Eiffel Tower, the *Normandie* was a floating temple to the leading French designers of the era. Enormous chandeliers and dozens of glass panels and pillars by René Lalique graced a glittering dining room that seated seven hundred passengers. In the grand salon, the corners were filled with four huge shimmering glass murals painted and gilded on the reverse (designed by Jean Dupas and executed by Charles Champigneulle). At the center of the grand salon, opposite the entrance, was a spectacular mural made up of gold and silver lacquered relief panels (designed by Dupas and executed by Jean Dunand). No wonder the *Normandie* was referred to as the "ship of

An elegant silhouette was created by an exaggerated, elongated figure. French bronze and ivory figure of a dancer by Paul Philippe.
c1930 22in (56cm) high V

light". It was promoted on posters, by Adolphe Mouron Cassandre and others, as the epitome of elegant travel.

Art Deco designers drew on a wide visual vocabulary and applied it across every aspect of daily life, whether they were creating the grand salon of an ocean liner, the exterior of a factory or cinema, or tableware for a domestic home. Pattern books by designers such as Edouard Bénédictus promoted fashionable motifs such as leaping deer. The focus lay firmly on flat, two-dimensional decoration, and ornamentation – firmly rejected by the modernists – was embraced by Art Deco.

POPULAR MOTIFS

Nature, which had so influenced and suited the requirements of the Art Nouveau elite, was now given the highly stylized treatment that the modern world demanded. The French used baskets and garlands of flowers, fountains, and clouds (borrowed from Japanese art), offering designers the opportunity for graphic repetition of an image. Animals such as deer and gazelles and the ubiquitous borzoi hound suited the elongated manner in which figures were often depicted.

The sunburst motif was particularly important and had a worldwide impact. This optimistic symbol represented both the dawn of a bright new future and the preoccupation with health and fitness. It is to be seen in the stained glass panels of suburban front doors, on the wrought iron of garden gates, and in the decoration of Clarice Cliff and Shelley tea services.

Sporting pastimes were now available to the new middle classes that were emerging in this brave new world. Jewelry, desk accessories, and sculpture featured horse racing, especially the circle of the winning post, motor racing, tennis, and golf. A new obsession with health and fitness – and clothes which allowed a

The glamor of travel inspired Lenci's 'Sul Mondo' figurine by Mario Sturani and Helen Konig Scavini. A young woman and her dog sit on a globe showing exotic destinations.
c1925 19.25in (49cm) high P

ART DECO TIMELINE

1922 Discovery and opening king Tutankhamun's tomb. The resulting "Egyptomania" saw Egyptian forms and motifs being used in many aspects of the decorative arts.

1923 First transatlantic wireless broadcast between London and New York. As communications became faster and easier ideas spread more quickly across the globe.

1925 The *Exposition Internationale des Arts Décoratifs et Industriels Modernes* is held in Paris. The exhibits are seen by 16 million people and help to define the Art Deco style.

1928 The Zeppelin airship's first transatlantic crossing. As air travel became a possibility for many more people, posters advertized the dream of exotic destinations and glamorous trips.

1929 The Wall Street Crash began on October 24 with the collapse of the New York stock market. By 1932 America was in the grip of the Great Depression with over 13 million unemployed.

Simplified streamlined shapes of railway tracks meeting at a star on the horizon draw the eye into Adolphe Mouron Cassandre's poster for the Pullman the Étoile du Nord.
1927 41.5in (105.5cm) high Q

The hand-painted geometric shapes in bold contrasting colors on this plate by British designer Susie Cooper are typical of her work c1927-c1931.
c1929 H

The stepped shapes of New York's skyscrapers inspired the 'Skyscraper Furniture' range by Paul Frankl. It included this elegant vanity, with a mirrored surface and semi-circular mirror, black lacquered body and chrome trim.
c1926 44in (112cm) wide NPA

greater freedom of movement – lead to figurines depicting women in energetic poses on the tennis court or enjoying gymnastics. In Germany the 1936 Berlin Olympics saw a host of Deco-style posters produced depicting athletes in bold blocks of color to create the impression of strength and physicality. The official poster for the 1936 games, designed by Franz Würbel and distributed in 34 countries, shows the muscular form of a Classical-style athlete picked out in a scheme of golds and yellows that give the figure a monumental yet modern look.

ESCAPISM AND EXOTICISM

The "talking pictures" had by this time become a global phenomenon, and it was the Hollywood directors who brought Art Deco iconography into the lives of millions of movie-goers every week. Busby Berkeley's synchronized and geometrical casts of dancers in *Footlight Parade* (1933) and *Dames* (1934), Fred Astaire and Ginger Rogers in musicals such as *The Gay Divorcee* (1934) and *Top Hat* (1935), and many others used over-the-top glamorous Art Deco film sets as part of their package of escapism from the Great Depression. The cinemas themselves were often newly built in the Art Deco style – bringing high fashion to neighborhoods across the world.

1931 Publication of *Brave New World* by Aldous Huxley which prophesied a futuristic world where advances in science and technology have helped to take man away from nature.

1932 Launching of the ocean liner *Normandie*. At the time she was the largest ocean liner in the world and was decorated by some of the greatest designers of the day including René Lalique.

1934 The Museum of Modern Art in New York's Machine Art exhibition marks the point at which machines could be considered aesthetic objects rather than just gadgets.

1939 Completion of the building of the Rockefeller Centre in New York. The Art Deco landmark covers 11 acres (4.5 hectares).

Exoticism became a powerful influence on design, and the movie industry was quick to recognize and promote it. Fans swooned to Rudolph Valentino in *The Sheik* (1921) and marveled at Claudette Colbert in Cecil B. DeMille's *Cleopatra* (1934) and Greta Garbo in *Mata Hari* (1932).

A fascination with history and with foreign countries and cultures was the underlying reason for many of the symbols given the Art Deco "treatment" throughout the 1920s and 1930s. Public taste for the exotic meant that one of the most famous women of the time was Josephine Baker, an African-American dancer and singer who became an instant success in Paris for her erotic dancing. Known as the "Black Pearl", she performed her *danse sauvage* wearing a costume of artificial bananas.

Back in 1910, a production of *Scheherazade* choreographed by Serge Diaghilev was performed in Paris by the Ballets Russes, with sets and costumes designed by the Russian painter Léon Bakst. The audience was wowed by the exotic costumes, and the vivid colors and fashion dictated that interiors and wardrobes henceforth should have a touch of the outlandish, romantic, and unusual about them.

ANCIENT AND PRIMITIVE CULTURES

Historical finds through high-profile excavations were another form of the Deco artist's muse. In 1922 Howard Carter discovered the tomb of Tutankhamun, the treasures of which caught the public's imagination. Jewels, compacts, cigarette cases, and furniture were receptacles for the Egyptomania that ensued, using its pharaohs, sphinxes, scarabs, hieroglyphs, and lotus flowers freely. The geometric patterns of Aztec and Mayan temples, pagodas, and ziggurats (temples in the form of stepped pyramids,

African tribal art masks inspired avant-garde designers in many fields. This black and red geometric Bakelite brooch with chromed steel eyebrows and mouth is redolent of the era.
1920s 2.5in (6.5cm) long B

built by the ancient Sumerians, Babylonians, and Assyrians) also played their part in Deco design.

It was the artists of the avant-garde art movements who wielded most effectively the emotional and spiritual pulling power of primitive cultures. Their works promulgated exotic imagery in a progressive way and subsequently influenced the appearance of myriad products. These cultures – from African tribal art to Native American handicrafts – were plundered for their naive imagery by the radical artists.

Within Art Deco we find the aggressive shapes and punchy shades of Cubism, the wild beasts and natural hues of Fauvism, the abstract explorations beloved of the Constructivists, the emotional journeys of the Expressionists, and the frightening, shadowy world of the Surrealists. In Germany the Bauhaus exerted its influence through its application of color and rectilinear forms. In Holland De Stijl was an art movement that promoted a philosophy of spiritual harmony and a sense of order that fitted with the new fashion.

THE NEW ARCHITECTURE

Architects around the world reacted with passion and conviction to the notion of Art Deco. They recognized that the authority conferred by the temples of ancient cultures could be tapped into by employing contemporary materials such as tubular steel, plate glass, and reinforced concrete.

The result was skyscrapers that towered over the populace. They represented power, success, and capitalism. In New York

Exotic finishes, popular with French designers, helped to create opulent interiors. A faux tortoiseshell finish was used on this Paul Frankl table which has raised sides, an open storage compartment, and flared pedestal base.
c1930 36in (91.5cm) wide K

Cubism influenced the decorative arts. A French pottery figure of stylized deer, modeled in a geometric style, features two animals standing amid stylized grasses.
c1930 11.75in (30cm) high B

City, for instance, the iconic Chrysler Building was the tallest building in the world after it was built – for less than a year. Designed in 1927 by William Van Alen and completed in 1930, it is 1,047ft (319m) tall and has a 77-floor structure with repeated arcs and triangular windows at the top. Like a cathedral to the motor car, it uses nickel-chromed steel, and the exterior brickwork is decorated with patterns of speeding automobiles. In 1931 another symbol of Art Deco – the Empire State Building – took its place in the record books at 1,453ft (443m) tall.

The Rockefeller Center, which spans 22 acres (9 hectares) and features 14 Art Deco buildings (completed in 1939), and the Daily News building of 1930 incorporated stone carvings with scenes of 20th-century working life, provide a machine age entrance for a temple of modernity. Throughout America – from the Hoover Dam (1936) to Los Angeles City Hall (1925–8) and Buffalo City Hall (1931), from Chicago's 333 North Michigan Avenue (1928) to Ocean Drive in Miami Beach (1930s) – new developments called for new architecture.

GEOMETRY AND MYTHOLOGY

Elsewhere, Art Deco's sharp geometry was combined with stepped structures, towers, and spires that dominated important cities. Shanghai has more Art Deco buildings than any other city in the world. In cities such as Mumbai in India and Ljubljana in Slovenia, architects combined patterns and motifs associated with their national heritage to decorate their buildings.

Many designers drew on the associations made with mythological figures. The British sculptor and typographer Eric Gill decorated BBC's Broadcasting House in London with Prospero and Ariel from Shakespeare's *The Tempest*. A heroic-sized sculpture of Atlas holding a celestial sphere is one of the Rockefeller Center's greatest icons.

The new style was also seen in Bakelite radios, fashions, and homeware, making it the first truly democratic design available to all. Art Deco was to prove so modern, so successful, and so appealing to the public consciousness that its design principles still inform every area of composition and construction today.

CARLTON WARE EGYPTIAN VASE

The discovery of King Tutankhamun's tomb in 1922 inspired a fascination with all things Egyptian. Pharaohs, hieroglyphs and sphinxes were among the motifs which were used on all manner of items. Carlton Ware used expensive luster glazes for its Egyptian wares, making them among the most expensive pieces the factory produced.

The cover is topped by a Pharaoh-shaped finial, based on the finials of Canopic jars found in the tomb.

The ovoid jar is covered with a lustrous glaze which resembles lapis lazuli, a semi-precious stone which was used by the ancient Egyptians for amulets and ornaments.

The decoration includes a frieze of lotus leaves. The lotus leaf is associated with Egyptian beliefs about death and the afterlife.

The jar is covered with hieroglyph motifs, many of them in gilt, which creates an opulent effect.

A Carlton Ware Tutankhamun jar and cover. c1930 10.5in (26.5cm) high K

1925 Paris Exhibition

Today, it's hard to imagine a trade fair – even an international one – having such a seismic impact on contemporary design, as did the 1925 Paris *Exposition Internationale des Arts Décoratifs et Industriels Modernes.* It was so influential that more than four decades later the term Art Deco was coined to describe the style associated with the exhibition, and soon it was being used to describe any between-the-wars design.

International exhibitions had promoted manufacturing and commerce ever since Britain held the Great Exhibition in 1851 to showcase current design and technology. The individual pavilions within the exhibitions were frequently as amazing as many of the exhibits.

Paris had staged international exhibitions on previous occasions. The city's most iconic symbol, the Eiffel Tower, was originally erected for the 1889 exhibition. The World's Fair held in the city in 1900 was not only a runaway success but also played a pivotal role in spreading the Art Nouveau style to the mass market. Plans to repeat this success were disrupted by the deteriorating international relations that led to World War One.

René Lalique built a glass fountain outside his pavilion, which lit up at night. His involvement brought him even greater success. Others were not so fortunate: many firms were crippled by the cost of exhibiting.

CELEBRATING MODERN DESIGN

The French authorities revived the idea after the war in order to demonstrate France's continuing cultural vitality, holding the fair in the heart of Paris between April and October 1925. Over 50 million people flocked to see it. The organizers' mission statement banned historical reproductions – the exhibition would celebrate modern design, not look back at the past.

No fewer than 34 countries took part, including Britain and Japan. The United States declined to participate (because Herbert Hoover, who was then Secretary of Commerce, had been informed that there were not enough American designers working in a modern style to participate). However, they produced an official report on the exhibition and obtained pieces for public collections. In addition, many American designers visited the exhibition, and it had plenty of press coverage.

The new style and the exhibition were promoted in Robert Bonfils' poster.
1925 Q

Following the exhibition many of the designers associated with it received commissions, including Fernand Léger who designed this geometric rug.
c1930 65.5in (166.5cm) long O

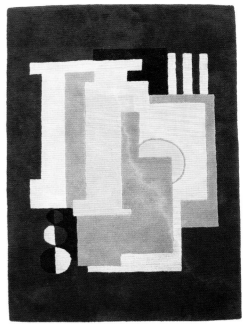

Naturally, the host country dominated the event. Most leading French firms exhibited and sold their latest products at the event. Scent manufacturers like Caron had individual boutiques in a perfume hall. Each of the city's four famous department stores – Bon Marché, Printemps, Galeries Lafayette, and Le Louvre – erected a pavilion. The luxury brands Sèvres, Lalique, and Ruhlmann showed wares in their own buildings as well as in other pavilions.

The exhibit of the French designers' organization, the Société des Artistes Décorateurs, portrayed an embassy abroad. Le Corbusier's outrageously avant-garde *Pavillon de L'Esprit Nouveau* antagonized the organizers and the public. From Jacques Adnet and Paul Follot to Fernand Léger and Jean Puiforcat, the stellar figures who contributed to the 1925 Exhibition reads like a *Who's Who* of artists of the time.

ART DECO EMERGES

Although there was no official "look", it soon became apparent that the same design vocabulary was used again and again, especially in the French exhibits. There were spirals, lightning rays, and ziggurats everywhere. Stylized fountains, garlands, and flower baskets cropped up abundantly, and dancing nymphs and graceful deer proliferated. What clearly emerged were the distinct motifs that have become associated with Art Deco.

The writer W. Francklyn Paris reported that the French designers had: "arrived at a style which is homogenous as well as characteristic, and which embodies ... a certain masculinity, a soberness of ornamentation and a dependence upon effects produced by proportion and a richness of material rather than by elaborate carving or applied ornament."

New ideas encouraged by the exhibition rapidly gained momentum and became a global movement. Many participants, such as Jacques-Emile Ruhlmann and Jean Dupas, went on to collaborate on projects like decorating the ocean liner *Ile de France*. Within a few years the modern French style had become an international one.

Sadly, the pavilions were never intended to be permanent. Once Edgar Brandt's magnificent iron gates closed for the last time, the site was demolished.

PAUL FOLLOT BERGERE CHAIR

A designer of interiors, furniture, metalware, jewelry, ceramics, and glass, Paul Follot is best known for his Art Deco furniture. However, he began his career working in the Art Nouveau style and ended it as a Modernist. In between he created Art Deco and, later, Cubist work. He became a member of the Societé des Artistes Décorateurs in 1901 and then became associated with Pomone, the interior design arm of the Paris Bon Marché department store from 1923. He designed Pomone's stand for the 1925 exhibition.

Follot furniture is elegant, luxurious, and often reminiscent of the Louis XVI style, but with a pared down, modern feel. This chair offers the comfort of deep, ribbed upholstery.

Simple, scroll carving embellishes the terminals of the arms of the chair and echoes the dramatic curve of the U-shaped seat rail.

The hard wood frame has been stained and polished.

A Paul Follot bergère chair.
c1920 20in (51cm) wide P

The fluted tapering legs have been ebonized and feature carved scrolls which stand proud of the wood.

French Furniture

Art Deco furniture began to appear in France after World War One. The majority of the designs drew on the perennially popular taste for 18th-century historicism. Shapes were often simplified and refined versions of Art Nouveau models. Elsewhere, opulent elements from the Louis XV and Louis XVI styles were combined with exotic woods and sleek, refined outlines to produce luxurious furniture of the highest quality.

LEADING DESIGNERS

A number of French designers created furniture that was to have worldwide influence. Louis Süe, an architect, and André Mare, a Cubist painter, came together in 1919 to produce sleek, museum-quality furniture. Made from highly figured woods such as walnut, mahogany, palisander, and Macassar ebony, the pieces featured elegant curves, sometimes with Rococo-style gilding and carving, and beautifully executed inlays with ivory, abalone shell, and mother-of-pearl. They designed extensively for the 1925 exhibition, but the partnership was taken over by the firm Fontaine in 1928 when it experienced financial difficulties.

Maurice Dufrène was one of the new *artistes décorateurs*, or interior designers. Despite working for La Maison Moderne, an Art Nouveau gallery, his preference was for a minimum of ornament and he worked in the Neo-classical manner. His reputation further increased when he took charge of La Maîtrise, a studio at Galeries Lafayette, in 1921. Stores like this played a major role in promoting Art Deco throughout France.

Another leading exponent of the classical look in French Art Deco furniture was Léon Jallot. He had managed the furniture workshops of Siegfried Bing's l'Art Nouveau gallery and he set up alone in 1903, being joined by his son Maurice in 1921. Their work heralded the shape of

A stylized acorn within a 'theater drape curtain' forms the back of Paul Follot Macassar ebony and rosewood chair. The carving is attributed to Laurent Malcles. **c1922 20in (51cm) wide 32in (81.5cm) high S**

DE COENE FRERES

The new French style was taken up by Belgium's largest furniture-maker, De Coene Frères. The company, established in Kortrijk, Flanders, in 1895 by brothers Jozef and Adolf De Coene, used exotic woods including Macassar ebony. Their Art Deco furniture resembled that of Léon and Maurice Jallot.

A lyre-shaped console by De Coene Freres.. **1930s 29.5in (75cm) high M**

Exotic woods such as plum pudding mahogany and exquisite marquetry decorate this dressing table by Maurice Dufrène. It features a folding adjustable triple beveled oval mirror and ribbed tapering legs. **c1921 52.75in (134cm) wide U**

furniture to come, with surface decoration dominating the design and employing unusual and technically demanding materials such as shagreen and lacquer.

Sculptor and designer Jules Leleu was a fine furniture designer, much inspired by the highly influential Jacques-Emile Ruhlmann. Leleu's delicate floral inlays used marquetry and ivory. In fact, many pieces of French Art Deco furniture also had ivory feet and handles, a sign of quality.

The interior designer Paul Follot joined La Maison Moderne in 1901, where he met Maurice Dufrène. Like Leleu, Follot had a love of traditional furniture and expensive woods such as amboyna, which he updated with contemporary ideas. Some of his pieces are decorated with garlands of flowers and fruit, in the early Art Deco style. In 1923 he took over the Pomone design studio for the department store Le Bon Marché and in 1929 became co-director, with Serge Chermayeff, of the modern French furniture design section of Waring & Gillow, the English firm with outlets in Paris.

SURFACE FINISHES

Clément Rousseau was a designer who used furniture as an opportunity to create extraordinary artworks in marquetry, shagreen, and ivory. His cabinet in Macassar ebony and violet wood was decorated with a dramatic bowl of flowers to the front. Marcel Coard, an interior designer with a shop on the Boulevard Haussmann, designed furniture for a select number of private clients, working with geometric shapes in shagreen, lapis lazuli, and mother-of-pearl.

The grand couturiers of the 1920s, who became the all-important patrons of the prestige French furniture designers, assisted the progress of Art Deco design. Jacques Doucet commissioned the artist and furniture designer Paul Iribe, as well as Marcel Coard, Eileen Gray, and Pierre Legrain. Paul Poiret, the first designer to free women from the confinement of corsets, also commissioned Paul Iribe, while Jeanne Lanvin's apartment was decorated throughout with the African-inspired, cast-bronze work of Armand-Albert Rateau. The legendary Madeleine Vionnet turned to the exemplary lacquered pieces of Jean Dunand.

LÉON AND MAURICE JALLOT CHAIR

Léon Jallot began making furniture c1890 and in 1898 became manager of the furniture workshop at Siegfried Bing's Paris shop La Maison de l'Art Nouveau. In 1903, he started his own decorating workshop. In 1921 he began working with his son Maurice who had studied furniture design at the École Boulle in Paris. Maurice used more refined techniques, including the application of leather and shagreen to the wood. They exhibited at the 1925 Paris Exhibition, showing furniture which was more modernist in style.

In the 1930s the Jallot's furniture was sleek and often featured metal or plastic elements.

The sides feature three chrome rails which are reminiscent of the rails on an ocean liner.

The ebonized tapered legs feature chrome mounts.

A Leon and Maurice Jallot dining chair.
1930 33in (84cm) high P

Jacques-Emile Ruhlmann (1879-1933)

In France, Jacques-Emile Ruhlmann set the benchmark for fine Art Deco furniture. His family owned a paint company, which he took over in 1907 when he was aged 28. Six years later he opened his own cabinet-making and decorating agency, and his work soon became synonymous with luxury and elegance. While today he is best known for his furniture designs, he also designed wallpaper, textiles, lighting, and metalware.

ART DECO

In 1919 Ruhlmann, whose first name is often given as Emile-Jacques, went into business with Pierre Laurent, a builder, to found R.E.L. (Ruhlmann et Laurent), which employed more than 600 people. By 1923 they had completed decoration projects for such high-profile clients as the Banque de France and the Elysées Palace, and Ruhlmann set up his own workshops to produce his models. He had his own pavilion at the 1925 Paris Exhibition, bringing him further recognition. Ruhlmann took charge of the Hotel d'un Collectionneur, selecting the designers who would show their work there.

Ruhlmann was a great technician. One of his assistants recalled: "With him, I learned subtlety in form and curve, as well as precision and originality in implementing an idea. These are things I would never have thought about had I not gone to Ruhlmann's: the perfection of the idea – not solely visual, but in production terms, too."

Ruhlmann's style initially combined Art Nouveau aesthetics with 18th-century shapes and craftsmanship. Desks and chairs often had very slender tapering legs, sometimes with delicate ivory feet. His cabinets floated upon central columns. Later his pieces were simplified to a true purity of line, becoming more Modernist in appearance.

He worked in precious hardwoods such as Bombay rosewood, ash burl, amboyna, purple heart, oak (black, gray, and light), walnut, Cuban mahogany, ash, cherry, tulipwood, kingwood, beech, and lime, as well as the macassar ebony with which he is most associated. Furniture frames were often made of oak. A veneer, such as Macassar ebony, would be applied over poplar battens – a technique of choice for

The height of luxury, Jacques-Emile Ruhlmann's "Lotus" dressing table is made of oak and mahogany with amaranth and andaman padouk veneer, ebony and ivory inlays, a silvered bronze mirror frame and fittings. **c1919-1923 47in (119cm) high NPA**

other Art Deco designers, too. Pieces were offered in different variants.

Details were executed using ivory inlays, crocodile skin, white and green shagreen (sharkskin), Havana leather, and lacquer. Specially designed handles were of ivory, silver, or bronze. The craftsmanship was always superb. The 'Bloch desk', for example, took 1,067 hours to make and used 54 shagreen skins and 27 meters (30 yards) of ivory "fillet".

Ruhlmann named some of his pieces after his wealthy clients – for instance, the 'Rothermere sofa' and the 'Ducharne armchair' were named after England's Lord Rothermere (publisher of the *Daily Mail*) and François Ducharne, a silk merchant from Lyon. Other pieces were known by the names of animals, such as the 'Elephant armchair' and the 'Gazelle chair'.

He claimed: "We must manufacture luxury furniture... [for] it is the elite that

launches fashion and determines the impetus." But he added: "It is by richochet... that the movement descends toward the masses." A cabinet by Ruhlmann could cost more than a reasonably sized house.

By the time of his death in 1933, Ruhlmann had created a remarkable 1,700 pieces. Only Jules and André Leleu produced more, at 7,000 pieces, but their careers spanned more than 70 years.

JACQUES-EMILE RUHLMANN FURNITURE

Leather covers the geometric frame of the 'Elephant' chair.
c1931 37in (94cm) wide NPA

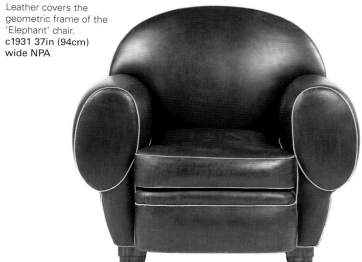

Stylized flowers decorate a gilded plaster ceiling sculpture, by Emile-Jacques Ruhlmann, from the Bon Marché department store.
47in (119.5cm) high M

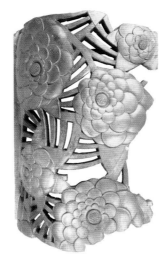

Burr amboyna armchair with ebony details and gilt metal sabots.
1913 27in (68.5cm) wide NPA

Intricate ivory inlays and a bowl of carved roses decorate this rosewood cabinet. The two curved side doors are inlaid in ivory with connected spirals of dots. The cabinet has four short fluted spindle legs.
c1919 50.75in (129cm) wide NPA

French Furniture in the Modern Style

As the 1920s progressed into the 1930s, French furniture designers tended to leave behind the historical references of the early 1920s and looked toward a more modern idiom. The "Ruhlmann style" grew increasingly important, carved decoration was largely abandoned, and inlays became more discreet. Angles were sharper, forms were often geometric, and curves almost disappeared. Eileen Gray and Le Corbusier were among the modernists experimenting with exciting, tubular steel furniture.

An ebonized frame and geometric frame enhance an armchair designed by Jacques Adnet.
1932 28in (71cm) high P

Jean-Michel Frank was an important French interior decorator who dressed elegant, modern apartments and houses for international clients such as the Rockefellers, the San Francisco millionaire Templeton Crocker, and the surrealist fashion designer Elsa Schiaparelli. Frank's austere, creamy leather sofas were set against high-sided chairs, which were decorated with panels of shagreen, and screens dressed in mica. An admirer of the sets Sergei Diaghilev had commissioned from artists such as Matisse and Picasso for the Ballets Russes, he is reported to have said: "I wish one could more often see artists collaborating in arranging houses. The result would be, at the very least, something of our time, and alive."

LIGHT, ANGULAR FORMS

The furniture designer, architect, and sculptor André Arbus enjoyed a long and illustrious career. He successfully made the transition from the traditional 18th-century styles of his father's cabinet-making firm to the light, angular forms of later Art Deco and then back to the highly decorative forms of the 1940s. He used finely grained veneers, parchment, lacquer, and bleached animal hide vellum as decoration.

Jacques Adnet, who had been appointed director of La Maîtrise at Galeries Lafayette in 1922, left there in 1928 to become director of the Compagnie des Arts Français (CAF), which had been founded by Louis Süe and André Mare in 1919. At CAF he promptly rejected Süe and Mare's classicist approach to Art Deco and instead introduced a range of modernist-influenced furniture and metalware. His work incorporated exotic woods, chromed metals, mirror, leather, parchment and smoked glass in linear styles minimal decoration.

Luxury materials and exotic woods separated the Art Deco furniture designers

Lacquered wood and tortoiseshell decorate an André Arbus secretaire. It is lined with vellum and has ivory drawer handles.
1937 53.5in (136cm) high NPA

An electrified central column illuminates the central glass panel of an Eric Bagge coffee table. The table is covered with a walnut veneer and a chrome trim enhances the geometric design.
c1930 35in (89cm) wide T

JACQUES ADNET (1900-1984)

Jacques Adnet has become an icon of luxurious French Modernism, although during his fifty year career (from c1920-c1970) he produced works that were continually relevant to the changing times. This means he can be called a Traditionalist, an Art Deco practitioner, a Modernist, a modern humanist or a post-war visionary with equal veracity. After taking over the Compagnie des Arts Français, he brought in painters like Raoul Dufy, Marc Chagall and furniture designers, such as Francis Jourdain, Charlotte Perriand and Rene Gabrielle, who helped him create his new 'Modernist' Art Deco style.

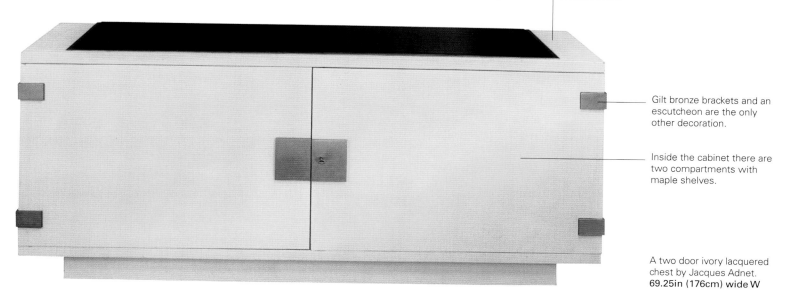

The overall effect is simple but luxurious. The black opaline top is encircled by a gilded bronze frame.

Gilt bronze brackets and an escutcheon are the only other decoration.

Inside the cabinet there are two compartments with maple shelves.

A two door ivory lacquered chest by Jacques Adnet. 69.25in (176cm) wide W

from the modernists. Companies such as Décoration Intérieure Moderne, or DIM (directed by the cabinet-maker René Joubert), and Dominique (founded by André Domin and Marcel Genevrière in around 1922) worked in woods such as purple heart (amaranth) and palisander, sometimes combining them with shagreen.

TESTING THE BOUNDARIES

The cross-fertilization of modernist and Art Deco convictions about design led to some of the most interesting furniture of the late 1920s and the 1930s. One designer who tested the boundaries of furniture design was Michel Dufet. His glossy, palisander dining table sported legs of aerodynamic aluminium, for instance, while a Cubist dining suite was executed in ebony and sycamore. These pieces still look shockingly radical today. The distinctive, modern furniture of Paul Dupré-Lafon combined limed oak, parchment surfaces, leather handles, and bronze feet.

Eric Bagge, architect and interior decorator, also designed furniture, fabrics, and

wallpapers. He designed pavilions at the 1925 Paris Exhibition and was a member of the Groupe des Architectes Modernes and a member of the French Exhibitions committee of the Société d'Encouragement à l'Art et à l'Industrie (SEAI) and was therefore influential. In 1930 he opened his own retail outlet in Paris. Bagge favored a clean,

Floral ebony carvings with mother-of-pearl highlights decorate the legs of a mahogany and glass coffee table by Rosel of Brussels. c1925 30in (76cm) wide M

streamlined look in his work that forms the basis of many furniture designs now.

In Belgium, companies such as Rosel were inspired by the leading French designers. Though using the same dark, highly figured woods, they frequently added their own trademark features such as mother-of-pearl inlays, to the pieces.

Squares of parchment create a geometric pattern on the doors of a sycamore cabinet designed by Jean-Michel Frank. c1930 41.25in (105cm) wide NPA

American Furniture

American Art Deco furniture was inspired by a number of design influences. From the luxurious French taste via European modernism and the glamor of Hollywood movie sets, American designers assimilated many elements to create a new "Moderne" style. Two of the defining features of this furniture are its resemblance to the architecture of the time and the impact on it of newly patented materials.

SKYSCRAPERS AND MACHINES

Art Deco furniture in the United States was predominantly linear, with the sections of a piece stacked, skyscraper-style, one upon another. The highly original skyscraper bookcases and desks by the Vienna-born designer Paul Frankl were based on the New York skyline, and he subsequently named his company Skyscraper Furniture. The machine aesthetic was also key, with products such as mirrored glass, steel, Bakelite, and aluminium appearing on traditional wood carcasses.

A number of the most progressive pieces of furniture came from industrial designers, who created products ranging from cars to cocktail sets. The furniture and radio cabinets by Norman Bel Geddes were metropolitan and futuristic, while German-born Kem (Karl Emanuel Martin) Weber, who was chief architect of the Disney studios at Burbank, California, dreamed up chairs that were streamlined and aeronautical. Meanwhile, the blonde wood furniture by Russel Wright was stark yet innovative.

One of the most successful designers was Donald Deskey. He visited the 1925 Exhibition in Paris and, two years later,

formed Deskey-Vollmer, Inc., with the designer Phillip Vollmer. Their interiors of the Radio City Music Hall in New York City's Rockefeller Center, completed in 1932, were awe-inspiring. During the Depression years of 1930–34, Deskey produced hundreds of economical designs in a wide range of materials, including chromium-plated steel tubing and Bakelite, for several furniture companies.

EUROPEAN INPUT

Gilbert Rohde founded his design studio in 1927, having discovered the concepts of Walter Gropius and the Bauhaus when he visited Germany. He used chromed metal and black enamel on mahogany and American maple for his designs. His work was produced by Herman Miller, based in Zeeland, Michigan, among others.

Similarly, Eugene Schoen had met both Josef Hoffmann and Otto Wagner while traveling in Europe and went on to create modern pieces in luxurious woods. Hoffmann's son Wolfgang was a success in the USA – from 1934 to 1942 he was the resident designer at the Howell Company, in Illinois, which offered ranges of modernist, chromed steel furniture.

The great Finnish architect and designer Eliel Saarinen moved to the United States in 1923. He produced Art Deco designs of restrained elegance and fluidity, such as the dining suite for his Cranbrook, Michigan, home and the lacquered "Blue Suite" originally fashioned for the studio of his wife, the sculptor Loja Gesellius. These pieces, like many items of Art Deco furniture, are still produced today.

Brass and ebonized wood pulls create the geometric decoration on the four-drawer chest designed by Gilbert Rohde for Herman Miller. **1930s 48in (122cm) wide L**

White paint and lacquer create a tiered effect on this Donald Deskey six-drawer D-shaped mahogany knee-hole desk. **c1935 50in (127cm) wide N**

SKYSCRAPER CABINET

As the 1930s progressed New York's skyline filled with skyscrapers as property developers vied with each other to build the city's tallest building. The Chrysler building gained the title in May 1930 only to lose it 11 months later with the completion of the Empire State Building. The designer Paul Frankl created a range of Skyscraper Furniture but he was not the only one to find inspiration there. Many anonymous furniture makers also took the shapes of these new monoliths and turned them into fashionable furnishings.

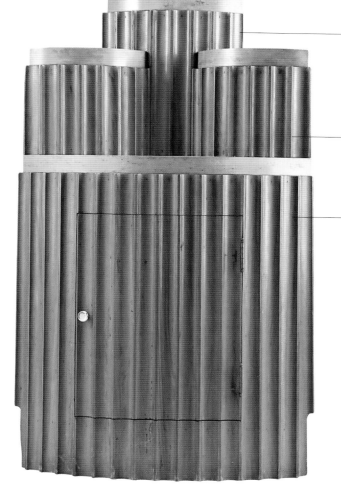

The excitement of the new skyscrapers is reflected in many furniture designs of the era.

The stepped, geometric top recalls the New York skyline.

The fluted sides make the cabinet appear taller than it really is and enhance the modernity of the design.

An Art Deco fluted corner cabinet of stepped form with single door concealing a shelf.
1930s 47.5in (120.5cm) high **G**

THE FRENCH INFLUENCE

French Art Deco design exerted its influence on American furniture of the 1920s, particularly in the use of rare wood veneers. The architect, interior designer, and furniture designer Pierre Chareau, was born in France, worked in Paris for the British furniture company Waring & Gillow, and emigrated to the United States in 1940. His work was modernist in outlook but incorporated exotic woods and fine materials. His celebrated minimalist desk, a study in angles and planes that prevented the surface from becoming cluttered, is still reproduced today.

An Art Deco macassar ebony circular dining table, with faux ivory inlay on pedestal base.
c1930 55.25in (140.5cm) diam **N**

ART DECO

FURNITURE GALLERY

Simple forms with geometric embellishments, from bases to handles, feet to mirrors, typify Art Deco furniture. Designers used exotic woods – or veneers of them – to create opulent finishes. Some pieces, such as cocktail cabinets, were made to suit the new, "modern" lifestyles. Others used the latest materials – chrome and Bakelite in particular – to great decorative effect.

A black granite top and matt black frame are embellished with gold-accented details on this occasional table.
32.5in (82.5cm) wide G

A gilt panel and reeded handles with brass backplates decorate this Laszlo Hoenig satin birch chest.
53.25in (135cm) wide G

The juxtaposition of the circular tops and cruciform bases add to the geometric design of a pair of lamp tables.
28in (70cm) diam M

Art Deco's geometric symmetry can be seen in this walnut veneered display cabinet.
43in (109cm) wide F

Blocks of color and texture enhance this Hille sycamore chair.
33.5in (85cm) high D

Contrasting surfaces decorate this illuminated bar of black lacquered and exotic wood veneer. The fluted doors of the center cabinet conceal a mirrored interior.
55.25in (140cm) wide O

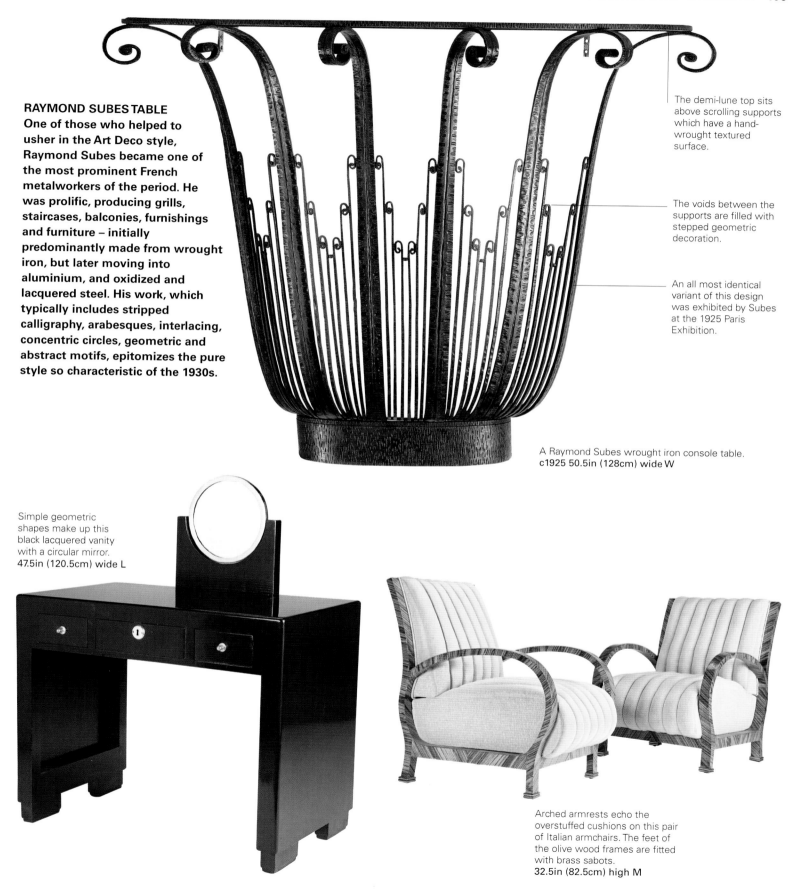

RAYMOND SUBES TABLE
One of those who helped to usher in the Art Deco style, Raymond Subes became one of the most prominent French metalworkers of the period. He was prolific, producing grills, staircases, balconies, furnishings and furniture – initially predominantly made from wrought iron, but later moving into aluminium, and oxidized and lacquered steel. His work, which typically includes stripped calligraphy, arabesques, interlacing, concentric circles, geometric and abstract motifs, epitomizes the pure style so characteristic of the 1930s.

The demi-lune top sits above scrolling supports which have a hand-wrought textured surface.

The voids between the supports are filled with stepped geometric decoration.

An all most identical variant of this design was exhibited by Subes at the 1925 Paris Exhibition.

A Raymond Subes wrought iron console table.
c1925 50.5in (128cm) wide **W**

Simple geometric shapes make up this black lacquered vanity with a circular mirror.
47.5in (120.5cm) wide **L**

Arched armrests echo the overstuffed cushions on this pair of Italian armchairs. The feet of the olive wood frames are fitted with brass sabots.
32.5in (82.5cm) high **M**

Stylized Nature

Ceramics provided the perfect medium for artists to express the zeitgeist of the 1920s and 1930s. Modern customers wanted dynamic designs, and manufacturers worldwide provided them with stimulating and sensational ornaments and tableware. Experimentation in glaze techniques in particular led to the wide range of finishes available to the Art Deco designer, while exhibitions and advertizing brought the new ceramics to the public's attention.

Stylized unicorns form a pair of bookends designed by Waylande Gregory for Cowan. They are covered in a mottled ochre and mahogany glossy glaze.
7.25in (18.5cm) high G

FRENCH SCULPTURES

In France, Jacques Adnet caught the sense of movement and controled power so associated with Art Deco with his perfectly formed dove of 1930. In white glazed faience on a stepped plinth, it is an iconic ceramic of the time. Joel and Jan Martel were twin brothers who were strongly influenced by Cubism. They shared a studio and executed small and large sculptures in a range of materials. Their designs included some powerful figurines, a sleek cat, and a series of pigeons.

The Swiss-born sculptor Edouard Marcel Sandoz, who lived in Paris and specialized in animalier sculpture, designed boxes and tea and coffee sets in the shapes of birds and animals. These were executed in polychrome porcelain by Haviland at Limoges.

The Boch Frères Kéramis factory in Belgium produced some of the most important ceramics of the period. From 1906 they employed the French designer Charles Catteau, appointing him as artistic director a year later. Catteau had studied at Sèvres and worked at the Nymphenburg Porcelain works in Bavaria. He encouraged hand-thrown pottery production and created sophisticated, layered effects with glazes that imitated cloisonné enamel. Catteau drew flora and fauna in *le style moderne*, frequently decorating them in a brilliant turquoise glaze on a crackled ivory ground. A series of vases exhibited at the 1925 Paris Exhibition brought him international acclaim.

In Hungary the new style was taken up by the Zsolnay factory. Its trademark irridescent glazes and low relief molded wares were an ideal medium for stylized naturalistic wares.

Advertizing was an essential tool in bringing the new wares to the attention of the public. Publicity gained from international fairs and exhibitions and widespread advertizing in newspapers and lifestyle magazines created markets for the new novelty products and modern designs.

AMERICAN ART WARES

In the United States, Reginald Guy Cowan, who had founded the pottery that bore his name in 1913, commissioned artistic wares from a team of talented artists. From 1927 to 1931, when the pottery closed, names such as Viktor Schreckengost, Waylande de Santis Gregory, and Margaret Postgate designed a range of artistic wares. Schreckengost's 'Jazz Bowl' (see p87) is the most famous of these, but it was Gregory who was the most prolific designer. He specialized in mythological subjects produced in a unique style.

Art Deco wares from the country's largest manufacturer – Rookwood – tend to feature simple, economical designs. These pieces were slip cast and feature matt, monochrome glazes. However, some art pottery was designed by artists such as Jens Jensen and Louise Abel.

THE SPIRIT OF THE TIMES

British ceramics were not well received at the 1925 Paris Exhibition. As a result, the Staffordshire-based factories, not wishing to be seen as the "poor cousins" of the more exciting European designers, focused on using designers who could capture the spirit of the times.

At Wedgwood, John Rattenbury Skeaping was commissioned in 1926 to produce highly stylized animal sculptures, which were made in earthenware or basalt and decorated in Norman Wilson's monochrome glazes. They bore a resemblance to Jan and Joel Martel's work for the Sèvres factory in France. Exotic

Stylized flowers on a striped ground cover this Boch Freres vase which was designed by Charles Catteau. They are echoed by a ring of smaller flowers at the rim. The bright colors are typical of Art Deco designs.
14in (35.5cm) high M

Panels of birds of paradise modeled in relief under lustered glazes decorate this Zsolnay tapering vase.
6.75in (17cm) high N

creatures included bison, sea lions, and kangaroos.

Carter, Stabler and Adams, of Poole, Dorset, had been established as a division of the Carter Company when John and Truda Adams joined Harold and Phoebe Stabler at the company. Working in earthenware, Phoebe was a figure modeller and Truda created quintessentially Art Deco floral designs that became a hallmark of Poole Pottery. (This name was in use from 1914 or earlier but was not officially adopted until 1963.) The leaping springbok motif, widely associated with the 1925 Paris Exhibition, was adopted by the company.

Charlotte Rhead was a designer who, with richly colored enamels, made Arts and Crafts-style floral decoration look perfectly right for the 1920s. She was the daughter of Frederick Alfred Rhead (see p43) who had worked at Minton's, and her elder brother was Frederick Hurten Rhead, who became a well-known potter in the United States. Working for Keeling & Co. at Burslem and then for T & R Boote, a successful tile-maker, she learned the art of tube-lining in which a raised impression is created on the surface. Moving on to Wood and Sons, she took charge of the tube-liners, and later began her association with Burgess and Leigh of Middleport – now known as the Burleigh Pottery – where she worked from 1926 to 1931. She joined A.G. Richardson in Tunstall in the 1930s, whose brand name was Crown Ducal, where she created patterns such as the highly collected 'Persian Rose'.

ARTISTS' WARES

Less well known are the ceramics of Vanessa Bell of the Bloomsbury Group. Bell designed stylized floral and abstract pieces, based on French Post-Impressionism, for the Omega Workshops. Later, Clarice Cliff commissioned Bell to decorate tableware for A.J. Wilkinson. Two of Bell's patterns were subsequently mass produced.

A collaboration between the Foley Pottery (E. Brain & Co) and A.J. Wilkinson led to other leading artists of the day being commissioned to produce ceramics. These included Dame Laura Knight, who devised tableware with a circus theme, Frank Brangwyn, and the teacher and writer Gordon Forsyth.

CHARLES CATTEAU VASE FOR BOCH FRÈRES

Charles Catteau is credited with single-handedly steering the production of the Art Deco wares of Boch Frères' Kéramis range from c1920 to 1945. The vases, bowls and other items produced were not designed to be high-end artistic wares but as fashionable accessories to be sold through fashionable galleries and department stores around the world. As such, they helped to promote the Art Deco style thanks to their bright colors and stylized decoration.

The vase is decorated with a frieze of stylized antelopes painted in Persian blue and green crackled glaze.

The rim is circled with a band of stylized leaves.

The creamy, crackled glaze on the body of the case of typical of the Kéramis range.

A Boch Frères ovoid vase by Charles Catteau.
14in (35.5cm) high L

Exoticism

The discovery of Tutankhamun's burial chamber by Howard Carter in 1922 sparked an Egyptian Revival that inspired the designs for myriad ceramic vases, boxes, and dinner services. Egyptian hieroglyphs as well as African masks and mythological figures all provided inspiration for designers – the public were hungry for exotic and glamorous foreign imagery, and Art Deco ceramics were an accessible way to acquire it.

A modernist Classical figure is picked out in silver on a matte green ground on a Gustavsberg Pottery 'Argenta' line designed by Wilhelm Kåge. 1930s 8in (20.5cm) high L

OLD SKILLS NEW WARES

In France, the Manufacture Nationale de Sèvres employed its historic skills to create Art Deco ceramics par excellence. While the factory continued to produce its traditional wares, it also employed Jean Mayodon, a painter and ceramicist as artistic consultant between 1934 and 1939. He later became the artistic director. Inspired by Persian and Middle Eastern ceramics, Mayodon immortalized odalisques (female figures), athletes, archers, and mythological subjects using metallic oxides highlighted with gold. Some of them spun around his plates in the manner of Henri Matisse's celebrated 1909 painting *Dance*.

René Buthaud was another important ceramicist who had trained as a painter, at the Ecole des Beaux-Arts in Bordeaux. He exhibited at the 1925 Paris Exhibition before returning to Bordeaux to establish his studio. Buthaud used crackle glazes to decorate simple stoneware, made for him by local potters. His surface effects included craquelure, lusters, and *peau de serpent* (faux snakeskin). Designs feature tribal figures and foliage, as well as the female nudes that are the most sought after. Under contract to Galerie Rouard in Paris from 1928 to 1965, he usually signed works for other outlets as J. Doris.

Fine earthenware and enamels were also produced at the Longwy factory. Longwy created pieces for the Parisian department stores Le Bon Marché and Le Printemps, and a number of the thickly enameled designs feature complex, stylized, floral decoration.

The Swedish firm Gustavsberg introduced a highly successful line called 'Argenta', designed by Wilhelm Kåge. The pieces had the appeal of exoticism, with mottled green glazes and stylized female figures, animals, and flowers picked out in silver.

The Italian design maestro and architect Gio Ponti also turned his hand to ceramic design during the Art Deco years, becoming prolific in this field. In 1922 he had founded Novecento, which brought together a group of designers whose philosophy was in direct contrast to that of the Futurists.

The Novecenti believed in "being Italian, being traditional, and being modern". He favored Neo-classical motifs that he brought up to date with modern styling, and he was also influenced by Italian folk pottery. Ponti designed ceramics for Richard-Ginori where he was art director from 1923 to 1930. He turned the company into a role model of industrial design excellence and decorated simple, traditional ceramic forms, which showed off elegant neo-classical motifs.

A geometric, odeonesque-style gilt plaque decorates a vivid blue and green mottled ground on this Sevres box and cover. c1925 6.5in (16.5cm) diam H

LONGWY PLATTER FOR PRIMAVERA

The Longwy factory in Eastern France created many pieces of fashionable ceramics for department stores, including the Atelier Primavera which was part of the Printemps store in Paris. Longwy, like Boch Freres, decorated wares using the traditional Japanese cloisonne technique. Notable designers included Maurice Paul Chevallier who was chief decorator from 1925 until 1972. During the 1920s Longwy began to use stylized floral and figurative motifs on its vases, tiles, and platters.

African themes were popularized by black American jazz age performers, above all, by Josephine Baker who – for the French particularly – epitomized the combination of American and African cultures.

The stylized jungle landscape is typical of Longwy's designs.

A Longwy Art Deco cloisonné pottery platter, made for the Primavera Design studio.
1920s 14.5in (36.75cm) diam N

Longway was known for its vibrant colors. This design has been created using several rich shades of blue.

LUSTERED GLAZES

Wedgwood introduced a range of lusterware with glossy, iridescent glazes. Imaginary worlds inhabited by fairies and pixies were portrayed on shapes that were modern and angular, in 'Fairyland Luster' pottery by Daisy Makeig-Jones.

Another British factory, Carlton Ware, the pottery division of Wiltshaw & Robinson of Stoke-on-Trent, produced lusterware that used as many as 12 colors,

on forms that were either traditional or modernist. Remarkably detailed, alluring illustrations of exotic gardens and magical places were transposed onto ceramic by highly accomplished painters. The charming and romantic patterns included 'Mikado', 'China Land' with a delicate pagoda, 'Paradise Bird and Tree', 'Tutankhamun' (see pp93) and the rare 'Babylon' design which features trailing tropical foliage.

Carlton's designer, Enoch Boulton,

moved to S. Fielding & Co. in 1929, where he introduced patterns that were remarkably close to those of Carlton. Popular designs included 'Fantasia' on a rich, cobalt blue background and 'Orient' with strong gilt, black, orange, and green coloring. The 'Mattajade' ground, which captured the spirit of jade but reinvented it for the new century in a matt sea-green hue, was decorated effectively with the 'Fairy Castles' and 'Chinese Dragon' patterns.

Geometric

Geometric shapes – whether squares, circles, triangles, hexagons, cones, or cubes –played an important role in Art Deco ceramics. Designers, greatly influenced by the avant-garde art movements of the first quarter of the 20th century, translated these concepts into a variety of home accessories. Used to create unusual forms or as surface decoration geometric patterns were key to much Art Deco ceramic design.

The angled, geometric form and stepped base of Roseville's Futura 'Tank' vase epitomize the Art Deco style.
1920s-1930s 10in (25.5cm) high V

WOMEN'S WORK

Clarice Cliff was a prolific British designer who recognized that geometric patterns could transform a conservative piece of china into a novel and stylish item. She had joined A.J. Wilkinson in Burslem, Stoke-on-Trent, as an apprentice lithographer in 1916. Around 1927, following a course at London's Royal College of Art, she was given her own studio there and was asked by the owner, Colley Shorter, to decorate some of the firm's old stock.

Although working with traditionally shaped, standard inexpensive earthenware, she applied hand-painted, banded, and geometric patterns in searing colors. They were marked with the name 'Bizarre'. Her studio mostly employed young, modern-thinking women who were encouraged to develop their own designs. Cliff was inspired by the Bauhaus and the Weiner

Werkstätte, while the *pochoir* (hand-stenciled) prints of the French designer Edouard Benedictus provided ideas for her color combinations. The effects can be seen in the 'Lucerne' and 'Lugano' designs for her 'Appliqué' range, which was launched in 1930.

Another innovative 20th-century female designer was Susie Cooper, who worked for A.E. Gray & Co. (Gray's Pottery) in Hanley, Staffordshire, between 1922 and 1929. She, too, initially designed hand-painted patterns that could be used on the traditional forms produced by the company. As well as geometric motifs, she worked with stylized animals, such as the gazelle, and flowers. By 1930 Cooper had set up her own company, Susie Cooper Pottery, where she was also able to design the shapes of the pieces. In 1931 she bought the Crown Works in Burslem.

INTERNATIONAL INSPIRATION

Designers in Stoke-on-Trent were fortunate to be exposed to the ideas of European modernism, with innovators, such as the modernist architect Serge Chermayeff, lecturing there in the 1930s. The Shelley Pottery, in Staffordshire, was a company

A vibrant geometric pattern decorates Susie Cooper's "Moon and Mountain" coffee set which she designed for Gray's Pottery.
c1930 Coffee pot 7.75in (20cm) high L

CLARICE CLIFF 'APPLIQUÉ LUCERNE' COFFEE POT
Cliff's early 'Bizarre' ware features Art Deco-inspired patterns handpainted onto old pottery blanks. However, by 1929 she was starting to introduce her own shapes which allowed her to combine Art Deco shapes and patterns. Some of these were strictly geometric while others were more playful, such as her concial sugar sifters.

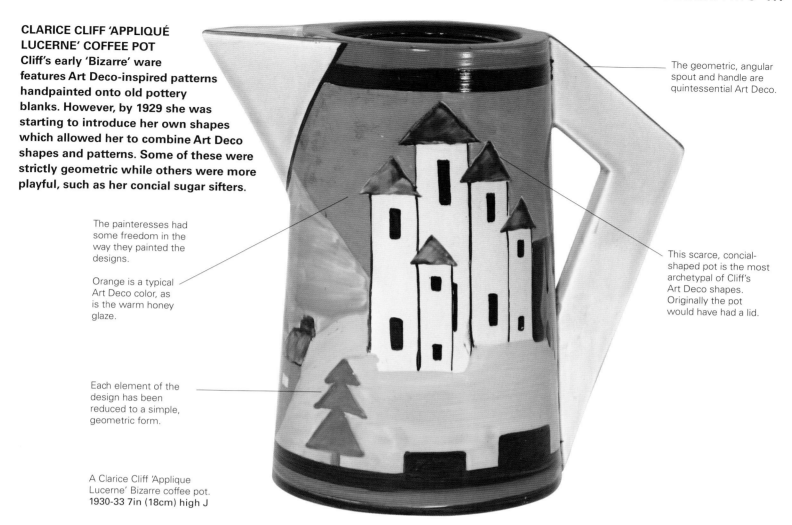

The painteresses had some freedom in the way they painted the designs.

Orange is a typical Art Deco color, as is the warm honey glaze.

Each element of the design has been reduced to a simple, geometric form.

The geometric, angular spout and handle are quintessential Art Deco.

This scarce, concial-shaped pot is the most archetypal of Cliff's Art Deco shapes. Originally the pot would have had a lid.

A Clarice Cliff 'Applique Lucerne' Bizarre coffee pot. 1930-33 7in (18cm) high J

that fully embraced the modern Art Deco style. The 'Vogue' and 'Mode' ranges were introduced in 1930, designed by Eric Slater. Conical with solid triangular handles, they were transfer-decorated with abstract and geometric designs. The 'Vogue' teapot was initially unpopular because it placed too much importance on form and too little on function – it was difficult to hold. However, when re-introduced under the name 'Eve' in 1932, with an open handle, it sold well.

The architectonic work of New Zealand-born Keith Murray for Wedgwood was sublime in its simplicity. Made in earthenware or basalt, his pieces are recognizable for their graduating grooves, which were made by hand. They were covered with monochrome, matt glazes. Many of his designs for glassmakers Stevens and Williams and for Wedgwood were produced in both ceramic and glass.

CONES AND CUBES

Cone and cube shapes were prevalent in ceramic design across Europe. In Czechoslovakia (now the Czech Republic) Pavel Janák promoted Cubist-inspired pieces, many in stark black and white. An inverted cone teapot with a press-molded disk handle by Grete Heymann-Marks for Hael-Werkstätten , was issued in Germany in 1930.

Russia was in the grip of Constructivism and Suprematism, with the State Porcelain Factory commandeering their revolutionary visual statements. Communist propaganda pottery was modernist rather than Art Deco and decorated with abstract art and slogans such as "The Land is for the Workers".

In the United States, the Arts and Crafts pottery Roseville – by that time one of the largest potteries in the country – launched its highly sought-after 'Futura' range in

1924. It featured exclusively futuristic forms, with geometric decoration in blended glaze colors, usually vivid contrast of pink with gray or blue. Futura is now considered to be the most progressive Art Deco pottery produced in the United States at the time. The Futura Tank vase is possibly the most iconic piece in the range – a large rhomboid shape with a commanding presence. Futura was followed by the Pinecone and Moderne ranges in the mid 1930s but neither of these caught the public's imagination in the way Futura had.

Aerodynamic styling, known as streamlining, swept across the United States in the 1930s, with Steubenville Pottery producing Russel Wright's popular 'American Modern' dinner service from 1939. Meanwhile, the Hall China Company drove the market with its 'Automobile' teapot, produced from 1938 to 1941.

Figurines

The 1920s and 1930s saw an explosion in the market for ceramic figurines. The middle classes were becoming increasingly affluent and sought ornaments for their homes that expressed the spirit of the times. Female figures were produced on a vast array of themes. The newly liberated woman was portrayed as a dancing flapper girl, playing tennis and golf, dressed in driving or bathing costume, or posing in elegant evening wear. Some figures wore nothing at all.

The new fashion for sunbathing is depicted in a 'Sunshine Girl' figure designed for Royal Doulton. The young girls is shown sitting dressed in a bathing suit beneath a parasol.
c1929 5in (13cm) high M

FANTASY WOMEN

Many of the sculptors modeled their fantasy women on the androgynous, super-thin body shape that was fashionable at the time. These figures often had impossibly long limbs and short, bobbed hair and wore the latest fashions and make-up. Exotic figures dressed in national costume, pierrots, children, and nursery figurines were also popular.

Goldscheider of Vienna produced thousands of figures – many are still believed to be unrecorded. Famous sculptors such as Josef Lorenzl and Stefan Dakon were commissioned by the company and their fluid lines and fabulous, highly decorated costumes created an unmistakable look for the firm.

The German company of Katzhütte, based in Hertwig, also produced colorful Art Deco ladies that were beautifully painted and expressed the sense of *joie de vivre* that society felt in the 1920s. Stefan Dakon also worked for Katzhütte, among many others.

In Britain, Leslie Harradine supplied figures to Royal Doulton for nearly 40 years. His sensual women and his "Bather" series, which included the cheerful "Sunshine Girl", were especially collected. Crown Devon introduced Art Deco figurines in 1931.

Lenci of Turin first produced ceramics in 1928 and they immediately received critical approval. The nude, white-glazed women wore jaunty accessories that contributed to the saucy air. Sandro Vacchetti, who designed for Lenci, went on to form a partnership in 1934 with Nello Franchini of Essevi. The company produced glazed terracotta figures in Georges Barbier-style dresses, or exotic female-animal combinations.

INTERNATIONAL INSPIRATION

Ceramics manufacturers far and wide rushed to take their share of the lucrative figures market, from the Weiner Werkstätte to Robj of Paris, who commissioned a jazz band, and Noritake of Japan, who produced a pierrot. Royal Copenhagen in Denmark, and Royal Dux in Czechoslovakia created an array of figurines, from snake dancers to Rudolph Valentino. Elly Strobach's busts and figurines for Royal Dux are sought after for their strong coloring and attractive features. At Rosenthal of Germany, Dorothea Charol created exotic dancers and Claire Weiss designed figures representing the Four Seasons.

WALL MASKS

Marlene Dietrich, Greta Garbo, Rita Hayworth, Gracie Fields, Ginger Rogers, Fred Astaire, and Bing Crosby were just some of the subjects portrayed as wall masks of the 1920s and 1930s. Goldscheider made around 1,000 masks and busts of women, the majority with the distinctive tightly curled hair.

"Google-eyes" masks are rare, with makers including Royal Dux. Clarice Cliff made a small number of masks in extraordinary headdresses. Beswick and Cope & Co. of Staffordshire modeled pretty women, while Leonardi earthenware masks by Leonardene of London featured mysterious, Latin-looking females.

A Goldscheider wall mask modeled as a stylized woman with a terrier dog.
c1930 9.5in (24cm) high F

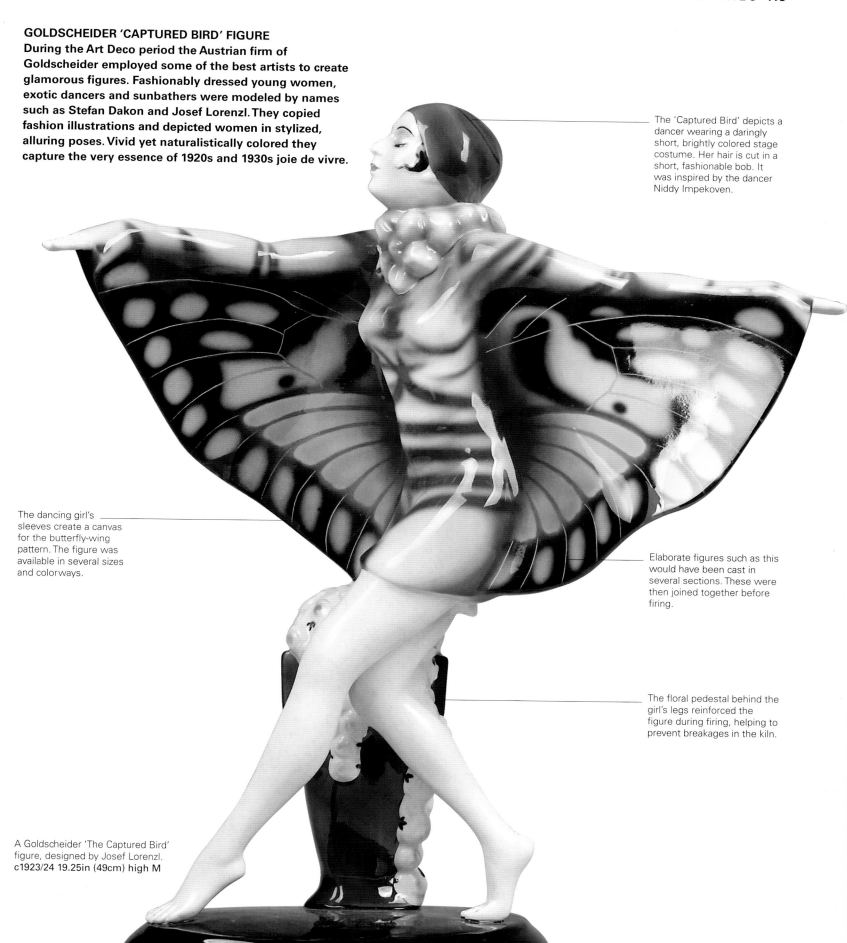

GOLDSCHEIDER 'CAPTURED BIRD' FIGURE
During the Art Deco period the Austrian firm of Goldscheider employed some of the best artists to create glamorous figures. Fashionably dressed young women, exotic dancers and sunbathers were modeled by names such as Stefan Dakon and Josef Lorenzl. They copied fashion illustrations and depicted women in stylized, alluring poses. Vivid yet naturalistically colored they capture the very essence of 1920s and 1930s joie de vivre.

The 'Captured Bird' depicts a dancer wearing a daringly short, brightly colored stage costume. Her hair is cut in a short, fashionable bob. It was inspired by the dancer Niddy Impekoven.

The dancing girl's sleeves create a canvas for the butterfly-wing pattern. The figure was available in several sizes and colorways.

Elaborate figures such as this would have been cast in several sections. These were then joined together before firing.

The floral pedestal behind the girl's legs reinforced the figure during firing, helping to prevent breakages in the kiln.

A Goldscheider 'The Captured Bird' figure, designed by Josef Lorenzl. c1923/24 19.25in (49cm) high M

CERAMICS GALLERY

Geometric shapes and patterns, figurines of fashionable young women and stylized tea services are among the ceramics produced in large numbers during the Art Deco period. All of them are typical of the era, but the best feature strong colors and bold designs. They were sold in fashionable boutiques around the world.

A Goebels pottery wall mask of a woman with stylized curly hair.
8.5in (21.5cm) long B

A plate decorated by Jean Lurcat features a stylized blue, black and white design.
c1925 9.75in (25cm) diam I

Ziggurats and stylized flowers decorate a Carter, Stabler and Adams Ltd. Poole Pottery vase, designed by Truda Carter.
9.75in (24.7cm) high L

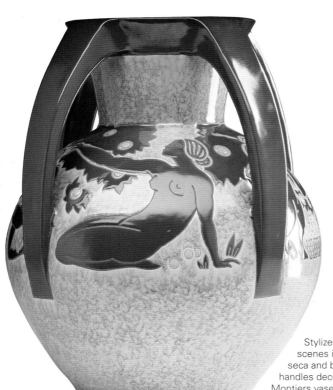

Stylized harvest scenes in cuerda seca and buttress handles decorate a Montiers vase.
16.5in (42cm) high M

The form provides the decoration of this modernist green-glazed 'Bombe' vase by Keith Murray for Wedgwood.
6in (15.5cm) high C

An elongated figure and fashionable bobbed hair feature on this Crown Devon figure of a dancer.
13.25in (33.5cm) high J

LENCI FIGURINE

From 1928 until the outbreak of World War Two Lenci produced an array of figures of young women. Founded in Turin in 1919 by Enrico and Helen (Elena) König Scavini, Lenci initially made hand painted dolls. Many of the best figurines were designed by Elena, who trained as an artist before her marriage. Gigi Chessa, Sandro Vacchetti, Giovanni Grande and Abele Jacopi also produced designs. Like those of Goldscheider, the elegant women depicted in Lenci figurines were tall and thin, with narrow waists and long legs. However, unlike Goldscheider, who were famous for reproducing contemporary couture, Lenci figurines often wore next to nothing at all.

Many Lenci figures had characteristic light yellow hair.

This girl is depicted in a characteristically nonchalant pose.

The frog on the back of her chair is a typically humorous addition to the design.

Black dresses like this one were fashionable at the time.

A Lenci pottery figure, from a model by Helen König Scavini.
1932 9.5in (24cm) high N

Triangular handles and a geometric design decorate this Shelley 'Green Block' pattern, 'Vogue' shape tea service.
c1930 I

A Rosenthal figure of an exotic snake dancer.
10.5in (26.5cm) H

Cut and Etched Glass

In the 1920s and 1930s, glassmakers across the globe recognized the potential of glass for creating fashionable new designs. The well-defined angular geometric shapes that were key to the Art Deco style were realized in the centuries-old technique of glass-cutting. The cut patterns – facets, grooves, and depressions – were created with a rotating iron or stone wheel and then polished to create a brilliant and sparkling surface.

CARVED MOTIFS

The Daum Frères glassworks, a prolific family-owned glassmaking factory based in Nancy, France, had exceled in the production of decorative glass since 1878. It thrived during the Art Deco period under the inspired guidance of the founder's grandson, Paul Daum. He forged a new artistic path in the 1920s, moving away from the ornate Art Nouveau style to concentrate on large, thick-walled vessels in single colors.

Lamps, bowls, and vases produced at this time by Daum feature etched or wheel-carved decorative motifs. These include eye-catching stylized flower blooms, birds resting on branches or flying above ocean waves, deer or gazelles silhouetted in verdant landscapes, or geometric or abstract Cubist-inspired Art Deco patterns. These were often acid-etched deeply into the thick glass, often with alternating bands of polishing and etching.

The imaginative designs were frequently set against monochromatic backgrounds, ranging from frosty white, butterscotch gold, and candy pink to vivid shades of emerald green, bright turquoise, and royal blue. These wares tended to be larger than their Art Nouveau predecessors, with internally decorated designs. Some were set into heavy wrought-iron frames designed by Edgar Brandt, Louis Majorelle, or André Groult, among others. The company showcased its fashionable designs to public acclaim at the 1925 Paris Exhibition and went on to provide glass for the oceanliner *Le Normandie*.

Possibly designed by Keith Murray, this Stevens & Williams vase is cut with geometric chevron design bands and lenses. The green color of the glass is typical of the company.
1930s 12in (30.5cm) high F

Angular twin-handles and a geometric cut design that follows the curves of the body, are epitome of Art Deco design on this Daum Frères vase.
c1925 5.75in (14.5cm) high I

STEUBEN 'GAZELLE' BOWL
After 1932 Steuben, which had been known for its colored glass, began to make many clear crystal pieces. The 'Gazelle' bowl was designed by Sidney Waugh, who was Steuben's chief associate designer from 1933–63. It was inspired by contemporary Scandinavian glass. The 'Gazelle' bowl is considered to be one of Waugh's most important works.

Leaping gazelles were a typical Art Deco motif.

The quality of the crystal allowed the engraver to depict an astonishing amount of detail: from the muscular body tone to the expressive faces of the twelve gazelles.

The thick glass walls are typical of the high-quality pieces produced by the factory.

The deep spherical bowl contrasts with the angular glass base with its linear cut decoration.

Steuben 'Gazelle' bowl designed by Sidney Waugh.
1935 7in (18cm) high V

Elsewhere in France, the Cristalleries de Saint-Louis, based in Lorraine, also took up the new trend, of creating contrasting polished and etched areas.

Also in Lorraine, the legendary Baccarat firm under the artistic leadership of Georges Chevalier embraced the Art Deco style. Glass was cut in bold multifaceted geometric patterns for glittering dressing-table sets, decanters and glasses, perfume bottles, lamps, and clocks. For the 1925 Paris Exhibition, Chevalier designed the Baccarat-Christofle Pavilion on a water theme which included a 3m (10ft) high chandelier representing a waterfall. It was a motif which was to inspire many designers.

SCANDINAVIAN INFLUENCE
Across the English Channel, the Art Deco glass designed by the New Zealand-born architect Keith Day Murray strengthened the international reputation of the Stourbridge-based glassworks of Stevens and Williams. Murray's cut-glass vases and tableware typically feature decorative architectonic fluting, consisting of parallel horizontal grooves as well as engraved motifs such as cacti. He visited Europe often in the 1920s and his spirited modernist designs reflect the influence of the new Viennese and Scandinavian glass that he had seen at the 1925 Paris Exhibition. Murray also designed modernist and Art Deco ceramics for

Wedgwood from the 1930s.

In the United States the celebrated Steuben Glass Works in Corning, New York, held sway as the premier American maker of decorative glass in the Art Deco style. From the early 1930s, the factory produced chic and contemporary Jazz Age glass engraved and etched with geometric designs by Walter Dorwin Teague and the sculptor Sidney Biehler Waugh. Waugh's majestic crystal glass compositions – 'Gazelle Bowl' and 'Europa Bowl' among them – were engraved with stylized Art Deco subjects which had been inspired by French and Swedish glass designs. Other artists were commissioned to create designs which were produced in limited editions.

Surface Decorated Glass

A host of highly original designs and surface treatments were used to decorate glass in innovative, exciting patterns and colors throughout the 1920s and 1930s. During this exhilarating period, art studios and factories alike answered the enormous demand for limited-edition, artist-designed glasswares in the new style. Led by trendsetting France, *le style moderne* influenced the production of stylish ornamental glass on both sides of the Atlantic.

Following the 1925 Paris Exhibition, glassmakers were inspired to use a range of traditional decorative techniques to create innovative designs. Surface treatments including enameling, acid-etching, casing and overlay, mottling, flashing, and trailing were employed to decorate tableware and ornamental glass. Clear glass vessels vividly decorated with lacquer, oil or enamel paints featuring stylized motifs such as female heads and nudes, birds, flowers, and fruits comprised the early work of Maurice Marinot, the leading maker of French Art Deco studio glass.

The technique was also adopted by Marcel Goupy at the Maison Rouard in Paris and by Auguste-Claude Heiligenstein for Leune in Paris. Goupy used it for his clear glass one-of-a-kind vases and bowls, highlighted with bold painted designs incorporating stylized classical figures and animals, chic ladies, and lush Cubist landscapes. Heiligenstein's distinctive enameled *objets* feature framed mythological motifs and flower, wave, or geometric patterns in the Art Deco style.

At the Steuben Glass Works in Corning, New York, the English designer Frederick Carder created a variety of art glass using new techniques, innovative surface effects, and a broad spectrum of lustrous colors. His intarsia glass with an etched design sandwiched between two colorless layers and his acid cutback glassware – usually two layers of cased glass in contrasting colors – bear a strong resemblance to wheel-carved cameo glass.

As an inexpensive alternative to labor-intensive hand engraving, acid-etching was another technique taken up on both sides of the Atlantic by glass designers who embraced the taste for decoration in the modern Art Deco style. These included France's Daum Frères, Italy's Venini glass factory under the artistic direction of Vittorio Zecchin and sculptor Napoleone Martinuzzi, and Sweden's Orrefors factory.

COLORED GLASS

The Orrefors glassworks – under the direction of the painters Simon Gate and Edvard Hald in collaboration with master glassblower Knut Bergqvist and other artists – developed Graal glass. A mosaic-like glass, it had cut and etched decoration that was flashed in clear glass.

Experiments at glass factories and art studios resulted in a variety of polychrome finishes – mottled hues in the same color family, subtle gradations of color from vibrant to pale, and mosaic-like glass – featuring a palette of rich, jewel-like colors. Ranging from emerald green to turquoise, sapphire blue to shades of ruby, citrus yellow, and orange, they demonstrate what a key role color plays as a foil for a wide variety of techniques to decorate glass.

Reflections in the glass multiply the number of fish and the amount of weed in this 'Fiskegraal' aquarium vase designed by Edward Hald at Orrefors.
5in (12.5cm) high E

Stylized flowers and leaves are wrapped around a vibrant Daum Frères vase. The design was acid-etched in amber over an internally speckled ground.
10in (25.5cm) high B

The exuberant Art Deco abstract pattern of flowers and flashes was created using enamels on a pair of Stuart candleholders.
3.25in (8cm) high B

STEUBEN ACID CUT BACK VASE
The acid cut back technique was used to great effect at Steuben to create glass decorated with Art Deco motifs. Pieces were usually made using two layers of contrasting colored glass. Hydrofluoric acid was used to remove the top or outer layer of glass to create a pattern. Many pieces were made using different shades of the same color of glass to create a subtle finish. But here, jade green glass has been cased with black to create a dynamic contrast.

The polished black glass decoration contrasts effectively with the matt surface of the green glass. Covering one layer of hot glass with a second layer of molten glass requires a great level of skill as the colors tend to cool at different speeds and this can result in cracking. The result here is simple yet striking.

Steuben glass from this era often features traditional shapes – such as this one – which are then decorated in the Art Deco style.

In the Art Deco style natural forms were frequently depicted in a stylized manner, as seen here in the simplified exaggerated curves of the petals and leaves.

The acid has eaten into the surface of the glass to leave a slightly pitted, matt surface. The black glass stands visibly proud of the surface.

The way the flowers and leaves appear to sway in the breeze suggests the work of a talented designer.

Hard stone colors such as jade green and rose quartz were often used by Steuben for its Art Deco wares.

Steuben acid cut back vase.
c1920 10in (25.5cm) high O

René Lalique (1860–1945)

The position of France as the leader in the production of innovative art glass during the 1920s and 1930s was largely due to the prolific and highly talented designer René Lalique. Widely imitated, most of Lalique's decorative glass in the Art Deco style – from vases, tableware, and perfume bottles to architectural panels, lighting, and clocks – was machine-made to a very high standard at his workshop in Alsace. The factory continues the tradition today.

Having established a career as a leading designer of exclusive jewelry in the Art Nouveau style, Lalique had by 1910 turned his attention to luxury glassmaking. He employed a variety of techniques including acid etching with sandblasting to produce a frosty opalescence, and his imaginative, highly original glassware was functional as well as decorative.

His reputation grew after the 1925 Paris Exhibition where he exhibited in two pavilions and within the grounds (see pxxx). Few designers made such a successful transition from the Art Nouveau to the Art Deco style.

Out of a modest but distinctive collection of glass scent bottles, atomisers, and powder boxes that he had developed for François Coty and other perfume companies and fashion houses grew an extensive repertoire of luxurious items: large molded vases, bowls, platters and centerpieces, lamps, and chandeliers. These featured decorative motifs such as sculptural animals, birds, elegant nude figures, and geometric or stylized blossoms.

Lalique's mass-produced yet high-quality smaller objects included car mascots and bookends. His workshop also produced a broad range of tableware as well as the occasional large-scale exhibition piece and limited-editions such as screens and fountains. He was also commissioned as an interior designer for large installations such as the *Orient Express* train and the oceanliner *Le Normandie*.

Color played a significant role in large-scale glass objects. Clear glass with a partially frosted finish was more common. Although some cased vases feature a white layer sandwiched between two layers of another hue to create luminous greens, blues, or reds, internal colors tended to be monochromatic or clear. Big, important vases dazzled in vivid shades of amber, turquoise, jade green, scarlet, and purple.

However, Lalique is best known for his lustrous pearl-white opalescent glass, which shimmers with a blue or yellow sheen depending on how it catches the light. The fact that the chemical formula for this popular glass was a closely guarded secret did not deter others from trying to create their own versions – with mixed results.

Classical maidens were a frequent decorative device. "Suzanne" statuette in opalescent amber glass.
c1925 9in (23cm) wide U

Perfume bottle for "Habanito" by Molinard in clear and frosted glass with a green patina.
c1929 4.75in (12cm) wide K

Vibrant colors include the blue of this "Espalion" vase which is molded with overlapping fern leaves.
c1927 7in (18cm) high M

ART DECO

The sumptuous and fashionable Grand Salon of the *Le Normandie* oceanliner featured glass fittings by Lalique.

LALIQUE IMITATORS

The inspired Art Deco glass designs conceived by René Lalique spawned imitations by factories around the world, though the copies were not always of the highest quality. The most successful of the imitators was the Sicilian-born Parisian Marius-Ernest Sabino, whose designs closely mirrored those of Lalique. Among the other glassmakers influenced by Lalique were Pierre d'Avesn – who had worked for the master for more than ten years – and the French firms Edmond Etling & Cie and Verlys. By 1933, Verlys had moved production to the United States. Typical of the factory's output are high-quality press-molded vases and bowls in deep-bluish opalescent glass – and more rarely in smoky gray, blue, or pink – boasting symmetrical patterns evocative of Lalique designs.

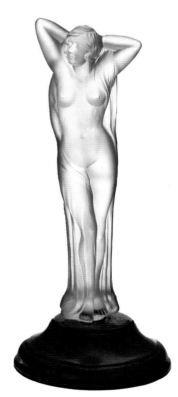

Lalique's work was widely copied. This frosted glass figure is probably French.
c1930 9.25in (23.5cm) high B

Red glass, like this Lalique 'Perruches' vase, tends to be costly to produce and is generally rarer than other colors.
c1919 10.5in (26.5cm) high N

Molded and pressed glass

The 1925 Paris Exhibition showcased the Art Deco style, and glass designers were quick to adopt this new fashion, which relied on sharp angular shapes, geometric decoration, and dramatic color combinations. To accommodate the growing demand for ornamental glass and tableware in the new style, glassmakers adapted these stylistic elements for less expensive wares by using techniques such as press molding and mold blowing.

This pressed glass vase shows the relief patterns popular with Art Deco designers to good effect. Rows of repeating geometric bands cover this vase designed by Simon Gate for Orrefors in Sweden. **c1930 6.25in (16cm) high B**

The pleasure-seeking lifestyle personified by the Jazz Age led to an overwhelming demand for affordable cocktail shakers, decanters, and glasses as drinking became socially acceptable. These were turned out in vast numbers and decorated with a wide variety of stylized Art Deco patterns, using mass-production methods like press molding. Along with vases, bowls, plates, compotes, pitchers, candlesticks, and other decorative objects, sets of cheap pressed-glass tableware – known as Depression Glass – became a key product of American glass manufacturers during the 1930s.

The process of pressing molten glass into a patterned metal mold proved an ideal technique for creating the complex angular and geometric designs that are hallmarks of the Art Deco style. Whether done by hand or machine, the press-molding process – whereby hot glass is dropped into a mold and then firmly pressed with a plunger to leave a decorative relief design on the object – was quick and efficient, although the definition is not as refined as on cut glass. In Europe, France, Britain and Germany pioneered the trend for press molding during the 1920s and 1930s.

Workshops from Bohemia to Scandinavia adopted press molding for tableware and vases alongside their more expensive ranges of ornamental art glass. Although European press molding tends to be softer than the sharp-edged designs produced in America, the crisp, clean wares designed by Simon Gate and Edvard Hald at Sweden's Orrefors factory set the standard for high-quality, highly original geometric shapes and bold colors for mass-produced inexpensive glass.

MOLD-BLOWN GLASS

At the same time, innovative mold-blown ornamental art glass boasting chunky forms, vivid color combinations, and

geometric patterning happily shared the stage with functional and inexpensive clear table glass decorated with a similar Art Deco vocabulary – angular geometric patterns, stylized animals, classical figures, flowers, and foliage. In Germany the colorful, internally decorated Ikora-Kristall art glass that was created by Bauhaus designer Wilhelm Wagenfeld at the Württembergishe Metallwaren Fabrik (W.M.F.) contrasted with serviceable clear glass domestic ware. Dramatic color was also a feature of the sculptural Art Deco shapes, surface textures, and internal color effects achieved by the Italian firms Barovier and Venini & C.

Mold-blown glassware often features robust modernist sculptural forms complemented by colorful internal effects – for example, air bubbles, metallic inclusions, or the *millefiori* technique

The dancer Isadora Duncan is reputed to have inspired this table centerpiece. The fan-shaped legs are typical of Art Deco pieces. **c1930 12in (30.5cm) diam B**

WALTHER 'SCHMETTERLING' VASE

The German factory Auguste Walther & Sohn was one of many inspired by the work of René Lalique. Like many Czechoslovakian glassworks and companies such as Jobling and Bagley in the UK it created decorative yet functional glasswares made from machine-pressed glass. Centerpieces and vases were especially popular – particularly as wedding gifts for middle class couples. Motifs included exotic women, birds and animals.

The symmetrical shape provides a geometric counterpoint to the exotic butterfly woman.

The Schmetterling – or butterfly – is depicted as an archetypal Art Deco woman with a slim but curvaceous figure. Instead of wearing the shocking short dresses that were fashionable at the time, she wears a flowing yet suggestively figure-hugging gown. The rim of the vase follows the shape of her outstretched arms.

The frosted glass enhances the woman's figure and provides a contrast to her polished "wings". She appears to be surrounded by a halo of light, an effect created by the texture of the molded glass.

The vase is a combination of frosted and polished glass. The frosting was created by covering some areas of the glass with a resist before placing the vase in an acid atmosphere which ate into the glossy surface and frosted the unprotected glass.

This example dates from the 1930s. Later copies tend to be completed polished. Modern fakes are sandblasted to achieve the frosted finish. These areas are rougher to the touch than acid etched glass.

A Walther & Sohn Schmetterling vase.
c1935 8.5in (22cm) high B

adopted by Frederick Carder at New York's Steuben Glass Works – or hand-finished decoration such as enameling and engraving. It may also imitate the effect of more expensive cut glass, although the decorative pattern can be felt on both the inside and outside of the object and the finish tends to be softer.

The clean, bold shapes and geometric motifs central to the Bauhaus philosophy were enthusiastically re-interpreted by a host of talented Art Deco designers. These included Michael Powolny at the Loetz factory in Bohemia, Napoleone Martinuzzi of Venini & C. in Italy, and Elis Bergh at Sweden's Kosta glassworks.

PATE DE VERRE

France was also the center for pâte de verre ("glass paste"). Known in ancient Egypt and revived in France during the late 19th and early 20th centuries, the technique involved making a paste from ground glass which was then applied in layers or poured into a mold and refired. Art Deco designers including Gabriel Argy-Rousseau, François-Emile Décorchemont, and Amalric Walter cemented the country's reputation for dramatic pâte de verre glass vases, bowls, boxes, trays, lamps and other objects in the sharp abstract shapes of the contemporary style, and complemented by deep yet muted colors.

GLASS GALLERY

A fascination with geometric shapes, exotic archeological finds in Egypt and South America, streamlining and a passion for color can all be seen in decorative and functional glass from the 1920s and 30s. At the same time, advances in technology allowed factories to mass-produce machine-molded glass at an unprecedented rate. As a result fashionable, decorative glass became affordable to many people for the first time.

A geometric design was etched and enameled onto this vase by French company Schneider for its Le Verre Français range.
c1930 3.5in (9cm) high K

Bands of horizontal ribbing give a modernist influence to this cased glass vase designed by Napoleone Martinuzzi, and made by the Italian firm Venini & C.
c1930 11.72in (29.3cm) high E

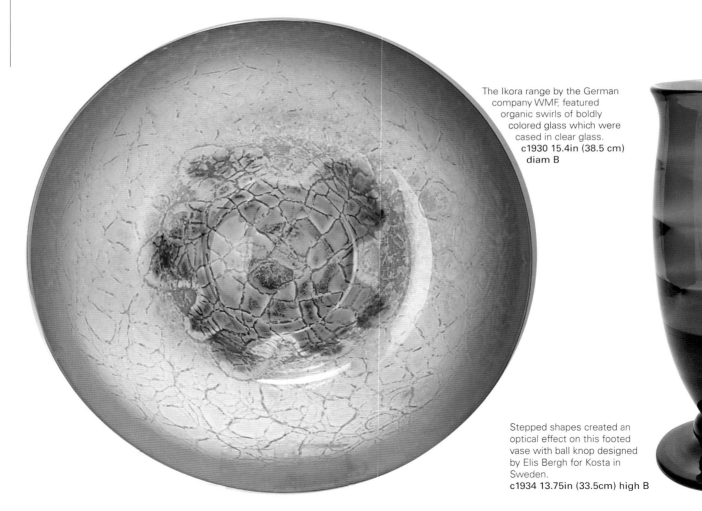

The Ikora range by the German company WMF, featured organic swirls of boldly colored glass which were cased in clear glass.
c1930 15.4in (38.5 cm) diam B

Stepped shapes created an optical effect on this footed vase with ball knop designed by Elis Bergh for Kosta in Sweden.
c1934 13.75in (33.5cm) high B

RUBA RHOMBIC VASE

In 1928 the Consolidated Lamp & Glass Co of Coraopolis, Pennsylvania, launched a new line of pressed glass it called "An epic in modern art". The Ruba Rhombic range, designed by Reuben Haley, was inspired by Cubist art and considered by many to be ahead of its time. Despite its commercial success, the Depression caused production to cease in 1932 and so Ruba Rhombic wares are rare today. A range included perfume bottles, decanter sets and bowls. Colors included Jungle green, Smokey Topaz, Sunshine, Jade, Lilac and Silver Cloud.

Ruba Rhombic was launched at the 1928 Pittsburgh Glass Show where it was given its own room decorated with antique gold walls highlighted with geometric apple green parallelograms.

It was said to be the very essence of Art Moderne.

The range was hailed as "true specimens of Cubist art" and the new shapes and colors were applauded by the critics.

The name Ruba Rhombic is a combination of ruba'i, a form of Persian poetry, and rhombic, a term in geometry for an irregular form with no parallel lines.

The geometric shapes create an intriguing interplay of light and shadow through the irregular planes of the glass.

A Ruba Rhombic vase.
c1930. 9.25in (23cm) high J

Simple, repeating horizontal fluting follows the tapered shape of this cut glass vase which was produced by Thomas Webb exclusively for the Rembrandt Guild in the UK.
c1935 7in (17.75cm) high C

A Val St Lambert geometric cut pink glass vase designed by Léon Ledru who was head of the design department at the Belgian factory from 1888 to 1926 .
7in (17.75cm) high S

This glass vase in a single bright color with a black rim is typical of the pieces created by the designer Michael Powolny for the Austrian Loetz factory.
c1920 6.25in (16cm) high B

An exotic Egyptian princess, lotus flowers and garlands of flowers decorate a perfume bottle by French designer Julien Viard for Dubarry's 'Blue Lagoon'. It was made by Depinoix.
c1919. 4in (10cm) high N

Metal Tableware

The icy glamor of silver cast a spell over Art Deco designers. In the 1920s and 1930s leading silversmiths stripped traditional hollowware and flatware design down to its bare essentials, letting the clean, elegant forms show through. Their bold work remains just as fresh and striking today. The arresting beauty of these designs was to percolate down to modestly priced tablewares.

Jean Puiforcat was one of the most influential silversmiths of the Art Deco era. A sculptor by training as well as a brilliant metalworker, the Parisian gold- and silversmith specialized in flatware and tea services, creating highly original pieces that were inspired by geometric lines. His designs are harmonious – a deceptively simple balance of shape and proportion. Handles and knobs made of exotic woods and rich materials such as lapis lazuli were transformed into ornament. He skilfully managed to create a lavish look while spurning surface decoration. His work was widely copied in continental Europe and the United States.

Puiforcat was not the only cutting-edge Parisian silversmith influencing tableware designs at the time. The firm Cardeilhac also produced outstanding minimal designs based on spherical and angular shapes throughout the 1920s and 1930s. They also incorporated wood, ivory and lapis lazuli into designs and used decorative finishes. The firm merged with Christofle in 1951.

GEOMETRY GAINS MASS APPEAL

The simplicity of the designs of silversmiths like Puiforcat and Cardeilhac offered an ideal template for the industrial production of cheap yet stylish metalwares. European silver-plate manufacturers like Christofle in France and Joseph Rodgers & Sons in England were among the first to pick up on the latest Parisian trends. They began producing clean-lined, geometric designs in the late 1920s and early 1930s and made the new style available to the masses.

Christofle met the demand for Art Deco pieces by commissioning designers such as Maurice Dufrène, André Groult, Louis Süe and André Mare, and Gio Ponti. At the beginning of the century the company had developed an improved form of silver-plate called Gallia, and this was used extensively on

Geometric shapes with minimal decoration were a feature of designs by Cardeilhac. This urn-shaped sterling-silver covered box has a contrasting lapis lazuli finial. **c1925 6in (15cm) high M**

THE COCKTAIL SHAKER

The martini, the daiquiri – these cocktails were de rigueur at any Jazz Age get-together. The rattle of ice in a cocktail shaker reverberated internationally between the wars. Redolent of good times and modish sophistication, they sold in vast numbers. The 1920s and 30s, when prolific partying contrasted with punitive prohibition, were one of the most inventive periods of shaker design. Every leading firm, from Georg Jensen to the Chase Brass & Copper Company, made them. Cocktail shakers were produced in various combinations of metal, glass, and plastic, and came in a range of sizes, including some as big as pitchers. Many had handles and spouts to make pouring easier. Some came in novelty shapes such as that of penguins – perhaps better for amusing guests than mixing cocktails.

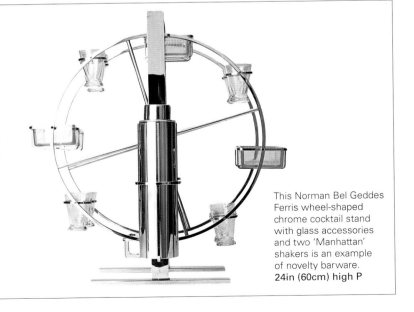

This Norman Bel Geddes Ferris wheel-shaped chrome cocktail stand with glass accessories and two 'Manhattan' shakers is an example of novelty barware. **24in (60cm) high P**

GEOMETRIC SILVER-PLATED TEASET
In the 1920s and 30s plastic was still a new and exciting material. It was often combined with precious metals to create pieces in the latest styles. For those who could not afford solid silver, silver plate continued to be an affordable alternative. It was crafted into some of the most innovative designs, making fashionable silver-colored tablewares available to the widest possible market.

Plastics such as Bakelite were often used in the place of ivory on handles and finials. Here the black plastic imitates ebony to insulate the handle from the heat of the liquid.

Innovative style was no longer the preserve of famous designers. Joseph Rodgers & Sons, one of the largest cutlery makers in Sheffield, England at the time, was among those who diversified into Art Deco designs to meet consumer demand.

The angular form of the teapot, hot water jug, V-shaped milk jug and sugar bowl are an ultimate expression of the geometric Art Deco style.

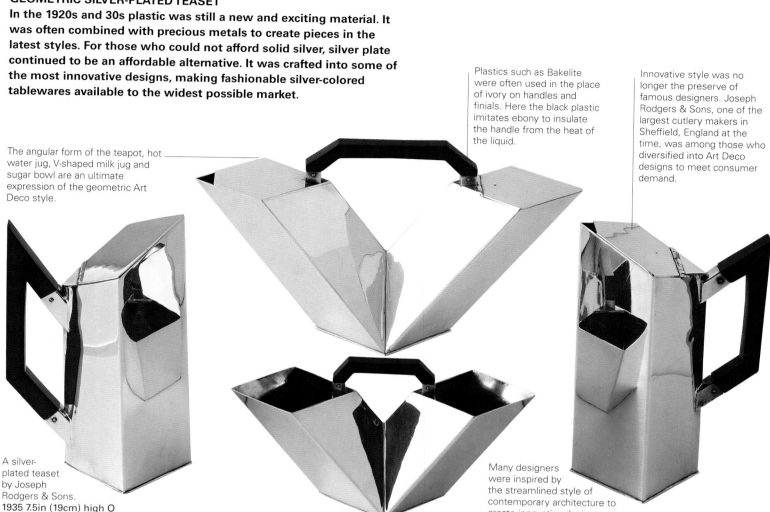

A silver-plated teaset by Joseph Rodgers & Sons.
1935 7.5in (19cm) high O

Many designers were inspired by the streamlined style of contemporary architecture to create innovative designs.

its Art Deco wares. It supplied most of the plated wares for the liner *Le Normandie* and other luxury cruise ships belonging to the Compagnie Générale Transatlantique.

INEXPENSIVE ALTERNATIVES
American manufacturers were slower to react to the new style. They concentrated on conservative metal tableware inspired by antique pieces until the Depression's devastating effect on sales forced them to rethink their complacent approach to design. Large firms like the Chase Brass & Copper Company employed such leading designers as Russell Wright to woo budget-conscious consumers with irresistible products. Wright also designed innovative Art Deco aluminium wares for West Bend Aluminum Company, Wisconsin.

Using inexpensive alternatives such as chrome and aluminium to replicate silver's dazzling allure, these designers introduced the fashionable European geometric style to the American market. The resulting designs were sleek and streamlined, expressing modernity. Many of these designs, like Norman Bel Geddes's acclaimed Manhattan cocktail service, were inspired by skyscrapers as these were thought to capture a distinctly American type of innovation. Other designs reflected current developments in technology, such as the 'Soda King' siphon bottle, also by Bel Geddes, that was shaped like a missile. Although standards were compromized by the Great Depression that started in 1929, manufacturers were able to combine mass production with innovative design.

GLOBAL LUXURY
Founded in the early 1900s, the Danish silversmith firm Georg Jensen was renowned for its quality and distinct designs. Its finely crafted silver appears to have been hand-made even though it was produced by machine. Classic Jensen designs have plain, curvilinear forms accented with a stylized animal or plant motif. However, in the 1930s designers including Harald Nielsen and Sigvard Bernadotte took Jensen in a radical new direction. They created a series of innovative designs characterized by an emphasis on form combined with restrained decoration, such as Nielsen's famous 'Pyramid' flatware composed of pure geometric shapes, which caught the minimalist Art Deco mood.

ART DECO

Decorative Metalware

The 1920s and 30s saw a revival of the use of metals for decorative purposes. Wrought iron, copper and brass became highly fashionable for interiors with simple, angular, or streamlined geometric designs. Stylized figural imagery, notably of animals was also popular. Industrial designers also experimented with the less expensive alternatives of aluminium, copper and sheet metal.

IRONWORK

Intricate iron gates, balcony grilles, and stair rails were once worked by hand, but during the 19th century this time-consuming technique was largely overtaken by easier and cheaper casting methods. The French metalworker Edgar Brandt played a key role in reviving wrought iron, which became particularly popular in France. His exuberant, complex work is characterized by stylized natural motifs including animals, vegetation, and jets of water. He mixed metals and finishes to create color and textural contrasts and experimented combining cast with wrought iron. Brandt also embraced new uses for wrought iron, including radiator covers, lamps, side tables, and even jewelry. He also made the gates for the 1925 Paris Exhibition.

Brandt was comfortable combining traditional methods with industrial technology and his pieces weres often composed of repeating motifs that could be put together on an assembly line. He also used new welding techniques that avoided the necessity to heat complex pieces in the forge.

Brandt's success at the 1925 Paris Exhibition helped promote the new French fashion across the Atlantic. He opened a branch of his company in New York, which encouraged other French manufacturers of wrought iron, such as Paul Kiss and Raymond Subes, to seek American commissions. The United States also produced its own ironworkers, like Oscar B. Bach, who also produced sculptural decorative objects, and Wilhelm

Abstract geometric patterns were a hallmark of Art Deco design. The contrasting silver and black pattern on this WMF 'Ikora' pedestal vase, designed by Rudolf Rieger, was enameled onto the metal.
c1930 25.75in (65.5cm) high D

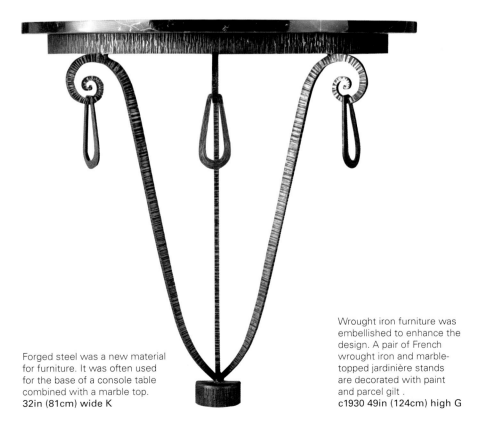

Forged steel was a new material for furniture. It was often used for the base of a console table combined with a marble top.
32in (81cm) wide K

Wrought iron furniture was embellished to enhance the design. A pair of French wrought iron and marble-topped jardinière stands are decorated with paint and parcel gilt .
c1930 49in (124cm) high G

Hunt Diederich, whose delicate openwork gates, screens, and fire screens were decorated with Art Deco animal imagery.

DINANDERIE

Another type of metalware popular in the Art Deco era was dinanderie. The name derives from Dinant, a Flemish town famed for its brass vessels during the Middle Ages. It became a catch phrase for hand-raised base-metal objects – usually brass or copper – with a variety of finishes, frequently used together. Dinanderie could be embossed and engraved as well as inlaid or encrusted with various colored metals. Some was finished with oxides or acids. One of Art Deco's foremost exponents, the Swiss designer Jean Dunand introduced the application of vividly colored lacquers embellished with crushed eggshell on dinanderie.

The French metalworker Claudius Linossier was a recognized master of dinanderie, combining meticulous craftsmanship with daring Art Deco design. Originally trained as a goldsmith and silversmith, Linossier studied briefly with Dunand before opening his own workshop in Lyon. Although he experimented with lacquer, he is best known for rich, burnished finishes and painstaking inlays. His early vases, bowls, and plates are influenced by ancient pottery from the Classical world while his later works are boldly geometric in design and decoration.

Striking dinanderie effects were imitated in cheaper, machine-made metalwork, from cigarette cases to the metal-covered wall panels so fashionable for interiors. In the 1930s, the German metal foundry W.M.F., which came to prominence in the Art Nouveau period, introduced their Ikora range of metalware featuring jazzy geometric decoration executed in enamel, inlay, and different surface finishes.

Stylized natural motifs are a hallmark of Edgar Brandt's work. This pair of wrought iron interior gates, by Brandt, feature a stylized water fountain and swirling stems of leaves and pierced flowers, above a base of pierced vines. Stamped "E. Brandt/France".
c1924 51in (129.5cm) high V

ART DECO

METALWARE GALLERY

Metalware designers took full advantage of the Art Deco style to create a plethora of designs. Streamlining, geometric patterns, stylized depictions of the natural world and Modernist structure influenced the decoration of everything from women's accessories and tablewares to architectural pieces. Skilled craftsmen used enamels, inlays and surface finish to create designs on silver and base metals. Items from cocktail shakers to compacts, fireplace furniture to tea sets were shaped into the latest fashionable styles.

The centuries-old technique of enameling was used to create dramatic geometric Art Deco designs on items such as this German compact.
1930s 3.5in (9cm) diam C

Japanese lacquer and eggshell techniques were used to great effect. Here they create a nautilus shell design on a cigarette case.
c1925 4in (10cm) wide I

Christofle made most of the silver plated wares for the oceanliner *Le Normandie*, including this compote, with Art Deco sphere base, designed by Luc Lanel.
c1934 13in (33cm) diam M

Fashionable metalware was a common feature of Art Deco buildings. New York designer Walter Kantack designed these iron window grates for the AT&T Building in the city.
1920s 68in (173cm) high M

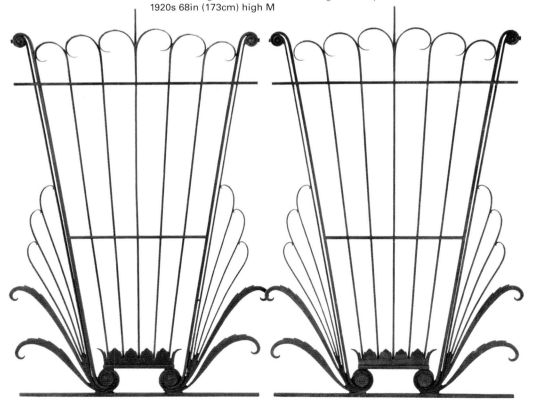

Polar bears were a common decorative form, thanks in part to François Pompon's sculpture of one at the 1925 Exhibition. This stylized cocktail shaker is typical.
10in (25.5cm) high M

NORMAN BEL GEDDES MEDALLION

Norman Bel Geddes designed this medallion for the General Motors 25th anniversary in 1933. It was minted by the Medallic Art Co. Around 2000 were made and presented at the 1933 Century of Progress World's Fair. Bel Geddes trained as a theater designer but opened an industrial design studio in 1927 where he designed a wide range of items, from saucepans, to furniture, to electrical appliances.

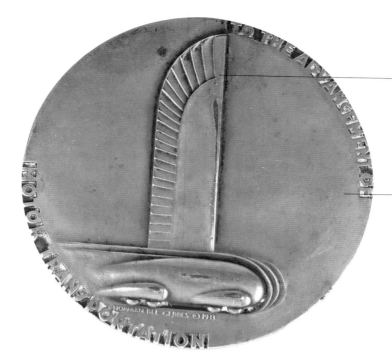

The teardrop-shaped vehicle features a dramatic, elongated wing rising from its roof. It gives a feeling of speed and movement which is typical of streamlined design.

The other side of the medallion shows a piston design.

The wording forms part of the design and is placed around the edge rather than across the center of the medal

A Norman Bel Geddes/ Medallic Art Company silver-plated bronze medallion.
1933 3in (7.5cm) diam L

Stylized and streamlined, leaping gazelles were a popular motif. They have been picked out in copper on a silver compact by the American Evans company.
1930s 3in (7.5cm) diam F

These American cast aluminum and bronze andirons feature a stylized water fountain motif.
1930 20in (51cm) high Q

This Jean Puiforcat silver-plated coffee and tea set has fashionable streamlined half-reeded bodies with contrasting hardwood covers.
1930s pot: 5.5in (14cm) high P

Sculptural Masterpieces

The bronze and ivory figures created in the 1920s and 1930s capture much that is exciting and modern about the Art Deco era. They reflect the very latest fashions and trends – often provocatively dressed women dancing or posing in exotic costumes. The epitome of glamor, they are synonymous with Jazz Age chic. Made from luxurious materials they represent the highest levels of craftsmanship.

For centuries artists had created sculptures using a combination of bronze (for the clothing) and ivory (for the exposed flesh). But this form of sculpture – which became known as chryselephantine in the 19th century, a word derived from the Greek for gold and ivory – reached a pinnacle in the 1920s and 1930s when an abundance of ivory from the Belgian Congo was available at a very low cost.

The greatest masterpieces of Art Deco sculpture were created by two men: Demêtre Chiparus and Ferdinand Preiss. They created sensous, animated figures of dancing women and Amazonian goddesses, using a combination of meticulous ivory carving and superbly detailed bronze casting. Their skill can be seen in the lifelike expressions on the faces, the elegant poses, and the movement in the folds of the fabric. Cold-painted decoration – a lacquering technique – was used to add vitality to the figures and vibrancy to the costumes, while rich embellishment with gilt, silver and gems enhanced the finish.

Each figure was designed individually and produced in limited editions.

Although he did a lot of the work himself Priess also had a team of sculptors to assist him, allowing him to produce many works. Many models were

Lithe dancers were a popular subject for sculptors. Ferdinand Preiss dressed this bronze and ivory figure in a figure-hugging costume with a fashionable pattern.
c1930 5.5in (14cm) high M

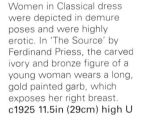

Women in Classical dress were depicted in demure poses and were highly erotic. In 'The Source' by Ferdinand Priess, the carved ivory and bronze figure of a young woman wears a long, gold painted garb, which exposes her right breast.
c1925 11.5in (29cm) high U

available in two or three sizes and with different finishes.

DEMETRE CHIPARUS

Demêtre Chiparus was undoubtedly one of the most highly skilled chryselephantine sculptors. Born in Romania, like many artists of his generation he lived and worked in Paris. Early in his career he produced religious and historic statuary. However, his real success came in the 1920s when he began modeling fashionably dressed women and stage performers in spectacular outfits.

Chiparus is famed for the way he encrusted the bronze costumes on his figures with lavish jewel-like decoration. Top cabaret acts of the day, such as the Tiller Girls and the Dolly Sisters, provided the inspiration for the high-kicking chorus lines and duos that were his forte.

FERDINAND PREISS

Ferdinand Preiss came from Erbach in Germany, a region famous for its ivory workshops. After serving an apprenticeship as a carver, he set up the Preiss-Kassler workshop in Berlin, with Arthur Kassler, in the early 1900s. They specialized in realistic representations of young children and active, independent women – principally Greek goddesses, athletes, and dancers. Some figures are portraits of contemporary celebrities such as the pilot Amy Johnson. Inspiration also came from revellers dressed as harlequins for the fancy dress balls that were all the rage between the wars.

Preiss's training ensured that his sculptures are celebrated for their superior carving, which can be seen in the expressions on the faces and elegant poses. He is also renowned for the way the bronze garments on his figures seem to ripple and flutter with movement.

Not only did Preiss design and execute his own figures, but he also produced figures by other sculptors. Like Preiss they favored studies of adventurous women. Leading sculptors who worked with Preiss-Kassler included Paul Philippe, Rudolph Belling, and Richard W. Lange. However, the workshop collaborated most closely with Professor Otto Poertzel – so much so that his designs can be hard to distinguish from those of Preiss.

The lithe dancer is realistically depicted.

Beautifully carved ivory face, fingers and toes show that the workmanship is the highest quality.

The racy pose would have been mildly shocking, yet the opportunity to have such a figure on display at home was exciting and exotic.

DEMETRE CHIPARUS FIGURE
Demêtre Chiparus' sculptures often depicted dancers from the Paris stage. In art, as in life, they wore tightly fitting costumes or otherwise revealing and strike elegant yet dramatic poses. The clothes were often highlighted with cold painting and gilt to add to the exotic aura.

The veined black marble base is engraved with the signature "D.H. Chiparus".

Demetre Chiparus bronze and ivory figure of 'Dancer with Ring'. c1925 19in (48.5cm) high T

ART DECO

Figurative Sculpture

Although Demêtre Chiparus and Ferdinand Preiss were the best-known creators of Art Deco figures, a number of other sculptors created their own versions of free-spirited, glamorous characters enjoying the liberated lifestyle of the age. Some were inclined to produce extraordinarily lifelike statuary, while others exhibited more stylized images. However, they had one aspect in common: their figures typically illustrated a joyful lust for life.

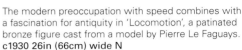

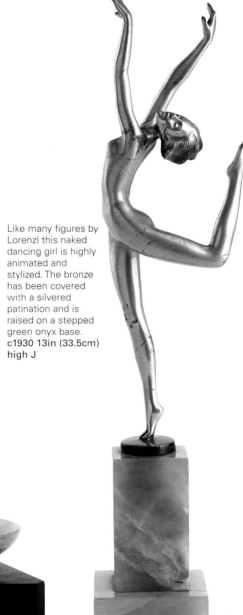

The modern preoccupation with speed combines with a fascination for antiquity in 'Locomotion', a patinated bronze figure cast from a model by Pierre Le Faguays. **c1930 26in (66cm) wide N**

One predominant theme in the work of the Art Deco sculptors was an evident admiration for the feminine form. A great many of the works showed representations of women, with the motivation for some – especially those of Bruno Zach – being overtly sexual. However, the 1920s and 1930s were a period of significant social change. Moral values were relaxing, and recent moves toward emancipation led women to take a more prominent role in society. Such provocative behavior as uninhibited dancing in public or wearing makeup was a key signal of women's changing lifestyles. Contemporary sculptors were inspired to capture this mood in their works.

DANCERS AND MAIDENS

With this level of feminine influence, it was fitting that one of the chryselephantine (bronze with ivory) figurative sculptors would be a woman. Claire-Jeanne-Roberte Colinet was a Belgian-born sculptor who found success in Paris. Like Chiparus, she was drawn to nightlife subjects, but she chose to depict Oriental dancers, often shown in fanciful versions of Indian, Turkish, or Russian dress, and demonstrating wild and exotic rhythms.

The French sculptor Pierre Le Faguays chose themes from ancient Greece and Rome, sculpting female figures, mainly in bronze, often taken from classical mythology and allegory. However, he took

Like many figures by Lorenzl this naked dancing girl is highly animated and stylized. The bronze has been covered with a silvered patination and is raised on a stepped green onyx base. **c1930 13in (33.5cm) high J**

A dancer by Stefan Dakon, dressed in a futuristic costume with geometric skirt and in an elegant, elongated pose. **c1930 7.5in (19cm) high K**

A dancer is caught mid-step to create a sense of speed and movement. The black patinated bronze figure, by Lorenzl, stands on tip toe, her other leg held gracefully aloft with arm outstretched behind. **c1930 19.5in (49.5cm) high K**

a more up-to-date approach in his sculptural design. It contained a strong geometric element and, despite the elongated and forceful poses, there is a stillness to his figures. He sometimes signed his work with pseudonyms, which included Fayral.

Many of the prolific Austrian sculptors of the day showed nude figures, often with simplified features and long, lithe bodies. One was Josef Lorenzl, who was evidently fascinated by Classical nymphs and dancing sprites. Unlike those of Le Faguays, however, Lorenzl's stylized maidens were highly animated. He preferred working in bronze, usually with a gilded or silvered finish, but he also produced figures wearing garments dotted with delicate cold-painted flowers.

The dancing maidens by sculptor Stefan Dakon were sometimes remarkably similar to Lorenzl's, perhaps because the two men had worked together at the Goldscheider (*see p112*) workshop in Vienna. Dakon is as well known as Lorenzl, but more for his ceramic designs.

The Austrian firm Hagenauer produced a wide range of affordably priced sculptures in materials like chrome, silver-plate, brass, and wood. The company's output included quite progressive designs, unusual for a large-scale operation, and they were known for highly abstracted sculptures of animals and people at work and play. Another speciality was African-style figures such as tribeswomen – perhaps in homage to the original African sculptures and masks that had such an impact on Western art in the first half of the 20th century.

ACCLAIMED BUT ACCESSIBLE

Not surprisingly, such figures were widely admired, and a market grew for work by sculptors who were prepared to reproduce their designs in sensibly priced editions for a broader group of consumers. Some of the leading Art Deco sculptors, including Pierre Le Faguays and Alexander Kéléty, designed specific ranges of more affordable figures for the style-conscious end of the mid-price market. Scaled-down and less detailed, these were usually made entirely from bronze, ivory, or spelter (an inexpensive alloy of zinc, lead, and tin) patinated to look like bronze.

PAUL PHILIPPE RUSSIAN DANCER
Paul Philippe is renowned for his chryselephantine figures, especially for his series of dancers from countries like Russia and Spain. His work was characterized by stylized dancing figures. He designed figures for several distinguished workshops, including Les Neveux de J. Lehmann in Paris and Preiss-Kassler (PK) in Berlin.

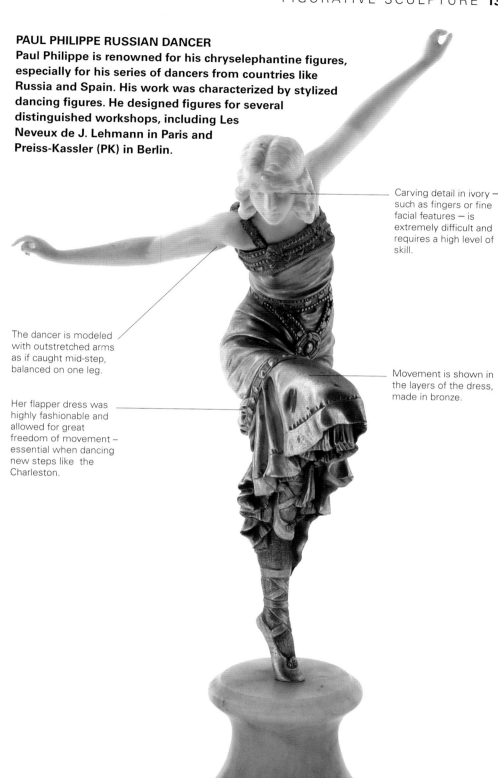

Carving detail in ivory – such as fingers or fine facial features – is extremely difficult and requires a high level of skill.

The dancer is modeled with outstretched arms as if caught mid-step, balanced on one leg.

Movement is shown in the layers of the dress, made in bronze.

Her flapper dress was highly fashionable and allowed for great freedom of movement – essential when dancing new steps like the Charleston.

A Paul Philippe bronze and ivory figure 'The Russian Dancer'. c1930 16in (40.5cm) high N

ART DECO

SCULPTURE GALLERY

As statuary gained more general appeal, firms developed less expensive models to capitalize on this interest, with stylish designs compensating for reduced standards of quality. Most manufacturers played it safe, endlessly repeating the successful formula of realistically styled dancing maidens, beauties, and babies. These pieces tended to be anonymous and unsigned, but a few daring retailers like New Yorker Rena Rosenthal commissioned, abstract figures very much at the cutting edge of design from workshops such as Hagenauer.

Nude maidens fascinated sculptors and public alike. This carved ivory figure runs her hand through her hair, and wears a fashionable gold metal arm band.
c1925 5in (13cm) high K

Elegant dancers were depicted by many artists. This patinated figure is in the manner of Ferdinand Preiss, and stands on a geometric marble base.
c1930 19.25in (49cm) high M

Newly discovered tribal art had a great influence on Art Deco. A Hagenauer stylized patinated bronze figure of a dancer.
c1935 10.5in (27cm) high D

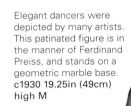

Talented artists showed the dancer's poise. Gilt metal figure, modeled balancing on one foot, on alabaster base.
c1930 9.75in (25cm) high B

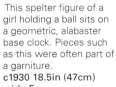

This spelter figure of a girl holding a ball sits on a geometric, alabaster base clock. Pieces such as this were often part of a garniture.
c1930 18.5in (47cm) wide F

ANIMAL SCULPTURE

Animals inspired many Art Deco designers, especially sculptors, who were fascinated by their elegance, power, and nobility. However, the resulting sculptures were stylized rather than realistic – animal shapes simplified and reduced to the geometric forms that are a hallmark of the Art Deco era. Big cats and deer were particularly popular subjects, depicted in all sorts of poses, but there are also many studies of horses, doves, and roosters. Reflecting contemporary love for the exotic, sculptors were also captivated by creatures such as cobras, monkeys, and borzoi hounds. François Pompon's celebrated marble polar bears launched a multitude of bear designs by sculptors like Gregoire. Other influential figures in animal sculpture included Edouard-Marcel Sandoz and Maurice Proust.

Leaping deer feature in many Art Deco designs. Their elongated forms provided scope for stylized depictions.

The speed and grace with which they moved reflected the fashions of the time.

The landscape show on the base shows Cubist inspiration.

A Gerhard Schliepstein, 'Leaping Deer' bronze , with dark-brown patina, probably executed by H. Noack, Berlin.
1924 10in (25cm) high M

Animals were shown in stylized form. The elongated body of this patinated bronze leaping gazelle was retailed by Rena Rosenthal.
c1930 9in (23cm) wide C

Stylized patinated bronze galloping horse retailed by Rena Rosenthal, on shaped bronze base.
c1930 7in (18cm) wide B

Powerful animals were shown in muscular poses. A silvered bronze centerpiece of two bears, cast from a model by Gregoire, on striated marble base.
c1930 20.75in (53cm) wide I

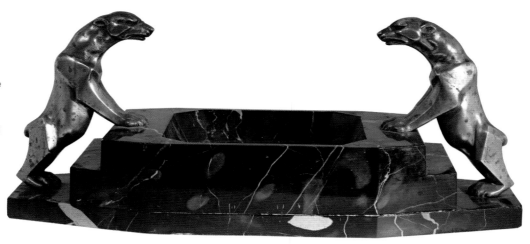

Lighting

Throughout the inter-war years lighting played an increasingly important role in exterior and interior design. It was realized that lighting could be used to create mood and atmosphere, and was therefore an important consideration in any decorative scheme. The style of wall sconces, chandeliers and even lamps was integrated into interiors to complement their design. Styles ranged from monumental, geometric shapes, to decorative metalwork.

NEW DIRECTIONS IN IRON

As with so many areas of Art Deco design, France led the way in lighting design. Metal sculptural lamps featuring subjects such as dancing maidens continued to be popular between the wars. But it was wrought iron workers such as Edgar Brandt and Raymond Subes, who developed innovative metal light fittings direction. These masters of their craft successfully scaled down their intricate architectural metalwork to create new types of lighting. The resulting table lamps, floor lamps, wall sconces, and chandeliers were based on highly stylized natural imagery with richly textured, hammered surfaces. They produced striking monumental light forms using a design vocabulary that harked back to Classical antiquity such as urns and coiling cobras. The results complemented the popularity for metalwork as part of interior design

ADVENTUROUS USE OF GLASS

Many celebrated French glassmakers, such as Paul Daum and Gabriel Argy-Rousseau, had had a reputation for creating exciting

glass lamps and shades since 1900. In the 1920s they continued to produce adventurous designs, introducing angular forms and pared-back organic shapes, along with vivid colors to replace the earthier tones that had been popular before. Effects such as marbling and texture were used to embellish glass surfaces. What little decoration there was tended to be highly stylized – usually based on floral or geometric motifs. As shape and material composition gradually usurped decoration in the late 1920s, brilliant colors were replaced by sophisticated neutral tones. Many of these glassmakers encased light

A French electrified torchiere, the stand made of sleek chromed metal with wood, supporting a clear and milky glass funnel-shaped shade.
c1930 28.75in (72cm) high E

A nickeled-bronze and peach-colored glass table lamp by La Maison Desny with a strong, geometric shape.
c1930 5.5in (14cm) high N

DONALD DESKEY (1894–1989)

The pioneering American industrial designer Donald Deskey worked in advertising before switching to design in the late 1920s. He made his reputation in 1932 by designing the interior of Radio City Music Hall, one of New York City's most famous Art Deco landmarks. Deskey used industrial materials like aluminum and Bakelite for his sleek designs. A commission for the impresario Roxy Rothafel's offices at the Music Hall – a chrome, black Bakelite, and cherry-wood desk and matching lighting suite – is especially noted for its influence on American modernism. He excelled at abstract angular lighting comparable to designs from Paris's La Maison Desny.

The stepped design and chrome-plated surface make this metal desk lamp by Donald Deskey a classic Art Deco lamp.
1927 13.25in (33.5cm) high EE

fittings inside the body of their table lights, which led to the development of illuminated glass sculptures.

Art Deco's most famous manufacturer of glass lights, René Lalique made a speciality of spectacular illuminated glass sculptures for fountains and interiors. These unique design schemes were produced for ocean liners restaurants, cinemas, and other businesses worldwide.

London's Savoy Hotel's Art Deco lighting designs, by the French designer Jean Perzel, are comparable in quality to Jacques-Emile Ruhlmann's furniture and Jean Puiforcat's silver. Perzel's shapes were based on an interplay of geometric forms. He was fascinated by the quality of electric light and how it could be used to achieve the best effect. To this end his designs provide both direct and indirect lighting. He also explored how glass could be used to diffuse the light and favored opaque glass sometimes flatteringly tinted beige or rose.

Other notable French designers, including Damon, Pierre Chareau, and La Maison Desny, produced daring lighting based on juxtaposed geometric forms.

INNOVATIVE MATERIALS
After the mid-1920s, torchères, or floor lamps that directed their light upward (indirectly), became fashionable and were often used in pairs. The bases might be wrough iron or sleek chrome cylinders.

When it came to exciting Art Deco lighting America was introducing new lighting designs by the 1930s. Industrial designers such as Walter Dorwin Teague, Walter von Nessen, and Gilbert Rohde used the latest materials like rubber, chrome, and plastic. Their sleek lighting designs, originally intended for use in the office or workshop, were soon adopted for mass production. Loosely inspired by speeding vehicles, their streamlined lights paid homage to the machine age and suggested optimism for the future.

Another innovation was the Anglepoise desk lamp, designed by George Carwardine in 1932. Also, fashionable sculptures by Demêtre Chiparus, Ferdinand Preiss, and others were fitted with lights to make eye-catching figurative lamps.

DAUM FRERES TABLE LAMP
The French Glassworks run by the Daum family were renowned for the quality of their glass. They had been making glass lamps since c1900 but in the Art Deco period began combining the glass with metal frames and making shades for wrought iron lamp bases. Designers such as Louis Majorelle and Edgar Brandt were commissioned to design the wrought iron elements, while Daum's talented glass blowers created shades in mottled glass, often with powder and enamel inclusions.

The lamp fittings have been designed as an integral part of the overall design.

The design of stylized leaves and berries is quintessentially Art Deco.

The shades are made from blown, mottled glass which was frequently used by Daum. Sometimes the shades were also decorated with etching.

A Daum Nancy glass and Amiot patinated metal three-light table lamp.
c1930 23.75in (60cm) high L

ART DECO

LIGHTING GALLERY

Craftsmanship and innovative design are the hallmarks of Art Deco lighting. Traditional skills such as glassblowing and wrought iron work were used to create elegant table and floor lamps. The latest materials – including Bakelite and chrome – were fashioned into Modernist shapes.

Stylized leaves and vines are wrapped around the shaft of this wrought-iron torchere in the style of Edgar Brandt.
c1930 75in (190.5cm) high L

Bakelite was used for many Art Deco lamps such as this French 'Jumo' streamlined desk lamp for Brevette.
c1940s 18in (45cm) high G

This Daum lamp is a stylized mushroom shape. Milky, mottled glass has been used for the base and shade.
c1925 18in high (46cm) U

Stylized flowers and leaves decorate the shade of this French wrought-iron and bronze table lamp.
c1925 17in (43cm) high N

Geometric Modernist styling with triple disk detailing embellish a French nickel plated candelabra.
1930s 13in (33cm) high K

The only embellishment on the shade are three engraved rings near the rim.

The upward curve of the top of the base complements the downward sweep of the shade.

BLACK ENAMELED TABLE LAMP
The trend for streamlined, Machine Age accessories brought with it a fashion for polished chrome lamps with simple domed shades and geometric bases. The chrome was often decorated with enameling or combined with Bakelite which created a strong contrast between the matt black of the plastic and the shiny metal. The futuristic result was equally suitable for domestic or business use.

A chrome and black enameled metal table lamp, with original shade and chroming.
1930s 18in (46cm) high F

The stepped base features a stepped disc design. Each step echoes the curve of the shade. Black enamel provides a contrast to the bright chrome.

The simple, flaring alabaster shade and scroll feet of this bronze torchère are typical Art Deco details.
c1930 71in (177.5cm) high L

Modernist discs decorate a pair of chrome and Bakelite candelabra-style boudoir lamps.
c1935 16.5in (42cm) high G

A stylized dove, berries and foliage for the base of a candlestick-style lamp designed by Edgar Brandt.
c1925 16.25in (41cm) high N

Statuettes transformed into table lamps. This exotic figure by Fayral holds a crackled glass globe shade.
c1930 20.5in (52cm) high E

Travel and Communication

The period between the wars was an era of bold technological achievement when people embraced science and engineering with enthusiastic optimism. Transport became faster, more comfortable and convenient. Air travel to exotic destinations was possible. Advertising posters celebrated the speed, luxury and magnificence of the latest cars, trains and ocean liners.

TRAVEL AND TRANSPORT

In the years following World War I, better transportation meant greater numbers of people traveled for pleasure. Journeys by rail, sea, road and air offered an enticing blend of technical innovation, speed and excitement. As a result travel became linked with modernity in the public's minds.

There was a growing market for all forms of transport – from day trips to the seaside to luxury cruises. Companies needed to advertise and the designers they used were at the forefront of fashion. Typography became a key part of design with new typefaces helping to set the style. The dynamic, streamlined appearance of many forms of transport such as Raymond Lowey's locomotives for the Pennsylvania Railroad Company re-enforced this spirit of progress. Indeed speedy, stylish travel became a matter of national prestige with countries competing to see whose liner could cross the Atlantic the fastest or who offered the best rail service. The latest cars from companies such as Fiat and Buick emphasized speed in their advertising or employed glamorous models to pose with them in magazines such as Vogue.

In this poster for Peugeot, André Girard depicts the car in an exaggerated perspective, zooming around the corner of a tri-color road and heading straight for the viewer. The company logo on the grille is a prominent part of the image.
c1929 63.75in (162cm) high M

The geometric design of this tray shows the wheels and bumper of a speeding car. The glass is in a chrome frame.
c1930 18in (45.5cm) wide D

The influence of Adolph Mouron Cassandre can be seen in the curve of the prow of this ship. Willem Ten Broek's poster glorifies the Holland-America Line and the concept of sea travel as a whole.
1936 38.5in (98cm) high N

IMAGE OF FASHIONABLE TRAVEL

Transport operators promoted travel's modern allure by employing pre-eminent Art Deco artists. René Lalique produced glass paneling for several rail services including the celebrated *Le train bleu* to the Riviera. The extravagant interiors of ocean liners set new standards in modern luxury. In fact the *Normandie* with its Jean Dupas murals, silver from Christofle and furniture by Jacques-Emile Rhulmann became the floating embodiment of the Art Deco style. Travel posters by designers like Cassandre and Willem Ten Broek conjured up a sensational vision of swift journeys to enchanting resorts.

Between the wars, transport and speed became incredibly popular themes throughout design, as a sign of modernity. The automobile, airplane, even the Zeppelin joined the canon of Art Deco motifs. This travel imagery featured on everything from jewelry to cocktail shakers. Meanwhile the move toward streamlining made utilitarian goods look more desirable.

ADOLPH MOURON CASSANDRE *NORD EXPRESS* POSTER

Adolphe Mouron Cassandre's travel posters have a bold, architectural style that influenced designers across the world. Here the stylized *Nord Express* locomotive is a graphic glorification of the Machine Age depicted using geometric shapes. Seen from track level, the train appears all the more massive and powerful, its speed emphasized by the way that it disappears into the horizon. The horizon itself is brought even closer by the telegraph wires. The typography is limited to the edge of the poster so it does not interfere with the image.

Nord Express poster designed by Adolphe Mouron Cassandre.
1927 41.25in (105cm) high M

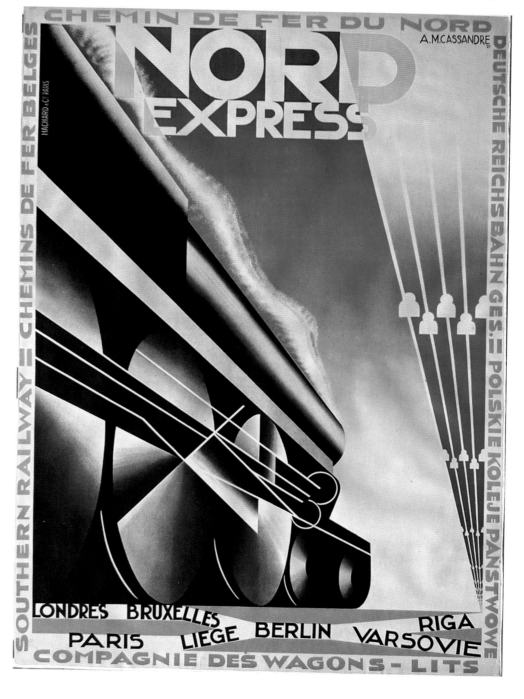

ART DECO

French Posters

The poster was one of the most effective forms of marketing in the 1920s and 1930s. Tapping into people's aspirations and desires, posters offered an open door into a world of fabulously dressed beauties, vacation resorts with sunny beaches, and jazz in chic nightspots. They presented images of travel undertaken by sleek, speeding motorcars, trains, and ocean liners.

Simple, geometric shapes and strong colors were used by many poster designers. The unknown hand behind this French poster for Pianos Daudé depicts a piano player seen from above. Art Deco artists recognized the power of type. Here the word "Pianos" is set at an angle and fitted effectively into the image.
c1930 63.5in (159cm) high K

France is considered the birthplace of the Art Deco style, and Paris was widely recognized as the premier cultural center of the early 20th century – a hotbed of modern art and design. Unsurprisingly, many of the greatest graphic designers of the Art Deco era lived and worked in France.

ICONIC FIGURE

The most celebrated and influential figure in Art Deco poster design was Adolphe Mouron Cassandre. Born in the Ukraine to French parents, Cassandre studied at the prestigious Parisian art school Académie Julian before launching his design career. Having founded his own advertising agency, Alliance Graphique, he produced posters for a wide range of products, from Philips radios to Ford cars.

In order to stress the advertiser's message he stripped his poster designs of all superfluous detail, using bold blocks of color and dynamic streamlined images to entice the viewer. The Cassandre style became a prototype for poster design worldwide. Classic Cassandre posters such as those for the train *Nord Express* (*see*

BORDEAUX
SON PORT · SES MONUMENTS · SES VINS

Strong shapes, elongated bodies and the influence of Surrealism can be seen in Jean Dupas' work. Here he advertises the ports, monuments and wine of his native Bordeaux.
1937 39in (97.5cm) high M

Cassandre advertises the Parisian furniture store Aubucheron using a striking and inventive design of a lumberjack swinging his axe against a background of radiating lines in abstract blue and black.
1926 161in (409cm) wide W

pp142–143) and the ocean liner *Normandie* are now considered Art Deco masterpieces. His work moved the novelist and poet Blaise Cendrars to write, "Here advertising approaches poetry."

DISTINCTIVE DESIGNS

One of the best known and most popular of all Art Deco artists, Jean Dupas developed a distinctive style for large-scale paintings and murals that translated well into poster design. His elongated sculptural figures and singular pastel palette are easy to recognize. Dupas had an international reputation with clients like the London Underground and the New York department store Saks Fifth Avenue who commissioned limited editions. As a native of Bordeaux he was the perfect choice when the French city needed a poster to celebrate hosting the 1937 World Fair.

Another notable French Art Deco poster designer, Paul Colin specialized in posters for the stage, a world he knew from his work as a costume and set designer. Colin's energetic angular style was ideal for capturing the dynamics of a performance. He is best remembered for his lively posters promoting the legendary entertainer Josephine Baker. Their association began in 1925 with the publication of his poster for *La Revue Nègre* at the Théâter des Champs Elysées, a music-hall where Baker had her Paris debut.

Colin ran his own school for graphic designers, and the poster designer Jean Chassaing was one of his students. Colin's influence can be seen in Chassaing's choice of subject matter and design, especially of faces. Chassaing also worked in Cassandre's studio, where he picked up airbrushing techniques.

The Italian-born artist Leonetto Cappiello, who settled in Paris in 1898, enjoyed a long and prolific career as a poster designer. Believed to have designed over 3,000 posters, he was very versatile and successfully made the transition from Art Nouveau to Art Deco. Broad strokes, strong color, and loose-edged elongated forms are typical of his work, together with powerful imagery such as lions or stallions. He often used a black background to make the product stand out. Cappiello's clients included Peugeot cars and Toblerone chocolate.

JEAN CHASSAING POSTER OF JOSEPHINE BAKER

Jean Chassaing's poster of the actress Josephine Baker was probably the most important commission of his career and is considered to be the best poster he designed. Chassaing may have met Baker while he was studying with Paul Colin but he did not design this poster until four years later. It was not made for a particular show or widely circulated at the time and so is very rare.

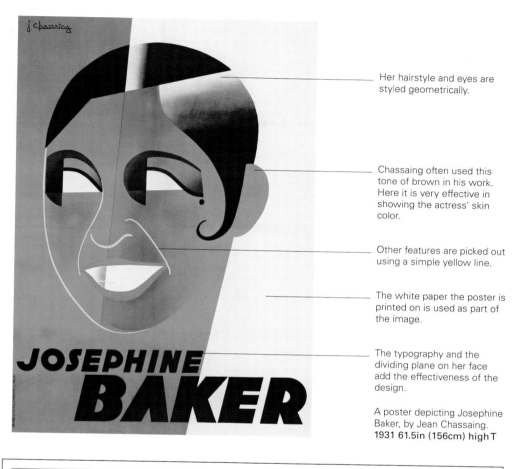

Her hairstyle and eyes are styled geometrically.

Chassaing often used this tone of brown in his work. Here it is very effective in showing the actress' skin color.

Other features are picked out using a simple yellow line.

The white paper the poster is printed on is used as part of the image.

The typography and the dividing plane on her face add the effectiveness of the design.

A poster depicting Josephine Baker, by Jean Chassaing. **1931 61.5in (156cm) high T**

MAGAZINES

Some of the most memorable images of the Art Deco era appeared on the covers and inside pages of magazines. Influential publications such as *Vogue, Harper's Bazaar* and *Vanity Fair* showed illustrations by designers like Georges Lepape and Erté. Although the work of each of these artists had an individual look, a recognizable style emerged: they all used linear images against a flat background to spectacular effect. The 1920s also saw developments in typography, when there was a rejection of "fussy" Victorian print styles in favor of an emphasis on the purity of letter forms, which created a distinctly modern look.

Issue of Vogue from 1932. **B**

International Poster Style

Where France led others followed. Geometric, stylized boldly colored posters were designed by artists around the world to advertise products from drinks to petrol, cafés to holiday resorts. Advances in printing technology made posters an effective way to gain publicity and today they offer a glimpse of the aspirations and desires of the 1920s and 1930s. Some of the most avantgarde posters were created for propaganda purposes in Eastern Europe, Russia and Italy.

BRITISH POSTERS

Shell Oil, Austin Reed clothing, and transportation businesses such as London and North Eastern Railway commissioned some of the most exciting and adventurous British posters of the 1920s and 1930s.

However, from around the beginning of World War I the greatest patron of modern design was the London Underground. Frank Pick, who was its publicity manager (and from 1928 its managing director), passionately believed that Art Deco's forward-looking images would be ideal to advertise the benefits of this modern mode of travel. To this end he employed many important British, European, and American artists, including Paul Nash, Jean Dupas, and Man Ray, to design posters for the Underground.

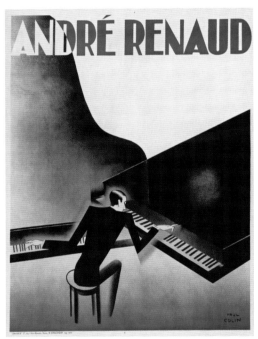

A graceful figure is depicted in the Spanish artist Tito Livio de Madrazo's poster for Jacqueline Elsane. The line of the letter "J" becomes the line of the woman's body, linking the text with the image.
c1930 47in (119.5cm) high K

Paul Colin used a Cubist approach to this poster for André Renaud, a virtuoso who could play two pianos at the same time.
1929 62in (155cm) high T

A bold composition style is used to give the impression of power in Edward McKnight Kauffer's poster.
1930 45in (114cm) wide J

NEW YORK WORLD'S FAIR POSTER
The 1939 New York World's Fair was planned to help to lift the city and country out of the Depression. It was the largest fair ever staged and received over 45 million visitors. Its theme was "The world of Tomorrow" and at its center were the geometric Trylon and Perisphere. Attractions included a futuristic city designed by General Motors, a life-size copy of the interior of Mayakovskaya station of the Moscow Metro and the first chance for many to see a television. The fair closed in 1940.

In so doing, he helped expose a generation of the British public to modern art.

Edward McKnight Kauffer, "the Picasso of advertising design", was an American artist based in London. Kauffer was one of the most popular artists designing for Pick and is considered one of the foremost between-the-wars graphic designers. Apart from his numerous Underground posters, Kauffer also received commissions from businesses such as Shell, British Petroleum, and the *Daily Herald* newspaper. His poster designs are characterized by the use of bold symbolic imagery and a simple composition, reflecting the influence of Cubism, Vorticism, and Futurism. Other leading names in British poster design include Austin Cooper, Fred Taylor, and Tom Purvis.

SOVIET PROPAGANDA POSTERS

In 1919, after the Russian revolution, the Soviet government saw experimental design as a tool to help build a new society. Under the influence of Russia's leading avant-garde artists such as Kasimir Malevich and Wassily Kandinsky, design was liberated from its traditional representational function. They used abstract geometry in posters that celebrated a new socialist nation.

In the late 1920s, with Stalin in power, Soviet design performed a reactionary about-face. Abstract imagery was now seen as decadent and anti-proletariat. A folksy realism was harnessed to put a populist spin on socialist propaganda. Posters featuring images of machines and happy farm workers were intended to promote the positive benefits of Stalin's programs – in reality, forced industrialization and farm

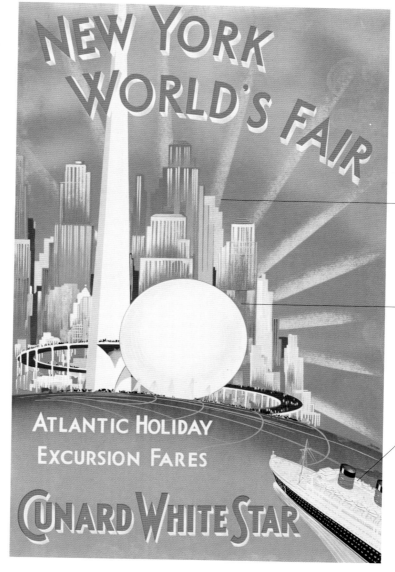

The sun's rays behind the skyscrapers promise a better tomorrow following the Depression.

New York's unmistakable, geometric skyline recedes into the background to be replaced by the fair's symbols: the Trylon and Perisphere. The result is futuristic view of the city with cars driving on a curved raised roadway.

A White Star liner sails toward a stylized green, orange and blue lower Manhattan.

Poster designed by Janno for New York World's Fair and Cunard White Star.
1939 39in (97.5cm) high
P

collectivization. Other totalitarian regimes such as Hitler's Germany and Mussolini's Italy would also use folksy realism as propaganda.

AMERICAN POSTERS

Colorful stylized imagery was an element of Art Deco design picked up by American artists. In 1923 Charles Mather began a series of work incentive posters which were intended to motivate workers using a bold image and short slogan.

By the early 1930s American designers were forging their own unique graphic style. Just as in Britain and other parts of Europe, travel operators such as New York's Central System liked to advertise their services with

posters. Some, like Leslie Ragan's poster of the Rockefeller Center, were commissioned by New York Central Lines in order to entice tourists to visit New York to see the city's awesome skyscrapers. Others promoted the modern comfort and convenience of traveling by train, ocean liner, or even airline – a service already on its way to becoming widespread in America.

In resources and technology America was way ahead of other industrial nations. Though the Depression hit the country hard, there was still great trust in American know-how and faith in progress. This optimistic attitude is patently clear in the futuristic posters used to advertise the 1939 World's Fair.

Textiles

Art Deco textiles are all about contrast. In the 1920s, fabric hues were dazzlingly bright, but by the 1930s they had become more subdued and neutral. They can be divided into two categories: stylized pictorials and dramatic geometrics. Because the public were happy to accept revolutionary design in fabrics while recoiling from radical modern painting, textiles became a medium for some of the most advanced artistic ideas of the day.

The work of Sonia Delaunay, whose colorful geometric designs were inspired by patchwork, can be seen in the embroidery on this handbag.
c1925 15.75in (40cm) high D

ARTISTIC IMPACT

From about 1914, avant-garde artist Sonia Delaunay began designing textiles in the manner of her Cubist paintings. She created cutting-edge fabrics, patchwork, and rug designs, juxtaposing bright colors with swirling prismatic imagery. In many ways her lively patterns were precursors to the psychedelic designs of the 1960s. Russian-born Delaunay worked in Paris and was widely imitated. After World War I her explosive motifs and vivid colors captivated a public in need of celebration.

The foundations for acceptance of the modern look had been laid before World War I. French avant-garde artist Raoul Dufy began producing experimental textile designs for the famous fashion designer Paul Poiret around 1910. Dufy re-interpreted France's traditional printed cottons, he updated historical toiles using contemporary scenes, and he revamped rosy chintzes and trellis calicoes with stylized floral sprays and geometric motifs. His bold, angular figures and imagery featured striking color contrasts. In 1912 he became design director of the prominent textile manufacturer Bianchi-Férier. Textile manufacturers like Bianchi-Férier produced pattern books containing fabric samples to show their customers. Valuable sources of design ideas, they helped to spread the new emerging Art Deco style. Today, because textiles themselves are so fragile, the pattern books are often the only surviving evidence of many of the amazing fabrics produced between the wars.

During the 1920s and 1930s, designers from other fields besides painting got involved in textile production. Interior decorators took a lead in consolidating a complete "look" for a decorating scheme. For example, Jacques-Emile Ruhlmann created special fabrics to harmonize with his chairs and sofas and commissioned

Geometrics combine with stylized flowers to decorate a Austrian woven cotton throw.
1930s 99in (251.5cm) long K

THE BALLETS RUSSES

The Russian Ballets Russes had a dramatic impact on the development of Art Deco. From the company's first visit to Paris in 1909, their spectacular stage productions had an immediate effect on design, especially of textiles and clothing. The company, led by Serge Diaghilev, introduced an Oriental flavor to design. This was largely thanks to Léon Bakst, whose costumes created a taste for brilliant jewel colors as well as dramatic yet simple prints. They started a trend for opulent textiles, particularly thick velvets, gold lamé, and boldly embroidered silks. But more than any other artist, it was the fashion designer and decorator Paul Poiret who popularized their colorful, exotic look.

Bright colors and geometric braid made up Leon Bakst's costume design for Lezghin in the ballet *Thamar*.
c1912 O

unique textiles from other designers to unify his lavish room schemes. The decorator Edouard Benedictus developed a reputation for using jazzy floral tapestries and rugs. As a result, manufacturers like Meunier & Co. hired him to create exclusive designs for them.

DESIGN OUTSIDE FRANCE

It was clear to anyone who visited the 1925 Paris Exhibition that French textile design was leading on fashion. Fabric designers in other nations did not really develop their own modern look until the 1930s. In keeping with the Depression, many of these designers returned to more muted, dusty tones. One of the best-known American designers, Ruth Reeves used this earthy palette for her pictorial fabrics portraying contemporary pursuits such as listening to the radio.

For other designers, texture became even more important than color. The English designer Marion Dorn developed a reputation for sculpted geometric carpets with rich, creamy grounds. Of course, in the 1920s radical experiments took place in the textile studios at Germany's Bauhaus art school, but these daring abstract weaves didn't impact on commercial design until after World War II.

LOUNGE CHAIR WITH GEOMETRIC UPHOLSTERY
Pattern and color filled Art Deco interiors. Upholstery, carpets, curtains and wallpaper or wallpanels decorated with stylized or geometric designs brought a sense of drama to fashionable homes. The result tended to be coolly sophisticated and the perfect setting for the wealthy to live their luxurious lives. Upholstered furniture was often sleek, simple and stylized in form but covered with vibrant fabrics in abstract patterns.

The strong, streamlined shape of the chair is enhanced by the fabrics.

The abstract design of the fabric, with its strong color contrasts, is pure Art Deco.

The sweeping curves of the arms of the chair are covered in gold velvet. The solid blocks of bright color frame the abstract pattern on the seat and back.

An Art Deco lounge chair.
35in (89cm) wide I

New Materials

In the 1920s and 1930s new materials were seen as innovative wonders that brought more consumer goods within the reach of greater numbers of people. Industry invested significant sums to develop the technology and materials to make mass-production cheaper and even more efficient. Chrome-plating and plastics are among the most important of these developments. These new materials helped make the Art Deco style accessible to everyone.

An early 1940s streamlined Fada model 1000 "Bullet" radio in butterscotch Catalin.
10.25in (26cm) wide F

AN IDEAL FINISH

Between World Wars I and II, metals such as steel were increasingly in demand for use in architecture and homeware. They were seen as both practical and modern. However, they needed an attractive, durable finish that would prevent rust and corrosion. Chrome-plating was ideal for this purpose. The word "chrome" is short for chromium, a tough, sparkling metal. Chrome-plating would help transform contemporary design especially in the second half of the Art Deco era.

Foundries producing decorative ornaments were among the first to pick up on the lasting shine created by chrome-plating. They used it as a gleaming, weatherproof finish on sculptural mascots for automobile hoods.

Bauhaus designers deliberately sought materials that could be used to create cutting-edge designs for mass-production. By the late 1920s their avant-garde experiments led to the development of chrome-finished tubular steel furniture.

Chrome-plating would go on to play a key role in stimulating the American economy during the Depression of the 1930s. The mirror-like finish became associated with distinctive streamlined and machine-styled designs. It enabled metal manufacturers such as Chase to produce easy-care Art Deco pieces, as glamorous as silver at an irresistibly modest price. Hoover and other appliance manufacturers adopted chrome-plating, together with streamlining, to add appeal to products like vacuum flasks and fans.

For furniture, geometric chrome-plated uprights were often combined with black lacquered wood to dramatic effect. On

A Paul Frankl chrome and black lacquer Art Deco console table with black glass top. The simple lines create a powerful design statement.
1930s 27in (68.5cm) wide S

wares such as coffee pots and cocktail shakers, the latest plastics were used for handles and finials in the way that ebony or ivory might be used with silver.

THE ROUTE TO CLASSY PLASTICS

Bakelite, a synthetic plastic made of phenol formaldehyde, was discovered by the Belgian chemist Leo Hendrik Baekeland in 1907. In homage to its inventor, Bakelite is often now employed as a catch-all name for any synthetic plastic produced before World War II. Before his discovery plastics served

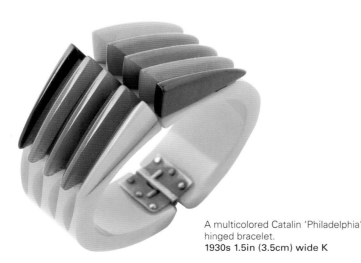

A multicolored Catalin 'Philadelphia' hinged bracelet.
1930s 1.5in (3.5cm) wide K

The cocktail bar located on the prow of the transatlantic ship *Queen Mary*. Chrome was often used to enhance the glamor of cocktail bars. Here the chrome-covered pillars, tables and bar stools bring added sophistication to a bar.

for the most part as a cheap substitute for more luxurious materials. For example, materials such as celluloid and Galalith were used to replicate ivory handles or tortoiseshell combs.

As phenolic-resin plastics such as Catalin improved throughout the 1920s, they became more widespread. They also acquired a new gloss and translucence along with the capacity to absorb eye-catching colors including jade, butterscotch, and cherry-red. By the late 1920s their design potential became more apparent – this revolutionary material could finally escape the role of a mere substitute.

Easily cast into streamlined and geometric shapes, the plastics of the 1930s were used for everything from jewelry to tablewares and appliances; designs for radios like Wells Coates's 'Round Ekco' and the 'Bullet' by Fada particularly stand out as examples of stylish design. Plastics were at once incredibly modern and stylish yet readily affordable. This winning combination helped restore faith in progress and modern life despite the Depression.

A René Lalique and Lucien Lelong 'Skyscraper' perfume bottle, with black enamel and chrome box. c1929 4.75in (12cm) high N

"What we call a good design is one which achieves integrity – that is, unity or wholeness – in balanced relation to its environment."
George Nelson

Mid-Century Modernism

Open-plan living with floor-to-ceiling windows that allowed plenty of natural light were the key to mid-century living. Furniture including 'Barcelona' chairs by Ludwig Mies Van der Rohe and George Nelson's 'Coconut' chair, lighting by Gino Sarfatti for Arredoluce and a table by Charles and Ray Eames created clean yet comfortable living space.

MID-CENTURY MODERN

Mid-Century Modernism

After World War Two designers were inspired by a renewed optimism and the new materials, new manufacturing techniques, new colors and new forms that were appearing. A more relaxed, fleshed-out form of Modernism began to appear in designs that were affordable and easily mass-produced.

A TIME OF RECOVERY

World War Two ended in 1945, but its influence on the world in general, and the design world in particular, continued into the 1950s. War-time frugality persisted, as almost all had come out of the war less affluent than they had been before the conflict began. There was also a strong general feeling that it was essential to return to normality and the Rational style pervaded.

The United States was the first country to recover financially, as it had escaped invasion, occupation or bombardment. Televisions and other new inventions helped foster a new sense of opportunity and American factories began achieving record-breaking levels of productivity. From this environment emerged designers like Charles and Ray Eames. In 1942, Charles had developed a way of molding plywood in more than one direction and now he and his wife adapted the technique to a host of innovative furniture.

The Marshall Plan was implemented during 1948-1951 and the United States used its considerable financial power to assist Europe's recovery. Nearly 13 billion dollars (almost $100 billion at present-day conversion rates) were pumped into Europe, and by 1951 the economy of nearly every country that had joined in the Organisation for European Economic Co-operation (OEEC) had grown well past pre-war levels and continued to grow. Italy, in particular, enjoyed continued industrial growth throughout the 1950s: a boom enjoyed by designers such as Gio Ponti, Carlo di Carli and the Castiglioni brothers, who went on to develop their own distinctive styles. Dino Martens, on the Venetian glass-making island of Murano, continued his exciting reinvention of traditional techniques into completely innovative designs.

Bright red celluloid spheres hang from metal rings using nylon wire to create an atomic-inspired lamp. Verner Panton 'Type H' dome lamp, designed for J. Lüber AG, Basel.
1969 17.25in (44cm) diam M

Meanwhile in Britain, the 'Festival of Britain' in 1951, encouraged a break from the past, launching the careers of a multitude of fresh new designers. For consumers who had spent years constrained by rationing and Government restrictions, the new alternatives to the plain utility furnishings were a revelation.

All over the world, economies expanded and as they grew a demand for goods increased. People wanted new designs and a greater choice. The designers, meanwhile, were excited by the host of new materials available to them and the possibilities even greater mass production offered. Councils and design bodies were established everywhere to promote national development. A consumer society bloomed.

A MATERIAL WORLD

Techniques and materials that had been pioneered for military purposes (mostly by aircraft designers) afforded the designers of the 1950s greater freedom. Lightweight and durable aluminum had been used in the interiors of military transport vehicles and was in abundant supply. The availability of increasingly narrow and lighter steel inspired the creation of lightweight wire-rod furniture, by designers including Harry Bertoia and Warren Platner. Innovative methods for bonding wood were also embraced by designers who were excited by the possibilities it brought.

A variety of new types of upholstery emerged in the 1950s. In Italy, tyre manufactures developed rubber padding. Meanwhile, the Scandinavians discovered a method of producing foam padding by steaming polystyrene beads. These could then be applied to a framework and molded into shape, making the design of pieces such as Arne Jacobsen's 'Swan' chair possible.

Traditional design techniques such as murrines were used in a new way and in bright colors on an 'Oriente' jug by Dino Martens for Aureliano Toso.
c1954 13in (32.5cm) high U

ARNE JACOBSEN 'SWAN' CHAIR

Arne Jacobsen designed the 'Swan' chair in 1957 as part of his commission to design the SAS Royal Hotel in Copenhagen. Jacobsen designed every element of the building – which was the city's first skyscraper – from the architecture to the door handles, curtains to cutlery, carpets to chairs. The 'Swan' chair is a perfect example of how the latest materials – including fiberglass and polystyrene – could be used to produce simple flowing lines.

The sculptural, organic form of this chair was meant to represent the simple outline of a swan and when arranged in the foyer of the hotel they looked like a small flock of birds on a lake.

Jacobsen used a new technique to create the frame of the seat and back: polystyrene beads were steam molded onto a fiberglass shape. The steam transformed the beads into a pliable foam.

The frames were upholstered in a range of colors and fabrics originally selected by Jacobsen.

Arne Jacobsen 'Swan' chair manufactured by Fritz Hansen.
30in (76cm) high K

However, the biggest change was the ready availability of petroleum-based plastics, which became relatively affordable during the oil glut of the 1950s and 1960s. Injection molding techniques allowed designers greater versatility, and they took advantage of plastic's ability to hold any form and to be made in a kaleidoscope of colors. The arrival of plastics also heralded a change in consumer attitude. Toward the end of the 1960s the age of timeless designs drawing to a close and the age of disposability was arriving. Items were made for the moment, to be thrown away when fashion changed.

A SOFTER SIDE TO MODERNISM

During the 1930s, Scandinavian designers had developed a distinctive, curvy style, now known as 'Soft Modernism'. It took the basic simplicity of modernism, but abandoned the coldness of mass produced materials such as plastic and steel. Alvar Aalto, a Finnish designer who was one of the first to experiment with this new style, famously remarked that modernist furniture was 'unsatisfactory from a human point of view'. He and other Scandinavian designers, including Bruno Mathsson, therefore set out to use natural materials, particularly those which could be found in abundance in Scandinavia (such as wood) and created correspondingly natural forms.

By the 1950s, Scandinavian glass designers, such as Per Lütken, had adopted a similar organic style in soft, relaxing colors. Meanwhile, many furniture designers had turned to the modern materials available. In particular, they embraced the new foam padding, with which the cold and unwelcoming surfaces of sheet metal could be softened. The work of Danish designer, Arne Jacobson, exemplifies the field, with stylish designs including the 'Swan' and 'Egg' chairs.

The comfort of Soft Modernism also appealed outside Scandinavia. In Italy Gio Ponti introducing sensuousness into his furniture. Local styles were incoporated in Japan and Germany to create a hybridized form of modernism, and French designers added decorative effects to the basic style.

AN IDEAL HOME

Case Study Houses first began to appear in California in 1945. These were a series of unique dwellings designed to examine new ways of living and were the creation of key designers and architects of the day, most significantly Charles Eames. The houses were ground breaking in their use of materials and featured open-plan spaces, transparent glass walls and lightweight construction. They were each decorated and furnished in a contemporary style, either with specially commissioned pieces or items selected from across the globe. The Museum of Modern Art in New York played its part, organizing an International Competition for Low-Cost Furniture in 1948 and its first 'Good Design Exhibition' in 1950.

The rapid growth of suburbia was a great opportunity for designers. The 'American Dream' had become synonymous with the constant acquisition of new goods to fill the home of your nuclear family. In the United States and Britain, the modern housewife, who was perhaps finding the move back into the home problematic, was provided with a range of enticing labor-saving appliances (refrigerators, washing machines and built-in televisions) tablewares and utensils to help her.

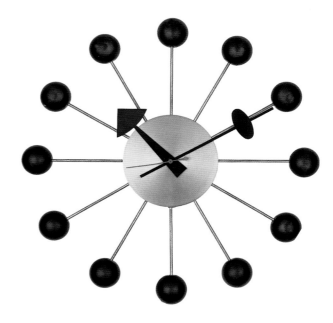

Advances in science, atomic power, and the Space Race inspired many designs, including George Nelson's 'Atom Ball Clock' for Howard Miller. 1947 13in (33cm) diam I

Some of the new mass produced furniture was designed for easy storage, such as Charles and Ray Eames's plastic and fiberglasss stacking chairs, produced by Herman Miller. 1954 31.5in (80cm) high F

A NEW GENERATION

The 1950s saw the first serious growth of a youth culture. The younger generation felt alienated by their elders, and were ready and able to rebel against political and social conservatism. Where their parents had encouraged them to sit upright, the young slouched and designers responded by creating comfortable chairs that people could drape themselves over. Where an older generation had 'made do and mended', the new one bought something to replace it the next day with the latest fashion: a trend epitomized by plastic furniture and paper dresses. Glossy magazines and the new newspaper color supplements promoted 15 minute crazes.

By the time John F. Kennedy, the youngest man ever to be elected president, assumed his place in the White House in 1961, the balance of power seemed to have shifted indefinitely in favor of this new, forward-looking generation.

The youth revolution was felt across film, music, art and all areas of design. Bright colors, once off limits, were now splashed around freely and new materials such as plastic were whole-heartedly embraced. So great was the role of plastic in Pop Art that even products not made from plastic (like Per Lutken's glass 'Carnaby' vases) were sometimes designed to replicate it.

TIMELINE

1948 The Museum of Modern Art organizes International Competition for Low Cost Furniture. Charles and Ray Eames design a molded-plastic armchair.

1951 The Festival of Britain brings the new design to public awareness. First direct-dial coast-to-coast telephone service begins in United States.

1954 Elvis Presley records his first record: 'That's All Right' on the Sun label. 'Rock Around the Clock', becomes first rock and roll number one for Bill Haley and the Comets.

1955 Arne Jacobsen designs the 'Series 7' chair. The most popular chair ever designed, over 6 million had been sold by the end of the 20th century.

Copper and steel "leaves" diffuse the light from Poul Henningsen's 'Artichoke' lamp which was designed for Louis Poulsen.
1957 18in (46cm) high M

Diagonal ribbons of blue and red glass create a chequerboard effect on a Barovier & Toso glass vase.
1955 9.75in (24.5cm) high N

Popular culture was taken more seriously and incorporated into the designs of the Pop movement. Brash, and gaudy, Pop took its influence from advertising, television and comic books, reaching its apotheosis in the work of such artists as Roy Lichtenstein and Andy Warhol. Other designs were influenced by the space-craze sparked by the first man orbiting the Earth in 1961. Much as the rod and ball atomic-style had followed the breaking of the atom, 'space-age' designs could soon be seen everywhere, in the silvery chair legs and space-helmet shaped television.

NOVELTY AND INNOVATION

During the 1960s the new materials and technology inspired novelty and experimentation in design. The Italian Gaetano Pesce designed a chair based on the female form for the manufacturer B&B Italia. The 'UP5' chair consisted on a high-density polyurethane foam "body" which was covered with stretch nylon. The chair was then vacuum packed, making it ten per cent of its original size. When the buyer arrived home they opened the packaging and the air seeped back into the foam, restoring the chair to its original size. Eero Aarnio's clear plastic sphere 'Bubble' chair suspended the sitter from the ceiling to make them appear to be sitting in the air. These rejections of traditional forms were a signpost to the future.

As the "Anti-Design" movement began its protest against society with ever more extreme designs, the stage was set for a rejection of everything the mid century modernists held to be true. In the next decade Postmodernism would turn design on its head.

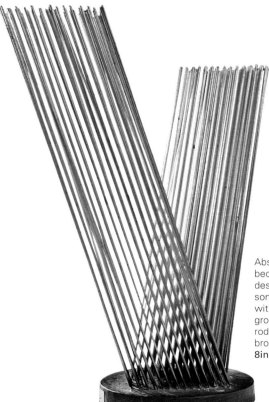

Abstract sculpture became part of interior design. Harry Bertoia sonambient 'V' sculpture with two opposing groups of gilded bronze rods mounted on circular bronze base.
8in (20cm) high K

1957 The 'Sella' stool is designed by Achille and Pier Giacomo Castiglioni. It uses a bicycle seat and pre-dates Postmodern design by over a decade.

1959 The Mini, designed by Alec Issigonis, is launched. It became the first successful small car.

1961 John F Kennedy sworn in as the 35th President of the United States. Yuri Gagarin becomes the first man to fly in space.

KENNEDY FOR PRESIDENT
LEADERSHIP FOR THE 60's

1966 The design groups Archizoom and Superstudio are founded in Florence. They are critical of modernist architecture and design.

MID-CENTURY MODERN

The Scandinavian Aesthetic

A new generation of Scandinavian designers took the clean lines of modernism and united them with the softer, more traditional properties of wood. The resulting fine-crafted furniture is at once redolent of innovative progress yet comfortably familiar. The organic shapes echo some of the socially conscious ideas that inform Scandinavian style. Stylish yet practical, such pieces have gained tremendous popularity throughout the world.

A discreet steel frame supports the leather-covered seat of a Poul Kjærholm PK22 lounge chair, designed in 1958, made by E. Kold Christensen.
28in (71cm) high N

A SIGN OF GOOD TASTE

During the 1950s and 1960s, Scandinavian Modern furniture was the epitome of Continental "good taste" among many style-conscious consumers. The metallic austerity of pre-war Modern design could be too cold and clinical for the home, while plastic remained a new and alien material for furniture. The sculptural elegance of wooden furniture was far more approachable. Beautifully proportioned and solidly built, it was reasonably expensive.

Attention to practicality and comfort is a characteristic of Scandinavian design. As Danish furniture designer Hans Wegner once said, "Things should do the job they are designed for." Scandinavian design philosophy put man – not machine – at the forefront when determining the look of objects. The designers believed in allying tradition with progress. This was the foundation of their attempt to fuse hand and machine craftsmanship, old and new materials, and modernity with historic

design. Danish furniture-makers in particular led the way. As new industrial production methods and materials were adopted after World War II, they successfully amalgamated skilled craftsmanship with mass production. Where furniture had traditionally been made in small workshops, now companies, most notably Fritz Hansen in Copenhagen, started to mass-produce furnishings.

TRADITION AND PROGRESS

Scandinavian designers tend to be split into two schools: those from the cabinet-making tradition, such as Hans Wegner, Ole Wanscher, Kaare Klint, and Børge Mogensen, all from Denmark; and those from the new breed of "designer". This second group included the Danes Arne Jacobsen, Finn Juhl and Poul Kjærholm, and Ilmari Tapiovaara and Antti Nurmesniemi from Finland.

Finn Juhl was probably the most influential of all the Scandinavian furniture

designers and is renowned for his sculptural forms. Hans Wegner is considered to be one of Denmark's finest cabinetmakers, combining traditional craftsmanship with modern needs in order to create functional classics. His most celebrated design is known simply as 'The Chair'.

Scandinavian designers had worked largely in isolation during the war years, and knew little of the developments in new materials happening abroad. Once the war was over the new influences – especially work being carried out at the Cranbrook Academy of Art in Michigan – had a great impact on their work. While many designers turned their backs on tubular-

Minimal form and decoration emphasize the natural tone and grain of the wood. Teak dresser by Børge Mogensen, sold by Illums Bolighus, Denmark.
1950s 60in (152.5cm) long NPA

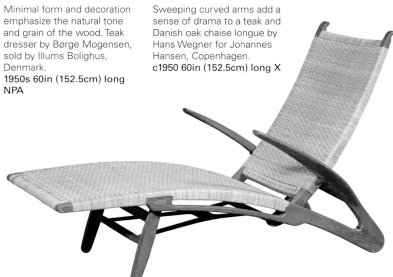

Sweeping curved arms add a sense of drama to a teak and Danish oak chaise longue by Hans Wegner for Johannes Hansen, Copenhagen.
c1950 60in (152.5cm) long X

steel furniture, Poul Kjærholm found that the new, thinner steel rods could be used in his furniture designs. Used as frames for chairs and tables, the rods do not detract from the visual appeal of his work.

Despite the Nordic countries' abundant forests, the wood used to make their furniture was mainly inexpensively sourced in the Far East. During the 1950s Denmark was the biggest European importer of teak. Furniture was also made from rosewood, beech and oak.

FINN JUHL 'CHIEFTAN' CHAIR
Finn Juhl helped to transform Danish design from a national style to an international phenomenon. His sculptural forms are some of the most easily recognisable. He was inspired by the work of abstract painters and African sculpture. His furniture has a freedom of form which sets it apart from that of his contemporaries.

Each element of the chair is curved – there are very few right angles or straight lines.

The struts that support the back are undulating, adding to the sculptural effect.

The top rail features stylized ears.

The curved arms were inspired by tribal art. The generous leather upholstery adds to the aura of comfort created by the chair.

The back and the seat of the chair do not join. This creates a feeling of light airiness despite the chair's size and sturdy frame.

The legs and other vertical wooden elements are made from turned wood. The horizontal parts are all carved.

Finn Juhl 'Chieftain' chair. **1949 40.5in (103cm) wide W**

The American and Italian Interpretation

In the years that followed World War II, designers in the rest of Europe and the United States took inspiration from the softer form of modernism that was taking shape in Scandinavia. Those in the United States and Italy lead the way and sought to combine their ideals of Good Design with emerging technologies to mass-produce honest pieces for consumers looking to shake off the deprivations of the war years.

GOOD DESIGN

The emphasis during this time was on producing furniture that was contemporary in design, yet durable; well made using the latest technology, yet affordable. Designers adopted the maxims of their Danish contemporaries, Finn Juhl and Hans Wegner, in adhering to the "form follows function" tenets of the modernist pioneers, while employing traditional cabinet-making techniques. In embracing the more sculptural, organic shapes emerging from Scandinavia, they succeeded in creating a far less austere form of the modernism that had dominated the inter-war years.

Wood was the material of choice for many of these designers. High standards of craftsmanship and a desire to remain true to materials epitomized this era and is evident in timeless, handcrafted pieces designed by Edward Wormley for Dunbar and Vladimir Kagan's sculptural forms made by Kagan-Dreyfuss in the United States, and Franco Albini's elegant cane and wicker pieces for Bonacina in Italy.

SELLING POWER

The rise of the furniture company during this period did much to push the realms of design into the public domain, with Knoll International and the Herman Miller Company dominating the scene in the United States, and Cassina leading the way in Italy. A new relationship developed between the manufacturer and the designer,

The organic forms favored by Vladimir Kagan include the angular, splayed legs seen on this walnut contour chair, designed for Dreyfuss.
28.75in (73cm) wide U

where the designer had more say in the production of his or her designs. George Nelson at Herman Miller and Florence Knoll saw the value of commissioning leading designers to produce pieces for them and did much to promote the careers of Charles and Ray Eames, Eero Saarinen, Isamu Noguchi and Harry Bertoia, among others. In Italy, Cassina forged strong relationships with Franco Albini and Gio Ponti. Coupled with annual competitions – such as MoMA's 'Good Design' exhibition in New York (from 1950) and La Rinascente's Compasso d'Oro awards in Milan (from 1954) – these firms ensured that furniture design of the very latest styles, made to high standards, reached the home of the mass consumer.

There was an overriding feeling that furniture needed to be smaller, more portable, and affordable to satisfy the needs of the consumer. In keeping with the ideals of 'Good Design', fitness for purpose was paramount. Furniture must be of exceptional quality with simple, modern lines and minimal superficial embellishment. Among the pieces that typify this period are innovative space-saving storage solutions, like Charles and Ray Eames's storage units and George Nelson's Comprehensive Storage System; multi-positional seating furniture such as

GIO PONTI (1891–1979)

Gio Ponti is often cited as the father of modern Italian design. An accomplished architect, he designed the Pirelli Tower in Milan, the city's first skyscraper and, until recently, Italy's tallest building. Among the highlights of a career that spanned over 50 years are his elegant ceramic designs for Richard Ginori in the 1920s and beautiful colored glassware for Venini in the 1940s. He was also founder of the highly influential architecture and design magazine, *Domus*, first published in 1928, and was its editor for the best part of 50 years. Ponti produced a wide range of furniture designs, enjoying a fruitful collaboration with Piero Fornasetti in the 1950s, and is perhaps best known for his 'Superleggera' chair. This design, Ponti's interpretation of the simple rustic chair, was hailed at the time as the lightest chair in the world and has since become an icon of the era.

Gio Ponti
'Superleggera'
dining chair.
1957 32in (81.25cm) high L

the 'D70' sofa by Osvaldo Borsani; and any one of a number of finely crafted sideboards – a seminal 1950s form.

ORGANIC DESIGN

A notable feature was a move toward more organic forms. Charles Eames and Eero Saarinen had already broken the mold with the award-winning chair they designed for MoMA's 'Organic Design in Home Furnishings' competition of 1940. With its curved wooden shell, it combined the "form follows function" ideal with a striking new organic aesthetic, setting a trend that came to dominate the era.

Again taking their lead from Scandinavia, and in particular the work of Finn Juhl, Saarinen's 'Womb' chair, Marco Zanuso's 'Lady' chair and Nelson's 'Coconut' chair highlight the move in this direction, where softly sculpted forms belie the comfort of a piece. Integral to the concept of a more organic approach was the idea that a piece should be aesthetically pleasing when viewed from any side. A natural progression from more abstract organic forms was biomorphism. Here, the Italian designer Carlo Mollino excelled. With a unique style of his own – later termed "Turinese Baroque" – Mollino's biomorphic approach was exemplified in sensuous daybeds and chairs whose forms were influenced by that of the female figure.

EDWARD WORMLEY FLAME MAHOGANY CREDENZA

Edward Wormley joined the Dunbar furniture company as a designer in 1931 and was its design director for over 30 years. During the 1950s, 30 of his designs received 'Good Design' designations at Museum of Modern Art Good Design exhibitions. Dunbar produced handmade furniture to Wormley's modern designs. He believed: "Modernism means freedom—freedom to mix, to choose, to change, to embrace the new but to hold fast to what is good."

Sideboards and credenzas suited the modern lifestyle of the 1950s which favored uncluttered interiors.

Designers relied on the grain of the wood for decoration. Pulls and handles were designed to be discreet yet add to the overall visual effect. Here the square pulls are made from ebony which contrasts with the flame mahogany case.

A flame mahogany credenza, by Edward Wormley for Dunbar.
65.25in (165.5cm) wide N

The short legs give a lightweight look and are reminiscent of some contemporary architecture.

Charles and Ray Eames (1907–78, 1912–88)

American husband and wife design team Charles and Ray Eames are mid-century legends on modernism. They designed everything from house interiors to multimedia presentations for the World's Fair. They were among the first designers to work in bent plywood and plastic and are universally renowned for their iconic chair designs. As the *Washington Post* once commented, the Eameses "changed how the 20th century sat down."

Charles Eames was an architect and draughtsman; Ray Eames an abstract expressionist artist. Together they expressed the modernist aim of combining industry and art for social good. They met at the Cranbrook Academy of Art in 1940. Among their friends at the academy were several other Mid-century Modern leaders such as Eero Saarinen and Harry Bertoia.

The couple married in 1941 and moved to Los Angles. Like many designers at the time, the couple were fascinated by the malleability of plywood. They were keen to develop exciting and affordable furnishings that served the overlapping needs of society, manufacturers and designers. They constructed a press that enabled them to bend plywood into three-dimensional shapes – previously an impossibility. They began to create experimental plywood products for their own purposes and that of U.S. Navy throughout World War II.

Inspired by an unusual source – a potato chip – they devised a unique chair design with a separate back and seat made from gently curving plywood. Christened the 'LCW' (Lounge Chair Wood) the couple exhibited it, along with a number of other plywood prototypes, in a solo exhibition at the Museum of Modern Art in New York in 1946. It was widely admired and the progressive furniture manufacturer Herman Miller put it into production right away.

The Eameses used the 'LCW' chair's soft contours as a template for many of their future designs. Its revolutionary design would help make them two of the most influential designers of the era.

An Eames '670' and '671' lounge chair and ottoman for Herman Miller, rosewood and black leather. The Eames's interpretation of the English club chair is made up of three laminated-wood shells, which are attached to a metal frame. Luxurious materials such as rosewood ensured these designs appealed to the high end of the market.
1956 Chair 31.5in (80cm) high N

In fact the 'LCW' chair would serve as a model for what many consider to be a milestone in Modern design, their 'DAR' (Dining Armchair Rod), the first plastic chair ever to be mass-produced. The couple developed the design after winning a competition held by the Museum of Modern Art in 1948, looking for ideas for low-cost furnishings for mass production. They originally planned to make the bucket-shaped chair from metal and plywood but switched to a sturdy plastic reinforced with fiberglass when the latest scientific developments made it available. Herman Miller put this seminal design into production in 1950.

The primary colors and amoeba-like form of the 'DAR' chair were very much in tune with the aesthetic mood of the 1950s. The Eames's created a number of variations on this design including a rocking version. Tremendously popular for the office and the home, it sold by the millions.

Their first attempt at design for the luxury market was an astonishing success. The '670' lounge chair with its matching '671' ottoman from 1956 is one of their most beloved classics. Inspired by the "look of a well-used first baseman's mitt", the chair comprised three leather pads nestled in plywood shells on a metal swivel base. They originally created it as a birthday gift for their friend Billy Wilder, the Hollywood film director. By this time the Eames's were renowned for their landmark designs throughout the USA and Europe, and the chair had its public debut on Arlene Williams's 'Home' show on NBC television.

Over the years the couple continued to experiment with new materials such as wire mesh and aluminum. They would go on to produce a number of classics including the 'Aluminum Management Chair' from 1958. The latest science and technology played a pivotal role in shaping their designs. Charles and Ray Eames passionately believed these innovations should be more accessible to the public at large. In the latter part of their careers they produced films and exhibitions to make the world of science and technology more easily understood.

Their mission was "getting the most of the best to the greatest number of people for the least amount of money".

EAMES FURNITURE

The Eames helped to pioneer fiberglass furniture. A Charles Eames/Herman Miller 'LAR' (Low Armchair Rod) fiberglass armchair.
c1950 25.5in (65cm) high G

Innovative materials and bright colors were a feature of the ESU-400 unit which Charles Eames designed for Herman Miller. It has dimpled sliding doors and polychrome side and back panels.
48.25in (122.5cm) wide O

Molded plywood was used by Charles Eames to design a child's stool for Herman Miller.
10.25in (26cm) wide L

A George Nelson and Charles Eames for Herman Miller 'Swag Leg' desk and a Charles Eames desk chair.
desk 39in (97.5cm) wide O

A dowel-leg table with square wood veneer top, designed by Charles Eames for Herman Miller.
c1955 21.5in (54.5cm) wide L

New Ways with Wood and Metal

The 1950s saw a number of designers returning to plywood and tubular steel as materials of choice. However, unlike the modernists of the inter-war years, the new pioneers of these materials were able to use technological developments to their advantage. As such they moved away from the rigid, strictly geometric forms of modernism, without compromizing on either the comfort or the function of a piece.

BENT PLYWOOD

Alongside new plastics and developments in upholstery, plywood became one of the seminal materials of this era. From the late 1940s, Charles and Ray Eames worked on plywood techniques they had developed for making splints during the war; their efforts were pioneering, and adopted by many designers in the Western world. They were also an influence in Japan, where Tendo Mokko became the first company to produce plywood furniture, attracting the country's most avant-garde designers.

There were several reasons for the tremendous success of plywood as a material for furniture design. Primarily, it was a low-cost material that lent itself well to mass production. Furthermore, it was light weight compared with solid wood and yet no less strong or durable. Finally, designers saw in plywood an opportunity to fulfil a common goal of constructing single-component furniture. An added bonus of plywood was that it could be sold in various finishes and a range of colors, so offering the consumer more choice.

Whereas laminated wood involves gluing layers of veneer together with the grain of one sheet running parallel to that of the next, plywood uses layers of veneer where the grain in one sheet runs perpendicular to that of the next. This affords a much greater flexibility, making it possible to manipulate the plywood into curved shapes.

Of course, the idea of using plywood was not a new one – Alvar Aalto and Marcel Breuer had enjoyed considerable success with the material in previous years. Now, however, designers such as Eames and Eero Saarinen were manipulating the wood to make three-dimensional forms for the first time. The beauty of the material was that it could be employed to make an entire chair form (seat and back) in one single piece, which made it extremely versatile and well suited to mass production. Taking their lead, Danish architect Arne Jacobsen used

George Nelson's bent plywood 'Pretzel' chair, designed for Hermann Miller, was only manufactured for a few years because of a lack of the manufacturing techniques needed to create its distinctive curves.
1957 30.5in (77.5cm) high J

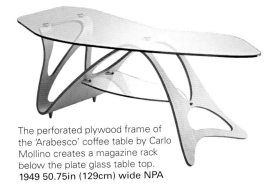

The perforated plywood frame of the 'Arabesco' coffee table by Carlo Mollino creates a magazine rack below the plate glass table top.
1949 50.75in (129cm) wide NPA

Arne Jacobsen's 'Ant' chairs consist of a molded plywood seat and three steel legs. They are still produced by Fritz Hansen today.
1952 30in (76cm) high D

Two strips of laminated bentwood were used to create the arms and legs of Eero Saarinen's Grasshopper chair for Knoll.
34.5in (86cm) high J

the techniques to develop Denmark's first mass-produced chair in 1952, the 'Ant' chair – which has sold in the millions – and a number of subsequent designs under the 'Series 7' group name. Comprised of a single-component molded plywood seat and back atop a tubular steel frame, the chair was easy and cost-effective to make – so easy that some examples required only one screw to attach the seat to the base.

The sheer versatility of this material is evident from the wide variety of forms that designers managed to achieve – from the surreal, sinuous curves of Carlo Mollino's 'Arabesco' coffee table to Sori Yanagi's sublime 'Butterfly' stool of 1954 or the exquisite, ribbon-like backrest and arms of George Nelson's 'Pretzel' chair for the Herman Miller Company in 1957.

WIRE REVOLUTION

While tubular steel had been widely adopted by modernist designers including Marcel Breuer and Le Corbusier, so perfect was it for achieving the rigid geometrical forms they favored that advances in technology now brought about thinner and lighter gauges of steel. This made it a more versatile and attractive material for designers looking to exploit its sculptural properties. Perhaps the most iconic metalwork pieces of this era were those designed by the sculptor Harry Bertoia for Knoll International. His famous 'Diamond' chair – whose intricate design had to be handcrafted – was made entirely from a wire mesh. The delicate appearance of the form belied its immense structural strength.

In Britain, steel rods were championed by Ernest Race, who used them to create a number of pieces, including the elegant 'Antelope' chair for the 1951 Festival of Britain. American sculptor Isamu Noguchi also experimented with steel rods. Famed for his sculptural designs he created the 'Cyclone' stool in 1954, which he developed three years later into a series of tables for Knoll. Central to these designs was an openwork column of chrome-plated steel rods. Notable steel pieces from the 1960s include Verner Panton's eye-catching wire 'Cone' chair and Warren Platner's tables and chairs for Knoll, which featured elegant, spindle-shaped bases that were made up of nickel-plated steel rods.

HARRY BERTOIA DIAMOND CHAIR

"If you look at these chairs," Harry Bertoia said of the five pieces he designed for Knoll in the 1950s, "they are mainly made of air, like sculpture. Space passes right through them." This set of chairs, which included the famous 'Diamond' chair, were made from a wire grid with upholstery. They were handmade because a suitable mass-production process could not be found. Despite this, the 'Diamond' chair – which won the Designer of the Year award in 1955 for Bertoia – became an immediate financial success. In fact, it sold so well he was able to give up furniture design and devote himself to his first love, that of sculpture.

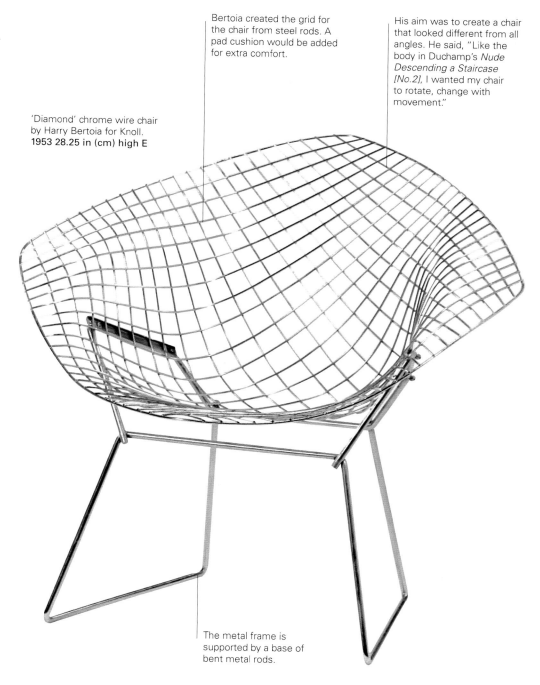

Bertoia created the grid for the chair from steel rods. A pad cushion would be added for extra comfort.

His aim was to create a chair that looked different from all angles. He said, "Like the body in Duchamp's *Nude Descending a Staircase [No.2]*, I wanted my chair to rotate, change with movement."

'Diamond' chrome wire chair by Harry Bertoia for Knoll. **1953 28.25 in (cm) high E**

The metal frame is supported by a base of bent metal rods.

The New Upholstery

The post-war years brought a greater emphasis on comfort in the home, as designers and consumers alike attempted to recover from the bleak deprivations of World War II. As a natural development of the softer form of modernism that began to emerge across Europe and in the United States, designers produced a wide range of upholstered chairs and sofas that made innovative use of new foams and stretch fabrics.

The 1950s saw a significant change in the way that consumers used, and therefore furnished, their homes. The latest must-have feature of the house, the television, took pride of place in the living room or lounge of many a dwelling, and presented a new focus for entertainment and relaxation at the end of the working day. Inevitably, there was a greater call for comfortable lounge furniture – and by association coffee tables – with which to furnish the room.

It seemed fitting that these pieces should reflect the more sculptural, organic shapes of the softer modernism that epitomized the work of Scandinavian designers like Finn Juhl and Hans Wegner, and from whom other designers of the time were taking their lead. In fact, Finn Juhl had proved as early as 1940 that new ways with foam and fabrics could help contribute to the overall softer aesthetic that designers of the 1950s sought. Gone were the harsh lines and

materials of modernism that had dominated the inter-war years, to be replaced, in the case of Juhl's biomorphic 'Pelikan' chair, with rounded shapes and all-enveloping comfort. Only four of these chairs were made at the time, however, and it was not until almost ten years later that such forms began to emerge for the mass market.

The organic shapes of Arne Jacobsen's 'Egg' chair and ottoman are upholstered in red wool.
1957 Chair 42in (106.5cm) high M

Two simple curves joined with metal bars make up Verner Panton's '1-2-3' lounge chairs. This pair is upholstered in blue bouclé fabric.
33in (84cm) wide M

One of the earliest designs to be made on an industrial scale was Earo Saarinen's 'Womb' chair for Knoll International in 1946. The basis of the chair was a molded fiberglass shell, not unlike those he produced for his 'Tulip' series almost ten years later. However, like Juhl's 'Pelikan', the shell was upholstered in fabric with foam cushions, and encouraged the sitter to curl up to get comfortable. The success of the chair was all too evident in similar designs that emerged across the globe. There was also a trend toward armchairs that you could practically lie on in order to lounge in even greater comfort. Saarinen's 'Grasshopper' chair for Knoll (1946), Hans Wegner's 'Flag-Halyard' chair for Getama (1950) and Robin Day's 'Lounger' armchair for Hille Co. Ltd (1952) all exemplify this perfectly.

BOLD SHAPES AND COLORS

As with the plastics that dominated design during the 1960s and 1970s, fabrics could be produced in all manner of strong and bright colors, which lent themselves perfectly to the bold sculptural forms that many of the designers were creating. For the seating furniture he designed for the SAS Royal Hotel in Copenhagen, Danish designer Arne Jacobsen was quick to recognize the value of the striking colors available to him. The now infamous 'Egg' chair he designed in 1958 for the hotel foyer used the same technology as Saarinen's 'Womb' chair; here the fiberglass mold was upholstered in foam that mirrored the shape of the human body. Although the chair was originally conceived in leather, Jacobsen finally settled on a dramatic red fabric for it.

Never one to shy away from provocative design, the Dane Verner Panton also embraced bright fabrics for a number of pieces, among them the 'Cone' chair – an upholstered version of his later wire model – which he designed for his parents' restaurant in Fünen in 1958. He also designed heart-shaped and square-backed versions of this piece. In the early 1970s, Panton created an entire series of organic pieces upholstered wool-fabric (20 in total), which made up the '1-2-3' group he designed for the American Herman Miller Furniture Company.

VERNER PANTON 'CONE' CHAIR

The 'Cone' chair, a thinly padded conical metal shell placed point-down on a cross-shaped metal base, was one of Panton's earliest designs and one of his most successful. The enthusiasm for the 'Cone' was so great that, when it was first shown in New York, the police ordered the chair be removed from a shop window where large crowds had gathered to see it. Ever outrageous, Panton arranged naked shop-mannequins and models over a set of 'Cone' chairs for a 1961 photoshoot by *Mobilia*, the Danish design magazine, causing a minor scandal.

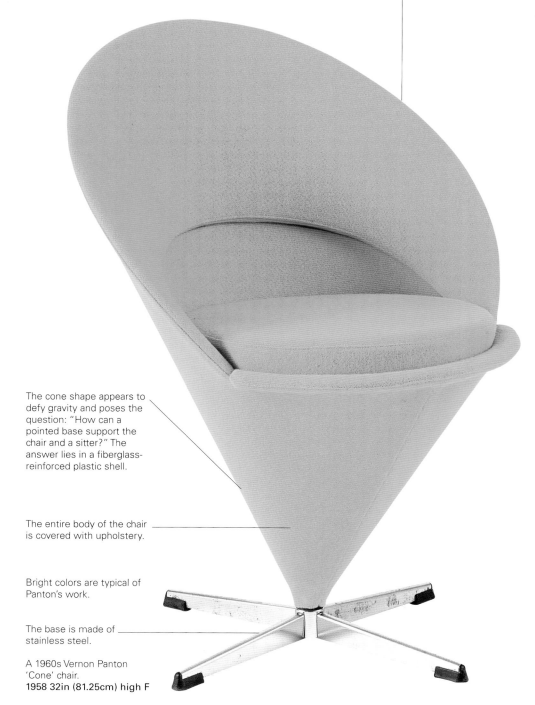

The tall, semicircular shell forms the chair's back and arm supports.

The cone shape appears to defy gravity and poses the question: "How can a pointed base support the chair and a sitter?" The answer lies in a fiberglass-reinforced plastic shell.

The entire body of the chair is covered with upholstery.

Bright colors are typical of Panton's work.

The base is made of stainless steel.

A 1960s Vernon Panton 'Cone' chair.
1958 32in (81.25cm) high F

Brazilian Furniture

Brazilian designers began a shift away from the old schools and toward modernism following the Week of Modern Art festival in São Paulo in 1922. This landmark event in the history of Brazilian art brought together the artists who are now seen as the founders of modern art in Brazil. The Week also introduced experimental ideas derived from European Expressionism, Cubism, and Surrealism to a wider public, while drawing on national folklore as a basis for making an art form more relevant to Brazilian society.

A high backed jacaranda Cantu chairs, designed by Sérgio Rodrigues.
c1959 39.5in (100.5cm) high NPA

EUROPEAN INFLUENCES

Many Brazilian design students of the 1950s and 1960s attended the Hochschule für Gestaltung in Ulm, Germany and this had considerable influence on the designs they created back in their home country. Consequently, when the first Brazilian school of design, the Escola Superior de Desenho Industrial (ESDI), a branch of the Rio de Janeiro State University, was founded in 1963 it was based on the Ulm methodology and interdisciplinary approach.

The masters of mid-century Brazilian furniture design, including Joaquim Tenreiro, Sérgio Rodrigues, Ricardo Fasanello, and José Zanine Caldas also worked (or, in Rodrigues's case, work) in Rio de Janeiro, typically in small workshops where they hand-produce each piece for a predominantly local clientele of wealthy businessmen and corporations. Most designs were site-specific and one of a kind. They were typically crafted in jacaranda, a wood which is now banned from use in furniture.

MODERN MASTERS

The son of a Portuguese furniture-maker, Joaquim Tenreiro is widely regarded as the father of 20th-century Brazilian furniture design. Tenreiro was among the first Brazilian designers to adopt a European modernist style in the 1940s. He eventually helped to steer his generation of designers away from copies of traditional European furniture and toward a new look that embraced emerging modern preferences, Brazilian culture, and indigenous materials such as Brazilian hardwoods and wicker.

Tenreiro considered himself a sculptor who made furniture. His pieces revel in obsessive attention to detail, with unique curves and hand-carved detailing that often is not immediately visible such as beveled edges found beneath a chair's arms or seat.

His early pieces, such as the 1942 'Poltrona Leve' (light armchair) met with considerable interest, and in 1943 he established his own company with factories in Rio de Janeiro and São Paulo. After great success, supplying illustrious clients such as the Brazilian architect Oscar Niemeyer, Tenreiro left furniture design in the late 1960s, to concentrate on painting and sculpture.

In 1956 Sérgio Rodrigues, who trained as an architect, founded Oca Industry in Ipanema, Rio de Janeiro, which went on to become one of the most important influences on modern design in Brazil. He left the company in 1968 to concentrate on furniture design.

Rodrigues utilizes traditional materials such as leather, and eucalyptus, jacaranda, peroba, and imbuia wood in his furniture. He combines Classical detailing and traditional woodworking with contemporary shapes and scale. His preference for the natural, and even sensual, imbues his furniture with a unique character.

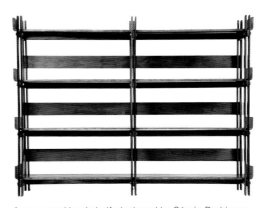

A rosewood bookshelf, designed by Sérgio Rodrigues.
1960s 81in (205.5cm) long NPA

A small jacaranda Eleh bench, designed by Sérgio Rodrigues.
1965 59in (150cm) long NPA

SERGIO RODRIGUES MOLÉ OR SHERRIFF CHAIR

Sérgio Rodrigues made his mark on the international design scene in 1961 as the creator of the Poltrona Molé or 'soft armchair', a chair he had designed four years previously. The Molé – also known as the Sherriff chair – won first prize at the International Furniture Competition in Italy where it was lauded for being unmistakably Brazilian in material, scale, and attitude. Rodrigues is considered to be one of the founding fathers of Brazilian design and the Poltrona Molé is his most famous creation.

The slouchy leather cushion slung across leather straps, has come to symbolize the relaxed, informal vernacular that informs Rodrigues's design and architecture.

The lush leather upholstery contrasts with the solid tapered cylindrical legs.

A 'Molé' chair, designed by Sérgio Rodrigues.
1957 40in (101.5cm) wide NPA

JOSE ZANINE CALDAS (1919–2001)

A self-taught artist, designer, and architect, José Zanine Caldas opened an architectural scale-model workshop in Rio de Janeiro at the age of 20 in 1939. It was here that he met and worked with some of the architects responsible for bringing Modernism to Brazil, such as Oscar Niemeyer and Lúcio Costa. In the early 1940s he started the Z Artistic Furniture line, which created plywood furniture. In 1952 he moved to São Paulo and worked as a scale modeller, furniture producer, landscape designer, and modeling teacher at the University of São Paulo. A few years later Zanine returned to his hometown on the southern coast of Bahia where he was inspired by local craftsmen to begin experimenting with a more elemental approach. Fascinated by the power of wood, he creates pieces of furniture by carving directly into huge logs, and in this way has redefined his style as a designer of organic, sculptural pieces.

A marine wood coffee table, designed by José Zanine Caldas.
1950s 27.5in (70cm) diam NPA

MID-CENTURY MODERN

Plastic and Fiberglass

The 1950s and 1960s brought revolutionary developments in the field of plastics that took leading-edge designers in a new direction. Rising to the challenge of producing groundbreaking designs for contemporary living, many designers created single-component pieces that could be produced swiftly and cheaply on an industrial scale. The futuristic furniture they designed has come to epitomise 1960s style.

Verner Panton's cantilevered 'S chair' was the world's first single-component plastic chair.
1959 32in (81.5cm) high M

NEW MATERIALS

The contribution made to the field of furniture-making by thermoplastics such as polyethylene (PE), polyurethane (PU), and polypropylene (PP) revolutionized furniture design after World War II. By the end of the 1960s, there was barely a furniture designer in Europe or the United States who had not experimented with these new, exciting materials. The arrival of thermoplastics and fiberglass-reinforced plastics meant there were now new materials suitable for furniture that were not only durable but also extremely versatile and cheap to use.

Chairs, in particular, caught the imagination of many designers, who sought to create pieces that were strong and hardwearing but also aesthetically pleasing and comfortable. With plastics the principles of ergonomics came into play as

chair seats and backs could be molded to fit the shape of the human body.

From as early as 1948, Charles and Ray Eames had been producing pieces using molded fiberglass, the seat shells interchangeable with a range of bases. Eero Saarinen, another great proponent of modern materials, produced his equally well-received 'Tulip Series' of tables and chairs, for Knoll International. These were famous for their elegant single-pedestal fiberglass bases and shells.

SINGLE-COMPONENT SEATING

The innovative Danish designer Verner Panton strove to design the world's first single-component plastic chair. He believed that "a less successful experiment is preferable to a beautiful platitude". He succeeded, with his incredible cantilevered 'S Chair', in 1959. Panton also appreciated

Molded polyester table designed by Eero Aarnio for Asko Lahti/Finland.
1967–68 51in (130cm) diam K

Plastic enabled designers to develop innovative forms. Luigi Colani designed the Zocker child's stool so that it could be used as traditional chair or, when used backward, as combined desk and chairs. Made by Burkhard Lubke of Germany.
1971–72 19.75in (50cm) high F

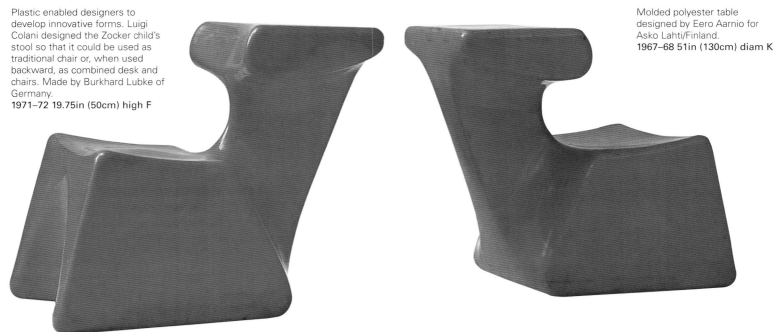

the color potential plastics brought with them. "Most people spend their lives living in dreary, beige conformity, mortally afraid of using colors," he said. "The main purpose of my work is to provoke people into using their imagination and make their surroundings more exciting."

In Britain, in 1963, Robin Day became the first designer really to exploit the use of thermoplastics for mass production. He designed the world's first injection-molded chair to be made on an industrial scale; over 14 million polypropylene chairs have been sold to date.

A year later, in 1964, Marco Zanuso and Richard Sapper developed a child's stacking chair for the Italian firm, Kartell – one of the first companies fully to embrace plastic as a material for furniture. The German designer Helmut Bätzner designed the single-component, reinforced-plastic 'Bofinger' chair in 1964 which took just five minutes to make. The race was on.

PLASTICS AND POP

The timing could not have been better. Europe and the United States were in the throes of a cultural revolution as Pop was taking center stage. Coupled with the increasing pressure to land someone on the moon, and the space age that ensued, this fueled a new generation of designers intent on using plastics to create ground-breaking furniture designs. Making the most of the relatively new injection-molding techniques at their disposal, and the wide range of bright colors that could be used, designers pushed the boundaries, experimenting with form in ways that had not previously been possible. And consumers loved them.

Among the important designers of this period were the Finnish designer Eero Aarnio, the Italian Joe Colombo and Luigi Colani from Germany. Aarnio's space-age designs really captured the zeitgeist of the times. His 'Globe' or 'Ball' chair of 1963–65 was a sensation, topped only by his re-working of the design to create the 'Bubble' chair in 1968 – a transparent ball suspended from the ceiling. Other seminal designs included molded polyester tables and chairs, among them the 'Pastil' chair, a circular disc-like piece which was molded to fit the shape of the sitter.

Joe Colombo, who had a fertile

EERO AARNIO 'BALL' CHAIR

The 'Ball' chair is one of the most iconic pieces of 1960s furniture and is, according to the *New York Times*, "the most comfortable [form] to hold up the human body". Eero Aarnio designed it for his first house where it was discovered by two managers from Asko. In 1966 the 'Ball' chair was presented at the international furniture fair in Cologne, where it was an instant success. Though very of his period in some ways, Aarnio refused to embrace the 1960s ethos of disposability and his chairs were of high quality and extremely durable.

The fiberglass shell is lined with upholstery. Cushions are added to create a seat.

The Vitra Design Museum describes the chair as, "something between a piece of furniture and a piece of architecture and at the same time embodies both the mobile and the established, the fixed."

The chair was designed as a sphere with a section cut away. The only design constraint was that it must be able to fit through a door. It creates a room within a room.

An Eero Aarnio 'Ball' chair on an enameled, metal swivel base.
1963–65 48in (122cm) high I

imagination for innovation, designed the first mass-produced, single-component, injection-molded chair in 1968, for Kartell. He was also quick to see the potential of using plastics to produce multi-use furniture such as his 'Tube' chair and 'Boby Storage' trolley.

For Luigi Colani it was important for a piece of furniture to work ergonomically as well as visually. Among his designs was the 'Körperform' (body form/shape) chair, a single-piece fiberglass chair that was molded to the human body. Colani was

also interested in developing multipurpose pieces, such as the 'Zocker' child's stool, which could also be used as a desk.

Among the other notable designers of this period were Vico Magistretti, who designed injection-molded 'Selene' and 'Gaudi' chairs for Artemide in Milan, and Anna Castelli Ferrieri, wife of the founder of furniture manufacturer Kartell, whose influential 'Componibili' storage pieces could be stacked in a number of variations to suit the user's needs.

FURNITURE GALLERY

New plastics and bent plywood played an important role in the design of the mid-century modern furniture. But this does not mean that upholstery and wood were ignored, they too were used to create furniture in the latest styles. The demands of the new open-plan homes were met with the creation of modular furniture and pieces that were easy to move as needs dictated.

A sculptural patinated bronze frame contrasts with the split cane seat and back of this 'Gazelle' line chair by Dan Johnson Studio, Rome, for Arch Industries Inc.
1950s 33in (84cm) high U

Wire struts radiate out from the base of a Verner Panton 'Cone' chair. With upholstered seat pad.
c1960 25in (63.5cm) wide F

Rows of velvet cushions on a steel frame make up George Nelson's 'Marshmallow' sofa for Herman Miller.
51.5in (131cm) wide R

A Jean Prouvé 'Standard' chair and 'Compass' desk.
c1950 desk 47in (119cm) wide T

Molded beech with a rosewood veneer have been used to make this 'Butterfly' stool by Sori Yanagi.
1956 15in (38.7cm) high C

A molded fiberglass easy chair '300', by Pierre Paulin for Artifort, with removable upholstered polyfoam pad.
1967 B

A bleached mahogany sideboard by Tommi Parzinger is embellished with brass hardware.
65.5in (166.5cm) wide N

Nickel-plated steel rods create the bases of a Warren Platner lounge chair and ottoman for Knoll. They are upholstered in Alexander Girard ocher fabric.
c1966 39in (99cm) high N

A pair of polished steel low-back chairs by Harvey Prober, who pioneered modular furniture.
24.75in (63cm) wide Q

ISAMU KENMOCHI CHAIR

From the 1950s to the 1970s, as Japan began to change from a largely rural nation into an imperial superpower, a new design ethos emerged: effectively the hybrid of Japanese and Western design. Isamu Kenmochi, who had spent the 1940s and 1950s traveling across Europe and United States, was a major champion of this style. He was lauded at home and internationally: in 1958 his 'Rattan' chair became the first piece of modern Japanese furniture to become popular in the West.

As with many designs of the late 1950s and 1960s, this chair shows the influence of Arne Jacobsen and Charles and Ray Eames.

A patinated mixed metal 'Chan Li' cabinet, by Philip and Kelvin Laverne. The design was influenced by Greek and Chinese metalware.
49in (124.5cm) wide V

Three shingle-style drawer fronts are the simple decoration on a Florence Knoll maple chest. The tapered legs are typical of the era.
36in (91cm) wide G

Isamu Kenmochi chair.
1961 27.75in (70.5cm) high C

The chair is made from beech with maple veneer. It was originally designed as an upholstered chair.

Piero Fornasetti

Piero Fornasetti is one of those rare idiosyncratic artistic figures who is a true individualist. While other prominent designers of the 1950s and 1960s turned their backs on tradition and ornament in favor of new unadorned forms Fornasetti positively embraced historic details and decoration. His distinct style transcends the mainstream of mid-20th-century design and yet it manages somehow to be of it.

Piero Fornasetti loved playing visual tricks. He often fooled his audience with smoke and mirrors. In a stunning publicity shot from the 1950s he bursts forth from a palatial façade made of window blind slats like a moustachioed magician. Though capable of transforming a Venetian blind into a building, this artistic conjuror was neither architect nor magic practitioner.

Fornasetti originally trained as a painter at Milan's Accademia di Belle Arti. Expelled for insubordination in 1932 he continued to hone his artistic skills. According to his son Barnaba Fornasetti, he mastered print-making by helping leading artists of the day like Lucio Fontana and Giorgio de Chirico print their lithographs. Fontana and de Chirico were associated with Surrealism whose haunting imagery dominated art throughout the 1930s. Fornasetti soon fell under the movement's provocative spell and rapidly developed his signature trompe l'oeil style.

Around this time Fornasetti met Gio Ponti, who greatly admired his display of scarves at the 1933 Triennale, Milan's cutting-edge design exhibition. Ponti, an influential architect and designer, was renowned for his generosity to up-and-coming designers and for championing contemporary Italian work at home and abroad. He featured Fornasetti's designs in his prestigious design magazine Domus and even commissioned several covers from the younger man.

After World War II the pair continued working together and collaborated on various high profile projects including a range of furnishings and the staterooms of the ill-fated luxury liner the Andrea Doria which sank in 1956. By 1960 Fornasetti had firmly established an international reputation for sophisticated work with an unexpected twist. He reportedly claimed: "My secret is imagination."

A Piero Fornasetti demi-lune chest appears in the guise of a Palladian villa. The black on white design also features brass pulls. Called 'Palladiana', it was designed in 1953 and is still in production.
40in (101.5cm) wide P

As a designer Fornasetti was far more interested in exploring surface effects than creating new forms. His genius was using decoration to transform banal objects into extraordinary mirages. Like many artists steeped in Surrealism he constructed his strange visions by juxtaposing found images. In Fornasetti's case these were derived from old engravings which he adapted so they could be transfer-printed by hand on to anything from fabric and umbrellas to ceramics and furniture.

Incredibly prolific as well as imaginative, Fornasetti created over 11,000 designs during his lifetime. He favored black and white designs, in homage to his printed source material. Fornasetti was particularly fascinated by images of architecture and classical antiquities. He also liked using newspaper pages, sheet music, playing cards, books on shelves and images of musical instruments as his source material. A dramatic image of the sun taking human form was another motif Fornasetti returned to frequently.

However his best-known design is a woman's face with big round eyes. It is based on a picture of the opera singer Lina Cavalieri, which Fornasetti discovered in a 19th century French journal. Cavalieri's face fired his imagination and inspired him to create more than 500 variations of this image. More than 350 of them were used for his popular plate series, Tema e Variazioni (Theme and Variation). This striking image was also applied to other items including lamps. He said he could not explain his fascination with Cavalieri, "What inspired me to create more than 500 variations on the face of a woman? I don't know. I began to make them and I never stopped."

Fornasetti's wit and irreverent appropriation of antique ephemera was welcomed in the drab 1950s. Two decades later his stylish historicism made him one of Postmodernism's greatest heroes.

Today Fornasetti's distinctive designs are more sought-after than ever. Following his death in 1988, Barnaba Fornasetti reissued more than 3,000 of his father's designs. By managing to be both utterly traditional and at the same time completely modern, Fornasetti ensured the timeless appeal of his work.

PIERO FORNASETTI DESIGNS

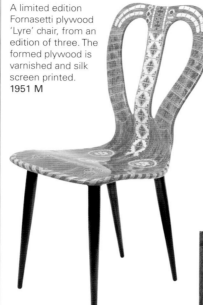

A limited edition Fornasetti plywood 'Lyre' chair, from an edition of three. The formed plywood is varnished and silk screen printed.
1951 M

A plate from Fornasetti's artists series featuring a black and white print of Tiziano Veneziano (Titian).
9.5in (24cm) diam B

Novel shapes were a feature of Fornasetti's work. A metal 'Doberman' umbrella stand.
34.25in (87cm) high F

A Fornasetti *trompe l'oeil* laminated wood folding screen depicts a sporting gentleman's wardrobe with shooting, golf, riding and fishing motifs.
78.75in (200cm) high R

A Piero Fornasetti single-drawer red metal file cabinet, printed with gold sunburst motif.
19.75in (50cm) wide K

Design for Mass Manufacture

The American movement in commercial ceramic design proved to be a major influence on the international adoption of the emerging new style. Following the war many of the European factories, particularly those in Staffordshire, England, were still looking to pre-war designs to inspire post-war wares. However, when change came, the results were radical.

A Steubenville Russel Wright Chartreuse sauce boat. The bud-like shape is inspired by nature, and was a move away from the angular forms of Art Deco.
7in (18cm) long B

CERAMICS FOR A NEW WAY OF LIFE

In 1937 designer Russel Wright created the 'American Modern' service for Steubenville. Its fluid and organic form was a dramatic departure from the angular shapes of the Art Deco era, and it was designed so that buyers could "mix and match" pieces from a palette of complimentary colors. These simple yet eye-catching designs were to continue into the post-war era when they inspired manufacturers across Europe.

Many of the wares produced in America were created as a result of the 'Organic Design in Home Furnishings' competition held by The Metropolitan Museum of Modern Art in 1940. The head of the museum's department of industrial design, Eliot Noyes, commented, "in the field of home furnishings there have been no outstanding design developments in recent years. A new way of living is developing however, and this requires a fresh approach to the design problems."

Designers who rose to the challenge included Eva Zeisel, whose range of organic-themed tablewares were manufactured by Castleton China.

An instant success, her simple, fluid forms hit the right note with design-conscious buyers. Ziesel also designed the 'Town & Country' range for Red Wing in 1947 as well as designs for Western Stoneware Co and Hall China Co. Other radical shapes were produced by Metlox Potteries, including Frank Irwin's 'Mobile' and 'Free Form' ranges. The latter included a boomerang-shaped relish dish with bold 'Aztec' decoration. Designers also worked on a freelance basis for a number of manufacturers, including: Belle Kogan for Red Wing, and Ben Seibel for the Pfaltzgraff Pottery.

SURFACE DECORATION

In Britain, the new style in ceramic design was slower to develop. The firm of Midwinter broke new ground with the development of its 'Stylecraft' and 'Fashion' ranges. During a selling trip to the United States and Canada in 1952, Roy Midwinter met with a senior buyer who declared, "I will shoot the next man who comes all the way over from Stoke to show me English roses." This prompted Midwinter to

WEST GERMAN CERAMICS

From the 1950s to the 1970s there was a revolution in West German mass-produced ceramic design. Form and finish changed constantly. Earlier designs feature new shapes, typically with fluid bodies decorated with bold, abstract patterns of primary colors. In later decades glazes became increasingly important, with volcanic, bubbling finishes developed in vivid hues accented with strong metallic oxides. Leading makers such as Bay Keramik Dümler & Breiden, Scheurich and Ruscha produced huge quantities of vases, bowls and other items.

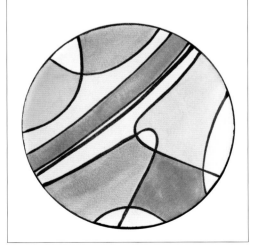

A Bay Keramik wall charger dish hand painted in the Bali pattern, designed by Bodo Mans. This was one of Bodo's earlier designs, and is typical of his work, with a colorful abstract pattern outlined in black.
1950s 10.25in (26cm) diam B

A Ridgway Potteries coffee service with Enid Seeney's 'Homemaker' pattern. The design depicted items from fashionable interiors of the day.
1956-57 Pot 7.5in (19cm) high C

JESSIE TAIT MIDWINTER TEAPOT

Jessie Tait represented a new breed of designer whose work is typical of the post-war period. She created colorful and stylish patterns for a new generation who desired modern designs at affordable prices. Her work was at the leading edge of post-war style and was an instant and huge success for Midwinter. 'Zambezi' remains one of her most recognized and imitated designs; launched in 1956 the simple, hand-decorated zebra pattern was accented with red and instantly caught the imagination of the young market.

Each piece is individually hand painted making every set unique.

The organic and fluid form and extenuated shape with its strong American influences was a huge departure for the Staffordshire potteries.

A Midwinter 'Zambesi' early morning teapot.
c1956 5in (13cm) high C

The addition of the red accent to the monochrome body perfectly reflected the taste and color palette of the period, with a nod to the exotic animal prints becoming ever more fashionable.

examine the comparative wares from the American market and realize the need for change. Midwinter's new ranges were a radical departure for a Staffordshire pottery, and the appointment of Jessie Tait and Terence Conran as designers resulted in ranges which became the "must have" for young, optimistic home-makers looking for something new. Textile-style patterns such as 'Primavera', 'Fiesta' and 'Plant' were inspired by fashionable interior schemes of the day.

Enid Seeney created the hugely successful 'Homemaker' range for Ridgways, decorated with images of design icons of the period such as a Robin Day chair and Gordon Russell cabinet in a striking monochrome palette. It sold for 22 years through Woolworth's stores.

There were different responses to mass-produced wares across Europe. Italy took a more artisan approach with products displaying classical references with a distinctly modern twist. The likes of Piero

Fornasetti decorated wares in an almost surrealist graphic manner with faces, suns, cities and optical trompe l'oeil effects.

In Germany the American influence was evident in Rosenthal's Service 2000. The elegant hourglass shape created by American industrial designers Raymond Loewy and Richard Latham, is instantly recognisable. As with Midwinter's 'Stylecraft' range, the service inspired many patterns including Lucienne Day's striking 'Regent Street' design.

Art Ceramics

Successful collaborations between artists and potteries brought the work of artists such as Pablo Picasso and Jean Cocteau into the homes of many people. The artists worked closely with the potteries, to create relatively affordable limited edition pieces that were characteristic of their work on canvas yet unique expressions of their art in clay.

A Madoura bird-shaped faience water pitcher, by Pablo Picasso. Common themes in Picasso's ceramics included figures, birds, portraits and bull-fighting.
9in (22.5cm) high P

A NEW MEANS OF EXPRESSION

Artists were commission by ceramic factories to design wares that offered consumers a new way to bring art into their homes. From America to Italy the post-war cross-pollination of studio, artist and commercial pottery grew at a pace. Many of the leading painters of the 20th century began producing decorated wares, from Henri Matisse to Pierre Bonnard.

The American designer, Henri Varnum Poor had trained as an artist in England and France, but felt that ceramics gave him even more control over his art. His painted and sgraffito decorated dishes were motivated by a mistrust of conformity and perfection that characterized corporate modernism in the United States.

The writer and artist Jean Cocteau was particularly successful in accomplishing the crossover from the visual arts to ceramics. Using a variety of decorative techniques, including a 'pastel' he invented himself, he designed, decorated and made small limited edition runs of simple vases, plaques and dishes at the Madeline-Jolly workshop in France. All his pieces were approached with a playful air and his characteristic style.

Others artists were encouraged to come to Vallauris, France by Suzanne and Georges Ramié who owned the Madura pottery there. They including Robert Picault, Roger Capron, and Jean Derval, who together created a lively forum for the exchange of artistic ideas Under the motto "utilitarian and beautiful", they created unique pieces and sculptures.

PICASSO AT MADOURA

During a visit to a friend in 1946 Pablo Picasso attended an exhibition of Vallauris pottery, where he was especially taken with the work of the Madoura pottery. He was introduced to the Ramiés and ended the day by producing two ceramic pieces. He returned a year later and was delighted to find his work. He then started working in earnest. The resulting collaboration is considered one of the most successful of the time.

Picasso developed two ranges of work: the first more unique and sculptural, where each piece was individually hand-crafted; the second a large number of wares that were issued in limited edition of 500. To create these pieces the pottery made a hardened plaster 'mold' of Picasso's original and then used them to make an impression in a piece of clay. These pieces

ITALIAN CERAMICS

The Italian market, like that of Scandinavia (see pp178–179), saw the hugely successful creation of high quality mass-produced art wares with an individual quality. The standard of design and execution of some pieces was high and some were overtly artistic. Artists such as Marcello Fantoni and Guido Gambone both created dramatic ceramics that were experimental and commercial in equal measure. Each developed a highly stylized method of decoration, often incorporating volcanic bubbling glazes in vivid hues with hand-decorated figures, animals or abstract patterns and sgraffito. Both experimented with glaze effects and as a result their works influenced the more commercial Italian ceramicists. The many wares that followed in the "fat lava" tradition in West Germany owe a great deal to the vision of such designers.

A large Fantoni bottle vase, with typical stylized decoration and glossy glaze.
6.75in (17cm) high G

A vase by Gambone, with simple, painted decoration of horses. His work often referenced Etruscan forms.
7.75in (19.5cm) high G

were marked "Original print of Picasso" and their subjects included mythical scenes, fish, fruit and clown-like faces.

Instantly recognizable as being by the artist, Picasso's Madoura wares immediately transferred his unique style to an accessible medium. The production of Picasso's highly sucessful ceramic wares was to have huge influence on many leading potters, ceramicists and manufacturers keen to follow the lead of such a great artist and successful designer.

ART CERAMICS IN BRITAIN

In post-war Britain the country's potteries were primarily concerned with more mass-produced wares. However, some potteries, such as Denby in Derbyshire had begun to introduce handmade and hand-painted lines, each piece of which was effectively unique. The 'Glynbourne' range designed by father and son team, Albert and Glyn Colledge was particularly successful.

Poole Pottery had been at the forefront of ceramic manufacturer for the best part of the century and now began to greatly expand the Poole studio, under the leadership of Robert Jefferson. Part of the brief that Jefferson had been given in 1958 when he was appointed resident designer had been to develop further the experimental approach to shapes and glazes, with the ultimate aim of producing a modern hand-decorated range that could complement or replace the traditional wares. To this effect, a new "Studio" line was released in 1961, which later became the 'Delphis' range. These pieces featured bold, colorful and abstract designs on new shapes created by Jefferson and Tony Morris, who joined the team in 1963.

The success of the 'Delphis' wares inspired Poole to open a Craft Section in 1966. New paintresses were hired, many with art school training, and they were encouraged to sign the pieces they decorated. The 'Atlantis' range, designed by Guy Sydenham in 1965–66, was decorated with geometric patterns forming strong textures and the decoration made as much use of the color of the clay as it did of any applied glaze. The new Craft Section led to ranges such as the darker 'Aegean' range, designed by Leslie Elsden in 1970 and the more elaborate 'Ionian' version (1974-75).

GEORGES JOUVE VASE

Georges Jouve was one of the grand ceramists of the post-war period having studied at the famous École Boulle in Paris. Primarily a sculptor, his passion for ceramics was ignited during the World War Two. Having been captured by the Germans he managed to escape and found himself in the village of Dieulefit where ceramics were key to the local economy. His grasp and understanding of this medium were both powerful and successful, and the work created after the war is still critically acclaimed as some of the most important ceramic art of the 20th century.

The handmade appearance of the vase enhances the primitive decoration.

Similar to the style employed by Picasso, the decoration is quick and confident, carved directly into the body, and picked out with simple flashes of glaze.

A Georges Jouve bulbous ceramic vase with applied plaque incised with bird, moon and starts on a gunmetal ground. 14in (36cm) high W

Jouve's development of glaze techniques, especially black oxides, became synonymous with his style.

Internationally recognized sculptor and ceramic modeller, Barbara Linley Adams joined Poole in 1972 and designed a series of stoneware wildlife sculptures and plates. The first of these was 'Wren on a Branch'. During her eleven years at Poole she designed 100 other models that also went in to production.

As with the Denby pieces, every piece of Poole Studio pottery from this period is unique. With time and a wide range of glazes to perfect their work, the designers produced pieces as one-off artistic expressions. Even unmarked Poole Studio pieces can be distinguished by the wider range of shapes and colors used. The decorators used even more than were used in the Delphis range. Poole pottery can be identified by its individual decoration, which brings pieces from the factory as close to the art-based ceramics of the studio potters as possible.

Scandinavian Ceramics

The post-war period in Scandinavian ceramics saw a large number of designers and factories producing a huge range of quality wares. Inspired by the fashion for simple, organic designs many pieces feature naturalistic shapes and decoration. Others looked to traditional Scandinavian forms and patterns as a starting point. The results were always thoroughly modern.

RETURN TO THEIR ROOTS

In Sweden, Gustavsberg was at the fore-front of the new developments. The factory embraced the new style under the director-ship of Wilhelm Kåge and his protégé Stig Lindberg. Kåge had created the 'Argenta' series in 1930, a range of top-end ceramics, usually in a mottled green glaze with ap-plied motifs in silver, that laid the founda-tions for Gustavsberg's market position in post-war years. Kåge used foliate and fig-ural themes, which were continued in de-signs by Stig Lindberg.

Lindberg took over the role of chief designer in 1949 and introduced a huge range of items from one-off pieces to mass-produced lines. His output was extremely diverse, including wall plaques with applied figural decoration through folk-inspired wares, to his starkly geometric and monochrome 'Domino' platters. However, his work is mostly associated with plates, dishes and bowls that mimic natural, organic forms. It was for these hand-decorated 'Faience' wares, which

A glazed 'Reptil' pattern by Stig Lindberg for Gustavberg. The assymetric form and natural texture are typical of this range. **7in (17.75cm) high C**

included leaf-decorated dishes, for which he became most noted. Lindberg's style was legendary – almost visionary – with light-hearted patterns and motifs. His wares were usually marked with a large 'G' and a hand motif and some also bear 'Stig L'.

FORM AND GLAZES

Ceramist Gunnar Nylund worked in his native Denmark, but is best known for his work at Rörstrand in Sweden. Despite training as an architect he was destined to follow in the artistic footsteps of his mother, a ceramist. He worked for Bing & Gröndahl in Copenhagen before deciding to start his own workshop, Saxbo, with Danish ceramicist Nathalie Krebs. He devel-oped shapes while Krebs devised glazes.

Nylund created elegant, modernist pieces in richly glazed stoneware as well as a series of utility ware in porcelain. He sought functionality and beauty in everyday objects. In 1930 he moved to Rörstand and remained there as one of its leading

A 1950s Royal Copenhagen ovoid Fayance vase designed by Inge-Lise Sorensen and Marianne Johnson. This is known as the 'Surreal' series, due to its unusual motifs.
7in (18cm) high C

STIG LINDBERG BOWL

Stig Lindberg's Faience range displays the crossover from art to domestic ware perfectly, with his range of simple sculptural forms beautifully decorated in fluid and whimsical designs. The shapes perfectly echoed the themes being seen in furnishings, metalware and glass and proved to be a huge success for the firm. His wares combined comical figures, stylized plant forms or simple repeat patterns in a palette of typical post war colors such as combinations of ocher, blue, green and red with black accents.

This large stylized leaf form shows a modern fluid organic style typical of the period. The subtle palette was inspired by nature.

The simple linear decoration is all hand applied and visually echoes the form.

A Stig Lingberg studio ceramic bowl.
c1950 9.5in (24cm) wide D

While designed as simple domestic objects, these became statement pieces as everyday items, and perfectly displayed the Scandinavian ethos of good quality hand craftwork even at a mass-produced level.

designers until 1958. The following year he returned to Denmark as art director at the Nymølle pottery. Later he worked as a freelance designer for Rörstrand and Strömbergshyttan.

Denmark upheld a market position with a huge selection of wares from the Royal Copenhagen factory with dramatically different designs. The 'Baca' Faïence range comprised standardized forms of dishes and vases but was decorated by a multitude of designers. Senior designer Nils Thorsson called on fellow artists Inge-Lise Sorensen, Marianne Johnson, Johanne Gerber and

others to develop floral, animal and abstract motifs picked out predominantly in blues, ochers, browns and greens. The result was a series that appeared individual and hand crafted while meeting the requirements of mass production.

Thorsson also designed earthenware for Royal Copenhagen that was produced by the Alumina factory. His 'Marselis' range of affordable, functional wares was decorated sparingly with ribs and geometric patterns picked out on solid glazes in natural tones.

Arabia was one of Finland's leading ceramic manufacturers. The mid-century

period saw technical and production advances combined with the successful collaboration of many new designers. Kaj Frank's appointment as design director in 1945 marked a time of great change.

Throughout the 1950s the firm's output was completely overhauled with the inclusion of both high-end art wares and domestic articles in a new style headed by the 'Kilta' range. The radical departure from old wares in terms of style, form and function was initially seen as a challenge, but the firm secured many international design awards during the 1950s.

MID-CENTURY MODERN

CERAMICS GALLERY

Mid-century ceramics reflected the mood of young homemakers, who sought to turn their back on the austerity of the war years with modern designs. While the search for new shapes and clean lines was a continuation of Art Deco, in other ways the new style was dramatically different. Inspiration was taken from organic forms: shapes were curved and organic rather than angular and geometric.

A Lenci pottery jug, shaped and decorated as a stylized bird form.
1950s 11.75in (30cm) high D

An H.J. Wood 'Piazza' ware vase, with a curved rim. The asymmetrical form and black and pastel colors are typical.
c1957 9.5in (24cm) high A

A Steubenville Mist Gray milk jug, designed by little-known designer Ben Seibel, for the popular 'Contempora' range.
4in (10cm) high A

A set of late Adam plates by Piero Fornasetti. Fornasetti broke away from his contemporaries, looking back to classical antiquity for inspiration.
c1970 C

A Hornsea jardinière, designed by John Clappison in 1963. The form is clean and unfussy.
10in (25.5cm) wide B

A Danish Royal Copenhagen 'Marselis' vase, by Nils Thorsson, with an organic texture and color.
1950s/60s 4.25in (11cm) high B

A Red Wing pitcher from the 'Smart Set' range with a hand painted yellow and black linear design. The simple, clean lines create a functional yet modern form.
12.75in (32.5cm) high C

MARCELLO FANTONI VASE

Italian ceramicist Marcello Fantoni was well established before the war, but continued to consolidate his reputation during the 1950s–70s. His combined interest in modern art and his Italian heritage led to the creation of new and unique forms, that were frequently more sculptural than functional. An interest in how glazes and forms work together can be clearly seen in his work, making pieces by his had easy to recognize. His bright colors and rough surface textures are very distinctive and were widely copied.

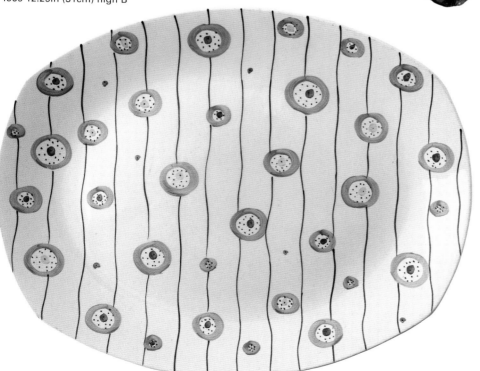

The bright colors and angular shapes suggest Cubist paintings.

The amorphous shape is enhanced by the polychrome glaze. Although there is a double-neck it is unlikely this piece would actually be used as a vase, as it is more sculptural than practical.

A Marcello Fantoni studio vase.
1955 16in (41cm) high M

The rough texture of the glaze is characteristic of Fantoni's work.

A Midwinter 'Festival' pattern charger, designed by Jessie Tait. The pattern of cells was inspired by developments in science.
1955 12.25in (31cm) high B

A 1950s Italian vase with painted and sgraffito design. The asymmetric shape is typically 1950s, and the figures are very similar to designs by Marcello Fantoni.
12in (30.5cm) high B

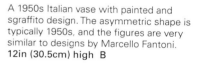

Murano Glass

Glass production on Murano in Vencie, Italy underwent a revolution as designers and glassmakers took centuries-old techniques and reinvented them to suit the new, post-war world. The result was some of the most significant and influential glass that re-established the pre-eminent reputation of glass from the island. The output created a signature note for interiors around the world and set the stage for future glass innovations.

Bold colors show the layers of glass, cased in clear glass, used in the sommerso technique. 'Valva' vase by Flavio Poli for Seguso Vetri d'Arte.
c1952 9.5in (23.7cm) high P

TIME FOR NEW BLOOD
The 1920s and 1930s had seen a change in fortune for the glassmakers of Murano as new blood began to pump into the heart of the island. Young and dynamic artists, sculptors, architects and designers were employed to rejuvenate factories such as Barovier & Toso and Fratelli Toso, or create new ones such as A.V.E.M and Seguso Vetri d'Arte. Generations of talented glass blowers and workers were quickly able to interpret the bold and experimental new designs. Artistry was the order of the day and the line between function and fine art became more blurred.

The mid-century modern look continued in this vein and was characterized by the use of centuries old techniques to create new organic forms and surface decorations. Suddenly a murrine cane was blown up in scale and fused with many others in a bright and bold kaleidoscope of color; glass was decorated with splatters of other colors, cut to simulate hammered metal or wrapped around metal foil to give a glittering finish.

UNSTOPPABLE ENTHUSIASM
By the 1950s the enthusiasm and expansion seemed unstoppable and established firms such as Venini flourished while many new ones were established including Cenedese and Vistosi. Many talented artists wished to be associated with Murano and increasingly inventive techniques and forms were created. The color scheme of the post war years suited the Italian palette, with its use of strong colors colliding across the bodies of vases and platters.

While the leading designers and factories created ever more dramatic and daring pieces, the smaller firms were quick to follow suit adapting the adventurous creations of the grand masters into

accessible gifts for the new breed of tourists who were visiting the city on the first package tours. This widened the popularity of Muranese glass by opening it to a wide and eclectic audience.

TRUE EXPERTISE
Technical excellence became the order of the day and from Seguso Vetri d'Arte to Vistosi the creations became ever more experimental and adventurous. At Seguso, Flavio Poli perfected the *sommerso* technique where layers of different colored glass created fluid organic forms, the dramatic simplicity of the final product belying the complexity of the technique. His 'Valva' range won awards at the Milan Triennale and Compasso d'Oro.

The multitude of variations of cane-worked pieces produced at the time stand as a testament to the skill of the maker in

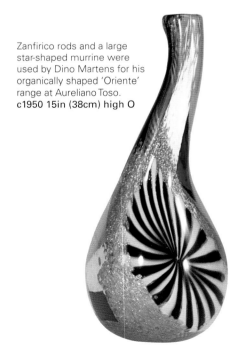

Zanfirico rods and a large star-shaped murrine were used by Dino Martens for his organically shaped 'Oriente' range at Aureliano Toso.
c1950 15in (38cm) high O

interpreting the idea of the designer. Complex techniques such as *murrine* (slices of patterned glass canes which can be pressed together or applied to molten glass before blowing to create a design); *lattichino* (white threads used to decorate clear glass); and *zanfirico* (threads of white or colored glass twisted together to form a filigree within clear glass), were used to produce many distinctive pieces.

At Salviati, Luciano Gaspari designed unusual, composite art-glass forms which became increasingly exagerrated as the 1950s went on. The attenuated shapes of his 'Pinnacolo' vases, which featured colored underlays, were the pinnacle of this form. Dino Martens' 'Oriente' pieces for Aureliano Toso used irregular-shaped bands of bright colors which were combined with over-sized murrines and aventurine inclusions. Aldo Nason's 'Yokohama' vases designed for A.V.E.M., used colored canes suspended over metal-tinted grounds to great visual effect. Meanwhile, Tobia Scarpa created his 'Occhi' wares, with fused panels of glass made up of a mosaic of *murrines*, for Venini. These now stand as stylistic symbols of the post-war era.

POLLIO PERELDA 'STELLATO' VASE FOR FRATELLI TOSO

Fratelli Toso was one of the long-established firms on Murano which was well-known for the re-interpretation of complex cane work pieces such as filigrana and murrine. The appointment of Ermanno Toso as artistic director in 1936 saw the introduction of a number of key ranges including the 'Stellato' series. Launched in 1953, the wares were created from designs by the painter Pollio Perelda.

The artistic freedom of the design shows the skill of the glassmaker in interpreting the ideas of a painter who is not familiar with the techniques used in glassmaking.

The clear glass helps to create an optical effect which is enhanced by the simple shape of the vase.

The combination of bright, strong colors are typical of the period.

The starburst murrines are large compared with the millefiori examples used previously.

Fratelli Toso 'Stellato' vase designed by Pollio Perelda.
1953 11.5in (28.5cm) high O

Paolo Venini (1895-1959)

Venini is a name synonymous with great design and excellence in glass. The factory's collaboration with many major artists including Carlo Scarpa, Ettore Sottsass, Gio Ponti and Fulvio Bianconi created some of the most important pieces of 20th-century glass design. Through the decades this factory on the island of Murano has promoted innovative designs created using traditional techniques. This philosophy has much to do with the company's founder Paolo Venini. It continues to be at the forefront of modern design today.

MID-CENTURY MODERN

Originally trained as a lawyer, Paolo Venini established the glassmaking firm that bears his name in 1921 when he formed a partnership with Venetian antiques dealer Giacomo Cappellin. Together they placed themselves at the forefront of the renaissance of Murano glassware. Known originally as Cappellin Venini, the company split in 1925, and the modern day Venini was created with a new artistic director, sculptor Napoleone Martinuzzi.

Paolo Venini sought to locate the best designers, artists and sculptors to help him realize his passion, and these collaborations are now recognized as the epitome of 20th century Venetian glass design. He had studied the techniques of other successful artistic directors and, by the 1930s, he took an increasingly visible role in the company's artistic direction. He was aided in this by a new creative mind, architect Carlo Scarpa.

Scarpa introduced an array of new decorative techniques including *bollicine*, where the body of the glass was filled with thousands of small bubbles, *coroso*, where acid was used to create a surface texture like rusted metal, *battuto*, created to look like beaten metal, countless decorative *murrine* cane variants, and *incalmo* techniques where blocks of glass were fused together in vertical, horizontal or panel formations. These techniques not only became a signature for the Venini workshop, they were also the envy of many of its rivals.

In the 1950s, Venini was a pioneer in introducing the mid-century modern style. Its new designs won it awards and accolades at the 1951 Triennale Design Fair in Milan. The new fashion for more fluid forms combined with unashamed and bold color palettes in primary and contrasting

Tesserae – squares of colored glass – were fused onto molten clear glass to create Fulvio Bianconi's 'Pezzato' vases. This example is in the 'Paris' colorway. **c1952 8.25in (21cm) high S**

shades instantly suited the firm's way of working and output increased dramatically. The introduction of the work of designers such as Fulvio Bianconi and Gio Ponti only served to increase the firm's creativity.

Fulvio Bianconi was an illustrator and graphic designer who was to become one of the most innovative Italian glass designers. After World War Two he went to Murano to study glass techniques and met Venini who saw his talent and hired him in 1947. Bianconi was the most successful designer of what is regarded as the Golden Age of Italian glass (c1945 to 1969). He brought a sensuality and excitement to glass showing in his work a passion for the female form. He believed, "artistic glass has to be unique, if it is repeated it loses its charm".

Bianconi developed a number of Carlo Scarpa's existing decorative techniques, creating new interpretations including *fasce, inciso* and *pezzato,* which were to become some of Venini's most popular designs. The walls of his 'Fasce Orrizontale' and 'Fasce Verticali' series were made up of horizontal or vertical stripes used with clear glass. During his time on Murano, Scarpa created many designs on a freelance basis for a number of firms, however it was his work for Venini which was to prove the most outstanding.

Gio Ponti had trained as an architect and also designed ceramics and furniture. He began designing for Venini in the 1940s using a palette of bold, Mediterranean colors including turquoise, red, green, gold, and ultramarine. Bi-colored and multicolored stripes were a feature of his 'A Canne' vases, decanters and tumblers. The human form also influenced Ponti's designs; for example his 'Bottiglie Crinoline' feature crystal glass frills which represent a woman's lace petticoats. These were applied to the blow glass bottle and decanter forms.

Venini worked with Bianconi on the design of the 'Fazzoletto' or 'Handkerchief' vase which is shaped like a falling handkerchief. Designed in 1948-49 it was a great success and has been widely copied.

Following Paolo Venini's death in 1959 the company passed into the hands of his son-in-law Ludovico Diaz de Santillana who continued to collaborate with the best artists the design world could offer.

VENINI GLASS

A mosaic pattern of square murrines is laid over clear glass to create the 'Occhi' range of vases designed by Tobia Scarpa.
1960 9in (23cm) high O

Horizontal strips of colored glass cased with clear glass form Fulvio Bianconi's 'Fasce' vase.
1953 14in (35.5cm high) D

Stacked red and cobalt glass elements form a glass lampbase designed by Gio Ponti.
58in (147.5cm) high R

A stoppered bottle designed by Paolo Venini, of blue glass with red mezza filigrana center.
15in (38cm) high H

Horizontal bands of colored glass form a tumbler-shaped vase by Fulvio Bianconi.
c1951 5in (13cm) high R

Venini pioneered the 'Fazzoletto' or 'Handkerchief' vase. The form was created by Fulvio Bianconi and Paolo Venini c1949.
c1950 5.8in (14.5cm) high M

Scandinavian Glass

Building on their pre-war experience and international success, Scandinavian glass designers of the 1950s and 1960s created a new aesthetic that became influential across the world. Classical, elegant, yet strongly inspired by nature, the "Scandinavian Modern" movement was much less exuberant than the design revolution on Murano, but no less inventive. Colors were cool; forms were balanced, often exploring the plasticity of the medium. The clarity of the glass and the skill of the glassmakers drew a global reputation.

ORREFORS

After the departure of Simon Gate and Edward Hald in the 1940s, the early post-war period was dominated by the designs of Ingeborg Lundin, Nils Landberg, and Sven Palmqvist. Landberg's landmark 'Tulpanglas' (tulip glass) range, exhibited at the Milan Triennale in 1957, exemplifed the balanced harmony and classicism of the emerging movement. Lundin's 'Apple' vase

was similarly influential, and further demonstrates the importance of nature as a key inspiration. Both were challenging to make, the elegant, elongated form of the 'Tulpanglas' in particular.

Complex technical advances based on the 'Ariel' technique were made with Palmqvist's 'Kraka' range of 1941, and the 'Ravenna' range of 1948. Brightly colored layers of glass were combined with a sandblasted pattern to great visual effect. In 1954, Palmqvist was also responsible for the opalescent 'Selina' range, developed with glass technician W.E.S. Turner and produced in gently curving, organic forms. The revolutionary centrifugally molded 'Fuga' range of tableware represented Palmqvist's entry into mass production.

KOSTA

In 1951, Vicke Lindstrand joined Sweden's Kosta factory as lead designer, having left Orrefors in 1940 and spent 11 years designing ceramics. His work showed a similar diversity to that of Palmqvist, using cutting, engraving, molding, and hot-glass techniques. His cut designs followed on from his work at Orrefors, being modern and stylized, and often feature the human form. Shapes had a more flowing, curving nature, echoing the lines of the cut design.

Lindstrand's inherent sense of harmony and rhythm can be seen in his series of cased vases with fine mesh or grid-like patterns that give a Scandinavian take on Muranese designs. He also produced designs for tableware, and made sculpture for both domestic and public settings.

For Kosta's sister company Boda, Eric

Holmegaard 'Duckling' vase, designed by Per Lütken in 1950. The bud-like and asymmetric form is typical. **1959 10in (25.5cm) high B**

Designed for Kastrup by Jacob Bang; the color and undecorated, linear form typify his post-war work. **1960 9.5in (24.5cm) high B**

The design of this vase, by Vicke Lindstrand for Kosta, combines Swedish and Muranese designs. **c1958 8.75in (22cm) high D**

INGEBORG LUNDIN 'APPLE' VASE

Ingeborg Lundin was the first female designer employed by Orrefors. When she joined the firm in 1947 her free approach to her work was in stark contrast to the more traditional formality of the factory's usual output. While she also developed cut and mold-blown pieces, it will be her 'Apple' vase for which she will be best remembered. Known for her humor, its free-blown form typifies the best of Swedish glass and has been called "the world's best-known piece of 1950s glass".

The form is a simple yet humorous design meant to represent an apple with its stalk.

This design was launched at the Milan Triennale in 1957 and won Lundin international acclaim. Today, examples are held in many museums worldwide.

Lundin was called "the Balenciaga of glass" by decorative arts historian Lesley Jackson, for her coolly elegant style.

Ingeborg Lundin 'Apple' vase designed in 1955 for Orrefors.
15in (37cm) high M

The free-blown body – which varies in thickness, giving variation to the color – is also symmetrical, requiring great skill on the part of the glassblower.

Höglund produced chunky, brightly colored works inspired by Primitive art and which reacted against the refined designs of his contemporaries.

HOLMEGAARD & KASTRUP

Jacob Bang left Denmark's Holmegaard in 1941, returning to glass design at Kastrup in 1957. Although he continued the modern aesthetic of his previous works, his designs from the late 1950s were more austere. Simple, linear forms in tableware and decorative glass were largely unembellished and executed in single, pure colors to give a striking, flawless look.

These were in direct contrast to the work of his successor at Holmegaard, Per Lütken, whose designs typify the 1950s interest in bud-like, curving shapes. One of his most iconic forms was the 'Duckling' vase of 1950, which was produced until the 1970s in a range of sizes and cool colors including ice blue, light green and smoky gray. Other typical forms include the heart-shaped vase of 1952. Lütken also designed the colored and cased 'Flamingo' series of vases in 1956. His exploration of and experimentation with studio glass techniques resulted in, among others, the 'Lava' range, produced from 1969.

This period also saw a sea change in Lütken's designs with the introduction of the 'Carnaby' range in 1969. Produced in vibrant colors such as red, blue and yellow lined with opaque white, they have an almost "plastic" appearance. Shapes were based around geometric forms, or combinations of them, including the cylinder, disc and sphere.

In 1970, Michael Bang, son of Jacob, produced a similar range known as 'Palet' which is often confused with 'Carnaby'. Also similar is Otto Brauer's earlier 'Gulvvase' bottle of 1962 for Kastrup, which continued to be produced in various single transparent and opaque colors after Kastrup and Holmegaard merged in 1965.

IITTALA

The theme of the natural Scandinavian landscape was fully explored at Finland's Iittala by designers Tapio Wirkkala and Timo Sarpaneva. Wirkkala's background in sculpture was combined with his

Per Lütken's 'Carnaby' range for Holmegaard lends itself to the Pop Art trend of the period.
1970s 11.75in (30cm) high G

experiences of nature, giving him a unique perspective for his works. These include his 'Jäkälä' (Lichen) vases of 1950, the 'Varsanjalk' (Foal's foot) vase of 1947, and his lyrical 'Kantarelli' (Chantarelle) vases of 1946. Inspired by mushrooms, they won a Grand Prix at the 1951 Milan Triennale.

He was also inspired by the rugged textures of rocky fjords, bark and ice, most notably in his range of drinking ware produced for Finlandia vodka in 1970. Similar was his textured and knobbled 'Ultima Thule' range of tableware, designed in 1968 and still in production today.

Sarpaneva also combined a curving, sculptural aesthetic with a feel for textured surfaces which became a leitmotif of glass design across the world during the 1960s and 1970s. In 1953 he designed the free-formed 'Orkidea' (Orchid) vase which, with its obelisk form and tiny aperture, is more a sculptural work of art than a functional vase. Winning a Grand Prix at the 1954 Milan Triennale, it also won *House Beautiful*'s "Most Beautiful Object of the Year" award in the same year.

His textured 'Finlandia' (see opposite) and 'Festivo' (1967) ranges were influential, and he ventured into household glass with the simple, functional forms of the mold blown 'i-line' range, introduced in 1956.

Key freelance designer Gunnel Nyman worked for Iittala, Riihimäki, and Nuutajärvi, producing work of a different character at each. Although at Iittala her designs were asymmetrical and angular, they took on gentler, curving forms at Nuutajärvi. Many contained networks of tiny bubbles, or ribbon-like patterns.

RIIHIMAKI

After the war, design competitions held by Finland's Riihimäki yielded talented new designers including Helena Tynell, Nanny Still and Tamara Aladin. Much of their work was mold-blown, allowing it to be mass-produced and exported globally. Forms were typically geometric, lobed or flanged, and executed in vibrant primary colors, and surfaces often textured.

This 'Piironki' vase, designed by Helena Tynell in 1968 for Riihimäen Lasi Oy (Riihimäki) was part of a series.
c1970 8.25in (21cm) high C

Sinuous figurative decoration was used by Vicke Lindstrand at Kosta, as seen here on The Bath vase.
1950s 8.25in (21cm) high C

TIMO SARPANEVA'S 'FINLANDIA' RANGE
Introduced by littala in 1961, the 'Finlandia' range arose from a happy accident. In a failed attempt to create textured surfaces, Timo Sarpaneva attacked the semi-hard surface of glass with a saw. However, the wooden molds the glass was held in became charred and created unusual surface textures in the glass. The result became one of Sarpaneva's most successful designs and included a selection of bowls and vases. Early examples were created from unique wooden molds that deteriorated with use. These were later replaced with metal molds which guaranteed the consistent results needed for mass production.

The molten glass was blown into an alderwood mold. As the hot glass burned the wood, it changed the textured interior each time it was used – therefore every piece was given a unique surface effect.

The casing and the different types of texture recall not only tree bark, but also ice and rock – all are features of the Scandinavian landscape.

Cool, muted colors were typical of the Scandinavian palette, and included smoky gray and an ice-like colorless glass.

The used and burned wooden molds were later exhibited as sculptures in their own right.

A Finlandia vase by Timo Sarpaneva for littala.
1960s 8in (20cm) high D

Czech Glass

Hidden behind the Iron Curtain, postwar Czech glass design underwent a revolution in style similar to that on Murano and in Scandinavia. While the glass was exhibited and exported internationally, it was not until after the Velvet Revolution in 1989 that the artists themselves, and the designs they produced, started to be recognized. This work is now being re-evaluated in the context of design developments across the world.

A NEW NATIONAL INDUSTRY

Following the devastating effects of German occupation, the new Communist government, which came to power in 1948, nationalized Czechoslovakia's vast glass industry. The new regime poured money into rebuilding and modernizing factories, and training a new wave of designers.

The goal was twofold; to demonstrate the success of Communism to the West, and to create glass to export and bring in valuable foreign currency.

Although other art forms were strictly controled and used as propaganda, the regime deemed glass unable to convey a social or political message. As a result, designers were free to create, with only a few exceptions. Many artists, such as Jan Kotík, even turned to glass to pursue an otherwise banned modern, abstract style. This combination created a unique melting pot of creativity.

Progressive and innovative designs were produced by leading designers such as Stanislav Libenský, René Roubícek, Pavel Hlava and Jií Harcuba. Many of these won major awards at a number of key international exhibitions, beginning with the 1957 Milan Triennale and the Brussels Exposition a year later.

Designs can be divided into two categories: experimental, progressive designs produced in limited runs or as unique objects for exhibitions, and mass-produced, factory-made designs inspired by them and produced for sale and export across the world.

BLOWN & MOLDED GLASS

Glass blown, molded, and finished at the furnace was largely a new direction for the Czechs. Forms reflected the plasticity of glass, being curving, asymmetric, and sculptural. Produced in bright colors, many are mistaken for, and may have been inspired by, designs from Murano. These include the work of Josef Hospodka for Chribskà, and Milan Metelák for Harrachov. Frantisek Zemek's 'Rhapsody' and 'Harmony' ranges, of 1956 and 1959

This vase design by Pavel Hlava was exhibited at the 1957 Milan Triennale, and later made by Exbor.
c1960 11.75in (29.5cm) high H

This unique 'The Town' cut vase by Jirí Harcuba uses a complex combination of cutting techniques to produce an abstract town plan, which resembles modern art.
1965 8.5in (21cm) high V

Frantisek Vízner's pressed glass vase for Hermanova is as much a sculpture as it is a functional object.
1962 7.75in (19.5cm) high C

respectively, for the Mstisov glassworks are also particularly noteworthy. With their cool colors and linear forms, vessels and sculptures by Miloslav Klinger for Železný Brod can be seen as a Czech take on Scandinavian designs.

The Škrdlovice glassworks, founded by the Beránek family, was a hotbed of experimentation. Innovative designers who worked there included Vladimír Jelínek, Lubomír Blecha, and František Vízner. They designed ranges in production runs of varying sizes that pushed the boundaries of glass design.

CUT GLASS

Czechoslovakia had been known for its fine-quality cut glass for centuries. After the war, traditional techniques were used in a new way. Designers such as Josef Pravec, Vladimír Žahour, and Ladislav Oliva broke from tradition to produce abstract and modern designs on simple forms. Using lens, prismatic, olive-shaped, and other cuts, designs focused on the optical and reflective properties of the cut itself. When natural or figurative motifs were used, such as by Jirí Harcuba or Josef Švarc, these were highly stylized and modern. Karel Wünsch updated flashed glass with contrasting colors cut through with sharp, angular abstract patterns.

ENAMELED & GILDED GLASS

Unique and highly influential exhibition pieces were produced from the 1940s to the 1960s by Vladimír Kopecký, Stanislav Libenský and others, and were effectively modern or abstract paintings on vessels. Unrelated geometric, banded, or stylized floral patterns were also used on mass-produced tableware and vases.

PRESSED GLASS

Pressed designs broke from the tradition of imitating cut glass, taking on sculptural forms, modern geometric patterns, and an interest in the optical effects created by surface decoration. The lens also became an important design motif. Key designers included František Vízner, Rudolf Jurnikl, František Pecený, and Adolf Matura. These were exported around the world by SkloExport, allowing Czech modern glass design to enter homes affordably.

BORSKÉ SKLO CASED BOTTLE VASE

For decades the leading glassmakers of central Bohemia produced flashed or cased works decorated with cut patterns and hand-enameled and gilded natural or floral scenes, or heraldic motifs. Here these traditional techniques have been unashamedly adapted to the postwar, modern age. This range was part of the successful Czechoslovakian contribution to the 1958 Brussels World Exposition.

Opaque white over red is challenging to make successfully due to the different cooling times for each color.

Red was traditionally associated with Bohemian glass, but this range can also be found in light blue or green.

Complex, traditional cuts have been replaced by simple sweeping cuts that emphasize the modern shape of the bottle itself.

Elements of modern art reminiscent of Picasso and Braque are used. This style of art was banned, but it was not considered subversive or decadent when it appeared on glass.

The repeated asymmetrical gilded Greek key motif creates a modern, abstract design.

Borské Sklo cased, cut, gilded and enameled bottle, by an unknown designer, the patterns by Jaroslav Lebeda. 1958 12.75in (32cm) high L

British and American Glass

In Britain and the USA, glassmakers were greatly inspired by the revolutions in glass design happening in Italy and Scandinavia. However, they did more than just re-interpret what they saw: they took the new themes and developed them into something uniquely their own.

BRITISH CUT GLASS

During the 1930s, factories in Stourbridge had made use of consultant designers such as Keith Murray and Thomas Pitchford. Directly after the war, a new wave of industrial glass design graduates from the Royal College of Art were employed by factories in Stourbridge, the heart of the British glass industry. These included Irene Stevens at Webb Corbett and David Hammond at Thomas Webb in 1947, and John Luxton at Stuart in 1948.

Until 1955, the industry was crippled by a 100 per cent luxury sales tax, and design progress was constrained by a largely conservative market that preferred traditional, safe and staid, cut designs. Nevertheless, Stevens and her colleagues took traditional cutting techniques and simplified their use, producing striking, bold designs on simple, classic forms. Miter, lens, and other linear and geometric cuts were spread across the body of the

piece to great visual effect. Where natural motifs appeared, they were both highly stylized and modern. From 1963–64, David Queensberry produced designs for Webb Corbett along a similar aesthetic that included 'Domino', 'Mitre' and 'Random'.

BRITISH BLOWN GLASS

During the 1950s, the influence of Scandinavian glass being imported into the UK, combined with the progressive Contemporary movement which grew from both the 1946 Britain Can Make It exhibition and the 1951 Festival of Britain, began to have a major effect on British glass design.

Perhaps the most important designer in this respect was Geoffrey Baxter, who joined the long established company of Whitefriars in 1954. A graduate of the Royal College of Art, he initially worked with William Wilson. Both produced innovative, organic and curving hot-worked designs that were a British take on Scandinavian design and production methods. These were also considered by David Hammond and Stan Eveson at Thomas Webb in 1961, the result being the free-blown and swung 'Flair' range. Scandinavian influences can also be seen in Baxter's 'Blown Soda' range of 1961, but it was his landmark 'Textured' range of 1966 that combined Scandinavian color, texture and form, but with a British twist. Baxter and his assistant Peter Wheeler also reflected the growing Studio Slass movement (see p.54) in their various 'Studio' ranges produced from 1969.

Also influenced by Scandinavian designs was Ronald Stennett-Willson, whose background was in importing glass by companies such as Orrefors. After

Dramatic, large decanters in unusual shapes are typical of Wayne Husted's designs for Blenko.
1958 20.5in (52cm) high G

Alternating acid-etched frosted and clear cut panels create a geometric optical effect on a Thomas Webb cut-glass vase designed by David Hammond.
1964 10in (25.5cm) high D

With each component being a separate piece of glass joined together when hot, Ronald Stennett-Willson's 'Sheringham' candleholder challenged glassmakers.
1967 6.25in (15.5cm) high B

**GEOFFREY BAXTER FOR WHITEFRIARS
'BANJO' VASE**
The 'Textured' range remains one of Whitefriars' most successful and iconic series. Designed in 1966 and launched the following year, the range was handmade and featured a number of vases in different, largely geometric shapes, each cased in clear glass over a single color. Inspired by the natural and manmade landscape around him, Baxter developed a new method of mold-making using pieces of bark, tacks, nails and wire to create different textured effects.

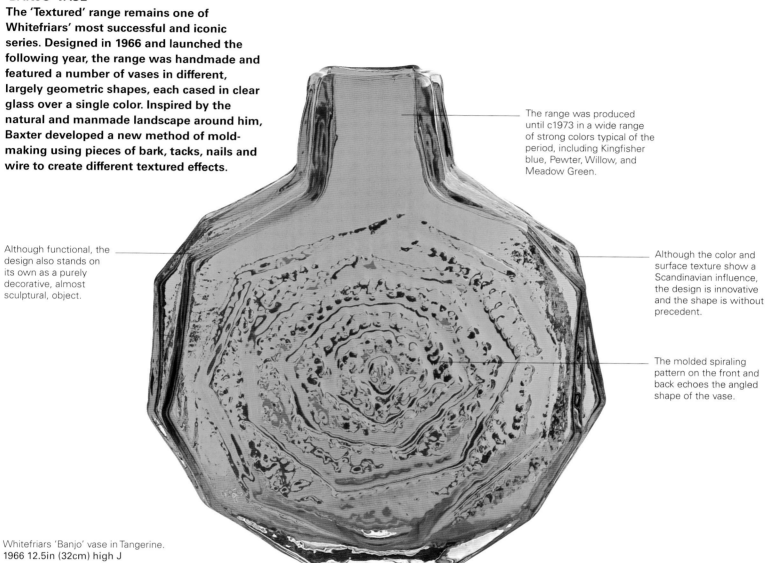

The range was produced until c1973 in a wide range of strong colors typical of the period, including Kingfisher blue, Pewter, Willow, and Meadow Green.

Although functional, the design also stands on its own as a purely decorative, almost sculptural, object.

Although the color and surface texture show a Scandinavian influence, the design is innovative and the shape is without precedent.

The molded spiraling pattern on the front and back echoes the angled shape of the vase.

Whitefriars 'Banjo' vase in Tangerine.
1966 12.5in (32cm) high J

producing designs for importers Wuidart, he founded his own factory at King's Lynn. As with Baxter, rather than purely imitate Scandinavian designs, he developed the themes that lay behind them. Particularly notable are his 'Sheringham' and 'Brancaster' candleholders, his 'Top Hat', 'Angular' and 'Studio' ranges, all of 1967, and his unique 'Ariel' designs of the 1970s.

Also working in a similar vein was Frank Thrower at Dartington Glass. Chance Glass mass-produced popular 'Handkerchief' vases, as well as modern tableware, with bright, printed designs.

AMERICAN BLOWN GLASS
With its heritage in stained glass windows, Blenko's vibrant colors were perfectly matched to the new modern movement. Three main designers were responsible for Blenko's postwar success. Winslow Anderson was the first in-house designer from 1947–53 and, like many others, was strongly influenced by Scandinavian themes. During his eleven year tenure from 1952–63, Wayne Husted became known for his dramatic, and often large, vases and decanters typified by the 'Spool' range. His successor, Joel Philip Myers, became closely

connected with the studio glass movement, leading to much experimentation. His forms led on from Husted's but are set apart by their extravagant profiles, sometimes with trailed decoration.

Other companies followed Blenko's lead, moving away from domestic, often pressed, glass to colorful freeblown decorative designs. Many were based along the Ohio River Valley, and included 'Pilgrim', 'Bischoff', 'Rainbow' and 'Viking'. Geometric or unusual, often lobed or ringed, forms in vivid colors are typical, with an emphasis on visual and decorative appeal.

GLASS GALLERY

Traditional techniques were given a new and modern twist by glassmakers and designers after World War II. In Murano, centuries-old decorative devices such as murrines were used in new ways and bright colorways. In Scandinavia the cool colors of the icy landscape inspired simple, organic shapes in pale tones. As a result, many long-established factories began to create revolutionary new ranges.

Geometric forms were a recurring motif. British mold-blown vase designed by Frank Thrower for Dartington. **c1970 5.25in (13.5cm) high B**

Traditional millefiori (a thousand flowers) murrines were updated in new styles and used on simple, modern forms. Murano glass vase designed by Ermanno Toso for Fratelli Toso. **c1960 8in (23cm) high O**

Functional forms were fashioned out of vibrantly colored glass. A Danish Kastrup vase from the 'Antik Grøn' series designed by Jacob Bang. **1964–70 6in (15cm) high B**

Decorative, oversized decanters and goblets, like this Pilgrim decanter, in bright colors were made in Italy and the U.S. **c1965 17.5in (44cm) high C**

Artists became involved with art glass as well as art ceramics. Marc Chagall worked with Egidio Costantini on this 'Anfora Sposi' vase. **1954 15.5in (39.5cm) high U**

An exuberant form and a painterly approach to color and decoration can be seen on this 'Finestra' vase by Anzolo Fuga for AVEM. **c1960 16.5in (42cm) high R**

ALESSANDRO PIANON 'PULCINO' BIRD
As well as functional and decorative vases, bowls and tablewares, some designers on Murano produced whimsical or eccentric animal forms. These were often copied widely by other factories. Alessandro Pianon's 'Pulcino' (chick) for Vetreria Vistosi combines an elongated blown glass sphere with murrine eyes and wire legs and feet.

The molten glass was pulled up from the body to create the beak, and the eyes are applied murrines – both create appealing character.

This was part of a series of birds with bodies reduced to simple, stylized forms, including the cube, ellipse and sphere.

The surface is textured, giving the impression of feathers.

The thin wire legs combined with the large spherical body create a humorous, almost cartoon-like appearance.

A Vetreria Vistosi 'Pulcino' bird designed by Alessandro Pianon. 1962 8.75in (22cm) high L

The traditional Venetian technique of applying triangular sections of glass to a surface was given a modern makeover in Barovier & Toso's key 'Intarsio' range. c1963 8.75in (22cm) high L

This Borské Sklo vase, designed by Pavel Hlava, combines studio and mass-production techniques. c1970 10.25in (26cm) high C

Decorative rather than functional, this Bischoff stoppered bottle was inspired by Blenko's successful designs. c1960 13.75in (35cm) high C

Designed by Vratislav Sotola for Exbor, this is typical of designs inspired by modern, abstract art produced by some Czech designers. 1966 7in (17.5cm) high F

Metalware

Following World War Two, technological developments made aluminum and stainless steel the perfect, less expensive, alternatives to silver and gold. Designers took these new materials and used them to make functional and decorative objects in the new, organic styles. These stylish pieces were easier to maintain than silver, as they did not tarnish, adding to their appeal with consumers. However, silver was still used for luxury items by companies such as Georg Jensen.

HARMONIOUS LOOK

The opportunities afforded by the mass manufacture of stainless steel, together with a return to precious materials such as silver, created a boom in the metalware market thanks in part to a new range of sleek and elegant wares.

The Scandinavian countries led the way with leading designers such as Arne Jacobsen. He created products such as the Cylinda-Line range for Stelton and the pared down AJ cutlery suite manufactured by Georg Jensen. Designed in 1957 it was deemed so futuristic that it was used by Stanley Kubrick in his 1968 film "2001: A Space Odyssey". Forms became fluid land organic and designers such as

Simple shapes were the hallmarks of Arne Jacobsen's 'Cylinda Line', which included this coffee pot.
c1970 8in (20cm) high

Nanna Ditzel, Bent Peter Gabrielsen, Erik Magnussen and Henning Koppel created jewelry and hollow wares that were modern and futuristic. Elegant in their simplicity, and working to a methodology of simple repeated forms and understated design, the style they delivered summed up the feel of the new era and was influential on an international scale.

Elegant, sculptural forms were created by Sigurd Persson, at his Stockholm studio. He also designed jewelry and glass and in 1960 won a medal at the Milan Triennale.

INSPIRATIONAL TEACHING

In the United Kingdom designers began to exploit the the new aesthetic. The catalyst for much of this new work was the Royal College of Art in London where designers

Curved shapes were the basis of David Mellor's 'Pride' electroplated tea service, which he designed for Walker and Hall.
c1959 Teapot 9in (23cm) long H

including Robert Welch, David Mellor, Gerald Benney and Stuart Devlin studied under Professor Robert Goodden. Goodden designed iconic pieces such as the 1951 'Festival' teaset and the 'Queen's Cup' made for the 1953 Coronation.

Robert Welch was at the forefront of the new mass production design movement. A visit to Sweden in 1954 made his aware of the stainless steel wares being designed by Sigurd Persson. Realizing the potential

A pair of Old Hall stainless steel triple candlesticks with teak feet, designed by Robert Welch.
1957 9in (23cm) high B

HENNING KOPPEL WATER PITCHER

Henning Koppel was trained as a painter and sculptor, before he found international fame as a silversmith. He was employed by the Georg Jensen firm in 1946, and his artistic expression is shown in everything from large sculptural bowls to jewelry and cutlery. He considered himself an anti-functionalist, and reacted strongly against the dominant ideal of the time that said form should follow function. At the first glance, Koppel's silver wares may appear uncomplicated and simple, but it demanded the highest skilled craftsmen to execute them. Koppel worked spontaneously, inspired by the moment and completely uninterested in the views of critics or the demands of mass production. He would first work out a design in line form, followed by a clay maquette before proceeding to the silver model. This would allow him to view a piece from all angles, ensuring that every plane would provide an elegant viewpoint.

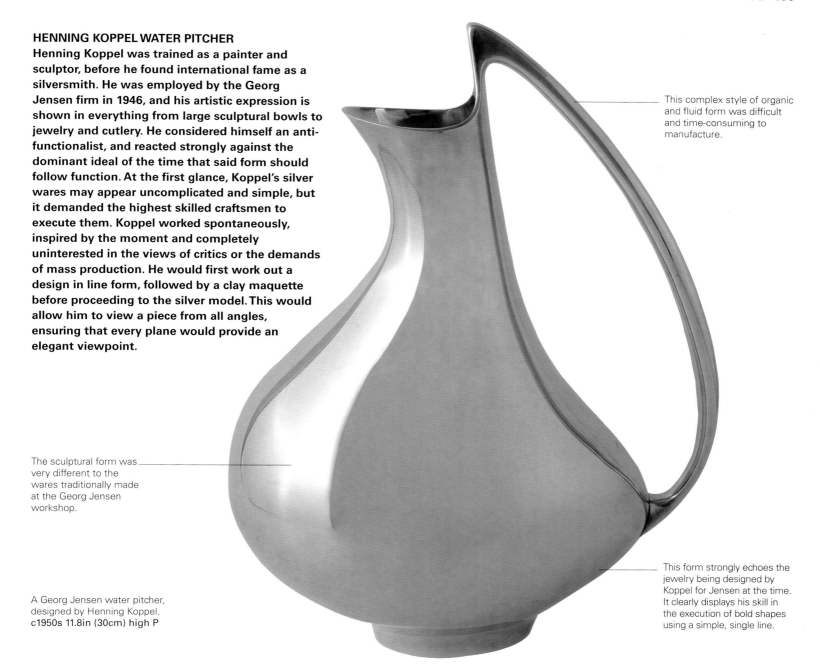

This complex style of organic and fluid form was difficult and time-consuming to manufacture.

The sculptural form was very different to the wares traditionally made at the Georg Jensen workshop.

A Georg Jensen water pitcher, designed by Henning Koppel. c1950s 11.8in (30cm) high P

This form strongly echoes the jewelry being designed by Koppel for Jensen at the time. It clearly displays his skill in the execution of bold shapes using a simple, single line.

of this material, he dedicated the last year of his studies at the college to the research and development of new designs. In 1955, Welch's appointment as design director of the tableware firm Old Hall was the start of a successful partnership. From simple toast racks to award winning designs, such as the 1964 'Alveston' range which included teasets and cutlery, the firm, and more importantly Welch, propeled stainless steel and Old Hall to a worldwide audience. Welch was design director at Old Hall until it closed in 1984.

After graduating in 1954 David Mellor, who had originally trained as a silversmith, worked for various manufacturers in Sheffield – his home town and the center of the British steel industry. Many of his designs are still produced including the 'Pride' cutlery service he developed while studying at the Royal College of Art. He was commissioned to design everything from a set of stainless steel cutlery for canteens, hospitals and British Rail to 'Embassy', a range of handmade silver tableware for British Embassies.

Gerald Benney developed a style that consisted of simple, clean elegant forms. He is also known for the textured finish he invented for silver, and later pewter, in the late 1950s. Australian Stuart Devlin decorated simple forms with rich embellishment which contrasted with the sleek lines inspired by Scandinavian design.

In the United States streamlined tablewares, many in aluminum, were made by ceramics designer Russel Wright. Tommi Parzinger, better known for his furniture, developed metalwares for Dorlyn.

METALWARE GALLERY

Many of the metalwares produced in the 1950s and 1960s feature clean, sleek lines inspired by Scandinavian design. Stainless steel and aluminum offered the possibility of affordable, modern homewares although silver, pewter, brass and copper continued to be used. Designs were modern and inventive whether for practical tablewares or decorative items.

A geometric base contrasts with an organic-shaped bowl designed by Henning Koppel for Georg Jensen.
1950s 14in (38cm) diam U

An elongated spout and simple handle enhance a Carl Auböck of Vienna metal watering can.
1952 6.25in (16cm) long E

Flared rims like opening buds feature on this pair of silver vases, by Hans Bunde for Carl M. Cohr.
1963 7in (18cm) high L

Stainless steel was combined with brass on this coffee pot by Tommi Parzinger for Dorlyn.
c1950 16.5in (42cm) high C

The interchangeable parts of this Nagel candleholder can be connected in a variety of ways.
c1970 35.5in (90cm) high F

Simple, clean lines feature on this Carl Auböck brass and leather magazine rack.
c1950 21in (53.5cm) long E

WILLIAM SPRATLING COFFEE SET

Though known as the 'Father of Mexican Silver', William Spratling was actually an American, who moved to Mexico in 1929. Spratling soon settled in Taxco, southwest of Mexico City. The city was a traditional site of silver mines, but had no silverworking industry of its own. Spratling hired local goldsmiths to produce his silver designs, decorated with pre-Columbian and traditional motifs. Having been successful himself, he began an apprenticeship program and many his students to continue to work in the Taxco area after finishing.

The modern shape of the silver is offset by the organic wooden handles.

The tray and handles are made from rosewood which creates an attractive contrast to the silver.

A four-piece sterling silver and rosewood coffee set, by William Spratling.
c1940 Pot 6.75in (17cm) high L

A Cachan enameled metal wall sconce by Serge Mouille.
11in (28cm) high N

A Christofle silver-plated architectural sculpture by Gio Ponti.
13in (33cm) high M

A sculptural metal and bamboo magazine stand by Carl Auböck.
c1950 (56cm) high E

A streamlined pewter pitcher, by Paul Evans, is set with a rosewood handle.
c1952 11in (28cm) high I

Abstract Sculpture

Evocative and sometimes challenging, abstract sculpture is non-objective or non-representational – it does not aim to "look like" something. Instead it uses space, scale, weight and texture to engage the viewer. Line, form and balance are all-important. During the 1950s and 1960s some abstract sculptors began working on kinetic sculpture. This was pioneered by artists including Alexander Calder and Harry Bertoia.

FURNITURE AND ART

Born in Udine, Italy, Harry Bertoia, who moved to the United States in 1930, enjoyed a highly successful career as a designer of furniture, jeweller and sculpture. In 1950 his first chair designed for Knoll Associates, the chrome-plated steel wire 'Model 420 Diamond', proved to be a stellar success. So successful was his furniture for Knoll, he was able to live on the royalties and devote his energies exclusively to sculpture.

Bertoia's highly accomplished kinetic sculptures – imaginative free-standing objects and sound sculptures combining constructed metal sculpture and modern design– define the marriage of art and science. By 1960, he had begun the exploration of tonal sculptures, sounding sculptures – or as they are frequently called 'sonambient' sculptures – which range in size and depend on a variety of metals including beryllium copper.

Throughout the 1950s and into the 1970s, Bertoia produced more than 50 public sculptures and completed numerous groups of constructed metal sculptures including forms based on trees and plants, screen forms and rods, and the popular starburst sculptures. Through his experimental work he was able to offer new possibilities to constructed metal art – most notably through his 'sonambient' pieces.

SCULPTURE WITH MOVEMENT

Born to a family of artists in Pennsylvania, the painter Alexander Calder revolutionized the art of sculpture by making movement one of its main components. Yet his invention of the 'mobile' – a word coined in 1931 by artist Marcel Duchamp to designate Calder's moving sculpture – was but one of his many impressive achievements. Although he numbered among his talents the creation of lithographs, toys, jewelry and tapestries, it was in his early wire figures and in his 'stabiles' – innovative static sculptures made from sheet metal – where Calder explored the aesthetic possibilities of non-traditional materials.

As a major contributor to the development of abstract art, Calder with his stabiles and mobiles challenged the prevailing notion of sculpture as a composition of masses and volumes by proposing a new definition based on the ideas of open space and transparency. With the giant stabiles produced during the latter part of his career, Calder launched a new type of public sculpture.

In the years after World War Two the abstract sculptures being made by artists such as Barbara Hepworth and Henry Moore inspired pieces of domestic

Stylized bronze sculpture of a man, by Eugen Gauss, untitled.
1946 26.75in (68cm) high S

An untitled mobile metal sculpture by Alexander Calder.
CC

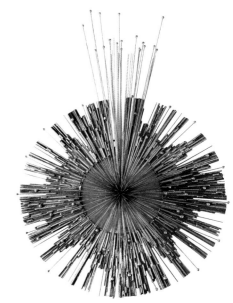

Atom-inspired mixed metal 'Shooting Star' wall sculpture by Curtis Jere.
58in (147.5cm) high I

HARRY BERTOIA DOUBLE GONG

Harry Bertoia began producing sculptures in his spare time while working at the Point Loma Naval Technical Lab and continued to do so when he joined Knoll Associates in 1950. Knoll exhibited his sculptures the following year and commissions followed. His early sculptures were abstract but in the late 1960s he began to experiment with tonal sculptures that make a sound when touched, beaten or moved.

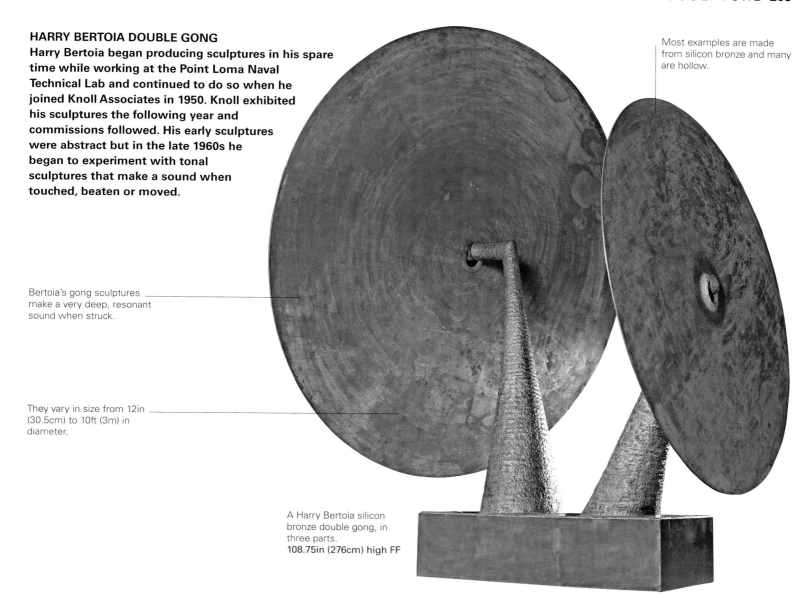

Most examples are made from silicon bronze and many are hollow.

Bertoia's gong sculptures make a very deep, resonant sound when struck.

They vary in size from 12in (30.5cm) to 10ft (3m) in diameter.

A Harry Bertoia silicon bronze double gong, in three parts.
108.75in (276cm) high FF

A copper and glass fusion sculpture, by Claire Falkenstein.
c1968 11in (28cm) high V

sculpture. Moore's work, which was concerned with human destiny, featured abstract, organic forms representing reclining figures, a mother and child, the family and the figure as landscape. Hepworth depicted the human form using the free assembly of formal elements – space, weight and texture – and used simplified, abstract and often pierced forms.

Eugen Gauss was equally comfortable working in the mediums of bronze, marble or steel. He is especially celebrated for his marble nude sculptures, which cleverly combine innovative abstraction and the traditional taste for naturalism.

Claire Falkenstein, who had created some of the earliest non-objective sculptures in the USA during the 1930s, began to experiment with glass and copper in the late 1950s. She discovered she could virtually 'fuse' chunks of colored glass with copper tubing by heating them together in a kiln. This tubing – bent, welded and hammered with pieces of glass melted within it – became her unique medium, with which she created many of her abstract 'thorny thicket' forms. The sunburst form was one of Falkenstein's favorite motifs, and it is perhaps the best illustration of a concept that she called 'expanding space.'

Technology

There was a technological explosion in the years that followed World War Two, leading to a revolution in private homes and office environments. Consumers sought to surround themselves with all manner of beautifully designed, state-of-the-art electrical appliances designed for modern living and communications. Globally, the precepts of 'Good Design' were now applied to a wide range of gadgetry, from televisions to coffee makers .

INDUSTRIAL DESIGN

The 1950s and 1960s saw a phenomenal increase in the number of industrially designed products being manufactured for the domestic and commercial scenes. Vacuum cleaners, food mixers, televisions, record players, hairdryers and electric razors all became standard features of the home, while offices were encouraged to keep up with the latest developments in typewriter and telephone technology. The demand for such products encouraged manufacturers to make the most of new materials and processes to produce wares more quickly and more cheaply than ever before. With built-in obsolescence, pieces also became easier and cheaper to replace.

Many designers took their lead from the United States, where the optimism that followed the Second World War appeared to be unshakeable. Already established as designers in the interwar years, Raymond Loewy (the "Father of Industrial Design") and Henry Dreyfuss had dominated the field in the USA and now served as role models for a new generation of designers. A master of reworking the appearance of a product to extend its shelf life, Loewy showed that the appearance of a product was as important as its function, perhaps more so in this era of the beautiful home. He believed that "between two products equal in price, function, and quality, the better looking will outsell the other". Such was his success that it is claimed that at the peak of his career over 75% of Americans came into contact with one or more of his products every day.

Henry Dreyfuss designed the innovative Bell telephone in 1937 in which both receiver and speaker were housed in the same component. He was also an early pioneer of ergonomics, a science which came to play such an important role in the post war years.

DEVELOPMENTS IN EUROPE

In Germany, product design was exemplified by the Braun appliance company, under the direction of German Industrial Designer Dieter Rams, who was appointed head of the design department in 1961. With a motto "Less Design is More Design" Rams reduced all of Braun's products to their simplest forms. The function of a piece was paramount, its use had to be clear from the very start. Basic, often geometric forms, spare use of color,

Color and style marry in this Trimphone telephone. The dial was replaced by buttons in 1974.
1964 7.75in (20cm) long B

and careful consideration as to a product's final application were all key components of the company's design process.

The recent developments in the production of plastics offered ideal materials for producing the ultra-smooth, flat, clean-line surfaces that epitomized Braun's wares. User-friendly, yet almost clinical in appearance, many of Braun's

JVC 'Videosphere' television, inspired by the space helmets worn for the 1969 lunar landing.
c1970 12.5in (32cm) high E

Dieter Rams brought pared-down, functional design to the home, including this Braun coffee grinder.
1960s 10.75in (27.5cm) high A

award-winning designs have become timeless classics. A similar approach was adopted by Jakob Jensen in Denmark, in his designs for sleek, slim-line audio equipment for Bang & Olufsen.

VERSATILE PLASTICS

The versatility of the exciting new plastics that had burst onto the scene, proved irresistible to designers of the avant-garde. This was a time of Pop culture and the Space Race, where designers were catering for a new youth-oriented market. The latest plastics were ideal materials for them, as they were cheap and durable, colorful and malleable – perfect for creating all manner of trendy, highly covetable domestic appliances. These included the Pop-styled cube televisions designed by Marco Zanuso and Richard Sapper for Brionvega in Italy in 1964 to Japanese televisions modeled on spacemen's helmets which were first seen in 1970.

Designers did not lose sight of the need for their pieces to be functional and user-friendly, but they imbued their designs with a more organic, sculptural look. Biomorphic forms introduced an ergonomic element to the designs, as was evident in designs like the very influential Swedish Ericofon telephone, where the entire mechanism – dial, receiver and speaker are housed in one single component.

ERICOFON TELEPHONE

The Ericofon – nicknamed the 'Cobra' because it was shaped like the rearing snake – has been named one of the best industrial designs of the 20th century by the Museum of Modern Art in New York . Based on a 1940s design, the all-in-one Ericofon was launched for domestic use in 1956 by the Swedish company Ericsson. It was designed to be easy and fun to use and remained the most popular one-piece telephone for over three decades. It was discontinued in 1972, though Ericsson released a version of the Ericofon to celebrate the company's 100th anniversary in 1976. It was re-issued again in 2001.

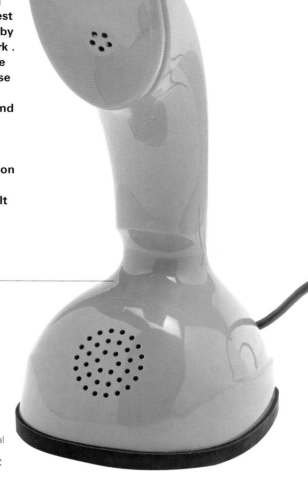

The rotary dial is hidden in the base of the telephone.

An Ericsson rotary dial Ericofon telephone.
8.25in (21cm) high C

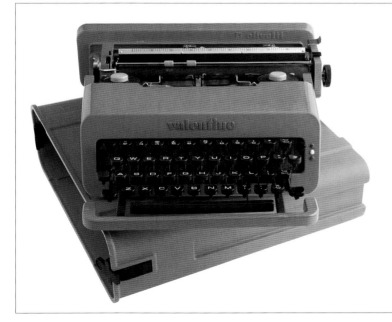

OLIVETTI TYPEWRITER

As the concept of brand awareness steadily grew, companies strove to make their products stand out above those of their competitors – not only using the latest materials and manufacturing processes, but also by employing well-known designers to create groundbreaking designs. Nowhere was this more the case than in Italy, where a number of perceptive companies, Olivetti and Brionvega among them, saw an immediate advantage in commissioning celebrated designers to make their products. Such practices guaranteed that a company's products reflected the very latest trends. Celebrated designers helped to revolutionize product design, introducing bold color to such mundane items as televisions, calculators and typewriters making them the absolute must-have products of their time. Advertisements were used to stress the fun and fashionable side of the designs.

Ettore Sottsass designed this colorful Olivetti Valentine typewriter.
c1969 16.25in (35cm) high C

MID-CENTURY MODERN

Sculptural lighting

New materials and advances in technology encouraged lighting designers to create inspired forms and shapes. The possibilities of the latest plastics meant a new range of sculptural shapes could be created for lighting. Practicality also played a part – open plan spaces required bright lights for illumination and lower lights to create an ambience.

A bulbous ribbed shade conceals the bulb in George Nelson's 'Bubble' lamp, designed for Herman Miller. **1955 20in (51cm) high D**

POLYMER COCOONS

The innovative materials used in the Pop furniture of the 1960s had a profound influence on lighting. One of these was liquid polymer. Its role as a protective material for shipping in New York Harbor in the late Forties, presaged the plastic's importance as a cocooning agent in the space age of the late Sixties. In the United States, Herman Miller produced George Nelson's 'Bubble' lamps, which were created by spraying liquid polymer over a wire frame. Made in 1955, the Bubble lamp was intended to be wall mounted and had a walnut panel and an adjustable-height tubular-aluminum arm.

Liquid polymer's central place in lighting design resonated in Italy where Flos – conceived by Dino Gavina and Cesare Cassina in 1960 – linked up with many top designers. One of the company's most notable products was the 'Gatto' table lamp – designed as a pair by Achille Castiglioni – which had a corseted wire frame concealed by a sprayed plastic cover. Joe Colombo, meanwhile, employed

plastic's versatility in his 1960s table lamp for Kartell. Its silvered plastic base echoed the chrome of earlier modernist light fittings, while its shade was of opaque plastic. Moreover, the way in which each element was welded into an organic shape was inspired by Gae Aulenti's 'Pipistrello' table lamp for Martinelli. This lamp featured a black-enameled metal base and a white, hard plastic shade. It also had a telescopic shaft, so that it could be used as a table or floor lamp.

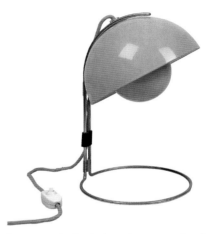

An orange plastic shade casts a warm glow from Verner Panton's 'Flowerpot' lamp for Louis Poulsen. **1968 13.5in (34cm) high G**

COMMERCIAL DESIGNS

While designers were preoccupied with the technological advances in their materials, many were also keen to make products that would be a commercial success rather than a critical one. High sales were seen to be a better reward than winning design awards. As a result they often created pieces which were icons of their time. For example, Vico Magistretti's use of bright colors and geometric shapes epitomized the Pop culture of the Sixties. He reinforced his preference for imaginative design with his 'Dalu' table lamps of 1969. Produced by Artemide, they were molded from hard red plastic in a single piece and were a clever take on spacemen's helmets.

In striking contrast to Magistretti's more prosaic approach to his work, Serge Manzon considered his objects as 'living aesthetic sculptures'. He covered the stand of his 'Sculptural' lamp with purplewood veneer, while the shade is made of ivory- and red-lacquered metal semicircles. Manzon went on to produce a range of "perfect" simple furniture forms in the 1970s, echoing the quest for ideal design of designers at the Bauhaus in Germany.

A white plastic hemispherical shade, and pivoting shaft, area feature of Franco Albini table lamp. **18.25in (46.5cm) high G**

Ivory enameled shades on a black metal base form a pair of Boris Lacroix table lamps. **19.5in (49.5cm) high I**

CASTIGLIONI BROTHERS TABLE LAMPS

Until 1952, the three Castiglioni brothers, Livio, Pier Giacomo and Achille worked together and were extremely influential, helping to establish the Milan Triennale exhibitions, the Compasso d'Oro awards and the Assocation of Industrial Design. When Livio left, his younger brothers continued to design together. Their designs included a range of minimalist lamps, such as the 'Luminator', 'Arco', and 'Taccia'. So popular was their 'Gatto' lamp, first designed in 1960, it was re-released by Flos in 2005.

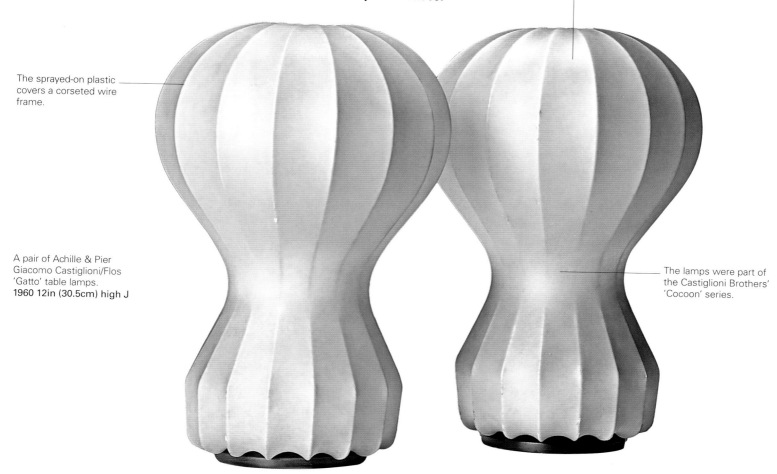

The sprayed-on plastic covers a corseted wire frame.

The covering of the lamps resembles a hot air balloon and creates a diffused light.

A pair of Achille & Pier Giacomo Castiglioni/Flos 'Gatto' table lamps. 1960 12in (30.5cm) high J

The lamps were part of the Castiglioni Brothers' 'Cocoon' series.

PAPER LANTERNS

It is perhaps no surprise that Isamu Noguchi, the Japanese-American sculptor, saw lighting as a fascinating medium to work with. He is reported to have said: "Everything is sculpture. Any material, any idea without hindrance born into space, I consider sculpture". He worked to align Eastern paper lamps with Western designs. An example of this approach was his Akari standard lamp design of 1951, which used paper made from mulberry bark and was produced in Gifu, Japan. It was a tubular, black-enameled metal design covered with Japanese paper and was inspired by the sculptor Constantin Brancusi's Infinite Column sculpture at Tirgu-Jiu in Romania. Noguchi was particularly fascinated by the idea of light as sculpture and said of his own lamps that "they seem to float, casting their light as in passing".

More broadly, the nascent drug-taking culture of the period also found expression in lighting design. Lights made from ABS hard plastic by Cesare Casati and Emanuele Ponzio resembled over-sized pills. Known as 'Pilloloa' lights, they were set on plastic ring stands and could be angled into different positions on the floor. The original and funky design was a cross between practical lighting and artistic sculpture. While the form was unusual, it conformed to the fresh design stance of the period.

Another characteristic of the Pop Art movement was the trend for taking everyday objects and enlarging them into ones of ridiculous proportions. Gaetano Pesce's 1970 'Moloch' floor lamp was a huge version of the 'Luxo' or 'Anglepoise' desk lamp he had designed. At 90.5in (230cm) tall, it scrupulously copied every detail of the original, and it could fill a room. Pesce explained: "Moloch was conceived for a practical need: to illuminate large American skyscraper lobbies".

Linear Lighting

Restrained and designed to be unobtrusive, futuristic lighting nevertheless included some eye-catching designs. Using aluminum and steel to create a minimalist look, designers and manufacturers created individualistic designs which transformed interiors. Often inspired by the Space Race they seem as futuristic today as they did when they were first designed.

GOING IN TO SPACE

Space exploration permeated mid-century lighting design which was characterized by futuristic objects. Designer Verner Panton produced several pieces that were emblematic of the period. One example was the pendant Moon lampshade produced by Danish firm Louis Poulsen in 1960. Nine white-lacquered rings revolved around a vertical axis and imparted bright or muted lighting, similar to the illumination of a waxing and waning moon. Panton also created a 'VP-Globe' lamp, which consisted of aluminum disks within a plexiglass sphere. The pervasive theme of space, saucers and satellites also led to designs such as Panton's 'Flower Pot' in 1968, notable for its psychedelic swirling patterns and deep blue and orange colors. Serge Manzon's metal lamp was inspired by flying saucers.

Many of the bold mid-century lighting designs were the antitheses of earlier ones, when the emphasis was on unobtrusive lighting that contributed to a harmonious interior. A good example of the prevailing individualistic flair was the PH Artichoke designed by Paul Henningson in 1958. This stunning piece was made up of 72 individual steel leaves which were placed on a cage of struts so as to represent the leaves of an artichoke. Originally commissioned for the Langelinie Pavilion Restaurant in Copenhagen Harbor, it was produced for retail by Louis Poulsen.

A NEW RESTRAINT

The design force behind the Italian company Arteluce – set up in Milan in 1939 – was Gino Sarfatti, who was responsible for most of the company's early designs. He sometimes worked with Victoria Vigano and together they produced sleek lighting designs. Many of Sarfatti's pieces were made from metal rods which give it a hand-crafted feel. Sarfatti often used colored shades which add a vibrant note. Later, the Arteluce worked with designers such as Marco Zanuso and Franco Albino.

Sarfatti also designed for Arredoluce, which was formed in 1946, and developed a more restrained treatment of lighting. With leading designers such as Sarfatti, Arredoluce embodied innovative style.

A Space Age brass and enameled metal lamp, by A. W & Marion Geller, for Heifetz.
36.5in (93cm) high N

A partially etched circular glass diffuser and polished steel shaft bring clean, modern lines to this Fontana Arte ceiling light.
62in (157.5cm) high J

Shades and handles in primary colors direct the light from a Gino Sarfatti for Arredoluce 'Triennale' three-arm brass floor lamp.
62.25in (158 cm) high M

The company helped to establish the Milan Triennale, which introduced many new designs produced by Italian firms. While fashionable interiors were home to Arredoluce's colored shades, the company's 'Cobra' lamp was an example of its more abstract products. As Arteluce's pre-eminence faded, it was taken over by Flos, which was home to the designs of the Castiglioni brothers.

Other fashionable lighting was made by Fontata Arte, which had been founded by Gio Ponti in 1932 and O-luce, founded in 1945 by Giuseppe Ostuni. O-luce commissioned designers including Joe Colombo and Marco Zanuso. The design company Azucena was set up to manufacture lighting and other furnishings by the architects and designers Luigi Caccia Dominioni.

SIMPLER STYLES

French sculptor Serge Mouille advocated a simpler style, as he considered the prevailing Italian designs as 'too complicated'. His aluminum shades allowed light to be dispersed over a wide area. Excited by the introduction of neon strip lighting, he experimented with both fluorescent and incandescent light. Such was influence of Mouille, whose most famous designs include the 'Oeil', 'Flammes' and 'Saturn' lamps, he was entrusted with providing lighting for universities and cathedrals.

ARREDOLUCE COBRA LAMP
While many fashionable interiors bore Arredoluce's colored lamp shades, the company also had a range of more abstract products, many of them designed by Angelo Lelli. He designed lamps for the company during the 1950s and 1960s, including the 'Cobra' lamp with its Cyclopic magnetic shade.

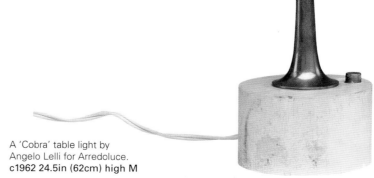

The brass stand features a Space Age 'eye socket' magnetic metal shade which can be adjusted to direct the light.

The central eye is surrounded by a ring of small lights which illuminate simultaneously.

A corseted brass tripod base and simple paper shade create the clean lines of T.H. Robsjohn-Gibbings table lamp for Hansen.
21.5in (54.5cm) high M

A 'Cobra' table light by Angelo Lelli for Arredoluce.
c1962 24.5in (62cm) high M

MID-CENTURY MODERN

LIGHTING GALLERY

Lighting was designed to be part of an interior and was used to create ambience within a room, as 'task' lighting illuminate a desk or work space, or as a sculptural form. Many designers were inspired to create futuristic designs that were inspired by space ships. Others took the latest plastics and used them to create futuristic, organic shapes. The results were inventive, glamorous and the height of fashion.

The clean lines of a chrome sphere form a 'Stilnovo' hanging lamp.
68in (173cm) high I

Futuristic enameled metal shades, on brass and walnut tripod base on a Lightolier table lamp by Gerald Thurston.
16.5in (42cm) wide L

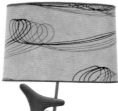

An American organic form table lamp, with original printed paper shade.
1950s 29.5in (75cm) high F

Futuristic brushed nickel table lamp with ribbed glass shade by Fontana Arte.
23in (55cm) high K

Blown-glass disc shades add color to a Vistosi floor lamp.
56.5in (143.5cm) high E

The spiraling brass stem and adjustable enameled metal shades resemble a futuristic stem of flowers. Arteluce floor lamp designed by Gino Sarfatti.
81in (206cm) high Q

A sculptural walnut French Rispal floor lamp, with suspended white spherical paper shade.
1950s 65in (165cm) high L

Swedish sleek teak tripod floor lamps by Luxus, with black enameled shades.
58in (147cm) high R

Futuristic Arredoluce three-arm polished chrome floor lamp, with black leather-covered handles and shaft, on white marble base.
69in (175cm) high H

The metal is covered in olive-green enamel.

Grossman was skilled at making heavy materials appear weightless. Here the substantial, enameled metal has been used to create an elegant lamp.

Space Age Italian polished brass floor lamp, with frosted glass diffuser.
80in (203cm) high I

GRETA MAGNUSSON GROSSMAN LAMP
A Swedish-born designer and architect, Greta Magnusson Grossman studied at Stockholm's prestigious School of Industrial Design. She was then apprenticed in a furniture factory and was the first woman to receive a prize for furniture design from the Swedish Society of Industrial Design. She and her husband settled in Los Angeles in 1941. She designed furniture and lamps for a number of companies, including Ralph O. Smith Co., for whom she created the 'Grasshopper' and the 'Cobra' lamp, which won a Good Design award in 1950.

Sleek floorlamp, with spherical plasticized paper shade hanging from a curving support on a black finished metal wire tripod stand.
1950s 55.25in (140cm) high E

Each leg of the tripod base ends in a disc-shaped foot.

A 'Grasshopper' metal floor lamp, by Greta Magnusson Grossman for Ralph O. Smith.
50.5in (128cm) high M

Posters

By the late 1940s many European poster designers had developed a new design style which put an emphasis on bold, simplified images with a humorous twist. This spirit continued into the 1950s and 1960s when visually elegant posters promoted everything from the latest 'package holiday' destinations to stylish shoe brands.

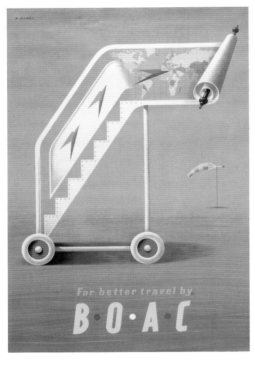

THE NEW STYLE

One of the most iconic and witty posters of the post-war years was produced by French artist Raymond Savignac in collaboration with graphic designer Bernard Villemot in 1948. Their most iconic poster was for Monsavon soap. It caught the public's imagination and made their names. Villemot worked for Bally, Perrier and Orangina among others creating humorous designs such as a woman with Perrier-bottles for spectacles. He created a total of 25 posters for Orangina.

Savignac started work under the direction of Adolph Mouron Cassandre. His work was noted for its simplicity and wit. This was at odds with the new style that was starting to appear in the United States which favored a photographic realism. French designer Jacques Auriac also worked for Bally as well as Gitanes and Air Afrique. He is known for his bold, colorful and extremely graphic posters.

Another designer who believed posters could achieve the biggest impact from the simplest design was the British artist Abram Games. He claimed: "I wind the spring and the public, in looking at the poster, will have that spring released in its mind." He was made Official War Artist during World War Two and created more than 100 posters for the war effort, including creating the 'blonde bombshell' for the ATS (Auxiliary Territorial Service). His posters, produced during and after the war, feature a sophisticated modern design and often use wit to get their message across. Games designed posters for London Transport and B.O.A.C. and created the emblem for the 1951 Festival of Britain.

After the war, posters increasingly gave prominence to what became known as "corporate identity". The graphic designer credited with establishing corporate identity as a necessity for any business was the American Paul Rand. His work included

Abram Games poster for B.O.A.C., shows surreal symbolism as a set of airline steps leads to a map of the world.
1952 30in (75cm) high K

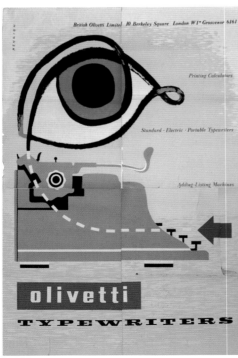

The link between the eye and the machine is created by a white dotted line in this post-Surrealist image by Frederic Henri Kay Henrion for Olivetti Typewriters.
1950s 119.5in (299cm) high L

This Bernard Villemot poster for Bally shoes created a stir as, although it focusses on the shoes, the positioning hints at a kiss. The flat planes of color on black are typical of Villemot.
1960s 24in (61cm) high C

TOM ECKERSLEY POSTER

By the 1930s, London Transport had become one of the country's most significant patrons of graphic design: Tom Eckersley was one of the designers who benefited from this, designing for them from 1935 to 1995. His designs included 'Cut Travelling Time' in 1968, a poster announcing the new Victoria line, then the most advanced underground system in the world, boasting computer-controlled trains and automatic ticket barriers. In his 1954 book, Eckersley wrote: "Really fine work never dates: it is only the posters which depend solely on the particular techniques of their period which today appear dull and dated."

A London Transport poster designed by Tom Eckersley of Eckersley Studio.
c1968 40in (101.5cm) high l

The scissors cutting the text in half get the message across simply and effectively.

The simple blocks of color are eye-catching and make the poster easy to read.

The London Underground logo replaces the pivot on the scissors.

the logos for IBM (International Business Machines) and UPS (United Parcel Service).

The pioneers of corporate design in Britain included Frederic Henri Kay Henrion and Hans Schleger. Henrion arrived in Britain from Germany in 1939, having studied in Paris with Paul Colin. His witty and revolutionary style incorporated elements of photomontage. Some of his work was inspired by the Surrealists and his poster for Olivetti Typewriters featured a giant eye and typewriter. Schleger had previously worked in Berlin and New York. His witty, innovative posters advertized The Ministry of Food, London Transport and Shell. Some of his designs feature

photomontage. Schleger had seen how effective what we now call "corporate identity" could be while working in Germany and the United States. He used this approach to great effect in his posters and his design for the 'circle-and-bar' symbol used to mark London Transport's bus stops.

TAKING TO THE SKIES

Air travel began to eclipse cruise liners as the preferred mode of long-distance transport during the 1950s. Posters promoted airlines in bright colors, such as Tom Eckersley's design for BOAC, which carried the slogan "It's a small world by

speedbird", and showed a globe with an abstract bird-plane flying past it. Another distinctive poster was Lee-Elliott's British European Airways, "The Key to Europe", which was produced in 1946.

In the 1960s, brightly colored, psychedelic posters, were used to publicize rock events and other "happenings". These kaleidoscopic posters typically incorporated surrealistic imagery with elements of Art Nouveau. The first examples were produced in San Francisco and were designed by underground artists such as Alton Kelley, Chet Helms and Stanley Mouse. They typified the music and drugs culture of the time.

Textiles

Mid-century Modern textiles celebrated a new beginning after the destruction and chaos of World War Two. They drew on the positive aspects of contemporary life – scientific discoveries, adventurous Modern art and the vitality of popular culture. In this optimistic, forward-looking environment designers created many of the most memorable textiles of the 20th century.

A SCIENTIFIC BASIS

The 1950s were an age of spectacular advance in technology and medicine. Scientific discoveries fired the imagination of post-war designers who created fabric patterns loosely based on atoms and other elemental forms. Floral prints were superseded by highly stylized botanical designs inspired by seed heads, bark, twigs and dry leaves. The emerging Space Race led to a wide-spread fascination with the Solar system and space ships, echoed in design. Edward Fields, the American carpet-maker, who developed the area rug, is renowned for his series of futuristic pile carpet designs with a celestial theme.

In reaction against the drab uniforms and austerity of World War Two, a keen appetite for colorful textiles took hold. Reds, blues, yellows, and dark greens dominated against a neutral ground. Arresting color combinations such as mustard, fawn and light gray accented in black and white were typical of the era.

Modern art made post-war fabric designers think more radically. The expressive colors and complex linear forms used by Paul Klee and Joan Miró were especially influential. Modern art had such an impact that many major textile firms actually commissioned designs from leading artists. British firm Ascher gained a reputation for inviting celebrity painters and sculptors of the day including Pablo Picasso, Henri Matisse and Henry Moore to design experimental fabrics.

A mounted Mira-Spectrum 'Large Curve' velvet fabric, designed by Verner Panton.
c1970 47.25in (120cm) wide J

John Piper large 'Chiesa Della Salute' curtains, produced by Sanderson Fabrics Ltd.
1959 Each piece 78.75in (200 cm) long NPA

A large Edward Fields area rug, with geometric patterns in yellow-green, blue and orange, signed on selvage.
216in (548.5cm) long L

An upholstered tête-à-tête, by Edward Wormley, for Dunbar, upholstered in floral fabric by Jack Lenor Larsen.
80.75in (205cm) wide O

Improved screen-printing technology revolutionized the printing of post-war fabrics. For the first time fabric manufacturers could replicate their watercolor brush strokes and the inky smudge marks from their pens, turning a designer's artwork directly into a printed fabric.

ARCHITECTURAL INSPIRATION

During the 1950s, abstract organic motifs generally prevailed but some cutting-edge textile designers drew inspiration from architecture. High profile Italian designer Piero Fornasetti's extraordinary trompe l'oeil fabrics (see pp174-175) often featured images of old buildings. Prominent British artist John Piper produced a number of fabrics printed with his haunting romantic architectural studies for firms like David Whitehead and Sanderson.

At first these contemporary patterns were predominantly used on home-furnishing fabrics. However they were so fresh and stylish that women, who had been used to turning old curtains to clothes as result of rationing, were very happy to use them for dressmaking. Entrepreneurial new clothing firms like Britain's Horrockes Fashions and Emilio Pucci in Italy were quick to pick up on this phenomenon and made names for themselves by providing patterned fashions ready-made.

In the 1960s large-scale geometric and psychedelic patterns were favored for textile design. Bright colors from acid yellow to day-glo pink and deep purple were incredibly popular. Op art by painters such as Victor Vasaérly with its undulating geometric patterns was a key influence. Danish furnishing and interior designer Verner Panton's vivid geometric fabrics typify the Op art style and influenced textile design internationally, especially in Britain.

Other fabric designs borrowed imagery from 1960s popular culture. Victorian, Art Nouveau and Art Deco designs were nostalgically evoked, too. The growing Hippie movement encouraged ethnically inspired designs. Jack Lenor Larsen's designs for woven and printed fabrics reflect this eclectic range of sources to sensational effect making him a dominant figure in American textile design at the time.

LUCIENNE DAY 'CALYX' FABRIC

'Calyx' is probably the most acclaimed fabric of the 1950s. Named after the leaf-like structure that protects a flower bud, this highly abstracted botanical played a seminal role in defining the look of printed textiles after World War Two. Retailed by Heal's, a progressive furniture shop, 'Calyx' first attracted attention at the 1951 Festival of Britain. It went on to win numerous international awards at events such as the Milan Triennale and helped make Day one of Britain's most successful and sought after fabric designers.

A panel of Lucienne Day 'Calyx' pattern fabric, in brown. c1950 48.5in (123cm) wide F

The fabric's spindly lines and curved shapes were designed to complement the lightweight appearance and graceful curves of her husband Robin's furniture.

The abstract depiction of the flowers influenced many other fabric designers.

"A table may need four legs to function, but no one can tell me the four legs have to look the same."
Ettore Sottsass

Postmodernism to Contemporary

American based architect, Frank Gehry's design for the Ray and Maria Stata Center at the Massachusetts Institute of Technology is a confusion of brick, mirror-surface steel, brushed aluminum, brightly colored painted walls and corrugated metal. The walls and columns are set an angles to each other, with random curves.

Postmodernism to Contemporary

Where the designers of the 1950s and 1960s had softened the harsh lines of Modernism, those of the 1970s and 1980s entirely rejected the belief that 'form follows function'. The eclectic, irreverent, fun pieces of Postmodernism were highly individualistic statements, rather than life-improving machinery. All notions of what constituted good design were disregarded, as wood and plastic, high technology and traditional crafts, the past and the future collided in a celebration of color and outrageous forms.

CYNICAL TIMES

The 1960s had been a time of space exploration, Beatles tunes and Flower Power. As the decade drew to a close the optimism and sense of progress that typified the post-war years were being replaced with a deep cynicism. Interest rates were increasing, inflation was rising and the number of unemployed was growing at an alarming rate. The United States' involvement in the Vietnam War had escalated out of control: their technological superiority failing to gain them an easy victory. For the first time scientists were warning about the damage being done to the planet. Then came the energy crisis.

In 1973 the oil-rich Arab nations, angry at the West's support for Israel, cut oil supplies in protest. An energy crisis ensued in the United States, Europe and Japan with dramatic price rises. Plastic, that wonderful new material, was now far less affordable. Consumers – many hit by gasolene rationing – lost further

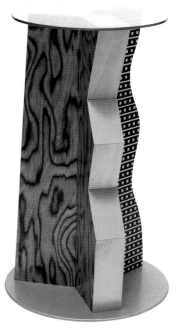

Ettore Sottsass gave a mix of shapes and laminates to the stand of this 'Ivory' table which has a circular glass top.
1985 40in (100cm) high L

confidence and, by 1975, a global recession was underway. The 'Summer of Love' seemed a long time ago. In the place of optimistic hippies stood the new Punk movement, which grew out of a strong sense of dissatisfaction and alienation. Punks, conceptual artists and satirical writers all came to the same conclusion: it was time for the world to change.

ANTI-DISPOSABILITY

There were effectively two apparently contradictory strands of design in the 1970s: Anti-Design and High Tech. The members of Anti-Design, which was based in Italy, were frustrated with a society they saw as damaged and dysfunctional. Some exponents created bright, colorful kitsch furniture to please the masses; others made pieces that were deliberately awkward. These pieces mocked high-minded Modernism and – it was hoped – would force consumers to make their own furniture rather than buy it.

By contrast, in the United States, the High Tech movement (named after *The Industrial Style Sourcebook* by Joan Kron and Suzanne Slesin) advocated a return to the severity of early Modernism as a reaction to cost-cutting by manufacturers. The movement also believed that timeless classic designs would stop the culture of disposability that was destroying the planet.

THE BIRTH OF POSTMODERNISM

By the end of the 1970s the theories of the Anti-Design and High Tech movements were being replaced. Designers began to consider the possibility that their work could be used to communicate ideas. *Mythologies*, by French philosopher and critic, Roland Barthes, had been translated into English in 1972 and Barthes's theories on semiotics (the study of signs and symbols as a means of cultural communication) had gradually permeated society. It was suggested that if objects were imbued with symbolism, users might well relate to them on a psycological level. This idea was willingly adopted by a host of designers who were eager to communicate their message.

Some designers advocated looking to the past. Though Modernism had also borrowed motifs from earlier styles, the new designers were interested in the symbolic value of these revival styles, rather than their structural qualities.

In 1966 the American architect Robert Venturi published *Complexity and Contradiction in Architecture*. It has become regarded as the seminal document of the Postmodern movement. Venturi's "gentle manifesto" put the case against "the puritanically

A limited edition 'Pink Cigar' asymmetric table centerpiece designed by Peter Shire for Vistosi. Bright colors and asymmetrical forms, made up of geometric shapes, are typical of his work.
c1985 16.5in (42cm) high L

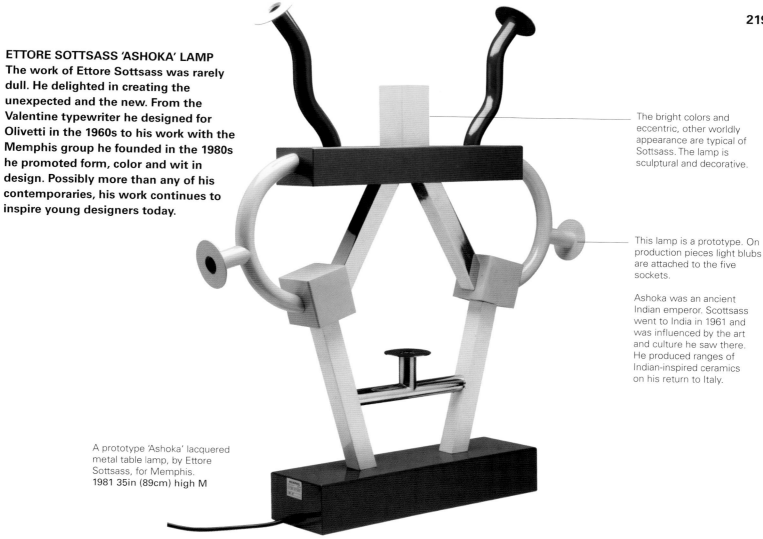

ETTORE SOTTSASS 'ASHOKA' LAMP
**The work of Ettore Sottsass was rarely
dull. He delighted in creating the
unexpected and the new. From the
Valentine typewriter he designed for
Olivetti in the 1960s to his work with the
Memphis group he founded in the 1980s
he promoted form, color and wit in
design. Possibly more than any of his
contemporaries, his work continues to
inspire young designers today.**

The bright colors and eccentric, other worldly appearance are typical of Sottsass. The lamp is sculptural and decorative.

This lamp is a prototype. On production pieces light blubs are attached to the five sockets.

Ashoka was an ancient Indian emperor. Scottsass went to India in 1961 and was influenced by the art and culture he saw there. He produced ranges of Indian-inspired ceramics on his return to Italy.

A prototype 'Ashoka' lacquered metal table lamp, by Ettore Sottsass, for Memphis.
1981 35in (89cm) high M

moral language" of late Modernism. He asserted that architecture had been simplified and clarified to the point of being separated "from the experience of life and the needs of society". Where Ludwig Mies van der Rohe saw that "less is more" Venturi claimed "less is a bore". By 1980 the design world was ready to listen. From the late 1960s there had been a movement away from Mid-Century Modernism. The old tenets had served their purpose and a new dogma had been installed. It has become known as Postmodernism.

ALCHIMIA AND MEMPHIS
The resulting anarchy of styles is best seen in the work of the Alchimia and Memphis design groups. Founded in 1976, the designers of Alchimia reveled in clashing colors, patterns and awkward forms, across a range of disciplines.

Led by the architect and designer Alessandro Mendini, the members of Alchimia produced work that was a "confusion of craft and industry", combining expensive and inexpensive materials in pieces of tremendous style. Mendini stated: "The act of making signs is everything." Though never a commercial succes, Alchimia was extremely influential (no design discipline remained unaffected) and laid the foundations for the Memphis group.

Based in Milan, but made up of a group of international designers, Memphis's leader was former Anti-Design and Alchimia member Ettore Sottsass. He summed the group up as follows: "Memphis tries to separate the object from the idea of functionalism. It is an ironic approach to the modern notion of philosophical pureness. In other words, a table may need four legs to function, but no one can tell me that the four legs have to look the same."

In the same way as their Alchimia predecessors, Memphis designers combined expensive and inexpensive materials. But they also mixed motifs from many cultures and periods of history to create work that was part functional, part art and part fashion. Witty, irreverent, colorful, when the movement launched itself as the "New International Style" it caused a sensation.

The Memphis group challenged what was expected of design. Wood was covered with plastic laminates in opposition to the way the mid-century modernists had worshipped its integrity as a material and the quality of its grain. Often laminates in several exotic finishes were used on the same piece to create outrageous effects, making the point that it was not necessary for the designer to be true to the materials.

POSTMODERN PRINCIPALS

Alchimia and Memphis were not alone in their rejection of form and function. Robert Venturi's simplified re-creations of historical chairs – from Queen Anne to Art Deco – made from bent wood laminates, exemplify this. They were designed in 1979 for Knoll International to showcase American Postmodern design. Venturi, and fellow American architect Michael Graves, brought architectural forms into product design. Other designers used asymmetry of shape, structure, color and materials as a reaction against the Modernist symmetry.

With the stress on visual impact, designers experimented with a wide range of surface decorations, with plastic laminates (imitating wood grains, animal hides and exotic textiles) proving popular. Color was used to enhance the new modular furniture, although the bright colors of the 1980s became more subdued in the 1990s.

Humor was a source of inspiration. Clementine Hope printed the outline of an 18th century table onto the plain carcase of medium-density fiberboard (MDF) one. Pop Art and cartoon characters inspired anti-intellectual, ironic, provocative designs that were the antithesis of those of Walter Gropius and the Bauhaus-inspired school of design.

Mickey Mouse inspired the 'Garriri' black leather and metal framed chair by Javier Mariscal for AKABA S.A.
1988 38in (96.5cm) high NPA

A CHANGE IN VALUES

Economies around the world began to pick up again in the early 1980s, but there was to be no immediate return to the sense of international community and cooperation that had marked design in the 1950s and 1960s. In the United States and the United Kingdom, President Ronald Reagan and Prime Minister Margaret Thatcher promoted capitalism and entrepreneurship. Doing things for the common good had been replaced by self interest.

The 1987 economic crash caused a further re-evaluation of beliefs. The environment became an important factor again following the 1986 Chernobyl nuclear reactor disaster and the discovery that the hole in the ozone layer was growing. Recycling in design returned to popularity. The 1981 designs of London-based Israeli designer Ron Arad, which included chairs made from car seats or corrugated cardboard, had never seemed more relevant.

A reaction to the excesses of Postmodernism brought about a return to Minimalism as designers and consumers grew tired of the visual anarchy. Clear glass or acrylic, untreated wood and metal, were all used to achieve this look, which aimed to be true to its materials. A new international style came about. Called "New Minimalism" or "Dematerialisation" or "Late Modern" it featured clean, uncluttered lines.

A Wendell Castle console table, with Caligari-decorated top, ebonized crossbars with metal rings and inverted V-shaped exotic wood supports.
1987 68in (170cm) wide N

A side table, comprized of panels of red and clear plastic clipped together, designed by Gaetano Pesce.
2002 19.5in (49cm) high NPA

TIMELINE

1976 The Punk movement starts to get global recognition as young people grow frustrated with society and its traditions.

1981 The Memphis design group, founded by Ettore Sottsass, holds its first collection in Milan.

1985 Philippe Starck's first chair designs are manufactured by Driade in Italy.

1987 The American stock market crashes.

A Frank Gehry for Knoll tall-back laminated bentwood chair, with enameled finish.
1992 43in (109cm) high G

RETURN TO HANDCRAFTS

The new sophistication in plastic injection molding allowed the production of a sleek finish. Simultaneously, the return to handcrafting which had happened in the late 1970s as a reaction against the machine aesthetic and unfashionable nature of plastics, metamorphosed in the 1980s and 1990s into the cult of the handmade. The newly affluent, buoyed by the profits of Wall Street and the City of London, had the money to pay for costly handmade, one-off items.

By the 1990s designers became fascinated by the potential of computer-aided design. Drawing up detailed designs and making models is no loner necessary with computer-aided design producing smooth and technical electronic consumer goods and decorative arts. At the same time, laser cutting allows for a precision and uniformity.

Communication over the internet and by mobile phone increased the speed and contributed to the international nature of design. Some websites act as idea generators and "weapons of mass communication" to allow ideas to be shared and assimilated immediately. Materials can be easily sourced from all over the world and even manufacturing can be (and often is) relocated to low-wage countries.

OUR CONTEMPORARY WORLD

The early years of the 21st century saw the continuing rise of the cult of the designer, which promoted expensive one-offs as a means of publicising wealth and individualism. But as economies faltered in 2008 visible displays of affluence began to lose their luster.

Designers are no longer tied to one discipline. Product designers such as Philippe Starck, Marc Newson and Tom Dixon design furniture, interiors, and accessories for clients around the world, becoming household names in the process. Meanwhile companies such as Cappellini and Alessi promote design and designers. Other designers lend their famous names to products that can be purchased by the "man on the street" in his local supermarket.

Design has now become an important part of daily life. Many items, from ball-point pens to electric hand-driers, coffee-makers to shoe horns, have been given a "designer" look. This transformation has not always happened in the studio of a named designer. Often an anonymous hand is at work behind the mass-produced yet stylish products we use every day. They may not always work any more effectively than their "undesigned" predecessors, but they always look the part.

Postmodernism had been a style that only the very rich could afford. Now, at last, design is truly for everybody.

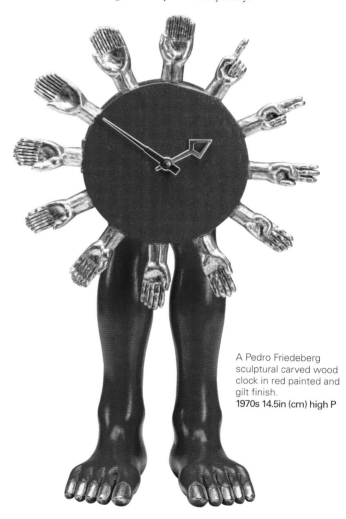

A Pedro Friedeberg sculptural carved wood clock in red painted and gilt finish.
1970s 14.5in (cm) high P

1989 The fall of the Berlin Wall heralds an end to the Cold War.

2000 By the end of the year more than 360,000,000 people worldwide use the Internet.

2009 Barack Obama is sworn in as the 44th President of the United States and its first African-American President.

Studio Alchimia

Murmurs of discontent began to emanate from the design world toward the end of the 1960s, particularly in Italy, where a number of anti-design groups formed. It was primarily architects who began to challenge the well-worn tenets of 'Good Design' that had dominated the post-war years. In its place they promoted 'Radical Design', the antithesis of modernism.

It was from this counter-culture that Studio Alchimia emerged, founded in 1976 by Italian architect, Alessandro Guerriero. Originally operating as a gallery showcasing cutting-edge designs, the Milan-based studio brought together a number of designers who sought to distance themselves intellectually from modernism. There was a feeling that modernism had run its course, that it was no longer avant-garde, but had rather become the stuff of consumerism, diluted in its application through the countless mass-produced goods that had flooded the market since the end of the World War Two.

EARLY EXHIBITIONS
The purpose of the gallery was for like-minded architects and designers to contribute one-off pieces for exhibition – in essence prototypes – that were totally experimental in their design and free from any constraints of the manufacturing process and mass production. Featuring work by Alessandro Mendini, Ettore Sottsass (see pp.224–225), Michele de Lucchi, and Andrea Branzi, among others,

the pieces on view certainly lived up to the studio's name. Italian for "alchemy" Guerriero's Alchimia sought, on one level, to produce highly desirable products from the cheapest and most kitsch of materials. Their rejection of modernism was clear from early exhibitions ironically entitled "Bau. Haus 1" and "Bau. Haus 2", in which classic Bauhaus furniture was audaciously parodied. Clean lines, purity of form and lack of surface decoration were replaced with bold use of color, dramatic patterning, mismatched legs and sloping surfaces. Ornamentation – the bugbear of the modernists – gained a new status, becoming a significant (if not the significant) feature of the pieces produced.

The idea was to provoke an emotional reaction in the user – be it laughter, complicity or even horror. Alchimia's designers wanted to reawaken the sensitivities of the consumer, which they felt had been numbed by the banal, characterless nature of the majority of goods that had been rolling off production lines. An energetic outburst, theirs was spontaneous,

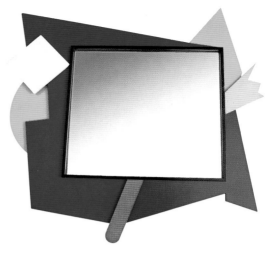

Brightly colored abstract shapes create the lacquered wood frame for an Alchimia 'Kandissa' mirror, designed by Alessandro Mendini in 1978.
c1978 39.5in (100cm) high NPA

creative and highly influential, and it was not long before the gallery became a design studio operating under its own steam.

A DRIVING FORCE
Alessandro Mendini became the group's intellectual driving force, setting an agenda of "redesigning" works from recent decades. In the early 1980s, he produced redesigns of such classics as Gerrit Rietveld's 'Zig-Zag' chair (giving it a cruciform back), Gio Ponti's 'Superleggera' chair (attaching colored pennants to the legs and stiles), and Marcel Breuer's 'Wassily' chair (adding superficial ornamentation). Other concepts included his *Mobili Infiniti* collection for which he invited designers to contribute a

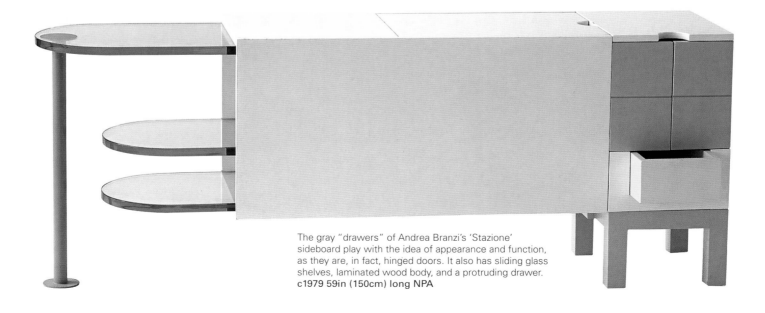

The gray "drawers" of Andrea Branzi's 'Stazione' sideboard play with the idea of appearance and function, as they are, in fact, hinged doors. It also has sliding glass shelves, laminated wood body, and a protruding drawer.
c1979 59in (150cm) long NPA

range of fixtures for pieces of furniture, which could then be applied and interchanged at whim by the user.

Studio Alchimia's success was all but over before the end of the 1980s. However, what had started as a small gallery in Milan became the most influential design studio of the late 1970s and early 1980s and laid the foundations for the Memphis design collective (see pp. 226–227) and the subsequent Postmodern movement that dominated the 1980s.

Colorful laminates decorate a 'Mikiolone – Nr. 2980' cocktail cabinet by Alessandro Mendini. The wood carcass stands on silver-gray enameled wooden legs, and has glass shelves. The cabinet's decorative appeal is more important than its practicality.
1983 65in (162.5cm) high P

Random transfer-applied dots and applied ceramic geometric shapes embellish a 'Mancini' ceramic vase designed by Alessandro Mendini.
1970s 12in (30.5cm) high K

The legs of this 'Atropo' table, designed by Alessandro Mendini, appear to be traditional turned wood but are gold colored metal. They provide a contrast to the hand-painted table top.
1984 28in (71cm) high O

Alessandro Mendini's 'Lassu' sculpture turns a simple chair into a work of art.
1983 11.5in (29cm) high NPA

Ettore Sottsass (1917–2007)

The Austrian born Italian designer Ettore Sottsass was always at the radical extreme of design. From the beginning of his career in the 1940s he made a significant contribution to design in every decade. However, what really earned him his place in the pantheon of 20th century masters is Memphis, the Postmodern design collective he founded which revolutionized the look of furnishing in the 1980s. Flamboyant, colorful and innovative he changed the face of design.

The free, sensual style of Ettore Sottsass's work was in part a reaction against the modernist style of his architect father. Ettore Sottsass senior was a leading member of the avantgarde Italian Rationalists, a group that promoted modernism in conflict with the Neo-classical styles favored by the ruling Fascist regime. Sottsass junior spent his career creating work that looked to the future, not to a rational or classical past. He said: "I believe that the future only begins when the past has been completely dismantled, its logic reduced to dust and nostalgia is all that remains."

Sottsass studied architecture at Turin Polytechnic before World War Two and worked for his father until 1946. A year later he opened a design studio in Milan. In those early years he mainly received commissions for furniture, ceramics and graphics. Intrigued by the organic forms and bright colors being used by American designers, he visited New York in 1956 where he spent a month working with George Nelson, the leading American designer. On returning to Italy a year later he became more focused on product design.

On his return to Italy, Sottsass became creative consultant to the Poltronova furniture factory. However, the first major contract he obtained for design consultancy came from typewriter manufacturers Olivetti in 1958. Sottsass designed a number of their typewriters and calculators, including the celebrated red 'Valentine' portable typewriter, which he designed in collaboration with Perry King, in 1969. His relationship with Olivetti lasted until 1980.

A man of boundless imaginative energy, Sottsass was always looking for new approaches to design. He photographed anything and everything that caught his eye.

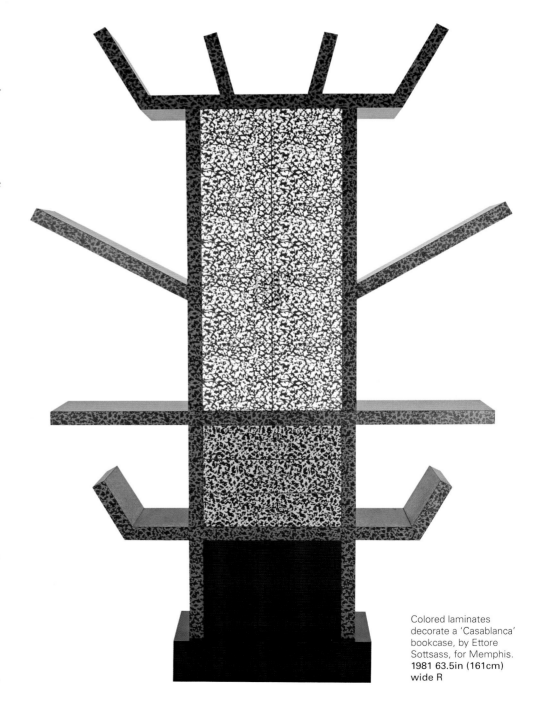

Colored laminates decorate a 'Casablanca' bookcase, by Ettore Sottsass, for Memphis. **1981 63.5in (161cm) wide R**

Toward the end of the 1960s his experimental activities led to a key role in the Anti-design movement. This group of mainly northern Italian architects and designers theorized about alternative living environments and objects as a protest against established modern design principles. They questioned the way consumer products were promoted as being in "good taste", which in their eyes, was just another tool to increase sales. In fact many designers, including Sottsass, became so furiously radicalized they practically ceased designing for a number of years.

In the late 1970s Sottsass was invited to join Studio Alchimia (see p222), a design group led by Alessandro Mendini whose aim was to amalgamate design with everyday life and culture. In 1981 Sottsass left Studio Alchimia, as ultimately, he did not share some of Mendini's intellectual preoccupations.

Sottsass's next venture, the Memphis collective (see p226), was founded in 1981. Aesthetically Memphis produced a more commercially-viable version of the design ideas first explored by Studio Alchimia. Wittily irreverent they are characterized by the emphasis given to their decorative qualities rather than their construction or utilitarian properties. Sottsass once proclaimed "our products are devoted to life, not posterity". Memphis made extensive use of plastic laminates for their furniture. Internationally celebrated architects and designers such as Michael Graves, Arata Isozaki and Shiro Kuramata were invited to join the collective.

The collective was skilled at marketing their work, which they exhibited in capital cities around the globe. Memphis design was eagerly sought after and widely imitated. At the height of its influence, in 1985, Sottsass quit the group having become increasingly disillusioned with the hype that surrounded it. In 1980 he had also set up Sottsass Associati, a studio that helped many young designers. Always one to move forward, he continued to work, concentrating mainly on architectural commissions such as Milan's Malpensa Airport. A few years before founding Memphis he wrote: "I am a designer and I want to design things. What else would I do? Go fishing?"

ETTORE SOTTSASS

Polychrome and printed laminates cover a 'Carlton' shelf unit, by Ettore Sottsass, for Memphis.
1981 75in (190.5cm) wide P

Geometric shapes and contrasting colors decorate an Ettore Sottsass 'Articolo 6000' vase for Bistossi..
c1991 30.25in (77cm) high L

Ettore Sottsass reworked the traditional tazza form with this 'Sol' glass fruit bowl, designed for Memphis.
1982 10.5in (26cm) high NPA

Architectural elements and marble and hardstone finishes combine on a 'Biedermeier' sofa designed by Ettore Sottsass. 1983 60in (137cm) high R

Memphis

From a small exhibition held in Milan's Arc 74 Gallery in September 1981 emerged an audacious design style that caught the imagination of the cash-rich consumer that epitomized the 1980s. The work on show was that of Memphis, a collective of like-minded Italian designers under the leadership of the master of innovative design, Ettore Sottsass. Their work created a style that came to define the look of the decade.

Accentuated geometric forms and zig-zags often appear in the work of Matteo Thun. This ceramic hanging light fixture was designed for Memphis.
15in (38cm) wide I

Much of the groundwork for the success of Memphis had been achieved through Studio Alchimia's (see pp. 222-223) contribution to design from the end of the 1970s, in which Ettore Sottsass and a number of his collaborators had played an important part. Under the direction of Alessandro Mendini, the focus of Studio Alchimia had been to challenge the precepts of "Good Design" that had dominated the post-war years. The emphasis, however, was on one-off pieces that sought to "re-design" classics of years gone by. As such the pieces were not always functional and Mendini proposed an increasingly intellectual agenda that some of the designers, notably Ettore Sottsass (see pp. 224-225), found stifling.

Toward the end of 1980, Sottsass – now in his sixties and at an age when others might have thought of retiring – met with a number of designers at his home, Andrea Branzi and Michele de Lucchi among them, to discuss ways of taking their concept one step further. Memphis famously took its name from the chorus of the Bob Dylan song "Stuck Inside of Mobile with the Memphis Blues Again", which was playing on the stereo during the first meeting of the group. Unlike Studio Alchimia, they were interested to see how their creations could be issued in greater numbers and sought to exploit the commercial potential of their work. Conscious of the fact that a strong marketing policy could accelerate their progress, the designers pursued a rigorous promotional campaign. They openly courted publicity, producing a book of their work, *Memphis: the New International Style* following their first exhibition, and soon gained widespread attention.

This new international style was intoxicating. Openly challenging what they saw as the conventional functionalism of "Good Design", Sottsass and his collaborators subordinated the function of a piece to its aesthetic appeal (though they did not seek to eradicate the function of the piece altogether). They produced ceramics, lighting, furniture and glassware that were emblazoned with all manner of decorative

Contrasting laminates cover a 'Kristall' table by Michele de Lucchi for Memphis. The wooden table is supported by rolled steel legs.
1981 19.75in (50cm) high NPA

elements from garishly printed plastic laminates to superfluous protrusions. Form ceased to be representative of the function of a piece, and whimsy appeared to be the design ethos. Motifs borrowed from bygone eras were re-appropriated to give them new meaning, while plastics, metals and glass were juxtaposed to create hybrid forms.

Central to many of the designs were the plastic laminates that were used to cover all manner of surfaces from tabletops to door fronts to plinths. Commissioned especially from Abet Laminati, these plastics – reminiscent of 1950s kitsch – bore a wide range of designs from animal fur to abstract patterns, and were often used in conjunction with more expensive materials. This practice was one of many that epitomized the Memphis agenda, so perfectly encapsulated in the group's name, with its ancient-Egypt-meets-Graceland connotations.

Besides Sottsass, Branzi and de Lucchi, founding members included British-born George Sowden and his French wife Nathalie Du Pasquier, among whose pieces was the brightly colored, tall-legged 'D'Antibes' vitrine, for which Du Pasquier designed the laminate. The French designer, Martine Bedin was also at the first meeting, held at Sottsass's house. Her 'Super' lamp featured at several Memphis exhibitions, was notable for being mounted on wheels. As the movement gained momentum, the collective continued to attract collaborators from all over the world. Later contributors included the American architect Michael Graves, whose 'Plaza' dressing table borrowed architectural motifs; Shiro Kuramata, a Japanese architect, who used cement for his 'Kyoto' table; and American ceramist, Peter Shire, whose collaboration with Memphis enabled him to experiment in other disciplines, such as furniture design.

Memphis marked an exciting new development in the world of design. Their work was not only coveted and sought after by the rich and famous when it was new, but also imitated for years to come. The group disbanded in 1988, Sottsass openly admitting that their intentions had been nothing more than a fad – so quickly do fashions change – but by that time, their work had been done.

MEMPHIS

Bright polychrome glazes cover a six piece ceramic totem by Ettore Sottsass for Memphis, made by Bitossi.
67.5in (171.5cm) high R

Contrasting patterns decorate a ceramic 'Carrot' vase, designed by Nathalie Du Pasquier for Memphis.
1985 12in (30.5cm) high NPA

Silkscreen printed decoration covers a 'D'Antibes' wooden display cabinet, by George J. Sowden for Memphis.
1981 23.5in (60cm) wide N

Geometric forms make up the 'Brazil' single-pedestal desk designed by Peter Shire for Memphis. It challenges the perception of what a table looks like.
1981 81.5in (207cm) wide L

A lacquered metal base, shaped glass column and perspex discs were used to create Ettore Sottsass's 'Bay' table lamp.
1983 19.25in (49cm) high NPA

Michael Graves (1934–)

Michael Graves's 'Whistling Bird' tea-kettle is one of the most recognisable "designer" products of the late 20th century. More than 1.3 million kettles have sold since it was launched by Alessi in 1985. Its popularity overshadows the fact that product design is something of a sideline for Graves – a leading American architect with buildings like New York's Whitney Museum of Art to his name.

After training as an architect at Harvard University in the late 1950s, Michael Graves went to work for the prominent architect-designer, George Nelson, who had created design classics such as the 'Atom Ball' clock. It was here that Graves was first exposed to modern product design.

Graves's time with Nelson was cut short after he was awarded the Prix de Rome fellowship in 1960. There then followed two years at the American Academy in Rome, where Graves visited many important Classical buildings and studied the writings of the great Classical critics and theorists. His time in Italy would have a profound effect on his subsequent career as both an architect and a designer.

Upon returning to America Graves forged a successful career as an architect and teacher, being invited to take a professor at Princeton University in 1962. His early works are typically modern in the sense that they are inspired by geometry and are free from ornament and color. In the mid to late 1970s he began to

Mickey Mouse's ears form the entrance to the Michael Graves-designed the Team Disney Casting Office at Walt Disney Studios, Burbank, California. It was built in 1986.

incorporate Classicism into his work along with what he termed "representational color", for example, sky blue for ceilings.

By the early 1980s, Graves was widely acclaimed for his ground-breaking Postmodern approach to projects like the Portland Public Service building in Portland, Oregon and the Humana Corporation headquarters in Louisville,

Kentucky. His growing reputation led to an invitation from the Memphis group (see p.226). Graves applied many of the exciting ideas he had been pursuing in architecture to his designs for Memphis. He frequently referenced historical styles – from Classical columns to Art Deco skyscrapers – and made extensive use of color. He mixed the highbrow with popular culture, for example

The 'Whistling Bird' kettle and sugar bowl Graves designed for Alessi.

A Swid Powell 'Little Dripper' transfer printed tea set, designed by Michael Graves. The red bases symbolize the heat under the teapot and the blue lines the water within it.
Teapot 9.25in (23.5cm) wide K

Art Deco skyscrapers inspired Michael Graves's architectural 'Plaza' dressing table and stool for Memphis. The rare set is made from bird's eye maple with an enameled finish and is illuminated by small light bulbs which celebrate pop culture and Hollywood.
1981 table 55.5in (141cm) wide NPA

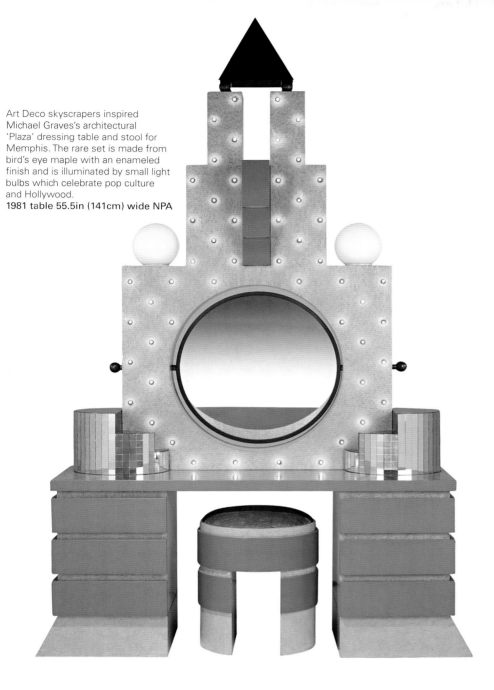

Michael Graves's work has been the subject of several exhibitions. This poster celebrates 30 years of his designs.
2000 24in (61cm) wide NPA

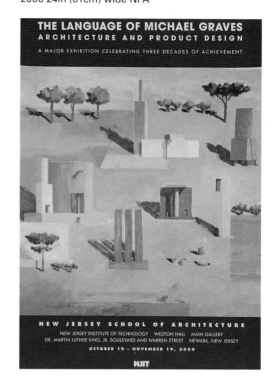

Classical architecture influenced the 'Mantel' clock Graves designed for Alessi.
1988 9.75in (24.5cm) high NPA

by combining rare wood veneers with cheap plastic laminates. Above all he put an inescapable aura of exuberance and fun into his design. Memphis produced pieces such as his 'Plaza' dressing table in limited numbers. The designs provided a template for many imitations during the 1980s.

Graves's major design venture with Alessi (see p.278) was more consumer oriented. The Italian manufacturer wanted to break into the American market and hired Graves to inject some Postmodern stylishness into a range of homeware. His designs for Alessi blend the quirky and the decorative with the functional and well-made. His iconic and bestselling 'Whistling Bird' tea-kettle revived the traditional "whistling" function of the kettle but humorously attributed the noise to a plastic bird attached to the spout. Fashioned from stainless steel with rivets around the base it recalls archaic industrial techniques. A range of similarly styled products was then created, followed by his 'Mantle' clock in 1986 and pepper mill in 1988.

Over the years Graves has designed everything from porcelain, rugs and lighting to wristwatches, posters and ballet productions. Many of these designs are now considered postmodernist classics.

Wendell Castle (1932-)

With a career spanning almost 50 years, American designer Wendell Castle has consistently blurred the line between art and design. Challenging conventional furniture shapes and how form relates to function, Castle has produced highly individual pieces in a wide range of materials including wood, plastic and metal, many of which betray his training in industrial design and a talent for sculpture.

One of the most remarkable aspects of Wendell Castle's work is its sheer variety, not just in the materials he has chosen to use over the decades, but in the visual nature of his pieces in response to changes in fashion and developing technology. Castle's creativity remains undiminished and, throughout his career, his sculptural pieces have stood out from the work of those around him.

Castle studied art and industrial design at the University of Kansas and made his first piece of furniture as a graduate student in sculpture. At no point did he study furniture design. "If I had, that would have been a disaster," he is reported to have said,

"industrial design and sculpture were a perfect combination."

An innovator, in the early 1960s Castle developed a new technique for laminating wood, in which the pieces of wood were no longer sheets of veneer, but one inch (2.5 cm) planks of oak or walnut, stacked one on top of the other. Castle used this technique to sculpt organic forms that rapidly came to epitomize his style. His first work was in oak and walnut, then he began to use other woods, sculpting them into biomorphic shapes. He once said, "To me the organic form offers the most exciting possibilities. It can never be completely understood in one glance."

From the 1960s, with the arrival of suitable plastics, Castle took his sculptural forms a step further, creating a range of large-scale pieces, among which his 'Molar' group seating of 1964 – huge tooth-shaped chairs – and giant, almost flexi-looking light fittings stand out in particular. Castle exploited the materials and techniques at his disposal to create ultra-smooth, biomorphic forms in the bold bright colors of the Pop era – primary yellow, bright red, lime green, and orange. Unlike many of the pieces emerging at the time that now seem dated (somewhat ironically as they were intended to impart a vision of the future) Castle's plastic pieces have retained a

A sculptured quilted maple cabinet, designed by Wendell Castle, with two doors, each enclosing an interior shelf, with partially painted and ebonized finishes.
1997 58.5in (23cm) long T

strikingly contemporary feel. However, they did not enjoy the reception that met similar experiments in Europe – such as Eero Aarnio's Ball and Pastil chairs and, with just 400 pieces made, he moved on.

Castle's work from the late 1970s and through the 1980s and 1990s epitomized the anti-design sentiment that was sweeping through much of the United States and Europe. In the United States, this manifested itself in the Craft Revival movement, with which Castle became associated and is often credited as its leading exponent – his work is sometimes described as "haute craft". He produced a series of one-off labor-intensive pieces. His work became an expression of art, forsaking function in favor of form and color. Pieces were made that emphasized the use of mixed media, skilfully combining painted or ebonized surfaces with patinated metals to create the desired effect.

As the Postmodern movement was increasingly championed through design, Castle's work began to incorporate elements of historical styles in a whimsical or ironic fashion. His sculptural background came to the fore during, allowing him to create his trademark biomorphic forms juxtaposed with geometric shapes at rakish angles.

In 2004, Castle's early plastic pieces were re-launched a limited number of them in just black or white. These included pieces from the 'Molar Group', a 'Cloud' shelving unit, which is suspended from the wall as if floating, and the 'Big Table', comprised of modular sections that could be arranged by the consumer.

Since then, Castle has returned to create striking, single-unit, biomorphic pieces in a range of materials including wod, gilded fiberglass, and stainless steel. With more refined, sleeker forms, the pieces are still unmistakably the work of this artist-designer. Of particular note is the predatory 'Black Widow' chair, where the wide fiberglass seat is slung low between three spider-like legs, and the elegant stainless steel 'Abilene' rocking chair with is strong yet sensuous curves. He has told *American Craft* magazine, "I don't see myself as part of tradition, and I don't see myself as part of the activity in American furniture." But as an artist and craftsperson, he explains, "you break new ground in different ways."

WENDELL CASTLE

A monumental study for a lighting fixture, by Wendell Castle, of gouache and marker pen on paper.
1995 88in (223.5cm) high M

An enameled and patinated metal sculptural maple and walnut anthropomorphic clock.
1989 21in (53.5cm) high Q

A pair of Wendell Castle yellow molded plastic 'Molar' chairs.
32in (81cm) wide L

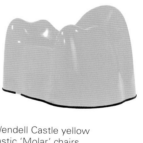

A Wendell Castle wall-hanging bookshelf and counter, with six blind drawers.
125.5in (318.75cm) U

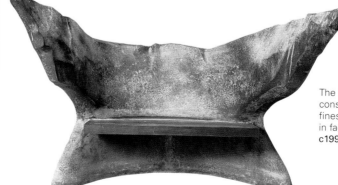

The 'Angel' chair series is considered by many to be Castle's finest achievement. This example is in faceted, patinated bronze.
c1990 63in (157.5cm) wide X

Philippe Starck (1949-)

The 1980s have been called "the designer decade". Design played such a major role in marketing and advertizing that everyone wanted products sanctified with a designer label. Design exhibitions attracted crowds of visitors and there was constant talk about design in the media. A new generation of designers emerged from behind their drawing boards and into the spotlight. None would have a more stellar role than French designer Philippe Starck.

Without question, Philippe Starck is one of the most influential designers of our times. Unusually for such a highly original thinker, Starck has never been very interested in being provocative. His aim is to create stylish product designs with mass appeal or, as he puts it, to "give the best to as many people as possible".

With an almost mythical ability to recognize what the public would regard as exciting and new, Starck put "Design" with a capital "D" into the products of the 1980s, 1990s and 2000s. He is charming and charismatic and has consummate marketing skills – never hesitating it seems to use himself to promote his designs.

Starck's parents – his father was a successful aeronautical engineer – encouraged his artistic nature and curiosity. As a child he spent endless hours taking apart his toys and putting them back together again just the way he wanted. After beginning an architecture course at the Nissim de Camondo school in Paris, he quit to start an inflatable furnishings and object company in 1968. A year later he joined Pierre Cardin where he worked as an art director for several years. In the mid-1970s he began working as an independent product and interior designer, rapidly acquiring for himself a reputation for designing nightclubs and as a man who likes to party.

He achieved wide acclaim in 1982 when he designed President François Mitterand's private suite in the Elysée Palace. Starck now works on projects globally and calls himself the "world's first truly international designer."

Starck's elegant organic style can be loosely linked to postmodernism. His designs are playful and humorous, for example his chairs sometimes feature animal legs. He happily incorporates references to popular culture and borrows ideas from the past, such as streamlining or

Philippe Starck's 'Juicy Salif' lemon squeezer, designed for Alessi in 1990, is a functional object designed as sculpture - it demands to be desplayed rather than stored away.

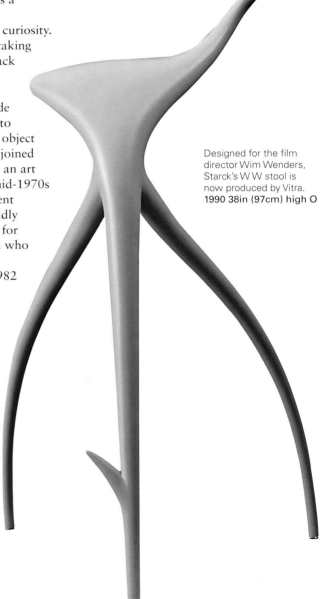

Designed for the film director Wim Wenders, Starck's W W stool is now produced by Vitra.
1990 38in (97cm) high O

elements of Art Nouveau. Such an example is his 'Louis Ghost' chair, made of transparent or colored polycarbonate, which references the Baroque style. He revels in color – from brilliant translucent greens to soft chalky pastel yellows.

The use of an enamel finish is another characteristic of his work. He likes to mix unusual materials such as plastic with aluminum or glass with stone. Where he differs from other Postmodernists is in his preference for sleek, stylized shapes decorated solely by color. He once described his chair designs as "surrealist or Dada objects" conceived to liberate the user "from the humdrum reality of everyday life".

When Starck is designing, it is the look rather than usefulness of a product that are uppermost in his thoughts. For example, his famous 'Juicy Salif' lemon squeezer has nothing to catch the pulp or juice and its spidery legs can scratch counter tops, yet it is still hypnotically attractive. Starck's designs are primarily intended to instil desire amongst consumers.

Stark's vast array of products encompass everything from stationery and toothbrushes to underwear, motorbikes and even the Olympic flame. So prolific is his output that it seems obvious that even for a man with his boundless energy, Starck must have a team of designers behind him.

During the early years of the 21st century, Starck lowered his profile slightly. These days you are less likely to see him in the newspapers and magazines. He has been concentrating more on interior design and architectural projects such as London's Sanderson hotel (2000), the seventh hotel Starck has designed with legendary hotelier and nightclub owner Ian Schrager, and re-decorating the lobby of Le Meurice in Paris. His most recent notable projects include wireless speakers for the Apple iPod and iPhone.

Starck continues to see design – or rather making things that improve people's lives – as his priority. He reportedly said: "First, we must remember that design is absolutely useless. It's absolutely not a priority, absolutely not important. The only final goal for design is to try to bring a better life to your friends."

PHILIPPE STARCK DESIGNS

Philippe Starck added sandals to his range of shoes for Puma in 2005. Typically for a Starck product, they are a sleek, single-color design.

A pair of side tables with elliptical plate-glass tops and cantilevered aluminum bases.
19.5in (49.5cm) wide J

A matte finish was used on this limited edition Daum teardrop-shaped 'Etrangeté 66' glass vase or display piece.
1988 22in (56cm) long NPA

A pair of high-back chairs, each with a single arm, designed for the Paramount Hotel in New York.
54in (135cm) high G

This 'Aleph' side chair, has simple, clean lines and just three legs, the rear leg was designed to trip up waiters.
34in (86.5cm) high L

WIRE FURNITURE GALLERY

Metal has been used to make furniture since the 18th century, but by the late 20th century developments in the manufacturing process made it possible to produce strong, thin wire that created new design opportunities. Offering more flexibility than traditional cast or wrought iron, furniture makers usedw metal wire to create textured and abstract designs, some of them more sculpture than seating.

A figural black wire lounge chair and ottoman by John Risley.
40.5in (103cm) high O

A Cappellini carbon fiber and epoxy resin 'Knotted Chair', designed by Marcel Wanders.
1995 28.75in (73cm) high M

A small Forrest Myers armchair with tubular black metal seat, and copper panel base.
31.5in (79cm) wide Q

A 'Trône' wrought iron chair by André Dubreuil, bent and welded, the shield back rising to an exaggerated scroll, slubbed fabric seat.
c1985 56.75in (144cm) high V

A Javier Mariscal 'Diagram Of Chair. One' wire chair.
2004 31in (79cm) high NPA

SHIRO KURAMATA 'HOW HIGH THE MOON' CHAIR

The Japenese designer Shiro Kuramata designed furniture that combined Japanese minimalism with Western irony, creating original and poetic furniture. His minimalist 'How High The Moon' chair, named after the song performed by Duke Ellington, is a re-evaluation of the armchair. Constructed entirely of steel mesh, without an interior frame or visible support, it suggests the mere outline of a chair.

This example is made from nickel-plated wire mesh.

The mesh gives the sitter a sense of floating. The reflective surface of the mesh suggests glowing moonlight.

The shape of the chair has been reduced to a minimum.

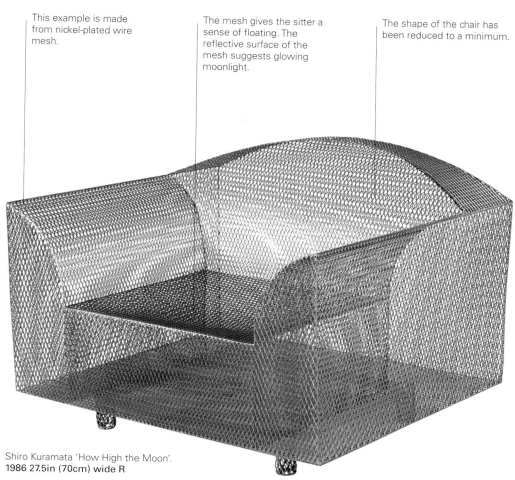

Shiro Kuramata 'How High the Moon'.
1986 27.5in (70cm) wide R

A Forrest Myers wire sofa with internal spring supports and rolled armrests.
80.5in (205.5cm) wide N

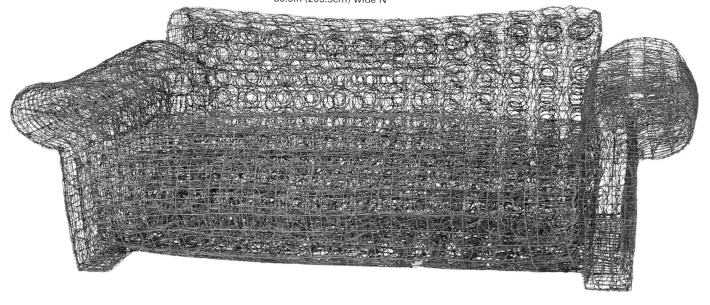

METAL FURNITURE GALLERY

Metal, whether steel, bronze, chrome or brass, offers a plethora of possibilities to the furniture designer. Inherently strong, it can be molded into sleek forms or given one of any number of textured finishes. It is perfect for indoor and outdoor pieces.

The legs of Sandro Chia's 'Tavolo' table form the letters in his surname. Cast bronze with verdigris patiation and glass top.
1989 31.5in (80cm) high NPA

A glass and steel Camel Console table, designed by Danny Lane.
2005 65in (165cm) long NPA

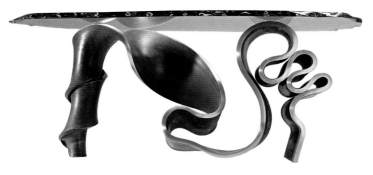

A mix of historical motifs include claw-and-ball feet feature on the arrow back chair, designed by Mark Brazier-Jones.
1995 43in (109cm) high P

An integral ice bucket is part of Willy Rizzo's revolving black laminate and stainless steel coffee table/bar.
c1972 45in (114.5cm) diam N

A Jonathan Singleton oak and steel dining table, with cerused oak top on curvaceous steel base.
89in (226cm) wide N

A Mats Theselius 'Älgskinnsfåtöljen' armchair. From his first collection which featured 360 metal chairs with leather upholstery.
1991 P

A unique 'Ring Couch', by Karim Rashid, manufactured by Galerkin, Gardena, CA, wood and steel frame with foam and vinyl upholstery.
2005 178.5in (453.5cm) diam U

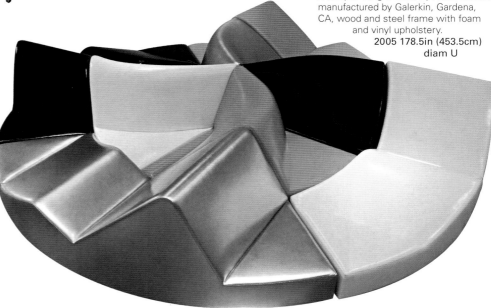

JONATHAN SINGLETON CHAIR

Jonathan Singleton studied to be an architect at Manchester University. When he graduated in 1992 the recession meant there was little work available and so he decided to cycle from his home town of Grantham to Barcelona. In Spain he opened a shop selling futons, and set up a workshop in his storeroom. There he made furniture using scraps of metal and glass he found on the streets. Eventually his designs outsold the futons and so he went into furniture design full time.

An 'Easy Number One' stainless steel chair, by Jonathan Singleton
41in (104cm) wide N

Singleton made his first Easy Chair in 1997. The red version has proved to be very popular.

This chair has a red enamel finish and leather cushion. It is also available in plain steel.

Singleton makes all his furniture by hand, welding the parts together himself.

Konstantin Grcic's Magis Chair One has legs of polished anodized aluminum and a die-cast aluminum seat painted with anthracite polyester powder.
32.25in (82cm) high C

A bronze 'Dragon' sofa table, designed by Mark Brazier-Jones, with glass top.
c1997 39in (99.5cm) diam W

A 'Peinador con Pestanas' dressing table and stool, designed by Edelmira Boller.
1991 58.25in (148cm) high O

WOOD FURNITURE GALLERY

An eclectic style, Postmodernism made use of many different materials, but wood – the traditional furniture material – maintained an important role. While there was a move toward re-examining the natural properties of wood, there was also an interest in re-interpreting styles of the past. Through this and other techniques designers sought to challenge conventional ideas about furniture, with hugely diverse results.

A beech chair designed by Toshiyuki Kita, Japan.
1984 171.5in (67.5cm) high D

The shelves on this 'Joy Rotating Shelf' unit by Achille Castiglioni revolve around the central axis to create an arrangement personal to the user while retaining its functionality.
1989 75in (190cm) high NPA

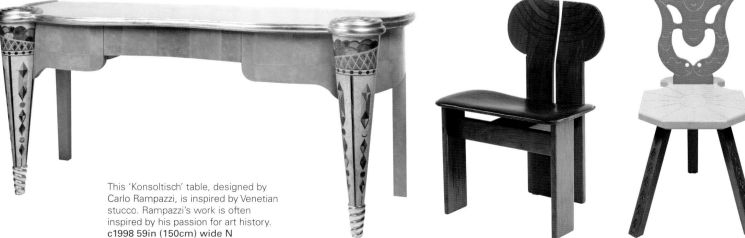

Rupert Williamson produces one-off pieces of wooden furniture. This banqueting table, with bright block supports, appears to be unstable and the legs protrude through the top.
1996 236.25in (600cm) long O

A Tobia and Afra Scarpa 'Africa' chair, inspired by Tribal thrones. The two-piece cherrywood back shows off the innate beauty of the wood.
1975 30.75in (78cm) high C

A painted wood 'Museum Chair', by Alessandro Mendini. He is interested in colorful and decorative 'redesigns' of typical forms.
1996 33.5in (85cm) high L

This 'Konsoltisch' table, designed by Carlo Rampazzi, is inspired by Venetian stucco. Rampazzi's work is often inspired by his passion for art history.
c1998 59in (150cm) wide N

'FRANKFURT SKYSCRAPER' F1 CABINET
Created by a trio of architects, Norbert Berghof, Michael Landes and Wolfgang Rang, the rare 'Frankfurt Skyscraper' F1 cabinet is regarded as an icon of Postmodern German design. The Frankfurt series cabinets (1985–87) and chairs (1985–90) were designed for the high-end German company Draenert GmbH. They were typically handmade in editions of 100 and included rich materials, such as marble, veneers or gold plating.

An assortment of rich woods are used to give a luxurious feel, including bird's eye maple, ebony, bruyère wood, maple, nut root wood and bubinga (African rosewood). The plinth and base are of Carrara marble, the drawer knobs of ivory, and there is gold leaf overlay decoration on the globes and the roof.

The design is made up of geometric forms, including the detailed interior which contains two secret compartments.

The piece is beautifully hand crafted and was clearly designed by architects. It is a postmodern update of an antique secretaire or bureau.

A 'Frankfurt Skyscraper' F1 cabinet, designed by Norbert Berghof, Michael Landes and Wolfgang Rang.
1985-6 92in (230cm) high V

FRANK GEHRY

Frank Gehry's low-cost 'Easy Edges' series of fourteen practical cardboard furniture pieces was designed in response to the greater awareness of environmental issues that arose in the 1970s, and to fulfill a need in the market for affordable furniture. Made from cardboard reinforced with laminate and metal rods at stress points, the series was released in 1972 and was immediately successful. Fearing that that this would detract from his reputation as an architect, however, Gehry withdrew the pieces from production and did not design furniture for another ten years. He then created the 'Experimental Edges' collection, also in cardboard, but intended as art furniture. Another eight years later, from 1990 to 1992, he developed a series of chairs for Knoll, constructed of woven strips of plywood.

A 'Wiggle' chair from the Easy Edges series. The layers of cardboard making up the chair have been manipulated into an attractive, flowing shape.
c1972 33.5in (85cm) high L

This monumental 'Easy Edges' table, uses the expressive qualities of corrugated cardboard.
183in (465cm) long W

SYNTHETICS FURNITURE GALLERY

From the 1960s onward consumers had an increasing amount of leisure time, and attention turned toward the home as a place of comfort and relaxation. Continued developments in synthetic materials provided designers with opportunities to create new products. Designs combined playfulness with practicality and the exciting with the everyday, creating innovative shapes and sensuous, tactile surfaces.

Eero Aarnio aims to challenge preconceptions, saying of his playful 'Pony' chair design, "A seat does not have to be a chair ... A seat could even be a small and soft pony on which you can 'ride' or sit sideways."
38in (96.5cm) long M

A 'Tomato' armchair, by Eero Aarnio, made of green polyester reinforced with fiberglass. This chair was designed to be stable while floating in water.
1971 55in (140cm) wide L

The 'Getsuen' armchair, by Japanese designer Masanori Umeda, is shaped like a flower with open petals.
1990 37.5in (100cm) wide L

This 'Cactus' coat stand is made of polyurethane foam. It was designed by Guido Drocco and Franco Mello for Gufram.
1972 66in (168cm) high K

A 'Maralunga' chair, by Vico Magistretti, with brown leather upholstery on steel frame. The Maralunga design was included in "Fortune" magazine's list of the top 25 design products of 1977.
38.5in (98cm) wide F

A 'Curved Chair', designed by Job Smeets, for Studio Job. The simple and functional design is made from laminated plywood bent over a mold.
1998 32.25in (82cm) high N

A 'TV-Relax' armchair, designed by Luigi Colani. The organic form of this chair is typical of Colani's work.
1969 37.5in (95cm) long J

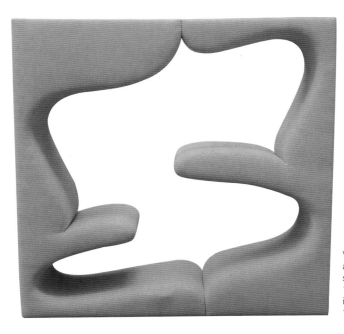

Verner Panton's 'Living Tower' accommodates four people. He sought to maximise the user's "experience" of the object by making it colorful, comfortable and playful.
1968–89 78.75in (200cm) wide O

'SUNBALL' CHAIR

The 'Sunball' chair was a piece of garden furniture: a Space Age sphere, with two flexible overlapping hemispheres that could be closed to keep off the rain, or opened for sunbathing and lounging. It was designed in 1969 by Günter Ferdinand Ris and Herbert Selldorf for Rosenthal in (West) Germany. Unfortunately, like a lot of modern designs, the 'Sunball' became expensive to produce after the 1973 oil crisis and few pieces were ever manufactured.

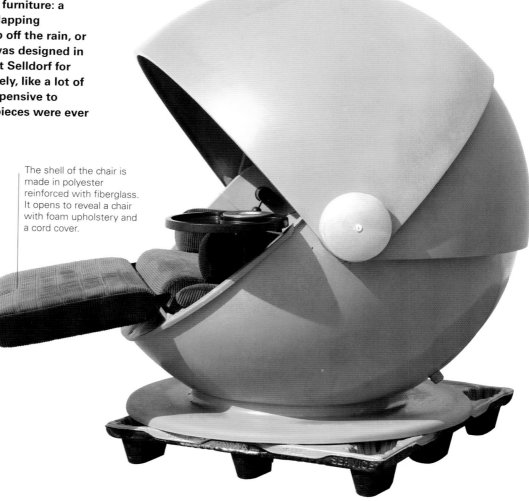

A large 'Sunball' lawn chair, designed by Ferdinand Günter Ris and Herbert Selldorf, for Rosenthal, Selb.
1969–71 62.25in (158cm) wide V

The shell of the chair is made in polyester reinforced with fiberglass. It opens to reveal a chair with foam upholstery and a cord cover.

JOE COLOMBO

One of Italy's most innovative product designers, Cesare "Joe" Colombo was part of the movement that attempted to introduce a more inclusive element to Italian design. As a young designer in the 1950s Columbo was excited by the possibilities of developing materials, such as plastics, and began to see himself as "creator of the environment of the future". During the 1960s he experimented with designs that increased the usefulness and relevance of everyday objects. The 'Tube' chair, which he designed in 1969, is one of the most striking examples of a chair that resists the more formal ideas of what furniture should be. It is easily carried (in its duffel bag) and can be assembled in a variety of ways, providing greater flexibility for the average sitter. Colombo's 'Multi' chair of 1970 operates under similar principles.

An Italian 'Tube' chair, Joe Colombo, of Flexform, consisting of vinyl-covered polyurethane foam, plastic cylinders, metal and rubber grips.
1969–70 Q Largest tube 17.75in (45cm) diam

OTHER MATERIALS FURNITURE GALLERY

The use of a wide range of materials is a notable characteristic of Postmodernism. From newly invented plastics and laminates, to traditional glass, leather and wood, there are few materials that have not been employed in search of groundbreaking furniture designs and unique effects. As well as using all-new plastics some designers have also made the use of recycled or salvaged material the focus of their work.

A 1970s molded armchair, designed by Ernst Moeckl. Due to the angled legs, this chair is often known as the "Kangaroo" chair. It is molded from a composite polyurethane manufactured by Bayer for Horn of Germany and is officially known as the 'Baydur' chair.
30.5in (76.5cm) high C

A 'Chaise Barbare' chair by Elizabeth Garouste and Mattia Bonetti, the seat of cow hide fastened to a bronze frame. Garouste and Bonetti are known for their designs inspired by primitive forms, ancient symbolism and mysticism.
c1981 118cm high L

A Walt Disney hardwood "Mickey Mouse" chair celebrates pop culture.
c1980 41in (104cm) high D

Designers became conscious of the need to consider the effect of their work on the environment. The 'McCain' chair, by Beata Bär, Gerhard Bär and Christof Knell, is made from recycled plastic frozen chip bags.
1994 18.5in (47cm) wide G

Czech designer Borek Sipek made this 'Picasso' stool' from Bohemian crystal, brass and Corian (a type of plastic). He is renowned for his work with glass and has referred to his own style as 'neo-Baroque'.
1990 21in (54cm) high NPA

ZAHA HADID

Zaha Hadid grew up in one of Baghdad's first Bauhaus-inspired houses and eventually settled in London in the mid-1970s. Though known primarily as an architect, Zaha Hadid has also designed several ranges of furniture for companies such as Dupont and Sawaya & Moroni. Her furniture, like her architecture, is challenging, original and dramatic. The 2001 Z-Scape range, manufactured by Sawaya & Moroni, for example, was inspired by glaciers, erosions, stalagmites and stalactites and is more an installation than a set of usable seating.

A sense of swirling movement is created by the uneven surface. The depressions in the table top also serve to visually connect the legs to the form.

Hadid is interested in how people interact with the objects around them. This table is of an irregular shape which affects the way it can be used.

The sculptural flowing shape and smooth, glossy surface are suggestive of a liquid.

A polyurethane gloss 'Aqua' table, designed by Zaha Hadid, for Established & Sons.
2006 120in (306cm) long W

The 'Suegiú' staircase chair, designed by Bruno Munari, for Zanotta, has a moveable unit that can be repositioned by the user.
1989 31.75in (80.5cm) high M

A Robert Venturi 'Sheraton' molded plywood chair with ebonized finish. The silkscreen-printed decoration to the cut-out back parodies the Neoclassical style of Thomas Sheraton.
33.25in (84.5cm) high L

A glass and steel 'Stacking Chair', designed by Danny Lane. Lane's work exploits the physical properties of his materials. The chair challenges the perception of how glass can be used.
4.5in (11cm) high NPA

Gaetano Pesce (1939–)

The Italian designer Gaetano Pesce burst onto the scene towards the end of the 1960s with a series of voluptuous chairs. More than any other designer he has exploited the latest available techniques, technologies and materials to produce innovative, colorful, controversial pieces. Always at the leading edge of avant-garde design, he has worked across a wide range of disciplines, from architecture to furniture design and lighting.

A trained architect, Gaetano Pesce's early work was closely associated with the Italian Radical Design movement that reacted against the "Good Design" philisophy that had dominated Europe and the United States in the 1950s and 1960s. Among his earliest works was a series of voluptuous armchairs and sofas made from polyurethane foam and upholstered in stretch nylon, launched at the Milan Furniture Fair in 1969. What was remarkable about these chairs was that they were vacuum-shrunk to some 10 per cent of their normal size before being heat-sealed in vinyl slipcases. When "released" from their packaging by the consumer, each form slowly inflated to its original size and rounded form as it gradually sucked in air. This 'Up' series, produced by B&B Italia, eptiomized the Pop culture that captivated designer and consumer alike.

A non-conformist at heart, Pesce challenged the precepts of Modernism – in particular that of standardisation. As such, he created several limited-edition designs that followed a specific model, but varied to some extent in the end result. This was particularly the case for a number of pieces he created for the pioneering Italian furniture manufacturer, Cassina, famous for its work with Gio Ponti in the 1950s. Cassina did much to promote Pesce's unconventional work. Among his designs for them was the 'Sit Down' series of chairs, produced in 1976 and reputedly inspired by the work of Swedish-born sculptor Claes Oldenburg. Each of these large, somewhat lumpy armchairs varied slightly depending on the quilting process of the upholstery

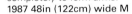

A Cassina 'Feltri' armchair, by Gaetano Pesce, of thick resin-infused wool felt and tied string laces, with padded, quilted fabric seat. The back of the chair can be bent and positioned as the user likes. For example, the wings can be folded down completely to form arms.
1987 48in (122cm) wide M

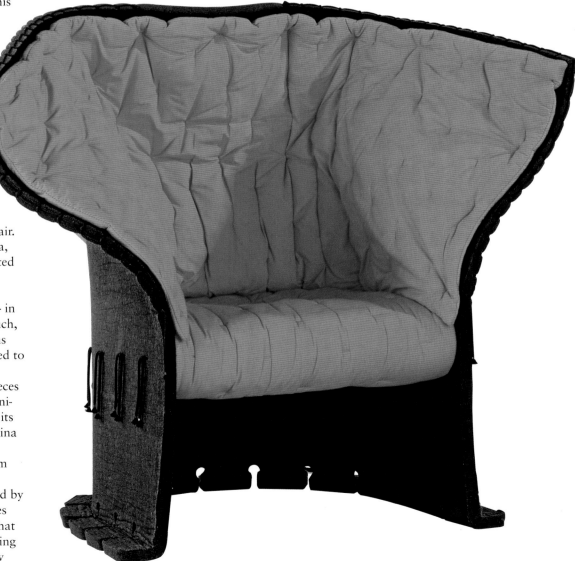

and the patterning of the fabric. Similarly, his resin 'Sansone' tables for Cassina in 1980 used a selection of shades from a specified palette, but the final combination of colors was chosen by the team of craftsmen that created the tables to his design.

Pesce reveled in creating experimental furniture where the interaction between user and furniture is as important as the function of the piece. To this end, he developed designs that behaved differently depending on who was using them. His 'Feltri' chair for Cassina (1987) epitomized the Postmodern fascination for producing pieces that were, in reality, not quite what they seemed on first viewing. Described by Pesce himself as an "object of uncertain form", the chair had a plastic frame upholstered with a resin-infused wool felt fabric that molded to the shape of the sitter's body when used. The high back of the chair could be folded down by the user to provide armrests if desired.

Similarly, Pesci's '543 Broadway' chair produced by Bernini in 1993 was a seemingly simple translucent resin chair, available in a range of colors – orange, green, blue and red. However, each of the chair's four feet was mounted on a spring. Depending on how the sitter adjusted his or her position, the chair bobbed and swayed to counteract that movement. A later, limited edition of the 'Broadway' chair, launched by Bernini in 2001, had no fewer than nine such feet and optional armrests. The seat and back of the chair – this time made from thermochromatic plastic in black, blue or red – changed slightly in color owing to the sitter's body heat.

Gaetano Pesce's work is by no means limited to furniture design and, in recent years, he has returned to the discipline of architecture in which he was originally trained. Towards the end of the 20th century, his lifelong passion for new materials, and in particular resin, saw him create wondrous, colorful, often translucent designs for all manner of vases, lighting and mirrors. Some of his most notable recent work has been for his own company, Fish Design – a playful reference to the English translation of his own surname – established in 1995 in New York where he now lives.

GAETANO PESCE DESIGNS

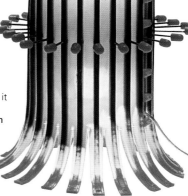

'Nobody's Chair' is typical of Pesce's interest in experimenting with materials. It is made from panels of polyurethane-based elastic resin inlaid with silk fragments.
2004 35in (88cm) high L

A polyurethane resin 'Alda' lamp. The lamp contains chips that create a jingling sound it is touched.
2004 28in (71cm) high NPA

An American Fish Design rubber '928' vase. This was a less expensive range intended for mass manufacture. Each piece is uniquely colored, patterned and shaped to avoid bland standardisation.
10.75in (27.5cm) high E

A rubber picture frame. Pesce always tried to incorporate an image of a face in these quirky designs – note the shape of the yellow and red designs, particularly on the left.
1996 9.75in (24.5cm) high D

A poured resin 'Waffle' table, from the office of the Chiat-Day advertizing agency. The combination of colors is unique to each table.
28.5in (72.5cm) high P

Marc Newson (1963–)

While most boys want to be astronauts when they grow up, Marc Newson dreamt of designing a spacecraft. It was a dream realized just over twenty years into what continues to be a remarkable career in industrial design. He has worked over a wide range of disciplines and received commissions from a host of influential international clients: from Qantas Airways in Australia to the Dom Pérignon champagne house in France, and from the Italian firm, Alessi, to American motoring giant Ford.

Something of an international superstar in the world of design, Marc Newson is one of a unique breed of designers who emerged during the late 1980s and early 1990s, in the wake of the Postmodernism that had gripped much of the Western world. Like his contemporaries – among them Jasper Morrison, Philippe Starck (see pp232–233) and Tom Dixon (see pp276–277) – Newson took inspiration from the more restrained forms that had emerged in the United States and Italy during the 1950s and '60s, combining these with the latest materials and techniques, to produce biomorphic designs in his own, individual style.

Born and raised in Australia, Newson first started exploring furniture design while studying jewelry and sculpture at Sydney College of the Arts. A grant from the Australian Crafts Council led to him staging his first exhibition in 1984. The exhibition featured his 'Lockheed' lounge chair, a curvaceous chaise longue fashioned from riveted aluminum. With a surrealism reminiscent of the work of Italian designer, Carlo Mollino, the piece caused an instant sensation. It also encapsulated the minimalist, biomorphic aesthetic that was to dominate Newson's style of furniture design in subsequent years.

In 1987 Newson moved to Tokyo and took a job with the innovative design company Idée. Four years later he moved to Paris to set up his own studio where he produced furniture forms in collaboration with the pioneering Italian furniture company, Cappellini, that met with international acclaim. Memorable examples

Marc Newson designed both the interior and the body of EADS Astrium's 'Spaceplane', launched in 2007.

The 'Embryo' chair, by Marc Newson, manufactured by Ideé, Japan, has an elegant waisted shape. It is covered in green neoprene, a wetsuit fabric.
c1988 30.5in (77.5cm) high P

include the narrow-waisted 'Embryo' chair (1988), the fiberglass, free-flowing 'Orgone' lounge chair (1989) and the versatile 'Felt' chair, which could be used for indoor or outdoor use, depending on the finish (1989). All three pieces feature Newson's characteristic sweeping, curved lines and bright colors, combined with his innovative use of modern materials, from the latest stretch fabrics to fiberglass.

In 1997 Newson moved to London and expanded his business. This gained him the capacity to take on more ambitious projects and his designs rapidly became sought after by a wide variety of clients. He diversified hugely, designing pieces for mass-production across several disciplines and for an impressive range of prestigious companies. His output included domestic wares for Alessi, furniture for B&B Italia and lighting for Flos. His broad outlook has continued into the 21st century, with designs for innovative products like the water-filled polypropelene 'Rock Door Stop' for Magis (2007), the Strelka cutlery range (2003) and 'Stavros Bottle Opener' (2007) for Alessi, and a range of watches for Ikepod (2006).

Newson's commissions have also included a number of transportation projects. In 1999, J. Mays of Ford – himself an innovator – invited Newson to design a concept car for the Tokyo Motor Show, in a bid to attract a younger clientele. That same year, Danish firm Biomega commissioned him to design a bicycle for their prestigious range, alongside bikes designed by Ross Lovegrove and Karim Rashid. In 2003 Newson designed a business-class seat for Qantas Airways, which led to a second commission the following year to design interiors not only for Qantas' new fleet, but also for first-class lounges in Melbourne and Sydney. In 2006, Newson became Creative Director of Qantas.

Newson's most recent – and ambitious – aircraft-related design was his 'Spaceplane' for EADS Astrium, launched in 2007. Commissioned to design both the shell and the interior of this suborbital jet, the result was the culmination of all aspects of Newson's design from the highly functional appearance of the jet, to the minimalist interior with its brightly colored sculpted seating and a prolific use of gentle curves.

MARC NEWSON DESIGNS

A 'Sci-Fi' ceramic vase. Newson admits to an eclectic range of influences, including the fantastical movie sets of Ken Adams.
1993 13.5in (34cm) high G

A Super Guppy floor lamp, in aluminum on casters. This was inspired by the Super Guppy cargo aircraft.
1987 73in (185.5cm) high N

A 'Gello Table' made from plastic with Perspex (Plexiglass) top. It was designed for mail order and so had to be flat-packed, light, and easy to assemble.
1994 23.5in (59cm) diam G

The body of this characteristically sculptural design, the 'Felt Chair', is made from reinforced fiberglass, on a leg of natural polished aluminum.
1989 26.5in (67cm) M

A fiberglass chaise longue, 'Orgone', with a sleek, free-flowing, organic form.
1989 70.5in (179cm) long U

A 'Bucky' chair, upholstered in red velvet, but also available in plastic. 'Bucky' chairs can also be fitted together to make a dome.
1995 40in (101.5cm) long L

Ron Arad (1951-)

Ron Arad has gone from enfant terrible to darling of the contemporary art scene. Yet the more internationally famous he grows the more radical and challenging his pieces become. One of a new breed designer-artists dealing with concepts rather than practicality or comfort, his provocative works can take on the qualities of sculpture. He leads the pack when it comes to straddling the divide between design and art.

Ron Arad is one of an elite group of avant-garde designers, including Marc Newson and the Campana Brothers, at the cutting edge of design. These designers produce convention-defying works that are hard to categorize and challenge their audiences.

Israeli-born furniture designer Arad was educated at the Jerusalem Academy of Art. He arrived in London in 1974 to continue his studies at the Architectural Association, an educational institute that promotes avant-garde architecture and design. Several fellow students like Peter Wilson, Nigel Coates, and Zaha Hadid have gone on to become acclaimed contemporary designers. Arad studied under architects Peter Cook and Bernard Tschumi. These two radical and influential design theoreticians believe

ideas and aesthetics are just as important as practicality. Their theories are considered important to the development of Postmodernism.

The London of that time was at the height of Punk and buzzing with possibilities. There was a freewheeling creative atmosphere about the city. After a brief stint in an architectural practice following his graduation, Arad started a furniture studio called One Off in Covent Garden with business partner Caroline Thorman. His early experimental designs were made from salvage and found materials. In 1981 Arad created his famous 'Rover' chair made from a used car seat mounted on a tubular steel frame. He followed it up in 1985 with 'Concrete

Sound', a turntable encased in distressed concrete.

Arad's use of concrete, twisted metal and discarded objects is suggestive of urban decay. His work expresses both environmental concerns and anti-consumerism. This provocative commentary on life after the demise of industry has led to his designs being categorized as Post-industrial.

His designs are more like conceptual artworks then conventionally useful objects. He intentionally distances his pieces from mass-produced furnishings with provocative design, unconventional materials and laborious craftsmanship. He stresses the fact that most of his designs are one-offs or limited editions. They hark back

This colorful 'Victoria & Albert' sofa makes a bold, sculptural statement. It is named after the Victoria and Albert Museum after a retrospective of Arad's work was held there in 2000.
2000 78.75in (200cm) long L

to 'ready-mades' of pioneering Modern artist Marcel Duchamp.

One Off became just like an experimental laboratory and attracted other unconventional designers. Arad began exhibiting work by Tom Dixon, Danny Lane, John Mills, and Tom Lynham. As his reputation grew he began to sell works to customers like Jean-Paul Gaultier. Most of his designs were used in cutting-edge interior decoration schemes for retail premises or offices.

In the late 1980s Arad moved to new premises in North London and in 1989 founded Ron Arad Associates. By this time he was exploring extremely sculptural seating made from steel. The 'Well-Tempered Chair' from 1986 is made out of sheets of stainless steel fastened together with bolts and wing nuts. All manufacturing was carried out on his premises until 1994 when the production of large metal pieces was moved to a workshop in Como in Italy.

Some of his work became more commercially oriented. He produced the Spring collection for Moroso, which included chairs like the 'Big Easy' from 1988, 'Big Heavy' in 1989, and the 'Little Heavy' from 1991. Commissioned by progressive Italian metal manufacturers Alessi to design some tableware, he came up with the distinct organic-shaped 'Babyboop' container. Since its introduction in the mid-1990s his plastic "Bookworm" bookshelf for Kartell has been a best-seller. Amongst Arad's more unusual commercial projects was a chandelier designed for the Swarovski crystal company. It incorporates LEDs (light-emitting diodes) so it can display messages that are sent to it by SMS text messaging. Since 1997, he has been head of the Design Products masters' degree course at the Royal College of Art in London.

Until recently, a booming contemporary art market has fueled interest in challenging pieces by designers like Arad. His work remains particularly popular with American collectors. Prices for his work have gone from several hundred pounds in the 1980s to several hundred thousand pounds for unique designs at auction today. Arad sees these prices as a vote of confidence in his pieces, firing his enthusiasm to make ever more complex designs.

RON ARAD DESIGNS

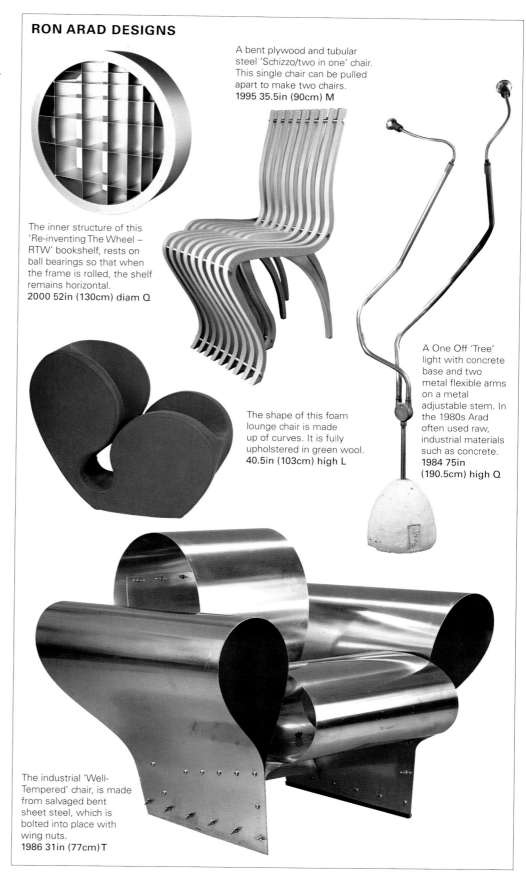

A bent plywood and tubular steel 'Schizzo/two in one' chair. This single chair can be pulled apart to make two chairs.
1995 35.5in (90cm) M

The inner structure of this 'Re-inventing The Wheel – RTW' bookshelf, rests on ball bearings so that when the frame is rolled, the shelf remains horizontal.
2000 52in (130cm) diam Q

The shape of this foam lounge chair is made up of curves. It is fully upholstered in green wool.
40.5in (103cm) high L

A One Off 'Tree' light with concrete base and two metal flexible arms on a metal adjustable stem. In the 1980s Arad often used raw, industrial materials such as concrete.
1984 75in (190.5cm) high Q

The industrial 'Well-Tempered' chair, is made from salvaged bent sheet steel, which is bolted into place with wing nuts.
1986 31in (77cm) T

Campana Brothers

Given that Humberto Campana studied law, and his younger brother, Fernando trained as an architect, they make unlikely candidates for having produced some of the most spectacular furniture of the late 20th and early 21st centuries. With a passion for the street culture of Brazil, and a fascination with the chaos of urban life in their capital city, São Paulo, they combine found objects and use the most innovative materials to create limited-edition pieces that have become highly sought after.

Collaboration between the two brothers began in 1984 when, on completing his training as an architect, Fernando (1961–) joined his brother Humberto (1953–) in his studio. Humberto had given up law to become a sculptor. From the very start they developed a working relationship in which Humberto's understanding of sculpture – form, color and texture – blended with Fernando's training in structure and design.

Their work was in tune with the low-tech, rough and ready furniture that was beginning to emerge toward the end of the 1980s, and which ran counter to the high-tech style that had dominated the first half of the decade. Along with designers like Tom Dixon and Ron Arad, the Campana brothers worked on

designs that incorporated scrap wood or fabrics, and items that were better known for more banal uses, including plastic hosing or drain covers. Working primarily on the aesthetic, and subsequently on the structure and ergonomics, their pieces have always retained an energetic, innovative, highly individual style.

The design that brought them international attention was the 'Vermelha'

chair (designed in 1993), which was constructed from a mass of red cord found in a São Paulo street market, wound and looped around a stainless steel frame. The design was taken up by pioneering Italian furniture company Edra, who even received a video recording from the brothers detailing every stage of the chair's construction. The concept of a jumbled mass is one that recurs often in their work.

Traditional local crafts led to the idea behind this 'Multidão' chair made from handmade rag dolls. The brothers made similar pieces using stuffed toys.
2003 25in (63.5cm) high V

For their 'Anemone' ('Anêmonas') chair (designed in 2002), the brothers used a similar technique as the 'Vermelha' chair, wrapping a length of vinyl hosing around a stainless-steel frame to create a low-slung basket-like seat. The 'Sofá Boa' (designed in 2002) is essentially a 295.25 foot (90m) mass of velvet polyurethane-foam-stuffed tubing, intertwined to give the sofa form.

In a series of domestic pieces commissioned by Alessi in 2003, the Campana brothers used stainless steel rods to make pieces including a fruit basket and a candle holder, where the rods are suspended in air as if they have been dropped like pick-up-sticks.

Among some of the Campana brothers' most notable designs are those that reference the cultural and social traditions of their native country. For their 'Favela' chair of 1991, for example, the brothers glued and nailed off-cuts of wood to one another in a seemingly random fashion. Retrieving the wood from city streets, they claimed as their inspiration the shantytowns (favelas) that had grown on the outskirts of Rio de Janeiro and many other Brazilian cities. Their 'Multidão' chair makes use of fabric figures that are traditionally made in the northeast of Brazil. Scores of the dolls are jumbled together. The piece makes for an unsettling comment on the hugely populated Brazilian cities.

Inspired by woven mats made in the favelas, the Campana brothers have long experimented with similar techniques for their 'Sushi' range of furniture. Here, waste textiles, including felt, wool fabrics, and synthetic materials of different thicknesses, are layered together and rolled up like a carpet. The roll is then sliced in cross-section to produce multicolored concentric rings with which sofas can be upholstered or tabletops covered. A variation on the 'Sushi' theme involves rolling strips of fabric, and stuffing them into a tubular frame to create a low, soft seat.

The country continues to inspire the brothers. They are reported to have said: "Brazil is our great fountain of inspiration. Everything inspires us – from the people and how they organize their lives, to the geographical, racial and cultural variety of our environment. This fusion is truly what we consider modernity."

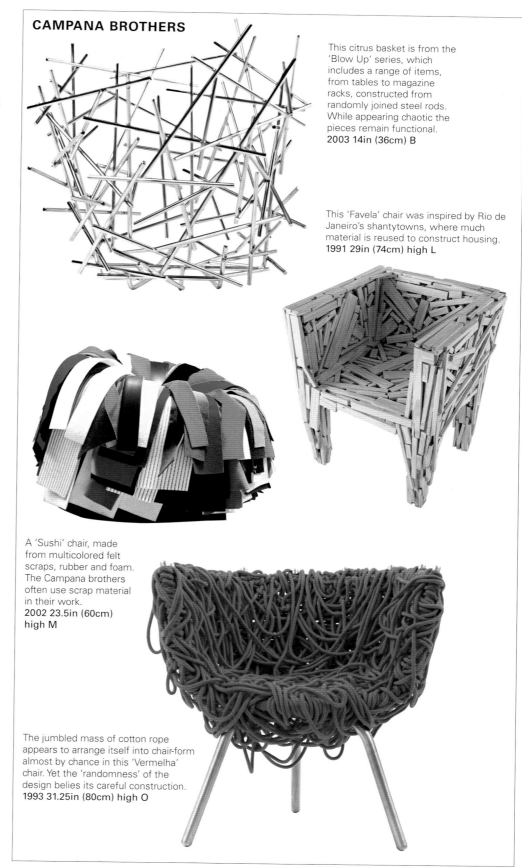

CAMPANA BROTHERS

This citrus basket is from the 'Blow Up' series, which includes a range of items, from tables to magazine racks, constructed from randomly joined steel rods. While appearing chaotic the pieces remain functional.
2003 14in (36cm) B

This 'Favela' chair was inspired by Rio de Janeiro's shantytowns, where much material is reused to construct housing.
1991 29in (74cm) high L

A 'Sushi' chair, made from multicolored felt scraps, rubber and foam. The Campana brothers often use scrap material in their work.
2002 23.5in (60cm) high M

The jumbled mass of cotton rope appears to arrange itself into chair-form almost by chance in this 'Vermelha' chair. Yet the 'randomness' of the design belies its careful construction.
1993 31.25in (80cm) high O

Julia Krantz (1967-)

The possibilities and sustainability of wood, together with the landscape of her native Brazil, motivate and inspire Julia Krantz. She says her furniture – which is carved from stack-laminated plywood – is made in partnership with the rainforest. Ecology and a fascination with nature are fundamental to her work in which she takes thin wood laminates and manipulates them into shape before polishing them to a smooth, glossy surface.

Her expertise in woodworking combined with a deep appreciation of design history and a love of nature allows Julia Krantz to create furniture that is elegant and beautifully handcrafted. A graduate of the School of Architecture and Urbanism at the University of São Paulo, she has run her own design studio – Julia Krantz Movelaria – in São Paulo since 2000.

There is a timeless quality to Krantz's work, which focuses on the unique histories of objects. Through her pieces she examines how people interact with the everyday objects that surround them.

Her 'Mesa Baum' table which features a bowl carved into its surface is one such example. The design has personal meaning for Krantz, as it was inspired by her mother's childhood memories of growing up in Germany during World War Two. The war was a time of deprivation, when many people had to manage without basic domestic objects. When her mother's family found they had no plates to eat from, her

mother's father – Krantz's grandfather – carved a bowl shape into the dinner table that was used to serve food.

The sculptural quality of Krantz's work almost creates the sense that her forms have emerged fully formed from the wood. She considers her work a continuous search for improved techniques with the wood, and she continually strives for a superior understanding of her material. She also seeks a more conscious connection to the

A stack-laminated plywood 'Mesa Baum' table by Julia Krantz. This piece, with its inset glass bowl, reconsiders how people use the objects around them. It was inspired by Krantz's family history.
2005 71in (180.5cm) long NPA

environment. Krantz describes her work as a "search". She says she views it as "a continuous quest for ways to manipulate wood with more precision, a better understanding of the material possibilities and a more conscious connection to the envrionment".

She uses a stack-laminated process to craft sensuous, organic, and monumental pieces, often inspired by the rich, lush landscape of her native Brazil, such as her

Unique in stack-laminated plywood 'Sofá Güell' by Julia Krantz.
2008 97in (246.5cm) long NPA

vessels with flowing lines that suggest the way water shapes a landscape over time. She once said: "A friend of mine says that my designs take the form of falling water. I never would have thought of such an image but it fits." For others, the sensual, organic curves seen in her furniture are also reminiscent of the undulating folds of a piece of fabric.

A champion of sustainable design, Krantz is continually developing methods to use her materials responsibly and in harmony with the environment. Wood scraps are re-used in imaginative ways, for example, to create surface patterns on carved bowls. Krantz never works with wood from endangered species of tree and is a certified member of the Forestry Products Buyers Group, which guarantees her commitment to use only materials obtained through responsible and sustainable management.

Part of a new generation of Brazilian artists who are exploring their relationship with their country, Krantz's "Brazilianess" comes through strongly in her creations. Not only does her work reflect the rich diversity of the rainforest, her style recalls the scale and organic curves of iconic Brazilian designers such as Sergio Rodrigues and Jose Zanine Caldas (see p168) while the level and quality of detail is similar to that of designer Joaquim Tenreiro (see p168).

Design critic Joseph Starr says: "Her pieces are so seamless that they appear to have emerged from the tree entire."

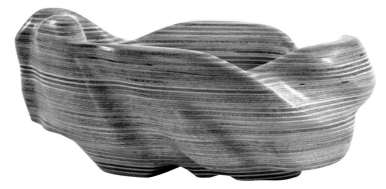

A carved Sumauma wood 'Oyster' bowl, designed and made by Julia Krantz. The shape of the bowl shows off the natural beauty of the wood.
2008 16in (40.5cm) wide
NPA

The flowing form of this lounge chair is inspired by nature. The design, named 'Poltrona Suave', meaning 'smooth armchair', is made from stack-laminated plywood ergonomically carved to make a comfortable seat.
2005 37.5in (95cm) high
NPA

HUGO FRANÇA

Working in the same tradition as modernist Brazilian masters, Hugo França seeks to reveal the beauty of the Brazilian hardwoods he uses as his raw material. Techniques include cutting layers into the wood to expose its natural features, and carving it into graceful shapes inspired by natural forms. After studying industrial engineering and a brief period at a computer company in the early 1980s, França moved to the jungle of northeastern Brazil in Bahia, where he lived and worked with the indigenous people for fifteen years. During this period França developed his passion for his native environment and learned traditional woodworking techniques. Well known for his respect for his material, França works exclusively with fallen trees and old canoes he purchases from the Amazon's Pataxó Indian tribes.

This solid 'Ayana' couch has been carved to show off the natural qualities of the pequi wood.
2007 74.75in (190cm) wide
NPA

Peter Voulkos (1924–2002)

From an early career designing tablewares, the Greek-American ceramicist Peter Voulkos forged a reputation for creating monumental sculptures. His pieces revolutionized our perception of ceramics as an art form. Voulkos' sculptures were decorated with glazes, or he created texture by cutting into the clay before it was fired. Later pieces were based on vessel forms and were often fired in wood-burning kilns. He encouraged a new generation of ceramicists to approach the medium in a new way.

Peter Voulkos is known for his highly original ceramic sculptures, which cross the traditional divide between ceramic crafts and fine art. He redefined the commonly held perception of pottery as a medium for studio work or a material destined for making functional everyday household wares. Instead he created clay sculptures that were to change the way the world views ceramics.

Born Panagiotis Voulkos to Greek immigrant parents in Montana, Peter Voulkos studied at Montana State College and the California College of the Arts before forging a career as a ceramicist, initially producing useful dinnerware in his home town of Bozeman, Montana. His first teaching post was in North Carolina, in 1953. A year later he established a department dedicated to the study of art ceramics at the Otis College of Art and Design (then called the Los Angeles County Art Institute). There, Voulkos turned his back on functional objects and concentrated on creating the sculptural ceramic designs which were to make his name.

Inspiration for these new works largely came from his encounters with the work of the Abstract Expressionists, especially the paintings of Franz Kline, during time spent in New York City. Among the beliefs of the Abstract Expressionists was that monumentalisation would redeem decorative art. The Abstract Expressionists worked in a seemingly spontaneous and

A wood-fired stoneware 'Siguirilla' sculpture by Peter Voulkos.
1999 45in (114.3cm) high NPA

intense style and their works have a dramatic impact – an attribute that can clearly be seen in Voulkos' methods and his finished work.

His move to the University of California at Berkeley in 1959, where he established a department dedicated to art ceramics, cemented Voulkos's reputation. Freely formed by tearing, ripping and gouging the clay surfaces, his eye-catching and bold pottery designs – lavishly decorated with painted brushstrokes or covered with rich colorful glazes, or left plain – have been widely influential and reinterpreted by ceramicists across the globe. His energetic and enthusiastic teachings inspired a generation of pupils, many who went on to become successful artists.

In the 1960s Voulkos set up a bronze foundry at the University and started to make monumental sculptures for public and private commissions. He was to work on bronze and ceramic sculptures for a decade.

After he retired from teaching in 1985, due to ill health, Voulkos continued to work full time from his own workshop. He returned to clay as his principal medium and from then on, nearly all his sculpture was based on vessel forms. These included what he called his clay 'stack pots' which were created by joining together a variety of shapes and sizes of ceramic pot to create a single object. He also made an array of sculptural ceramic compositions which were cast in bronze.

Voulkos had been introduced to the use of wood kilns by ceramic artist Peter Callas in 1979 and much of his later work was fired in wood kilns. The effect of the wood smoke and charcoal on the fired vessels gave him new surfaces to explore. He also experimented with new clay bodies that he discovered while working in Japan, including sandy, orange-colored clay from Shigaraki.

His sculptures were hand-built, many created using the ancient technique of coiled pots where ropes of clay are built up to create the walls of a vessel before being smoothed by hand.

Voulkos made the University of California at Berkeley a major center for experimentation with clay. His bold, organic, aggressive and energetic works changed the world's perception of ceramics.

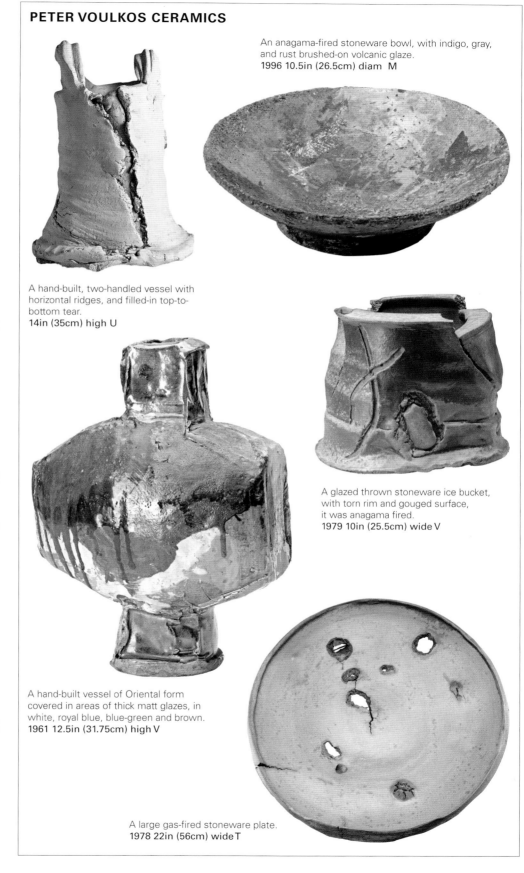

PETER VOULKOS CERAMICS

An anagama-fired stoneware bowl, with indigo, gray, and rust brushed-on volcanic glaze.
1996 10.5in (26.5cm) diam M

A hand-built, two-handled vessel with horizontal ridges, and filled-in top-to-bottom tear.
14in (35cm) high U

A glazed thrown stoneware ice bucket, with torn rim and gouged surface, it was anagama fired.
1979 10in (25.5cm) wide V

A hand-built vessel of Oriental form covered in areas of thick matt glazes, in white, royal blue, blue-green and brown.
1961 12.5in (31.75cm) high V

A large gas-fired stoneware plate.
1978 22in (56cm) wide T

SCULPTURAL CERAMICS GALLERY

From the 1970s onward ceramicists became particularly interested in combining sculptural and pottery techniques, producing pieces that occupied a rich middle ground between functional ceramics and fine arts. Many potters used traditional forms – such as teapots, chargers, and vases – as their starting point, although the more sculptural a piece became, the less likely it was to be of practical use. Others abondoned the need for their creations to be tied to recognisable forms altogether.

This powerful piece depicting a wrapped figure cradled in a pod-like structure is inspired by African fertility sculptures. Artist Edwin Scheier frequently represented figures within other forms.
19in (48cm) high J

A ceramic sculpture, 'The Conqueror' by Beatrice Wood. An accomplished potter but untrained in sculpture, Wood deliberately creates "primitive" figures.
9.5in (24cm) high N

In his work Michael Lucero explores different cultures, and contrasting ideas of beauty, as in this hand-built carved and glazed ceramic sculpture, 'Island Dreamer'.
1983 27in (68.5cm) wide

This glazed faience double-vessel, was designed by inventive ceramic sculptor Michael Lucero. Lucero uses diverse cultural influences in his work.
11.5in (29cm)high L

A large glazed earthenware sculptural charger, by Viola Frey. The energetic and colorful high relief decoration is typical of Frey's work.
1983 25in (63.5cm) wide Q

A hand-built stoneware vessel decorated with colored slip, 'Lightning Spout III' by Elizabeth Fritsch.

A figural 'Ohio' ceramic sculpture, by Jack Earl. Earl creates humorous works often incorporating cultural references.
26in (66cm) high N

A large glazed terracotta gourd-shaped sculpture, by Graham Marx.
30in (76cm) high S

A large porcelain teapot by Tom Coleman, multi-fired with lithium-barium glazes.
23in (58.5cm) high S

GRAYSON PERRY VASE

"It's about time a transvestite potter won the Turner," Grayson Perry said as he accepted the 2003 Turner Prize. His ceramics are typically traditional forms – described by Perry as "classical invisible … a base that people can understand" – decorated with collage, graffiti, photography and drawing. The colorful, naïve decoration deals with often disturbing themes – including issues drawn from his own life and that of his alter ego, Claire. Some pieces satirize the work of other artists.

'Moon Jar' by Grayson Perry. 2008 24.5in (62cm) high

There is often a disparity between the form and the content of Perry's work, especially the relationship between the pots and the images that decorate them.

The ceramic is often covered with sgraffito drawings, handwritten and stenciled texts, photographic transfers and rich glazes. In this way a functional object becomes a piece of art which tells a story.

References to Perry's childhood, his family and his transvestite alter ego Claire can be seen in the decoration.

David Regan's work is typically highly sculptural, yet closely based on traditional forms. This porcelain 'Pot Belly Stove Teapot,' shows an interior scene. 1989 10.25in (26cm) high **M**

An earthenware pot by Noi Volkov, 'Van Gogh/Venus', with painting after Botticelli and Van Gogh. 2004 17in (43cm) high **O**

The Hong Kong Chinese/American artist, Hui Ka Kwong, narrowed the gap between ceramic craft and art. 20.5in (52cm) high **M**

A large ceramic vessel by Rudy Autio, 'Razz-ma-Tazz'. Autio drew on Western American folklore for inspiration. 1998 31.5in (80cm) high **W**

David Gilhooly (1943–)

A leading member of the Funk ceramic movement, David Gilhooly, is best known for his light-hearted FrogWorld pieces, although his work consists of more than these. Ceramic works range from representations of animals named after old acquaintances, to enormous pieces of junk food, but the work is always colorful and often humorous. Gilhooly has also worked in other media, most notably in Plexiglas, as well as papier-mâché, printmaking and assemblage (collage).

Brightly colored, humorous or satirical ceramics, often with a political message, characterize the Funk ceramics of David Gilhooly. Born in California, Gilhooly earned an MA from the University of California, at Davis, in 1966. While studying there he became a key member of what was later to be called the Funk Ceramic Movement of the San Francisco Bay Area. This group included professor Robert Arneson, the leader of the movement, and Gilhooly's fellow Davis students, Peter Vandenberge, Chris Unterseher and Margaret Dodd.

Gilhooly has created a broad range of inspired Funk ceramics throughout his illustrious career. Never deterred by the size of a kiln, he cut the pieces of his large-scale sculptures in a variety of places and fired it in instalments. He exploited the possibilities offered by the new low-firing white earthenware body that had been developed by Robert Arneson and Peter Vandenberge at Davis. Gilhooly allowed large sculptural pieces to be constructed in stages and encouraged a greater use of color.

It is for his whimsical 'Frog World' series that Gilhooly is best known. The frogs came about during a cup-making session. Gilhooly remembers: "We all tried to make the most far-out, grotesque, unusually handled cups possible while still keeping the cups functional. I made a giant mushroom for a handle and set frogs below it. I also put one in the bottom of the cup itself unknowingly tying myself to a joke that went at least as far back as Babylon."

He went on to create a frog universe. "Some people kept telling me that they must be going to take over after we had wiped ourselves out with some nuclear holocaust. Others just thought them cute

A ceramic sculpture, by David Gilhooly, 'BreadFrog Making a Vegetable Stew of Himself'.
17in (43cm) high N

and whimsical, but I, having no special feelings for them either way, thought that they were, in the end, just us, using a different body. The body we use is unimportant, any body might do, frog bodies seemed as adaptable as some lemur. Bodies are after all just a tool for us to use. So why couldn't there be "frogs" just like us in some parallel universe where the

choice was made 65 odd million years ago to use a frog body rather than that of some protopig or lemur?"

From 'FrogEgyptian' Gods and Goddesses to busts of historic luminaries such as Queen Victoria and George Washington – called 'FrogVictoria' and 'FrogWashington' respectively – these highly original large-scale frog sculptures frequently parallel the human condition. They are bizarre and comical expressions of Gilhooly's own opinions about religion, political issues and contemporary events.

After moving to Ontario in 1971 to teach part-time, he added a host of colorful vegetable and food shapes including doughnuts and pizza slices which he would sell from a stall at art exhibitions. Gilhooly also made large-scale papier-mâché animals such as crocodiles and alsoturned his attention to printmaking.

By 1983, Gilhooly had tired of working in the "demon clay", sold his kilns and potter's wheel, and turned to Plexiglas as a medium. Alternating between Plexiglas and clay, with occasional departures into wood and print, he continued to work with food themes alongside cityscapes that often incorporated "found" objects or real food. In 1996 he abandoned clay to work on what he calls "shadow boxes" – playful sculptures of fruit of vegetables, for instance – that are framed to hang on the wall like pictures.

PLEXIGLAS (PERSPEX)
Gilhooly relished the challenge of working with this material – a transparent form of acrylic that diffuses light. Better known for its use for signs and advertizing, Gilhooly found the bright colors appealing. He enjoyed the challenge of not knowing how the colors would work together until the piece had been assembled.

'The Modern Airport' by David Gilhooly
36in (91.5cm) high NPA

DAVID GILHOOLY CERAMICS

A sarcophagus, glazed ceramic, in two halves. In this piece Gilhooly playfully represents the Ancient Egyptian culture in frog form, with a humorous attention to detail.
1970 28.5in (71cm) L

A glazed earthenware sculpture, 'Jelly Belly Bear in Art'. Gilhooly's efforts to resolve his eating problems have led him to represent junk food in his work.
1981 17in (43cm) high L

This large sculptural piece with pigeons perched on an imposing frog-like face is called 'The Count of Crumbs in Central Park or The Death of the Count of Crumbs'.
22.5in (57cm) high O

The frog figures in this piece entitled, 'The Cosmic Egg', seem to be emerging from the surface of the "egg".
1975–78, 20in (51cm) high L

The first of the frog pots, this is modeled with frogs as Mount Rushmore icons.
13in (33cm) high M

A marbleized ceramic two-piece sculpture, 'Trip to California Stelae', featuring anthropomorphized frogs.
1975 29in (74cm) high N

CERAMICS GALLERY

By definition, postmodern ceramics are remarkably diverse and therefore difficult to summarize. A great number of ceramicists have explored working with near abstract creations. While not all pieces have moved away from traditional forms or themes, freedom from the need to produce functional wares has given potters huge scope to experiment with new techniques, forms and surface finishes.

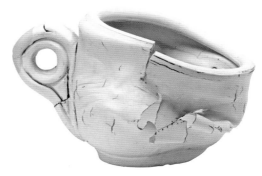

The influence of Peter Voulkos, can be seen in this porcelain sculpture of a crumpled teacup, by Irv Tepper.
14in (35.5cm) wide N

A piece of stoneware by Michael Cleff from the series 'On Addition'.
2004 15.5in (39cm) high NPA

Howard Kottler took inspiration from modern art, as in this bold and colorful sculptural glazed earthenware 'Lemon Punch Pot'.
1986 19.5in (49.5cm) high L

This tall wood-fired totemic vessel, by Paul Chaleff, has an elegant waisted form, two applied handles and a closed-in rim. The textured surface has a deep red and matt mustard finish.
1984 30.5in (77.5cm) high I

A Ken Ferguson oversized stoneware teapot, with characteristic rabbit-form handle, in verdigris glaze. Ferguson used rabbit forms with flowing ears in many of his later works in clay.
23in (58.5cm) high P

In this stoneware bowl Emmanuel Cooper has explored texture and color by using crater glazes.
4.75in (12cm) diam C

FUNK CERAMICS

Centered around the San Francisco Bay area, the Funk movement borrowed from Dadism and Pop Art to create brightly colored, fun ceramic sculptures with a strong political and social agenda. The movement was lead by Robert Arneson, a professor at the University of California at Davis and was carried on by Arneson's students, who included David Gilhooly, Peter Vandenberge, Chris Unterseher, and Margaret Dodd. Other key figures include Hui Ka Kwong, who created boldly decorated, symmetrical forms that displayed an individual, emotional response to the world.

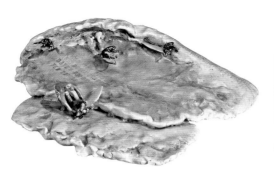

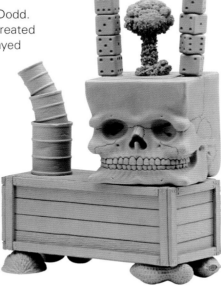

Chris Unterseher was at the University of California at Davis with Gilhooly where he created this Funk ceramic sculpture, 'Champion Surfer Mike Doyle Teaches Dave's Frogs a Few Tricks'.
1969 14in (36cm) wide F

A Richard Notkin stoneware teapot. Richard Notkin's outspoken criticisms of social and political issues are evident in his work, such as the sculptural re-interpretations of the Yixing teapot.
1999 9in (23cm) high P

A Funk pottery lamp, by Hwa Kwan Hui, with five sockets and two rows of arms, painted in bright yellow and gold on a cobalt base. The trumpet-like form emphasizes the fun in the Funk aesthetic.
38in (96.5cm) high M

An Otto Natzler ceramic sculpture. The iridescent, vibrant red revealing blue veining is typical of Natzler's inventive glazes.
1979 13in (33cm) high O

A slab-built abstract sculpture, by Paul Soldner. Soldner experimented with firing techniques to try to re-create traditional Japanese raku effects.
1981 35in (89cm) wide V

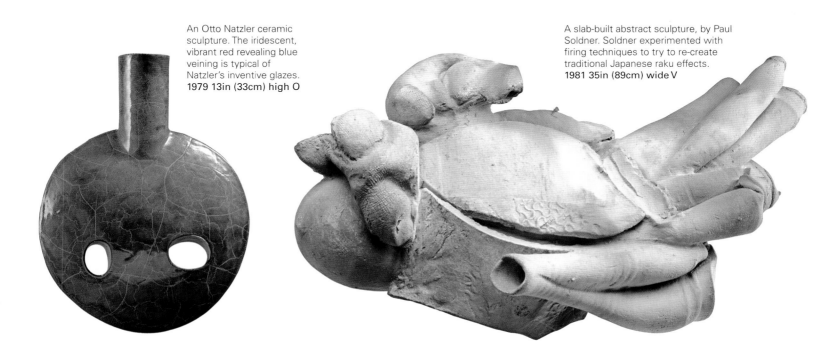

POSTMODERNISM TO CONTEMPORARY

MASS-PRODUCED CERAMICS GALLERY

Ceramics designers have taken their inspiration from the past and from other cultures to create intriguing pieces for mass production. Working with long-established companies such as Lladro, and newer concerns such as Droog, they have created designs which push the boundaries of ceramic design.

Spanish designer Jaime Hayon created 'The Rocking Chicken Ride' as part of his Fantasy Collection for Lladro.
2008 G

Marcel Wanders 'Turtle' plate from a series of 30 different designs.
2003 5.5in (14cm) diam C

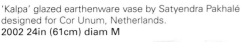

Based on the design for a disposable plastic cup, the porcelain 'Blooming Over Cup' was designed by Mina Wu and Jan B for Droog Design.
2005 A

'City Brunch' porcelain set by Matali Crasset manufactured by Guy Degrenne.
2006 C

'Kalpa' glazed earthenware vase by Satyendra Pakhalé designed for Cor Unum, Netherlands.
2002 24in (61cm) diam M

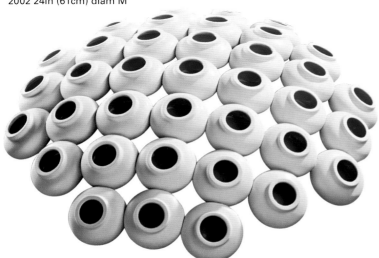

The pastel colors on black, combined with the geometric motifs, made a striking scheme that was typical of the period.

SWID POWELL

Founded in New York in 1983 by Nan Swid and Addie Powell, Swid Powell produced works by many of the major Postmodern designers, including Michael Graves, Ettore Sottsass, Zaha Hadid and Robert Venturi, who designed one of Swid Powell's most popular patterns: 'Grandmother'. This pattern was an ironic re-imagining of a grandmotherly chintzy tablecloth. Venturi believed that although the style of our immediate past (our mother's style) seems dated, the buffer of a generation can make our grandmother's style appealing.

Steven Holl was one of a number of leading architects who designed homewares for Swid Powell.

A 'Planar' pattern transfer printed dinner plate, designed by Steven Holl in 1986.
12in (30.5cm) diam C

A Swid Powell 'Medici' pattern transfer printed teacup and saucer, with fashionable, stylized motifs. Designed by Ettore Sottsass in 1984.
Saucer 5.75in (14.5cm) diam. C

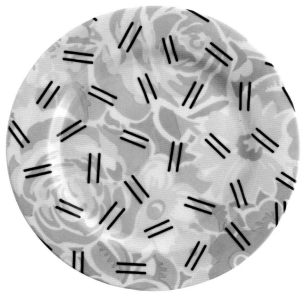

A Swid Powell transfer decorated 'Grandmother' pattern ceramic plate, designed by Robert Venturi in 1984.
9in (23cm) high C

Murano Glass

The ancient decorating techniques of Murano were transformed between the 1950s and 1970s. Larger *murrines* were used in vibrant colors: typically primaries or clashing colors. Dino Martens was a major catalyst for change. As well as exciting work for Aureliano Toso, he reinvented the *zanfirico* technique for A.V.E.M., using revolutionary color combinations, although the basic glass forms stayed essentially the same. By the 1980s, however, even that had begun to change.

A Barovier & Toso vase, designed by Toni Zuccheri, with a dark violet exterior and white interior, with colorless vertical ribs. The elegant design is typical of the 1980s.
c1985 12.5in (32cm) L

POSTMODERNISM'S INFLUENCE ON MURANO

The influence of Italian postmodernism groups such as Alchimia and Memphis began to show on Murano as artists such as Ettore Sottsass, Mario Zanini and Matteo Thun turned to the experienced craftsmen of Murano to realize their outlandish glass designs. These were often brightly colored vessels of geometric, architectural form. Some appeared to be made from Perspex, rather than glass. The Memphis glass manufactured by Toso Vetri d'Arte was innovative and exciting, combining fantasy with function.

Venini, which had prospered under the leadership of Paolo Venini, began to develop a set of glass windows in bright colors that could be used like screens. These were made under the guidance of Paolo's son-in-law Ludovico de Santillana and his daughter (Paolo's granddaughter), Laura,

who worked as a designer at Venini until 1986. Italian artists Riccardo Licata and Toni Zuccheri designed for various Muranese companies, including Venini and Barovier & Toso. Other Venetian artists, such as Paolo Martinuzzi, were not part of the new design movement, but nevertheless produced work that epitomizes the Postmodern spirit. Martinuzzi's vessels are lightly engraved with small, child-like figures with large eyes. They rest on bases that suggest washed up debris, such as wood and rust-covered metal. Livio Seguso, an independent artist in Venice since 1965, abandoned the Murano glassmaking heritage in the 1970s and began to focus on clear crystal. His sculptures of crystal and blown glass became images of light.

MURANO'S INFLUENCE ON POSTMODERNISM

Murano had been an almost closed community for many years, the craft of glassmaking passed down through families. Now they began to open their doors to the newly emerging studio glass-artists. A number of foreign artists were invited to share designs and expertise.

Dale Chihuly was one of the Americans who went to Murano in the 1960s and to learn traditional glassmaking skills. Twenty years after his first visit, he collaborated with the Muranese *maestro*, Lino Tagliapetra on a series of glass pieces that were inspired by 1920s and 1930s Venetian glass, but of wildly exaggerated forms. Richard Marquis (see pp56-57), another American, also spent time in Murano, where was inspired to use *murrines*. His *murrine*-decorated, blown, fused, slumped and carved vessels are referred to as 'Marquiscarpa' – a fusing of his name with that of Muranese designer, Carlo Scarpa.

A Venini 'Klee' glass vase, by Laura Dias de Santillana, the design inspired by the colorful paintings of the artist Paul Klee.
1983 9.25in (23.5cm) high K

A four-fold screen by Makio Hasuike for Venini. The five patterned panels each demonstrate different decorative techniques.
Each panel 19.5in (50cm) wide Q

Kyohei Fujita was known for his glass boxes with detailed surface decoration, such as this example with gold and silver leaf, and white and red plum pattern.
6.5in (16.5cm) Q

LINO TAGLIAPIETRA VASE

Born and raised on Murano, Lino Tagliapietra learned the island's traditional techniques before he left for the USA in 1979. There he taught traditional Italian glassmaking techniques and in return was inspired by the work of American glassmakers, such as Dale Chihuly. As a result his own work became richer and more dramatically colored, but was always based on traditional Venetian techniques. Tagliapietra's influence undoubtedly contributed to the fashion for free-blown glass in the 1990s.

The vase is a Classical baluster shape in a modern style.

The glass would have been very complicated to make. There are several layers of glass, one of them made up of *zanfirico* stripes, and applied glass 'wings'. The outer layer of glass was cut to show the multi-colored layer beneath.

The bright colors are typical of Murano glass.

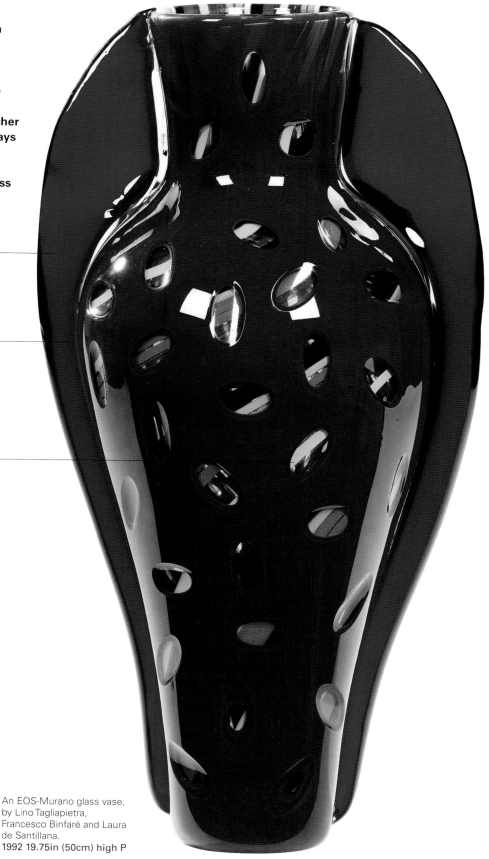

Japanese artist, Kyohei Fujita, is said to have spent one month of every year in Murano from the 1970s. Fujita made two types very different kinds of glass, both inspired by Venetian techniques. The first, of colored canes in pastel shades and gold foil, very obviously echoes the Venetian hot-glass techniques. The second, cast glass caskets, for which Fujita is perhaps most famous, are heavily influenced by Japanese *kazaribako*. The technique he used to create them was first used by Carlo Scarpa.

Another Japanese artist, Yoichi Ohira, began designing for the Vetreria de Majo in 1987. In collaboration with the glassblower Livio Serena he began creating unique pieces in vase forms inspired by classical Japanese ceramics and the brilliant, swirling palette of Venice.

An EOS-Murano glass vase, by Lino Tagliapietra, Francesco Binfaré and Laura de Santillana.
1992 19.75in (50cm) high P

Dale Chihuly (1941–)

Dale Chihuly is part of long tradition of celebrated American glass designers that can be traced back to Louis Comfort Tiffany at the beginning of the 20th century. His extraordinary glass objects are prized by collectors and museums while his experimental creations are often referred to as sculptures and installations. Chihuily's category-defying glass has long provoked considerable controversy as part of the "is it art or craft?" debate.

Dale Chihuly first developed his passion for working glass while studying interior design at the University of Washington in the early 1960s. Even as a college student his glass created a sensation. An innovative tapestry design incorporating glass helped win him a postgraduate scholarship to the University of Wisconsin where Harvey Littleton had just established the USA's first glassworking program. He then continued his education at the Rhode Island School of Design. Awarded a Fulbright Fellowship upon graduation, he took the opportunity to visit the famous Venini glass factory on the island of Murano (see pp186–187).

He once described how he became fascinated with glass. "One night in 1965, I melted a few pounds of stained glass in one of my kilns and dipped a steel pipe from the basement into it. I blew into the pipe and a bubble of glass appeared. I had never seen glassblowing before. My fascination for it probably comes in part from discovering the process that night by accident. From that moment, I became obsessed with learning all I could about glass."

When Chihuly returned from Europe in 1969 the Studio Glass movement (see pp54-57), which encouraged designer-makers to work alone, was really gathering momentum. The Rhode Island School of Design was so impressed by Chihuly's designs they invited him back to develop a glassworking program for the college. He was to teach there for the next eleven years. Many of his students, such as Dan Dailey and Toots Zynsky (see pp56–57), would go on to become leading studio glass artists. Simultaneously he founded an independent institution to teach glassworking in Seattle called the Pilchuck Glass School with help from art patrons John and Anne Gould Hauberg. Today, Pilchuck is one of the largest and most influential educational bodies.

For a designer early in his career Chihuly was receiving significant recognition. This gave him the confidence and the freedom to work on large-scale environmental

A spectacular manganese blue Venetian glass vessel, by Dale Chihuly, with a dramatic single full-height coil and contrasting colored yellow lip to rim and to base.
1991 31.75in (80.5cm) high W

installations and architectural projects, such as the Cast Glass Door he produced for Pilchuck in 1972. At that time he often used combinations of neon, argon and blown glass for his creations. Chihuly drew inspiration for his designs from a number of sources including West Coast Native American baskets and Navajo blankets. Most significantly he was also already developing his characteristic plant-like imagery.

Gifted designer-makers of studio-glass like Chihuly tend to experiment technically as well as creatively. An example of this is the technique he developed in 1974, in collaboration with colleague James Carpenter and a group of students at the Rhode Island School of Design, for picking up drawn glass threads. These threads went on to feature in his work.

During the 1970s Chihuly often collaborated on major projects with his students or colleagues like Carpenter, but he tended to produce most of his glass designs himself. However, after losing the sight in one eye in a car accident in 1976, then badly dislocating his shoulder in another accident in 1979, it became impossible for him to blow glass comfortably. He remembered how the glassmakers at the Venini glass factory would work on pieces together in groups. Chihuly decided he would behave "more like a director than

'Carnival Pheasant Macchia' by Dale Chihuly, made of four pieces. The 'Macchia' series takes its name from the Italian for "spot". Pieces from this range are typically spotted with color and shell-like in form.
2002 21in wide W

A clear and yellow overlaid glass 'Basket' bowl, by Dale Chihuly. This piece is decorated with multicolored spots and fine iridescent threads spun around.
1989 10in (25.5cm) diam M

actor" on projects from now on. He would pick a team of exceptional glassblowers and oversee them in the execution of his designs.

This new collective way of working allowed him to create incredibly complex glassworks on a grand scale. Chihuly set the trend. Soon other studio-glass workers were copying his cooperative approach for their larger and more elaborate projects.

Chihuly is well known for his multipart blown-glass compositions resembling fantastical sea anemones, tendrils of vegetation, and bunches of fruit. His colorful organic imagery derives from a variety of sources, ranging from icicles, foaming sea waves and Japanese fishing floats, to medieval Persian and Art Deco Italian glass. His use of floral forms harks back to the blooms that grew in profusion in his mother's garden.

In the early 1990s Chihuly began producing massive ceiling installations which he called "Chandeliers". These vibrantly colored creations with masses of intertwined forms were affixed to specially engineered steel armatures. They started out relatively modest in size but have now grown significantly in scale and can weigh over a ton. Perhaps the most extravagant example of a Chihuly chandelier is the eighteen-foot blue and yellow glass example that decorates the entrance hall to London's Victoria & Albert Museum.

Chihuly continues to explore new shapes and techniques. He has created major installations for events including the Academy Awards and the Salt Lake Olympic Winter Games 2002. Chihuly's largest work to date, the 'Fiori di Como', was installed in the lobby of the Bellagio hotel in Las Vegas in 1998. He has also worked on stage sets including the Seattle Symphony Orchestra's production of Béla Bartók's opera 'Bluebeard's Castle'.

Dale Chihuly's 'Rio delle Torreselle' chandelier installed at the Columbus Museum of Art, Ohio as part of its 1996 Chihuly Over Venice exhibit. Each part was blown separately and then assembled on a metal frame.

A large 'Macchia' vase of vermilion, manganese, and turquoise striped glass. Chihuly uses the asymmetric form to emphasize the delicate quality of the glass. **1988 27in (68.5cm) wide U**

Central European Glass

During the 1970s, the artists of Czechoslovakia – following the example of style leaders, such as Stanislav Libenský and Jaroslava Brychtová – drew attention to themselves by producing glass that was demonstrably art, rather than purely an example of skilled craftsmanship. Many explored the possibilities of optical glass, whilst others experimented with free-blown glass. Czechoslovakia was a major European glass powerhouse, and by the 1980s it had become the undisputed leader in optical glass.

OPTICAL GLASS

Optical glass, the flawless glass used in the manufacture of lens and prisms, was first made available to artists from the 1940s. By the 1970s a whole generation of Czech artists had become obsessed with the reflective and refractive properties of this material, and it became a dominant feature of Czech glass production.

The most influential figures in this field were undoubtedly husband and wife team, Stanislav Libenský and Jaroslava Brychtová, who first worked together in 1954. Their collaboration resulted in the famous 'Head Bowl' of mold-melted glass. The couple married in 1963 and continued to work together, producing work with carefully modeled interior voids.

During the 1970s Libenský and Brychtová's work was predominantly in colorless glass. Setting themselves apart from other artists, they made monumental glass charged with emotion. The 72 foot (22m) long sculpture they created for the Czech Pavilion at the Osaka World Expo in 1970, 'River of Life', so clearly evoked the political repression in terms of a progression from happiness to misery that it was deemed unacceptable by the authorities. Despite such pressures they managed to retain their artistic integrity throughout the Communist regime. In the 1980s they began to introduce color in their work.

Even before the regime collapsed in 1989, the influence of Libenský and Brychtová on the international scene was enormous. At home the effect was even more pronounced.

A monolithic, sculptural glass form 'Free Through II' by Stanislav Libenský and Jaroslava Brychtová.
1992-2006 30.5in (77.5cm) high NPA

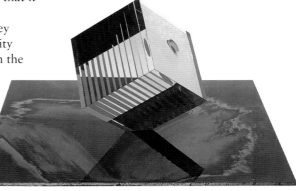

An optical and laminated cut-glass form, 'Würfel', by Vaclav Cigler.
1986 base 19.5in (50cm) square O

The natural elements within this piece of glass by Slovakian artist Yan Zoritchak create a magical, imaginary landscape, which is reflected in its title, 'Jardin Celeste' ('Celestial Garden').
1998 17.75in (45cm) long U

A gray-blue bowl by Frantisek Vizner of cut, sandblasted and polished glass. The pure and minimal form and deep color is typical of Vizner's work.
1987 11in (28cm) diam V

As a professor at the Prague Academy Libenský had taught some of the best young Czech glass artists. Frantisek Vízner's solid, geometric-shaped blocks of colored glass, for example, owe a great deal to Libenský's teaching. Where Libenský and Brychtová cast glass to create light effects, Vízner illuminated his glass by cutting it to varying thicknesses. His colors are typically monochrome and the overall effect is one of effortless simplicity and harmony. Another of Libenský's pupils, Yan Zoritchak settled in France in 1970. His forms have clean lines with plain outer surfaces and complex internal decoration, as in his 'Messager de l'Espace' series.

Václav Cigler, who taught at the Academy of Fine Arts in Bratislava, was also a major inspiration on Central European glass. Using optical cutting he creates reflections and optical illusions that allow the viewer to enter the work. Ciglar rarely uses colored glass, instead letting the glass reflect the colors of the world around creating an interactive experience. Geometrical, architectural glass was made by Hungarian artist, Zoltán Bohus. His wife, Mária Lugossy, tends to produce more emotional pieces, often incorporating other materials including cast bronze.

Other glass artists experimented with engraving. The foremost figure in glass portraiture is Jiri Harcuba, who creates three-dimensional depictions of artists and writers, such as Mozart, Wagner and Kafka, in blocks of clear glass. When viewed from the front the engravings cast shadows on the flat surface. This creates images that go beyond physical likeness, delving instead into the psyche of the subject in an attempt to capture their creative genius.

HOT GLASS

In contrast to the cool cut and cast glass of Libenský and Brychtová, other artists experimented with blown glass in a riot of color and free flowing forms. From the 1950s, René Roubícek and his wife, Miluše Roubícková, worked on independent projects. In the 1970s they collaborated on a number of ideas, including a series of blown 'Heads'. Pavel Hlava created elaborate glass sculptures, while Dana Vachtová also explored the play between the inner and outer spaces of the glass.

RENE ROUBÍCEK

René Roubícek's hot glass sculptures of imaginary objects, familiar yet unfamiliar, display an intense enjoyment of color and form. Though initially lauded (he was sent to represent his country at the Brussels Expo in 1958), after 1970 he became one of those punished for artistic excess by the Communist regime but continued to make glass. Roubíček and other Europeans became pioneers in hot glass, mirroring the American studio glass movement.

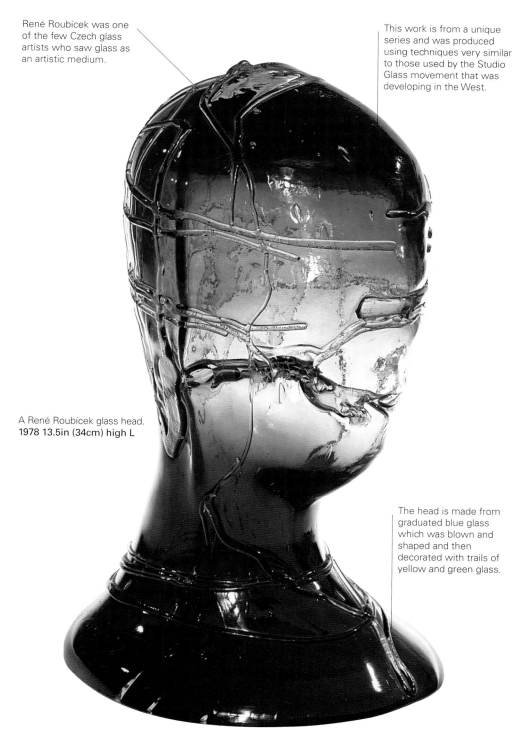

René Roubícek was one of the few Czech glass artists who saw glass as an artistic medium.

This work is from a unique series and was produced using techniques very similar to those used by the Studio Glass movement that was developing in the West.

A René Roubícek glass head.
1978 13.5in (34cm) high L

The head is made from graduated blue glass which was blown and shaped and then decorated with trails of yellow and green glass.

GLASS GALLERY

Many glass artists used traditional techniques such as pâte de verre, cutting and engraving in new ways to create glass that made a statement. Meanwhile others experimented with optical glass and sandblasting to make intriguing, functional, and decorative – often sculptural – glass.

An American glass sculpture, by Ginny Ruffner in the form of a vase, surmounted by a fish balancing an artist's palette on its head.
1989 39.5in (100.5cm) high N

A glass 'Blue Lightning Jar' vessel, by John Lewis, on black glass base.
1988 10.5in (26.5cm) high M

A Graal 'Slottsfroknar,' glass vase, by Eva Englund for Orrefors.
1990 12.5in (32cm) high Q

A glass 'Bipede' figure, designed by Robert Zeppel-Sperl, with two feet and head with big ears, legs with malachite stripes and ten opaque-white glass cabochons for toes.
1998 23in (58.5cm) high Q

Layers of fused glass make up 'Compacted Solarized Blue with Dual Ring' by Tom Patti.
1989-91 6in (15.5cmm) wide Y

A glass sculpture by Kit Karbler and Michael David of Blake Street Glass Studio, hand-blown, cut and hand polished.
2003 11in (28cm) high V

A French Gilles Chabrier 'Cube with Faces' sculpture.
c2002 11in (28cm) high O

A large 'Whopper' vase, by Dante Marioni, pale gray and blue glass with orange trim.
1988 25.5in (64.5cm) high N

DAVID REEKIE GLASS SCULPTURE

British artist David Reekie creates images of the human figure using the lost wax technique. A wax model is encased in a plaster mold and the wax replaced with glass. This creates an opaque, white finish to the glass which gives depth to the hands and head of each piece. He paints the rest of the figure with enamel paint. Many of his sculptures are comical, conveying futile tasks or unnecessary urgency, drawing attention to the absurdity of human behavior.

The inside of the mold is painted with enamel paint before it is filled with glass.

Heads are a recurring theme in Reekie's work. Here they appear to be looking for something.

The glass appears white as a result of the lost wax process used to cast it.

This sculpture has a wood base which has also been decorated with enamel paint.

A 'Something is Missing' pâte de verre sculpture by David Reekie.
1990 15.25in (39cm) high P

A Dan Dailey 'Zila Woman' sculptural glass vessel.
1990 24.25in (61.5cm) high U

A Marvin Lipofsky mold blown, cut and sandblasted glass sculpture, 'IGS VII 2000-03 #9'.
2000-2003 16in (40.5cm) wide U

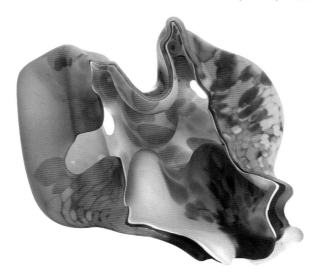

A William Morris blown glass with glass powders 'Crow Vessel' urn.
1999 20.5in (52cm) high Z

METALWARE GALLERY

Silver- and goldsmiths and other metal workers experimented with form to create functional and decorative pieces which used traditional techniques to create new forms. Many took advantage of the reflective quality of polished metals to create optical illusions.

Cast bronze 'bowl' by Michael Anastassiades. The title 'bowl' refers to the shape rather than the function of the piece.
2008 13in (33cm) diam L

A gold leaf vase with copper base by Professor Yasuki Hiramatsu.
c2000 11.5in (29.5cm) high S

A hand-folded bowl by René & Sach, made from raw, unpolished brass with polished edges. Inspired by origami, the hand-folding technique ensures each piece is unique.
c2008 16.5in (42cm diam) J

Copper 'Grid' vase by Jaime Hayon for Gaia and Gino. The range is made by Turkish craftsmen.
2008 13.25in (33.5cm) high H

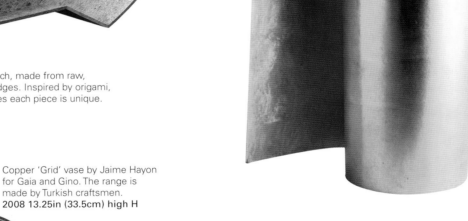

A Lino Sabattini 'Servizio Rialto' silver-plated four-piece tea set on a tray.
1970s Teapot: 4.5in (11.5cm) high R

CARLO SCARPA JUG FOR CLETO MUNARI
Italian designer Cleto Munari first met
Carlo Scarpa in the early 1970s. Scarpa, an
architect and designer, offered to create a
piece of silver for the design company
Munari had founded. It was the first of
many pieces of cutting edge silver designs
to be created for the company by other
designers. By 1980 a collection of limited
edition silver pieces had been designed by
architects and designers such as Mario
Botta, Michele De Lucchi, Ettore Sottsass,
Vico Magistretti, and Hans Hollein.

The interior of the jug has
been covered with a gilt
wash.

The cut-away spout puts the
emphasis on form rather
than function, while the
notched handle promotes
the jug's function.

The surface of the jug has a
textured, hammered effect.
The clean lines give it a
contemporary feel.

A limited edition Cleto Munari .925
silver jug, designed by Carlo Scarpa,
numbered 22 from an edition of 300.
1970s 8.75in (22cm) high L

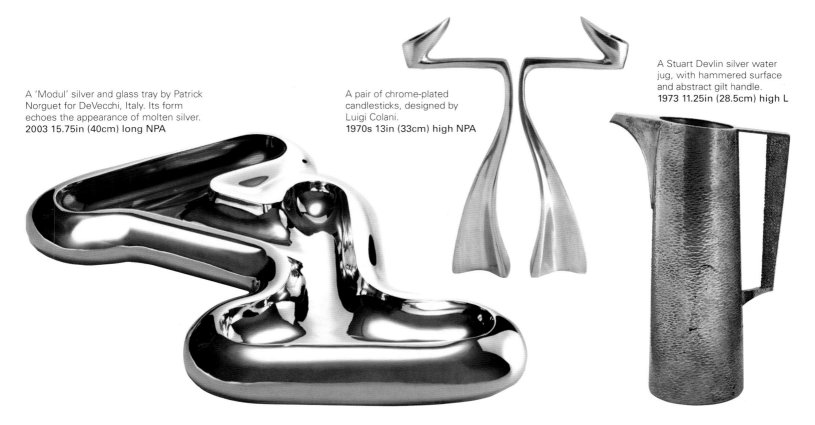

A 'Modul' silver and glass tray by Patrick
Norguet for DeVecchi, Italy. Its form
echoes the appearance of molten silver.
2003 15.75in (40cm) long NPA

A pair of chrome-plated
candlesticks, designed by
Luigi Colani.
1970s 13in (33cm) high NPA

A Stuart Devlin silver water
jug, with hammered surface
and abstract gilt handle.
1973 11.25in (28.5cm) high L

POSTMODERNISM TO CONTEMPORARY

Sculpture

From its pre-World War One beginnings, Abstract Art went on to become the most characteristic art form of the 20th century. However, as the 1980s and 1990s progressed many artists took a renewed interest in figurative subjects. For public spaces, Postmodern sculptors created large, abstract site-specific sculptures which were often charged with political meaning.

ART WITHOUT BOUNDARIES

Abstract artists embraced the idea that art no longer had to depict a recognisable object – a work of art could exist for its own sake. However, some continued to create simplified representational forms. Others made non-representative forms or believed in "free" expression. To the Postmodernist, art was allowed even greater freedoms. American writer and gallery owner Mark Del Vecchio states: "Postmodernism never made the proposition that anything is art, it merely offers the freedom that an artist can use anything to make art. The boundaries are all gone."

The American artist Mark Dion aims to explore our perception of history and the natural world. He is among those sculptors whose art exists without boundaries. He often incorporates taxidermy in his work, or uses collections of items displayed in curiosity cabinets which are similar to museum exhibits or the *Wunderkabinetts* owned by 16th century noblemen.

THE NATURAL LANDSCAPE

A major influence on sculptors was the natural landscape, which stood in contrast to waste and excess, now widely condemned by sculptors in Britain and America. However, where inspirational landscapes had historically been Arcadian groves, the new artists focused on less welcoming areas, such as the desert, which was used to great effect by American Michael Heizer in 'Double Negative': two deep trenches gouged into the desert.

Many landscape-conscious sculptures were necessarily site-specific: the choice of space adding to the meaning of the piece, which would be diminished by removing the sculpture from its original location.

Denis Mitchell's visual language was inspired by his knowledge of working in and on the landscape while mining tin during World War Two, as well as his tenure as chief assistant to Barbara Hepworth. After working with wood, slate and stone, the British artist chose to focus on tall, abstract sand-cast bronze sculptures.

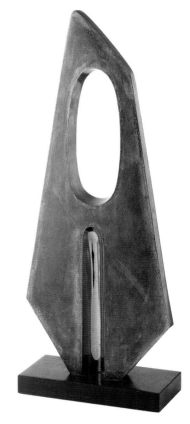

A Denis Mitchell 'Sawanna' polished bronze abstract sculpture, mounted on a slate base.
1974 25in (63.5cm) high M

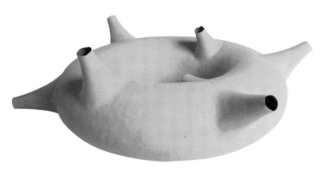

A Jonathan Bonner copper sculpture 'Yellow Vessel', with multiple protrusions and painted yellow finish.
1994 48in (120cm) diam K

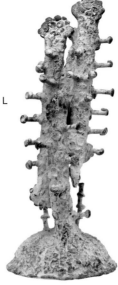

A Klaus Ihlenfeld phosphorous bronze 'Sundew Plant' sculpture.
2006 14.25in (36cm) high L

A Claire Falkenstein welded and patinated copper 'Living Curve' sculpture.
c1973 32in (cm) high R

BETTY WOODMAN SCULPTURE

Betty Woodman taught at the University of Colorado, where she was instrumental in the growth of the ceramics program. When she moved to New York in 1980, she turned her attention to art pottery. However, she soon began to explore the relationship between ceramics, sculpture and painting. Her sculptures typically feature a vase, which she points out "holds and pours all fluids, stores foods, and contains everything from our final remains to flowers. The vase motif connects what I do to all aspects of art".

This piece is made from canvas, terra sigillata, glazed earthenware, epoxy resin, lacquer and paint.

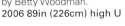
Vases are a prominent part of the design.

'Reflective Vases' sculpture, by Betty Woodman.
2006 89in (226cm) high U

ART AND SCIENCE

Other sculptors were less aggressive in their approach. American artist Jonathan Bonner often combines art and science in his site-specific sculptures, such as his series of weathervanes and 'Noon Marks': a series of sundials. Bonner's slender, fluid reinventions of these familiar garden objects challenge the viewer's expectations about what garden furniture and sculpture ought to be. Bonner's work also typically embodies the minimalist trend of much postmodern sculpture.

Artists including the Americans Donald Judd and Scott Burton began to explore the intermingled relationship between "art" and "design" and the role of art in society. They experimented with sculpture that was based on useful products, such as furniture and ceramic forms. Judd once explained: "The intent of art is different from that of [design], which must be functional." Burton, on the other hand, felt the art world was becoming too elistist and wanted to make furniture/sculpture that was "intelligible to a non-art audience".

German-born American Klaus Ihlenfeld has also produced many abstract works in bronze, although his style is more organic, displaying a 'warped complexity' and 'twisted humor' that is typical of postmodern design across all disciplines.

There was also a renewed interest in figurative sculptures. While many sculptors still preferred to create the abstract forms that had been ubiquitous in the 1950s and 1960s, such as American Claire Faulkenstein's 'thorny thickets' of copper tubing and melted glass, by the 1980s, the human figure had returned to sculpture. The long period of artistic absence allowed sculptors to look at the body afresh. Some focused on their own imperfect forms, whilst others, such as the German-born American artist Kiki Smith, focused on the internal make-up of the body. The idealized human form that had been portrayed in ancient Greek marble statues and Art Deco ivory figurines was largely abandoned.

Paul Day, a British artist who works in France, creates terracotta sculptures which depict contemporary scenes. His use of perspective recalls formal, Renaissance sculptures.

Tom Dixon (1959-)

Tom Dixon has come a long way from his early anti-establishment roots. The British design star first made an impression in the 1980s with his convention defying do-it-yourself furniture made out of salvage. He still makes waves with thought provoking designs like his Rubber Band chair. He also attracts important commissions from big businesses such as Habitat, and expounds the virtues of classic design by mid-century modernists including Verner Panton.

Born in Sfax, Tunisia, Tom Dixon was brought to England in 1963 and grew up in London. After dropping out of Chelsea Art College in the late 1970s he worked as a graphic designer and colorist on animated films by day, and as a bassist in the band Funkapolitan by night. He then drifted into organizing and promoting warehouse parties.

As design debuts go, Dixon's was exceptional. In the early 1980s he began making chairs from scrap metal as an avant-garde stage spectacle at Titanic, a London nightclub. In post-punk London at that time, a "do-it-yourself" artistic spirit reigned supreme. If you wanted to be a musician you picked up a guitar. If you wanted to be an artist you aimed a can of spray paint. And if you were Dixon, and you wanted to make furniture, you reached for your welding equipment.

Dixon's lack of formal design training is frequently remarked upon. He claims it allowed him to experiment uninhibitedly, make mistakes and develop his own style. He originally taught himself welding in order to repair his motorcycle after a crash. The artistic possibilities of this technique excited him enormously. He began scavenging for pieces of metal to weld into furniture. For example, his 'Kitchen Chair' was made from reclaimed frying pans, ladles and steel. He also liked using rubber tubing and experimenting with cut-up road bollards in his designs. His unique 'found' furniture created a sensation and by the mid-1980s the entrepreneurial Dixon was running Creative Salvage designs.

In many ways Dixon's audacious approach to design was an ironic response to Western society's move from manufacturing to a service based economy

during the 1980s. Dixon himself says he designs "mainly through an interest in materials and technologies" and does not start with an object's form. His aim is to create structures rather than superficially attractive surfaces for mass-produced pieces. In the early days he made his furniture himself and he also reused discarded items from the manufacturing past. Critics were quick to call his boundary-pushing style 'Post-industrial'.

Dixon's first commercial success came in 1989 when the Italian firm Cappellini put his 'S-chair' into production. The chair's slim organic shape evoked Verner Panton's plastic 'Panton Chair' from the 1960s. This homage to Panton became one of the most instantly recognisable designs of the era and can be found in New York's Museum of Modern Art.

By the late-1990s, Dixon was internationally renowned for his innovative designs. He had scored another success with his 'Bird Lounger.' He had been invited to work on large-scale projects and had opened Space, a shop in London's fashionable Notting Hill Gate. He had mass manufactured items including Jack, a pronged plastic light. Yet Dixon says he was floundering. "I had gotten involved in design, craft, factory management, design consultancy, marketing, sales and retail – all with no training or funding," he explains. "Frankly it was unsustainable, and it was time to grow up."

Salvation came in 1998 in the form of an invitation from British furnishing chain Habitat to be their design director. He later became the company's creative director. Dixon seized

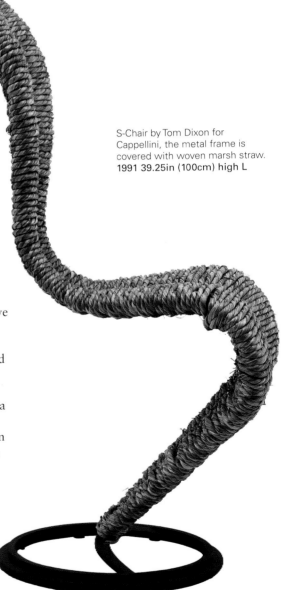

S-Chair by Tom Dixon for Cappellini, the metal frame is covered with woven marsh straw. 1991 39.25in (100cm) high L

this opportunity to get a proper grounding in business while also continuing with his independent career. He once explained: "My friends and acquaintances were horrified. I would have my creativity compromized... For me, however, it was as though I had a giant toy box... There was no other job like it in Europe! I went from maverick to high street overnight."

He is very proud of the fact that while he was at Habitat he made classic pieces accessible and affordable to wider audiences. These included work by Panton, Ettore Sottsass, and Robin Day, as well as adventurous new work by designers including Ronan and Erwan Bouroullec, Ineke Hans, and Marc Newson. He was part of the team that returned the firm to profit. He left Habitat in 2008.

Dixon emerged from the experience with a new professionalism and more imagination then ever. In 2004, while still working for Habitat, he had also been made creative director of Artek, the Finnish furniture manufacturer founded by the architect Alvar Aalto in the 1930s. Dixon says: "Artek is probably the only company from the modernist era to remain in its original form. It has an extraordinary cultural and historic heritage and a unique position in Finnish society, but it will vanish without new products and thinking... I am engaged in a process of investigating the latest innovations in wood and natural materials technology to develop a new aesthetic for the company based on a superior knowledge of the latest developments in sustainable materials and processes."

The now business-aware Dixon is likely to be seen at prestigious institutions such as the Milan Design Fair. He says he has a mission to revive the British furniture industry. By 2009 he had more than 45 lighting and furniture designs in production. Highlights of these included wire furniture in his characteristic elongated organic shapes; a series of mirrored plastic lamps; and "Eco Ware", tablewares which are made from biodegradable bamboo fiber.

As you would expect from a designer who once made furniture from salvage, Dixon is keen to raise awareness of sustainability with design.

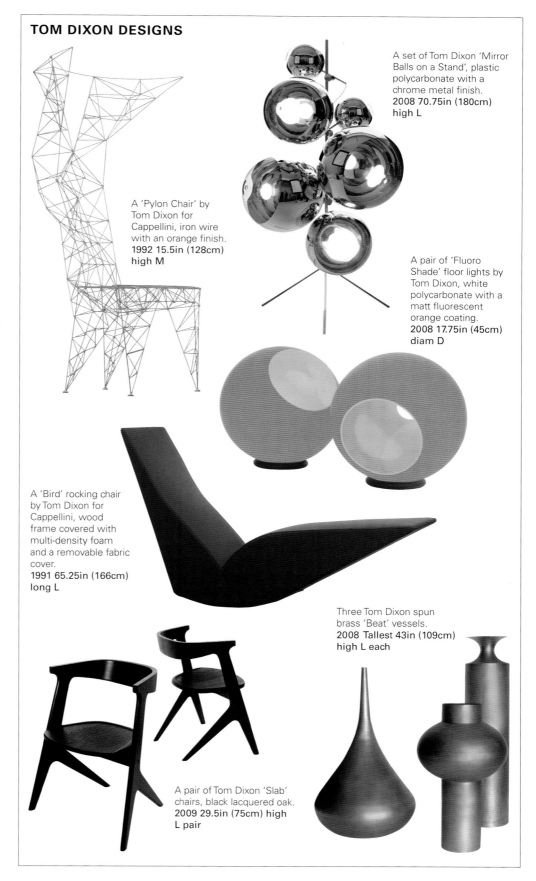

TOM DIXON DESIGNS

A 'Pylon Chair' by Tom Dixon for Cappellini, iron wire with an orange finish.
1992 15.5in (128cm) high M

A set of Tom Dixon 'Mirror Balls on a Stand', plastic polycarbonate with a chrome metal finish.
2008 70.75in (180cm) high L

A pair of 'Fluoro Shade' floor lights by Tom Dixon, white polycarbonate with a matt fluorescent orange coating.
2008 17.75in (45cm) diam D

A 'Bird' rocking chair by Tom Dixon for Cappellini, wood frame covered with multi-density foam and a removable fabric cover.
1991 65.25in (166cm) long L

Three Tom Dixon spun brass 'Beat' vessels.
2008 Tallest 43in (109cm) high L each

A pair of Tom Dixon 'Slab' chairs, black lacquered oak.
2009 29.5in (75cm) high L pair

Alessi

In the 1980s Alessi became renowned for its striking, unconventional homewares which were designed by some of the most avant-garde designers of the time. Each piece was imbued with the Postmodern style that came to dominate the decade. These wares reflected the Zeitgeist of the times so brilliantly that many in the Western world soon had a piece of "designer" whimsy on display in their home.

The Alessi company was founded in 1921, in Omegna, Italy, by Giovanni Alessi, and was originally a foundry and metal workshop. During the 1920s, Giovanni designed coffee pots and trays, establishing the brand name "Alessi" for the first time in 1924. When his son Carlo joined the firm in 1932, the company began to take a more serious interest in industrial design, experimenting with stainless steel and developing new forms with a view to mass-producing household wares.

From the 1950s Carlo Alessi established a new direction by seeking to commission celebrated designers to create the company's wares. However, it was not until the late 1970s that the concept began to work on an unprecedented scale. Headed by such innovative designers as Alessandro Mendini and Ettore Sottsass, groups like Studio Alchimia, and Memphis started to create all manner of controversial, unconventional pieces – furniture, glassware, lighting and ceramics – that abandoned the austerity of Modernism in favor of a deliberately haphazard, colorful, irreverent approach. The results were groundfiberaking and attracted Alberto Alessi, son of Carlo, who was now running the firm (and still is today).

Alessandro Mendini became a consultant for Alessi from 1983 and invited eleven international architects, including Aldo Rossi, Michael Graves, Charles Jencks, Kazumasa Yamashita and Richard Meier to design tea and coffee sets for the firm. The Tea and Coffee Piazza, as it was known, was revolutionary. Although each of the designers had the same materials and techniques at their disposal, their highly individual contributions were wildly diverse. Alessi wasted no time in establishing a new product line, Officina Alessi, which was dedicated solely to

An Alessi 'Viso' large ceramic vase, with multicolored transfer applied decoration, designed by Alessandro Mendini.
2001 35.75in (91cm) high NPA

limited-edition ranges by "celebrity designers". The move was a stroke of genius, with Alessi rapidly gaining notoriety for the original avant-garde pieces that its heavyweight designers created.

Throughout the 1980s and well into the 1990s, Alessi produced a wide range of domestic wares which combined quality craftsmanship with an avant-garde edge, each betraying something of the personality of its designer. Items were intended to be visually stimulating as well as functional – conversation pieces, even – and this was reflected in all manner of quirky, eye-catching forms and the decorative details employed to make them stand out. With origins steeped in the anti-design sentiment of the Postmodern era, sleek and shiny polished steel was often juxtaposed with bold, brash, brightly colored plastics.

The best-known designs from this period are often listed as Michael Graves's 'Whistling Bird' kettle of 1985, Philippe Starck's 'Juicy Saliff' lemon squeezer from 1990, and Mendini's 'Anna G' corkscrew designed in 1994. However, Alessi's output during this time was phenomenal, each piece a work of art in its own right. Other memorable designs include Ettore Sottsass's 'Nuovo Milano' cutlery set of 1989, timeless in its simplicity; Frank Gehry's 'Pito' kettle of 1992, its wooden fish whistle a pun on 'fish kettle'; and Guido Venturini's 'Firebird' gas lighter with its brightly colored biomorphic handle.

Today, Alessi produces a wide range of products using all kinds of materials from durable plastics through ceramics, glass and copper to wood and leather. The firm continues to commission independent designers to design their wares, ensuring they remain ahead of the latest trends. To date, some 500 designers have contributed to Alessi's back catalog and they are as diverse as the pieces they have created, from Mario Botta to Ron Arad and from Richard Sapper to Patricia Urquiola and Zaha Hadid.

The company continues to produce many designs from previous decades. Alessi has even released classic designs that they did not commission, such as a Christopher Dresser toast rack from 1881 and Marianne Brandt's stainless steel bowls which were designed at the Bauhaus.

ALESSI DESIGN

A pair of sculptural and architectural 'Crevasse' vases, designed by Zaha Hadid for Alessi, polished stainless steel.
2005

'La Conica' stainless steel coffee pot, designed by Aldo Rossi.
1980-83

A limited edition Alessi 'Tea and Coffee Piazza' service designed by Charles Jencks, comprising coffee pot, teapot, milk jug and sugar bowl.
1983

Mario Botta 'Mia' and 'Tua' water and wine carafes.
2000

Alessandro Mendini 'Anna G' corkscrew.
1994

POSTMODERNISM TO CONTEMPORARY

Technology

The late 20th century saw a dramatic leaps in technological advancements, which included the arrival of the personal computer, the cell phone, and the Internet. No longer satisfied by the purely functional appliances of the modernist age, consumers were offered technology that was as beautiful as it was useful. Companies including Apple and Dyson stepped forward to satisfy this desire for attractive, functional wares.

ATTRACTION OF GOOD DESIGN

An important commercial asset in an increasingly competitive market, the idea of 'good design' has become a high priority for many technology companies. Hartmut Esslinger, the German-American industrial designer, notably claimed that "in computers, design isn't decoration, it's the essence": a philosophy that Apple Computers, in particular, strives to uphold. The best technological designs are generally the product of a close collaboration between the manufacturer and the designer. This means that the design and the function are developed side by side, rather than the aesthetic design for a product being secondary.

During the 1980s and 1990s the fashion for designer goods encouraged manufacturers to invest in the outward appearance of their devices as well as the ergonomics of the designs and the technology inside them. The result was visually appealing, user-friendly appliances. Stylish forms, often in bright colors, could be integrated into the home rather than

hidden away. At the same time, as people became more familiar with machines such as computers they came to expect devices that were attractive and easy to use. They became smaller as advances in technology allowed the component parts to shrink.

Designers often give the appearance of audio equipment particular attention. Many sleek, well-detailed appliances have been designed for Bang & Olufsen, notably by Jacob Jensen. His products for the firm include the Beolit 600 Portable Radio of 1970 and the BeoGram 4000 Record Deck from 1972. Jensen has also designed an astronomical clock for Max René, the Comet telephone for Standard Electric Kirk (1976), and loudspeakers for Dantax.

Bang & Olufsen designers often disguise the function of an object in favor of highlighting its contemporary style. Similarly, Marc Berthier's 'Tykho Radio' of 1997 has a body made of single color synthetic rubber, without any dials.

ADVANCES IN TECHNOLOGY

The digital watch was introduced in the late 1960s and quickly became extremely popular. As a result, the Swiss analogue watch industry went into decline until the launch of the Swatch watch in 1983 revitalised interest. Marketed as a casual, fun, and relatively disposable accessory, the quartz Swatch watch was designed for manufacturing efficiency and with fewer parts (the movement was built into the case). In the past the quality of the movement had been important to many watch buyers. Now, due to a reliable quartz movement, it was the case and strap that appealed to the buyer. Innovative colors and plastics were used and well-known designers, such as Vivienne Westwood and Paloma Picasso, were asked to contribute designs. So

Left: A Swatch 'Rave' wristwatch, from the D.J. Ten-Strikes series, with decorated clear strap. **1991**
Right: A Swatch 'Silver Patch' wristwatch, from the Nespolo series, with multicolored strap. **1993 A**

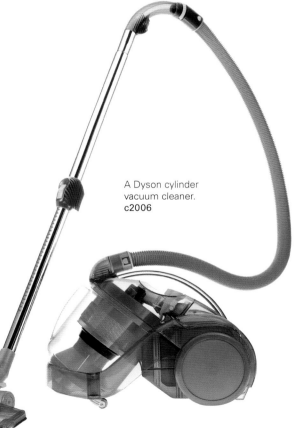

A Dyson cylinder vacuum cleaner. **c2006**

Marc Berthier's 'Tykho' radio for Lexon features a brightly colored synthetic rubber case. **1997 5.5in (14cm) wide A**

THE APPLE iMAC
The iMac was hailed as the most original new personal computer since the first Apple Mac in 1984 when it was launched in 1988. As well as integrating the monitor and the central processing unit within a single case, the iMac came in five bright colors: blueberry, strawberry, lime, tangerine and grape, rather than the usual off-white or gray. It also featured an unusual circular mouse. It saw the start of computers as fashion accessories rather than work machines.

The colourful translucent plastic case was revolutionary.

It was designed to have aesthetic as well as technical appeal. Apple claimed: "the back of our computer looks better than the front of anyone else's." It was designed to suit home offices as well as appeal to the growing media industry.

The "i" in iMac stood for "Internet" because the user only needed to go through two steps to set up the computer and connect to the Internet.

The original 'Bondi Blue' iMac G3 which was introduced in 1998.

successful was the Swatch that, in 1992, the 100 millionth watch was produced.

Like the Swatch, James Dyson's bag-less vacuum cleaner, designed in 1983, was revolutionary in its technology and also in its appearance. With transparent casing and brightly colosred motor parts, the Dyson vacuum cleaner was a striking object. It appeared on the cover of *Design Magazine* in its first year and became a status symbol in Japan after winning the 1991 International Design Fair prize.

The cell phone has become an indispensable part of life for many. The first practical handset was created in 1973 by Dr. Martin Cooper of Motorola in the United States. However, the cell phone was not approved for public use until 1982: the year the GSM (Global System for Mobile

Communications) was introduced. Cell phones took a few more years to arrive in Europe and were typically too large to be carried around, so most were installed as car phones. This changed in 1989, with the introduction of the 'MicroTAC Pocket Cellular Telephone', which was designed to fit into a shirt pocket. The subsequent miniaturisation of components and the development of more sophisticated batteries allowed for smaller and lighter designs.

One of the most desirable cell phones of the early 21st century, Apple's iPhone was launched in 2007. Its appeal lay more in the design of its software than its outward appearance which was very simple. Apple Computers has been at the front of product design since 1977 when it unveiled the Apple II computer, designed by Jerry

Manock. Not satisfied, Apple founder Steve Jobs continued to seek the "best design in the world" that would turn Apple into a world-class company. With the help of Hartmut Esslinger and his company, frog design, he did just that. Apple released the resulting Snow White design program (characterised by horizontal lines and an off-white or light grey color) in 1984 and it became a resounding success.

By the late 1990s, computer design had started to move away from the bulky 'grey box' to shiny, compact machines that are at the cutting edge of design. British designer Jonathan Ive further enhanced Apple's reputation with the brightly colored iMac in 1998. Ive is also credited as the principal designer behind other Apple products, such as the MacBook, iPod and iPhone.

LIGHTING GALLERY

Developments in technology and new materials encouraged designers to create ever-more sculptural and futuristic lights or to reject technology in favor of traditional crafts. Others created witty or whimsical designs with fantastical flourishes. Concern for the environment brought about lamps made from recycled items or which helped to reduce energy use.

A chromium-plated aluminum desk lamp, designed by Hans-Peter Rainer.
c1985 124in (315cm) long U

A table lamp by Garry Knox Bennett, titled 'A Nite on Lindquist Ridge'.
1990 22in (56cm) wide I

A pair of cast plaster candlesticks shaped as hands, by Richard Etts.
1976 9.5in (24cm) high L

A 'Little Buildings' polished stainless steel floor lamp, by Jonathan Singleton.
74.75in (190cm) high L

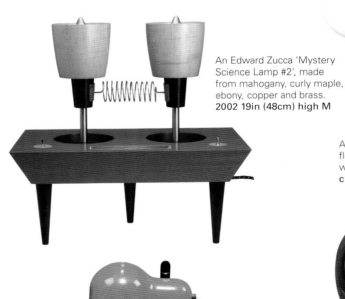

An Edward Zucca 'Mystery Science Lamp #2', made from mahogany, curly maple, ebony, copper and brass.
2002 19in (48cm) high M

A carved and laminated oak floor lamp, Robert Worth, with branded mark.
c1970 58in (147.5cm) high N

A 'Topolino' table lamp, designed by Joe Colombo, for Stilnovo.
1970 13.75in (35cm) high E

A Herman Miller 'Leaf' personal light, designed by Yves Béhar of fuseproject in San Francisco. It is set with 20 energy-saving light-emitting diode (LED) bulbs. **2007 36.5in (92.75cm) high when extended E**

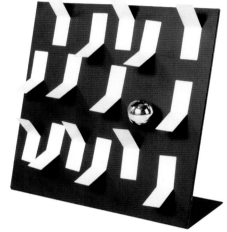

A Gianni Villa 'Kalamo' enameled magnetized metal lamp, with movable magnetic strips. **1972 18.25in (46.5cm) wide M**

The lamp still has the paper tag from 'Artisan House, the studio set up by Jerry Fels and Curtis Freiler.

CURTIS JERE LAMP

The name Curtis Jere is the company name of two costume jewelry artisans Jerry Fels and Curtis Freiler. They teamed up in the late 1950s to design and manufacture by hand wall sculptures and household accessories – 'gallery quality art for the masses' – at their California studio Artisan House. They sold the company in 1972. It continues to make sculptures and other items.

A 'Flashlight' floor lamp/ sculpture, by Curtis Jere. **1981 67.5in (171.5cm) high N**

The head of the lamp is shaped like a torch.

A 'Synchronis Serpents' sculptural candleholder and occasional table by Jack Larimore, made from red oak, cherry and crystal. **c2002. 53in (134.5cm) wide N**

Albert Paley (1944-)

The work of metal sculptor Albert Paley has been celebrated around the world. His creative approaches to form and technique helped to revive American metalworking as an art form. Both his early jewelry and his later public sculptures exhibit a sensuous, organic form which appears to contradict the unyielding nature of the metals they are made from. Paley's work has been described as "archisculptural" because of the way it enhances – and is in turn enhanced by – its setting.

Albert Paley was born and raised in Philadelphia, Pennsylvania. He left school at 16 and went to work in the art supply section of a local department store. While there he met a student from Temple University's Tyler School of Art who persuaded him to apply to study there. He was successful and went on to study sculpture, and then took a master's degree in gold-smithing.

By 1969, Paley had become one of the top jewellers in his field. He moved to Rochester, New York, where he taught gold-smithing at the Rochester Institute of Technology and continued to create his

jewelry – large, bold pieces designed to move with the human body. Eventually, tired of the perception of jewelry-making as a craft rather than art, he began to experiment with iron and steel, making tables, candlesticks, mirrors and planters.

When the Smithsonian Institution took over the Renwick Gallery in Washington D.C., Paley was one of thirty artists asked to submit designs for a new pair of internal gates. Though he had never designed anything on such a large scale, Paley won the contract. The gallery opened in 1972 as the home of the Smithsonian American Art Museum's contemporary craft program.

The gates were a turning point in Paley's career. They won him national awards and made his name, as well as demonstrating how the skills he had acquired through jewelry-making could be utilised on larger projects. "If you look at the forms – the gate and the jewelry – they actually are very similar," Paley points out. "The design sensibilities are the same. The Smithsonian project allowed me to use my design sensibilities and interface that with architecture. It allowed me to break out."

He gave up jewelry making in 1977 and concentrated instead on his large-scale iron-work, which displayed Medieval, Gothic,

Albert Paley's monumental metal sculptures feature ribbons of colorful, twisted steel. Here his sculpture 'Sentinel' is being installed at the Rochester Institute of Technology.

Baroque and Art Noveau influences, and used ornamentation that bolstered the piece's structural integrity. Throughout the 1980s and 1990s he was commissioned to create gates, railings, screens and columns and created the organic-looking accessories such as lamp stands, and furniture in steel, brass and copper, that provided much of his income.

Paley's plant stands, tables and candleholders are forged from mild steel. The metal can be twisted into tendril-like forms because it is a low carbon metal that is particularly pliant at superheated temperatures. His sinuous flowing lines were inspired by Art Nouveau and northern European ironwork. Paley's organic style, combined with his experimental approach to metal, and his unique forging processes, led the way to a revival in American metalsmithing.

He says people should not be surprised by the sinuous shapes he creates: "Usually people think of metal in its industrial state – bars and rods and plates – but metal is very plastic. It can be formed and shaped into anything: cold, through hydraulic bending, or by heating it to a yellow state. People are amazed at how fluid the steel is in my work, how alive it seems... tendril ribbon shapes are woven through the structure to indicate water, and I had to make solid steel seem translucent."

In 1982 Paley created the first of the public sculptures for which he is perhaps most famous, for Rochester's Strong Museum. He continues to design and create enormous metal sculptures, despite being caught in a life-threatening propane explosion in 2002 while at work. The largest (125ft or 38m long) and most complex figurative sculpture of Paley's career to date, 'Animals Always' was installed at the St. Louis Zoo in 2006. It features more than 600 elements, including trees, water, birds, beasts and fish. It was first produced as a scale cardboard model which was then converted into a series of computerized images. A computer then drove a torch that cut the steel plates to Paley's specification.

In 1995, Paley was the first sculptor to receive a Lifetime Achievement Award from the American Institute of Architects: the AIA's highest award to a non-architect.

ALBERT PALEY

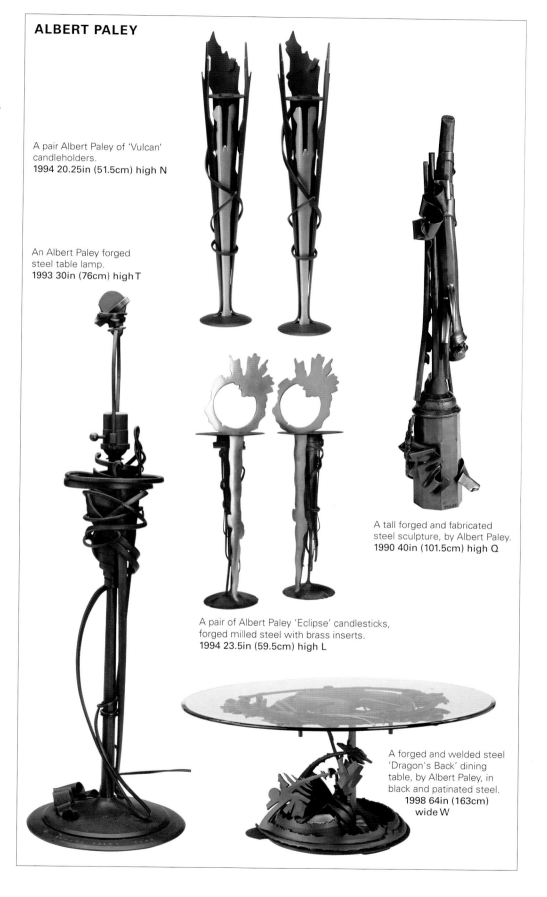

A pair Albert Paley of 'Vulcan' candleholders.
1994 20.25in (51.5cm) high N

An Albert Paley forged steel table lamp.
1993 30in (76cm) high T

A tall forged and fabricated steel sculpture, by Albert Paley.
1990 40in (101.5cm) high Q

A pair of Albert Paley 'Eclipse' candlesticks, forged milled steel with brass inserts.
1994 23.5in (59.5cm) high L

A forged and welded steel 'Dragon's Back' dining table, by Albert Paley, in black and patinated steel.
1998 64in (163cm) wide W

Posters

The posters of the late 20th and early 21st centuries were unlike anything that had come before. They were used by businesses and politicians to sell – and sometimes to surprise. Despite the ever increasing importance of television advertizing, the poster remains an important means of conveying a message and controversial examples retain the ability to shock.

COMPETITION FOR THE POSTER

Following World War Two, the importance of the poster declined in many countries, where magazines and television became strong competitors in the advertizing industry. However, poster art continued to evolve in Switzerland, where the International Typographic Style, or Swiss Style, was developed. It favored stark photography and typographic elements in black and white, all based in a mathematical grid.

Meanwhile, in the United States and Poland a new illustration style that borrowed from Surrealism, Pop Art and Expressionism evolved, described by graphic designer Philip Meggs as 'Conceptual Image'. Tadanori Yokoo initiated an artistic revolution in Japan when he introduced Pop Art and Western imagery into Japanese graphics, resulting in outrageous collages.

International Typographic Style was the leading international graphic design style in the 1970s, but by the 1980s some began to criticize its cold formality. Swiss designer Wolfgang Weingart started to produce chaotic and playful posters and ushered in the style known as postmodern design.

At this time, the work of famous artists was also employed in advertizing. In 1983 Andy Warhol was commissioned to paint the Absolut vodka bottle after confessing a fascination with its artfulness to Michel Roux, the CEO of Absolut's American import company. The image was a great success and became the start of the now-famous 'Absolut Art' series.

By the 1990s computer-aided design had revolutionized poster art. A smooth, technical look was possible and previously time-consuming design was accomplished

'Absolument', a poster for Absolut vodka using artwork by Andy Warhol.
68.5in (174cm) high J

Japanese artist Hajime Sorayama designed his first 'sexy robot' in 1978 and has gained international recognition for his hyper-realistic female cyborgs.
B

Designed for controversy, this United Colors of Benetton poster was called 'Embraced in a Blanket'.
1980s 36in (91cm) high C

in an instant. The famous Barack Obama 'Hope' poster, for example, took a single day to design. The poster, by street artist Shepard Fairey, shows the then-presidential candidate gazing into the distance in bold red, white and blue stripes.

SHOCK TACTICS

More recently charities, businesses and governments have all employed graphic imagery and blunt slogans in an attempt to make their messages linger in the public consciousness. The master of this sort of 'shockvertizing' is the Italian clothing manufacturer United Colors of Benetton. In 1989 creative director, copywriter, art director and photographer Oliviero Toscani produced two posters for the company that controversially failed to feature the company's clothes at all. 'Handcuffs' – a black and a white hand cuffed together – and 'Breastfeeding' – the image of a black woman breast feeding a white baby – were much talked about. However, the talk was not all positive. Many were convinced that 'Breastfeeding' harkened back to slavery, although to date it is the Benetton poster which has received the most awards. The 1990 campaign, which included 'Embraced in a Blanket', continued the "concept of equality in diversity" and won many international awards.

DAVID HOCKNEY POSTER
In the 1970s David Hockney designed theater and opera sets and costumes, as well as numerous posters for stage productions. These included Stravinsky's 'Rake's Progress' and Mozart's 'Magic Flute for the Glyndebourne Festival and a triple bill of works by Satie, Poulenc and Ravel at the Metropolitan Opera in New York. While Eric Satie's 'Parade' is less widely popular than many other operas, Hockney's poster has become a classic.

The image, with Hockney's neo-pop décor and costumes, showcase a juggler whose contortions fit eye-catchingly into the elongated format.

The repetition of the colors in the two parts of the design unify them.

A Metropolitan Opera poster for 'Parade', designed by David Hockney. 1981 80in (203cm) high L

PUBLIC FEELING AND THE POWER OF THE POSTER

Some of the most successful posters manage to mirror and enlarge cultural issues. Though this is true of many posters, it is particularly true of political posters. These can present opponents unfavourably and help to turn public opinion. The 'Gordon Brown's Debt' poster, issued as the 2009 recession began to bite in Britain and shown below, is a clear successor to War-time posters depicting imperiled children. Conversely, other posters are simple celebrations of their party, such as the red, white and blue Barack Obama 'Hope' poster discussed above. Though not officially commissioned, the striking image became one of the most widely recognized symbols of Obama's campaign message, depicted variously as 'Progress', 'Change' and simply 'Hope'. It was a message the American public embraced after the events of 9/11 and the Iraq war.

Dad's Nose. Mum's Eyes. Gordon Brown's Debt.

Labour's Debt Crisis: Every child in Britain is born owing £17,000. They deserve better.

NOW FOR CHANGE   conservatives.com

Textiles

After a century of continuous novelty, textile designers felt the need to impart something familiar. Throughout the 1970s, 1980s and 1990s they created textiles with an increasingly retro feel. The full breadth of textile history, right up to 1960s Op Art geometrics, provided a rich seam for designers to mine. As a result they created some sensational fabrics with a contemporary feel by revitalizing old designs and traditions.

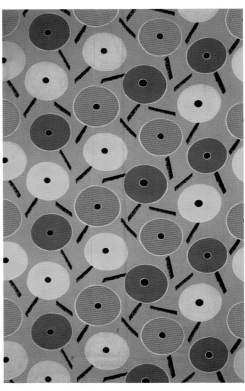

Sixties Op Art for a new generation. Fabric in the LEK pattern by Birgitta Hahn for Tiogruppen, Stockholm.
1980 NPA

LOOKING TO HISTORY

By the early 1970s there was a growing awareness of the adverse affects of the modern industrial society. People began to realise that unlimited progress had unforeseen negative consequences – from environmental damage and the controlling tendencies of big business to the bland uniformity of many machine-made products. It brought about a shift in attitude to what the past had to offer. Textile designers were in the vanguard of this re-engagement with history.

Numerous fabric producers rejected industry altogether. They returned to time-honored methods of weaving and printing their own designs by hand. Although many remained committed to mass production, they disliked the anonymity of working for a large-scale manufacturer and the creative restrictions that often came with it. The economic crisis in the 1970s made the manufacturing sector even more risk-averse. Designers who wanted to regain control over their creations either struck out on their own or formed collectives loosely inspired by traditional craft guilds. They reversed the status quo and employed factories to make their textiles and took direct responsibility for marketing themselves.

For instance, in 1970, a group of designers tired of having their designs rejected as "unsaleable, too advanced and

A 1980s geometric wool area rug, from the Guggenheim Museum, New York City.
1980s J

The Timorous Beasties' 'London Toile' celebrates their love of London. It features landmarks such as the London Eye and Tower Bridge as well as vagrants and drug dealers. It is a play on the design of 18th century French toile de Jouy.

non-commercial" established Sweden's Tiogruppen. They wanted to participate actively in the supply chain, from initial sketch to retail, of finished fabrics in their own shop. Typical Tiogruppen fabrics have bold primary colors and strong graphics. Designs tend to be either geometric patterns or folk art inspired. They have become internationally renowned thanks to special collections commissioned by IKEA.

Other textile designers were more overtly reactionary. The 1970s will be forever associated with Laura Ashley fabrics. After the wild futuristic patterns of the 1960s, her delicate floral prints were based on scraps of 18th century wallpaper. During the 1980s, English textile designers referenced elements from the past even more adventurously. Husband and wife team Timney Fowler found success with striking Neo-classical prints "sampled and wittily re-mixed" from old black and white engravings, just like Piero Fornasetti's designs. Textile designer Georgina von Etzdorf was acclaimed for her rich hand-printed velvets. Her designs are often compared with the sumptous fabrics of the Renaissance.

By the 1990s textile designers had grown so confident in their use of historicism that they began to subvert traditional textile designs with a contemporary twist. Neisha Crosland revitalised a fabric popular in the 1920s called devoré – velvet imprinted with acid to remove some of the pile to create a relief effect. She made this "antique" fabric very much her own with distinct muted colors and delicate abstract motifs. Scottish firm Timorous Beasties played with the traditional bucolic imagery printed on toile de Jouy in France since the 18th century. They replaced these archetypal scenes with nightmarish visions of crack addicts and prostitutes against a backdrop of dilapidated inner city tower blocks.

In uncertain times many fall back on classic designs. Textile designers such as the team behind Eley Kishimoto – Mark Eley and Wakako Kishimoto – have no allegiance to any particular historic source. Their striking patterns are sparked by everything from 1930s floral chintzes and Argyll knits to the swirling geometric patterns on 1960s Op Art fabrics.

ALEXANDER CALDER TAPESTRY
The sculptor Alexander Calder was one of the artists who turned their talents to tapestry design. He created a number of tapestries that were created by teams of traditional weavers in Masaya, Nicaragua. These abstract designs feature the bold primary colors, whimsical forms, and geometric shapes that are typical of Calder's graphic style. The craftsmen worked in teams and used jute, European dyes, and many of needles to make the tapestries.

The tapestry is signed with an embroidered copyright "AC 74 57/100".

Large red discs frequently feature in Calder's work.
The design is similar to that of his sculptures.

A maguey fiber 'Balloons' tapestry, by Alexander Calder.
1974 96in (244cm) wide P

Glossary of Marks

Marks and modern trademarks were used as publicity by large firms (such as Minton and Wedgwood) and could also be used by the retailer so re-orders could be correctly placed. They can be very useful in not only identifying the manufacturer of a piece, but also in dating it – sometimes to the exact year of production as many firms used private dating systems.

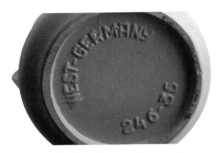

Bay Keramik, West German factory active 1933-96.

Bitossi, Italian pottery active 1921-present. Impressed mark and label for Danish retailer.

Boch Frères, Belgian factory active 1841-present. Charles Catteau designed c1922-45.

Carlton Ware Ltd, British ceramics factory active 1890-1989. From 1935-61, the backstamp read "Registered Australian Design" to prevent Far Eastern copies being sold.

Clarice Cliff (1899-1972) British ceramics designer. This mark used 1931-34.

Doulton, British factory, active from 1815, became Royal Doulton in 1901. This mark 1932 to the present.

Marcello Fantoni, (1915-) Italian potter and ceramics designer.

Fulper Pottery Company, American factory active 1899-1935 (purchased by Stangl in 1930). This printed 'racetrack' mark used 1922-28.

Goldscheider, Austrian factory active 1885-1953. This mark 1920-30.

Stig Lindberg (1916-82) Swedish ceramics designer, mark used during the 1950s at the Gustavsberg ceramics factory

Bernard Leach (1887-1979), British studio potter, impressed BL personal seal mark.

Martin Brothers, British studio potters, active 1873-1923, this mark 1874.

Marzi & Remy, West German factory active 1879-1994.

Midwinter, British ceramics factory active 1910-1987. Stylecraft range launched 1955.

Keith Murray (1892-1981), worked for Wedgwood 1933-48. Mark introduced 1932.

Newcomb College, American pottery factory active 1895-1944. 'MW' mark denotes 1922.

George Ohr (1857-1918) American potter, Biloxi Mississippi.

Poole, British pottery: (Carter & Co.1873-1921); Carter Stabler & Adams, active 1921-34, mark used 1925-34 (known as 'Poole' from 1934).

Poole, British ceramics factory, active 1934-present, mark used 1955-59.

Rookwood, American pottery active 1880-1967. The Rookwood mark is very prescriptive. The flame mark with Rookwood monogram was used from 1886 with an extra flame used each year – by 1900 there were 14 flames. In 1901 the Roman Numeral I was added below and changed accordingly with each year. XXI denotes 1921. 2551 is the shape number. Below this is the artist's monogram for Sara Sax.

Rorstrand Studio, Swedish pottery active 1825-present.

Roseville, American pottery active 1892-1954. This mark added to new moulds 1932-37.

Royal Copenhagen, Danish factory active 1775-present. This mark used 1924-34.

Ruskin Pottery, British pottery active 1904-33. This mark used 1904-15, with year below.

Saxbo, Danish pottery active 1930-68. 'DANMARK' used with 'Ying Yang' mark from 1931-49, with 'DANMARK' only used until 1949, and 'DENMARK' used from 1950 onwards.

Shelley, British pottery active 1925-66. This mark used 1925-45.

Artus and Anne Van Briggle, American studio potters active 1899-1912.

Peter Voulkos (1924-2002) American studio potter.

Weller, American Pottery active 1893-1945.

Russel Wright (1904-1976), designer for Steubenville Pottery, Ohio 1939-59.

Alvar Aalto (1898-1976), Finnish architect and designer. Furniture retailed by Finmar Ltd.

Selectform Centrum Mobler St Merlose, Danish furniture maker, active in the 1960s.

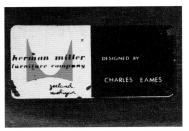

Charles Eames (1907-78) American designer. Label from an early design for Herman Miller (1923-present).

Paul Frankl (1886-1958) American furniture designer, began Skyscraper range in 1926.

Garouste & Bonetti, French design company active 1980-present. Founded by Elisabeth Garouste, (1949-) and Mattia Bonetti (1953-).

Paul McCobb (1917-69) American furniture designer, design for H. Sacks & Sons, c1960.

Gaetano Missaglia, Italian furniture manufacturer active in the 1960s/1970s.

Verner Panton (1926-98) Danish furniture designer.

Tommi Parzinger (1903-72), German-born American designer. Parzinger Inc founded 1939, became Parzinger Originals in 1946.

Gilbert Rhode (1894-1944) American designer. Label from a design for Herman Miller.

Mobili Saragoni, Italian furniture maker, active from c1930s.

Karl Springer (1931-91) German-born, French-educated American designer.

Gustav Stickley (1858-1942) American Arts & Crafts furniture maker and architect. This United Crafts mark used 1905-12.

Tecno, Milanese furniture company founded in 1953 by Osvaldo Borsani (1911-85).

Hans Wegner (1914-2007), Danish furniture designer, design for Carl Hansen of Denmark.

John Widdicomb Co., American furniture company active 1897-present. T. H. Robsjohn-Gibbings (1905-76) designed 1943-56.

Blenko, American factory active 1893-present. This sandblasted signature used 1958-61.

Daum, French factory active 1878-present.

Michael Harris (1933-94) British Studio glassmaker. Rare signature used 1968-72.

Holmegaard, Danish glass factory active 1823-present, with artist's cypher for Per Lutken (1916-98).

Kosta Boda, Swedish glass factory, began 1742. Goran Wärff designer name and model number.

Dominick Labino (1910-87), Studio glassmaker.

René Lalique (1860-1945). 'R' initial was not used after 1945. Lalique & Cie active today.

Loetz, Austrian glass factory active 1836-1939. After 1918 a stamped etched mark used.

Orrefors, Swedish glass factory active 1898-present. Followed by model number.

Verrerie Schneider, French glass factory active 1913-40, mark for 'Le Verre Francais'.

Val Saint Lambert, Belgian glass factory active 1826-present.

Venini, Italian glass factory active 1925-present.

Demetre Chiparus (1886-1947), Romanian sculptor.

Fayral (Pierre le Faguays) (1892-1935), French sculptor.

Josef Hoffman (1870-1956), Austrian designer, metalwork mark for Wiener Werkstatte (1903-32).

Georg Jensen (1866-1935), Danish silversmith, factory active 1904-present. This mark c1905.

Josef Lorenzl (1892-1950), Austrian sculptor.

Dirk van Erp (1859-1933), American Arts & Crafts metalworker. Opened Dirk van Erp Studio in 1909.

Artists & Designers

Alvar Aalto (1898–1976) Finnish architect and furniture designer

Eero Aarnio (1932–) Finnish furniture designer

Jacques Adnet (1900–1984) French architect and furniture designer

Tamara Aladin (1932-) Finnish glass designer

Franco Albini (1905–1978) Italian architect and furniture designer

Michael Anastassiades (1967-) British designer

Winslow Anderson (1917-2007) American glass designer

Ron Arad (1951-) British/Israeli furniture designer

André Arbus (1903–1969) French architect, furniture designer and sculptor

Gabriel Argy-Rousseau (1885-1953) French glass designer

Alfred Arndt (1896-1976) German architect

Gertrud Arndt (1903–2000) German textile designer

Robert Arneson (1930-1992) American sculptor

Charles Robert Ashbee (1863–1942) British furniture designer

Carl Auböck (1900-1957) Austrian metalware designer

Gae Aulenti (1927-) Italian architect and designer

Jacques Auriac (1922-) French poster designer

Rudy Autio (1926-2007) American ceramic artist

Ralph Bacerra (1938-2008) American ceramic artist

Oscar B. Bach (1884-1957) American metalware designer

Leo Hendrick Baekeland (1863-1944) Belgian inventor of Bakelite

Eric Bagge (1890–1978) French furniture designer

Léon Bakst (1866-1924) Russian artist, theatre and costume designer

Jacob Bang (1899-1965) Danish glass designer

Michael Bang (1944-) Danish glass designer

Beata Bär (1962-) German furniture designer

Gerhard Bär (1962-) German furniture designer

Sidney Barnsley (1865-1926) British architect and furniture designer

Ernest Barnsley (1863-1926) British furniture designer

Helmut Bätzner (1928–) German architect and furniture designer

Geoffrey Baxter (1922-1995) British glass designer

Herbert Bayer (1900–1985) Austrian architect and graphic designer

Harry Beck (1902–1974) British graphic designer

Martine Bedin (1957-) French ceramicist

Yves Béhar (1967-) Swiss designer

Peter Behrens (1868-1940) German architect and furniture designer

Norman Bel Geddes (1893–1958) American industrial designer

Vanessa Bell (1879–1961) British artist and interior designer

Rudolf Belling (1886-1972) German sculptor

Edouard Benedictus (1878-1930) French chemist, glass and textile designer

Gerald Benney (1930-2008) British metalware designer

Garry Knox Bennett (1934-) American furniture, metalware and lighting designer

Elis Bergh (1881-1954) Swedish glass designer

Norbert Berghof (1949-) German architect and furniture designer

Knut Bergqvist (1873-1953) Swedish glass designer

Sigvard Bernadotte (1907-2002) Swedish metalware designer

Lucian Bernhard (1883-1972) German/American graphic designer

Marc Berthier (1935-) French architect and designer

Harry Bertoia (1915-1978) Italian/American furniture designer and sculptor

Fulvio Bianconi (1915-1996) Italian glass designer

Lubomír Blecha (1933-) Czech glass artist

Zoltán Bohus (1941-) Hungarian glass artist

Mattia Bonetti (1953-) French furniture designer

Robert Bonfils (1922-) American poster designer

Pierre Bonnard (1867 - 1947) French artist

Jonathan Bonner (1947-) American sculptor

Osvaldo Borsani (1911–85) Italian architect and furniture designer

Rudolf Bosselt (1871-1938) German metalware designer and sculptor

Mario Botta (1943-) Swiss architect and designer

Ronan Bouroullec (1971-) French designer

Erwan Bouroullec (1976-) French designer

Will Bradley (1868-1962) American artist

Edgar Brandt (1880 - 1960) French metalware designer

Marianne Brandt (1893-1983) German artist and metalware designer

Frank Brangwyn (1867-1956) British artist and ceramic designer

Andrea Branzi (1938-) Italian architect and furniture designer

Georges Braque (1882-1963) French artist and sculptor

Mark Brazier-Jones (1956-) New Zealand/British furniture designer

Hin Bredendieck (1904-1995) German metalware designer

Marcel Lajos Breuer (1902–1981) American architect and furniture designer

Alison Britton (1948-) British ceramic artist

Jaroslava Brychtivá (1924-) Czech glass artist

Hans Bunde (1919-1996) Danish designer

Paul Bürck (1878-1947) German artist

René Buthaud (1886–1986) French ceramic artist

José Zanine Caldas (1918–2001) Brazilian furniture designer

Alexander Calder (1898-1976) American sculptor

Fernando Campana (1961-) Brazilian furniture designer

Humberto Campana (1953-) Brazilian furniture designer

Giacomo Cappellin (1887 - 1968) Italian glass designer

Leonetto Cappiello (1875-1942) Italian poster designer

Roger Capron (1922-2006) French ceramic artist

Frederick Carder (1863 - 1963) American artist and glass designer

Michael Cardew (1901-1983) British studio potter

George Carwardine (1887-1947 German lighting designer

Cesare Casati (1936-) Italian architect and lighting designer

Adolphe Mouron Cassandre (1901–1968) Ukranian/French poster designer

Achille Castiglioni (1918 - 2002) Italian furniture designer

Pier Giacomo Castiglioni (1913-1968) Italian furniture designer

Wendell Castle (1932–) American furniture designer

Charles Catteau (1880–1966) French ceramic artist

Gilles Chabrier (1959-) French glass artist

Marc Chagall (1887-1985) French artist

Paul Chaleff (1947-) American ceramic artist

Pierre Chareau (1883-1950) French architect and furniture designer

Dorothea Charol (1895-1963) Austrian sculptor

Jean Chassaing (1905 - 1935) French poster designer

Sandro Chia (1946-) Italian sculptor and furniture designer

Dale Chihuly (1941-) Amercian glass artist

Demetre Chiparus (1886-1947) Romanian sculptor

Hans Christiansen (1866-1945) German architect and furniture designer

Václav Cigler (1929-) Czech glass artist

John Clappison (1937-) British ceramic and glass designer

Michael Cleff (1961-) German ceramic artist

Clarice Cliff (1899–1972) British ceramic designer

Marcel Coard (1889–1975) French furniture designer

Nigel Coates (1949-) British architect and furniture designer

Wells Coates (1895-1958) Canadian/British architect and appliance designer

Jean Cocteau (1889 - 1963) French writer, artist and ceramic designer

Luigi Colani (1928-) German car designer

Paul Colin (1892-1985) French poster designer

Claire-Jeanne-Roberte Colinet (1880-1950) Belgian/French sculptor

Albert Colledge (1891 - 1972) British ceramic designer

Glyn Colledge (1922-2000) British ceramic designer

Joe Colombo (1930–71) Italian furniture designer

Claude Conover (1907-1994) American ceramic artist

Terence Conran (1931-) British designer

Peter Cook (1936-) British architect and furniture designer

Susie Cooper (1902–1995) British ceramic designer

Emmanuel Cooper (1938-) British studio potter

Austin Cooper (1890-1964) Canadian poster designer

Hans Coper (1920-81) German studio potter

Reginald Guy Cowan (1894-1963) American studio potter and ceramic designer

Matali Crasset (1965-) French designer

Carl Otto Czeschka (1878-1960) Austrian printmaker and artist

Dan Dailey (1947-) American glass artist

Stefan Dakon (1904-1992) Austrian sculptor

Paul Daum (1888-1944) French glass designer

Pierre d'Avesn (1901-1990) French glass designer

Robin Day (1915-) British furniture designer

Lucienne Day (1917-) British textile designer

Michele De Lucchi (1951-) Italian furniture designer

Laura de Santillana (1955-) Italian glass artist

Ludovico Diaz de Santillana (1931-1989) Italian glass artist

Waylande Desantis Gregory (1905-1971) American sculptor

Joseph-Theodore Deck (1823-1891) French potter

Francois-Emile Décorchemont (1880-1971) French glass artist

Sonia Delaunay (1885-1979) French artist and textile designer

Christian Dell (1893-1974) German metalware designer

Jean Derval (1925-) French ceramic artist

Donald Deskey (1894–1989) American furniture designer

Stuart Devlin (1931-) Australian metalware designer

Richard DeVore (1933-2006) American ceramic artist

Carlo di Carli (1910-1999) Italian furniture designer

Erich Dieckmann (1896-1944) German furniture designer

Wilhelm Hunt Diederich (1884-1953) American metalware designer

Nanna Ditzel (1923-) Danish furniture and textile designer

Tom Dixon (1959-) British designer

Margaret Dodd (1941-) Australian ceramic artist

Marion Dorn (1896–1964) American textile designer

Christopher Dresser (1834–1904) British textile, ceramic, glass, furniture and metalware designer
Henry Dreyfuss (1904-1972) American appliance designer
Guido Drocco (1942-) Italian architect and furniture designer
Nathalie Du Pasquier (1957-) French furniture and textile designer
André Dubreuil (1951-) French furniture designer
Marcel Duchamp (1887-1968 French artist
Michel Dufet (1888–1985) French furniture designer
Maurice Dufrène (1876–1955) French ceramic designer
Raoul Dufy (1877–1953) French artist
Jean Dunand (1877-1942) Swiss metalware designer
Jean Dupas (1882-1964) French artist, poster designer and designer
Paul Dupré-Lafon (1900-1971) French architect and furniture designer

Charles Eames (1907–1978) American furniture designer
Ray Eames (1912–1988) American furniture designer
Jack Earl (1934-) American ceramic artist
Tom Eckersley (1914-1997) British poster designer
Jan (Johannes Wigbold) Eisenloeffel (1876-1957) Dutch metalware designer
Harvey Ellis (1852-1904) American architect and furniture designer
Eva Englund (1937-1998) Swedish glass artist
Wharton Esherick (1887-1970) American sculptor and furniture maker
Paul R. Evans (1931-1987) American furniture designer

(Frank) Shepard Fairey (1970-) American graphic designer
Claire Falkenstein (1908-1997) American sculptor
Marcello Fantoni (1915-) Italian ceramicist
Ricardo Fasanello (1930-1993) Brazilian furniture designer
Ken Ferguson (1938-) American ceramic artist
Anna Castelli Ferrieri (1920–2006) Italian furniture designer
Edward Fields (-1979) American carpet maker
Paul Follot (1877-1941) French furniture designer
Grahame Fowler (1956-) British textile designer
Piero Fornasetti (1913-1988) Italian artist and furniture designer
Gordon Mitchell Forsyth (1879-1952) British ceramic designer
Hugo França (1954-) Brazilian furniture designer
Kaj Frank (1911-1989) Finnish glass designer
Jean-Michel Frank (1895–1941) French furniture designer
Paul Frankl (1886-1958) Austrian furniture designer
Viola Frey (1933-2004) American ceramic artist
Pedro Friedeberg (1937-) Mexican artist and furniture designer

Elizabeth Fritsch (1940-) British ceramic artist
Roger Fry (1866-1934) British artist and critic
Anzolo Fuga (1915-) Italian glass designer
Kyohei Fujita (1921-2004) Japanese glass artist

Bent Peter Gabrielsen (1928-) Danish goldsmith
Guido Gambone (1909-1969) Italian ceramic designer
Elizabeth Garouste (1949-) French furniture designer
Luciano Gaspari (1913-2007) Italian glass artist
Simon Gate (1886-1980) Swedish artist and glass designer
Eugen Gauss (1905-1988) American sculptor
Dino Gavina (1922-) Italian industrialist and designer
Frank Gehry (1929-) American architect and furniture designer
David Gilhooly (1943-) American ceramic artist
Ernest Gimson (1864-1919) British architect and furniture designer
John Glick (1938-) American ceramic artist
Robert Goodden (1909-2002) British architect and metalware designer
Marcel Goupy (1886-1954) French glass artist
Duncan Grant (1885-1978) British artist
Werner Graul (1905-1984) German artist
Michael Graves (1934–) American architect and designer
Eileen Gray (1878–1976) Irish furniture designer
Konstantin Grcic (1965-) German furniture designer
Charles Sumner Greene (1868-1957) American architect and furniture designer
Henry Mather Greene (1870-1954) American architect and furniture designer
William Grueby (1867-1925) American ceramic designer
Walter Gropius (1883-1969) German architect and furniture designer, director of the Bauhaus
Greta Magnusson Grossman (1906-1999) Swedish/American furniture designer
Maija Grotell (1899-1973) Finnish/American studio potter
André Groult (1884-1966) French furniture designer
Alessandro Guerriero (1943-) Italian architect and furniture designer

Ludwig Habich (1872-1949) German sculptor
Zaha Hadid (1950-) British/Iraqi architect and furniture designer
Brigitta Hahn (1938-) Swedish textile designer
Edvard Hald (1883-1980) Swedish glass designer
Reuben Haley (1872-1933) American glass designer
Shoji Hamada (1894-1978) Japanese studio potter
Ineke Hans (1966-) Dutch furniture designer
Jiri Harcuba (1928-) Czech glass artist

Leslie Harradine (1887-1965) British ceramic designer
Michael Harris (1933-1994) British glass artist
Makio Hasuike (1938-) Japanese glass artist
Jamie Hayon (1974-) Spanish designer
Auguste-Claude Heiligenstein (1891-1976) French glass artist
Chet Helms (1942-2005) American artist and poster designer
Poul Henningsen (1894-1967) Danish architect and designer
Frederic Henri Kay Henrion (1914-1990) British artist and poster designer
Barbara Hepworth (1903-1975) British sculptor
René Herbst (1891-1983) French architect and furniture designer
Sam Herman (1936-) American glass artist
Yasuki Hiramatsu (1926-) Japanese metalware designer
Pavel Hlava (1924-2003) Czech glass artist
David Hockney (1937-) British artist
Josef Hoffmann (1870–1956) Austrian architect and designer
Wolfgang Hoffmann (1900–1969) Austrian furniture designer
Eric Höglund (1932-1998) Swedish glass designer
Ludwig Hohlwein (1874-1949) German poster designer
Steven Holl (1947-) American architect and ceramic designer
Josef Hospodka (1923–1989) Czech glass artist
Elbert Hubbard (1856–1915) American author, publisher and designer
Patriz Huber (1878–1902) German metalware designer
Wayne Husted (1927-) American glass designer

Klaus Ihlenfeld (1934-) German sculptor
Arata Isozaki (1931-) Japanese architect and furniture designer
Alec Issigonis (1906-1988) Greek/British car designer
Johannes Itten (1888-1967) Swiss artist and graphic designer

Arne Jacobsen (1902-1971) Danish architect and furniture designer
Léon Jallot (1874–1967) French furniture designer
Maurice Jallot (1900-1971) French furniture designer
Pierre Jeanneret (1896-1967) Swiss architect and furniture designer
Vladimir Jelinek (1934-) Czech glass artist
Charles Jencks (1939-) American architect and ceramic designer
Jakob Jensen (1926-) Danish designer
Georg Jensen (1866-1935) Danish metalware designer
Georges Jouve (1910-1964) French ceramic artist
Finn Juhl (1912–71) Danish furniture designer
Rudolf Jurnikl (1928-) Czech glass artist

Vladimir Kagan (1927–) German/American furniture designer
Wilhelm Kåge (1889–1960) Swedish studio potter

Wassily Kandinsky (1866-1944) Russian artist
Walter Kantack (1889-1953) American metalware designer
Kit Karbler (1954-) American glass artist
Eric McKnight Kauffer (1890-1954) American poster designer
Peter Keler (1898-1982) German furniture designer
Alexander Kéléty (active 1918-1940) French sculptor
Alton Kelley (1940-2008) American artist and poster designer
Isamu Kenmochi (1912-1971) Japanese sculptor
Paul Kiss (1885-1962) French sculptor
Toshiyuki Kita (1942-) Japanese furniture designer
Poul Kjærholm (1929-1980) Danish furniture designer
Gustav Klimt (1862–1918) Austrian artist
Miloslav Klinger (1922-1999) Czech glass artist
Kaare Klint (1888-1954) Danish architect and furniture designer
Dame Laura Knight (1877-1970) British ceramic artist
Florence Knoll (1917–) American architect and furniture designer
Belle Kogan (1902-2000) Russian glass and ceramic designer
Vladimír Kopecký (1931-) Czech glass artist
Henning Koppel (1918-1981) Danish metalware designer
Jan Kotík (1916-2002) Czech glass artist
Howard Kottler (1930-1989) American ceramic artist
Julia Krantz (1967-) Brazilian furniture designer
Michael Lucero (1953-) American ceramic artist
Valentina Kulagina (1902–1987) Russian poster designer
Shiro Kuramata (1934-) Japanese furniture designer

Dominick Labino (1910-1987) American glass artist
Boris Lacroix (1902-1984) French lighting designer
René Lalique (1860-1945) French glass designer
Nils Landberg (1907-1991) Swedish glass designer
Michael Landes (1949-) German architect and furniture designer
Danny Lane (1955-) American/British architect and furniture designer
Luc Lanel (1893-1965) French metalware designer
Jack Lenor Larsen (1927-) American textile designer
Richard Latham (1920-1991) American designer
Peter Layton (1937-) Czech/British glass artist
Le Corbusier (born Charles-Édouard Jeanneret-Gris) (1887-1965) Swiss/French architect and furniture designer
Pierre Le Faguays (Fayral) (1892-1925) French sculptor
Bernard Leach (1887-1979) British studio potter

ARTISTS & DESIGNERS

Léon Ledru (1855-1926) French glass artist
Pierre Legrain (1888-1929) French furniture designer
Jules Leleu (1883–1961) French furniture designer
Stanislav Libensky (1921-2002) Czech glass artist
Riccardo Licata (1929-) Italian artist
Roy Lichtenstein (1923-1997) American artist
Charles Limbert (1854–1923) American furniture designer
Stig Lindberg (1916-1982) Swedish glass, ceramic and textile designer
Vicke Lindstrand (1904-1983) Swedish glass designer
Claudius Linossier (1893-1953) French ceramic artist
Harvey Littleton (1922-) American glass artist
Raymond Loewy (1893-1986) French/American car designer
Adolf Loos (1870-1933) Austrian/Czech architect and furniture designer
Josef Lorenzl (1892-1950) Austrian sculptor
Charles Loupot (1892–1962) Swiss poster designer
Ross Lovegrove (1958-) British appliance designer
Raymond Loewy (1893-1986) American industrial designer
Mária Lugossy (1950-) Hungarian glass artist
Ingeborg Lundin (1921-1992) Swedish glass designer
Jean Lurçat (1892-1966) French artist, textile and ceramic designer
Per Lutkin (1942-1998) Danish glass designer

Frances MacDonald (1873-1921) Scottish artist
Margaret MacDonald (Mackintosh) (1865-1033) Scottish artist
Charles Rennie Mackintosh (1868–1928) Scottish architect and furniture designer
Herbert MacNair (1868-1955) Scottish artist and furniture designer
Vico Magistretti (1920–2006) Italian architect and furniture designer
Erik Magnussen (1940-) Danish ceramic artist
Louis Majorelle (1859-1926) French furniture designer
Daisy Makeig-Jones (1881–1945) British ceramic designer
John Makepeace (1939-) British furniture designer
Kasimir Malevich (1879-1935) Polish artist
Jim Malone (1946-) British ceramic artist
André Mare (1887–1932) French artist and furniture designer
Filippo Marinetti (1876-1942) Italian artist
Maurice Marinot (1882-1960) French glass artist
Dante Marioni (1964-) American glass artist
Javier Mariscal (1950-) Spanish furniture and textile designer
Richard Marquis (1945-) American glass artist
Aino Marsio (1894-1949) Finnish architect and furniture designer

Joel and Jan Martel, (twin brothers both 1896–1966) French ceramic designers
Dino Martens (1894-1970) Italian glass designer
Robert Wallace Martin (1843-1923) British studio potter
Edwin Martin (1860-1915) British studio potter
Walter Martin (1857-1912) British studio potter
Paolo Martinuzzi (1933-) Italian glass artist
Napoleone Martinuzzi (1892-1977) Italian glass designer
Bruno Mathsson (1907-1988) Swedish furniture designer
Henri Matisse (1869-1954) French artist
Adolf Matura (1921-79) Czech glass artist
Jean Mayodon (1893–1967) French ceramic artist
Serge Manzon (c1935-1998) French designer
Warren McArthur (1885-1961) American furniture designer
Paul McCobb (1917-1969) American furniture designer
Edward McKnight Kauffer (1890-1954) American artist
Philip Meggs (1942-2002) American graphic designer
Richard Meier (1934-) American architect and ceramic designer
David Mellor (1930-2009) British metalware designer
Alessandro Mendini (1931-) Italian architect and furniture designer
Dino Martens (1894-1970) Italian glass artist
Percy Metcalfe (1895-1970) British ceramic designer
Adolf Meyer (1881-1929) German architect
Hannes Meyer (1889–1954) Swiss architect and furniture designer
Joan Miró (1893-1983) Spanish artist and ceramic designer
Denis Mitchell (1912-1993) British sculptor
Ernst Moeckl (1931-) German furniture designer
Børge Mogensen (1914-72) Danish furniture designer
László Moholy-Nagy (1895-1946) Hungarian artist and photographer
Carlo Mollino (1905–1973) Italian architect and furniture designer
Piet Mondrian (1872–1944) Dutch artist
Henry Moore (1893-1986) British sculptor
William Morris (1834–1996) British artist, furniture, textile designer and critic
Jasper Morrison (1959-) British designer
Koloman Moser (1868-1918) Austrian artist
Serge Mouille (1922-1988) French lighting and metalware designer
Stanley Mouse (1940-) American artist and poster designer
Georg Muche (1895–1987) German artist
Albin Muller (1871-1941) German metalware designer
Bruno Munari (1907-1998) Italian artist and furniture designer
Keith Murray (1892–1981) New Zealand architect, glass and ceramic designer
Hermann Muthesius (1861–1927) German architect and furniture designer
Forrest Myers (1941-) American furniture designer and sculptor

Joel Myers (1934-) Danish studio glass artist

George Nakashima (1905-1990) Japanese/American architect and furniture designer
Paul Nash (1889-1946) British war artist
Aldo Nason (1920-) Italian glass artist
Otto Natzler (1908-2007) Austrian studio potter
Getrud Natzler (1908-1971) Austrian studio potter
George Nelson (1907–1986) American furniture designer
Jessie Newbery (1864-1919) British textile designer
Steven Newell (1948-) Amercan glass artist
Marc Newson (1963-) Australian furniture designer
Harald Nielsen (1892-1977) Danish metalware designer
Isamu Noguchi (1904–1988) Japanese/American sculptor
Richard Notkin (1948-) American ceramic artist
Eliot Noyes (1910-1977) American architect and ceramic designer
Antti Nurmesniemi (1927-2003) Finnish furniture designer
Gunnar Nylund (1904-1997) Danish/Finnish ceramic designer
Gunnel Nyman (1909-1948) Finnish glass designer

Yoichi Ohira (1946-) Japanese glass artist
George Ohr (1857-1918) American ceramic artist
Edvin Öhrström (1906-1994) Swedish glass designer
Josef Maria Olbrich (1867–1908) German/Austrian architect and metalware designer
Claes Oldenburg (1929-) Swedish sculptor
Ladislav Oliva (1933-) Czech glass artist

Albert Paley (1944-) American architect and metalware designer
Sven Palmqvist (1906-1984) Swedish glass designer
Verner Panton (1926–1998) Danish furniture designer
Tommi Parzinger (1903-1981) German furniture designer
Tom Patti (1943-) American glass artist
Bruno Paul (1874-1968) German architect and furniture designer
Pierre Paulin (1927-2009) French furniture designer
František Pečeny (1920-1977) Czech glass artist
Dagobert Peche (1887-1923) Austrian ceramic, furniture and textile designer
Pollio Perelda (1915-1984) Italian artist and glass designer
Charlotte Perriand (1903-1999) French architect and furniture designer
Grayson Perry (1960-) British ceramic artist
Sigurd Persson (1914-2003) Swedish metalware designer
Jean Perzel (1892-1986) French lighting designer
Gaetano Pesce (1939-) Italian architect and furniture designer
Paul Philippe (1870-1930) French sculptor
Alessandro Pianon (1931-1984) Italian glass artist

Pablo Picasso (1881-1973) Spanish artist and ceramic designer
Robert Picault (1919-2000) French ceramic artist
Henri C. Pieck (1895–1972) Dutch architect and graphic artist
John Piper (1903-1992) British artist and printmaker
Warren Platner (1919–2006) American furniture designer
Otto Poertzel (1876-1963) German ceramic designer and sculptor
Paul Poiret (1879-1944) French fashion designer
Flavio Poli (1900-1984) Italian glass designer
Jacqueline Poncelet (1947-) British ceramic designer
Gio Ponti (1891–1979) Italian architect and furniture designer
Emanuele Ponzio (1923-) Italian lighting and ceramic designer
Philip Lloyd Powell (1919-2008) American furniture designer
Michael Powolny (1871-1954) Austrian glass designer
Josef Pravec (1928-) Czech glass artist
Ferdinand Preiss (1882-1943) German sculptor
Jack Pritchard (1899-1992) British furniture designer
Jean Prouvé (1901-1984) French furniture designer
Otto Prütscher (1880-1949) Austrian designer
Jean Puiforcat (1897-1945) French metalware designer
Tom Purvis (1888-1959) British artist and poster designer

David Queensberry (1929-) British glass designer

Ernest Race (1913–1963) British furniture designer
Leslie Ragan (1897-1972) American poster designer
Carlo Rampazzi (1949-) Italian furniture designer
Dieter Rams (1932-), German designer
Paul Rand (1914-1996) American poster designer
Karim Rashid (1960-) Egyptian/Canadian/American furniture designer
John Rattenbury Skeaping (1901–1980) English sculptor
Man Ray (1890-1976) American artist
David Reekie (1947-) British glass artist
Ruth Reeves (1892-1966) American artist and textile designer
Lilly Reich (1885-1947) German furniture designer
Grete Reichardt (1907–1984) German furniture and textile designer
Charlotte Rhead (1885–1947) British ceramic designer
Frederick H. Rhead (1880-1942) British/American ceramic designer
Gilbert Rhode (1894-1944) American furniture designer
Lucie Rie (1902-1995) Austrian/British studio potter
Richard Riemerschmid (1868–1957) German architect and furniture designer

Gerrit Thomas Rietveld (1888–1964) Dutch architect and furniture designer

Günter Ferdinand Ris (1928-) German architect and furniture designer

John Risley (1919-) American furniture designer

Willy Rizzo (1928-) Italian/American photographer and furniture designer

T. H. (Terence Harold) Robsjohn-Gibbings (1905-1976) British architect and furniture designer

Sergio Rodrigues (1927-) Brazilian furniture designer

Gilbert Rohde (1894–1944) American furniture designer

Johan Rohde 1856-1935 Danish metalware designer

Charles Rohlfs (1853–1936) American furniture designer

Aldo Rossi (1931-1997) Italian architect and ceramic designer

René Roubicek (1922-) Czech glass artist

Miluše Roubícková (1922-) Czech glass artist

Clément Rousseau (1872–1950) French furniture designer

Ginny Ruffner (1952-) American glass artist

Jacques-Emile Ruhlmann (1879–1933) French furniture designer

John Ruskin (1819–1900). British critic

Sydney Gordon Russell (Sir) (1892-1980) British furniture designer

Eero Saarinen (1910–1961) Finnish-American architect and furniture designer

Eliel Saarinen (1873–1950) Finnish architect and furniture designer

Lino Sabattini (1925-) Italian metalware designer

Edouard Marcel Sandoz (1881–1971) Swiss sculptor

Richard Sapper (1932–) Italian designer

Gino Sarfatti (1912-1984) Italian lighting designer

Timo Sarpaneva (1926-2006) Finnish glass designer

Raymond Savignac (1907-2002) French poster designer

Carlo Scarpa (1906–1978) Italian architect and glass designer

Tobia Scarpa (1935-) Italian glass designer

Helen Konig Scavini (1886-1974) Austrian/German ceramic designer

Edwin Scheier (1910-2008) American ceramic artist

Mary Scheier (1908-2007) American ceramic artist

Hans Schleger (1898-1976) British poster designer

Eugene Schoen (1880–1957) American furniture designer

Viktor Schreckengost (1906-2008) American industrial designer

Paul Schuitema (1897-1973) Dutch graphic artist

Heinz Schulz-Neudamm (1899-1969) German graphic artist

Kurt Schwitters (1887-1948) German artist

Enid Seeney (1931-) American ceramicist

Livio Seguso (1930-) Italian glass artist

Ben Seibel (1918-1985) American ceramic designer

Herbert Selldorf (1929-) German furniture designer

Livio Serena (1942-) Italian glass artist

Peter Shire (1947-) American artist, furniture designer and sculptor

Kataro Shiriyamadani (1865-1948) Japanese-born American ceramic artist

Jutta Sika (1877-1964) Austrian ceramic designer

Jonathan Singleton (1969-) British furniture designer

Borek Sipek (1949-) Czech furniture designer

Eric Slater (1896-) British ceramic designer

Job Smeets (1970-) Belgian/Dutch furniture designer

Paul Soldner (1921-) American ceramic artist

Pauline Solven (1943-) British glass artist

Hajime Sorayama (1947-) Japanese poster designer

Inge-Lise Sorensen (1939-)

Vratislav Sotola Italian glass designer

Ettore Sottsass (1917–2007) Italian architect and furniture designer

George Sowden (1942-) British architect and furniture designer

William Spratling (1900-1967) American metalware designer

Karl Springer (1931-1991) German/French furniture designer

Mart Stam (1899-1986) Dutch architect and furniture designer

Philippe Starck (1949–) French architect and appliance designer

Thomas Stearns (1936-2006) American glass artist

Ronald Stennett-Willson (1915-) British glass designer

Gustav Stickley (1858–1942) American furniture designer

Nanny Still (1926-) Finish glass and ceramic designer

Niklaus Stoecklin (1896–1982) Swiss poster designer

Mario Sturani (1906-1978) ceramic designer

Russell Sturgis (1836-1909) American architect and critic

Raymond Subes (1893-1970) French metalware designer

Louis Süe (1875-1968) French metalware designer

Nikalai Suetin (1897-1954) Russian artist and ceramic designer

Gerald Summers (1899-1967) British furniture designer

Josef Švarc (1928-) Czech glass artist

Guy Sydenham (1916-2005) British studio potter

Lino Tagliapietra (1934-) Italian glass artist

Jesscia Tait (1928-) British ceramic designer

Toshiko Takaezu (1922-) American ceramic artist

Ilmari Tapiovaara (1914-) Finnish furniture and textile designer

Fred Taylor (1875-1963) British artist and poster designer

Walter Dorwin Teague (1883-1960) American architect and glass designer

Willem Ten Broek (1905-1993) Dutch poster designer

Joaquim Tenreiro (1906-1992) Brazilian furniture designer

Irv Tepper (1947) American ceramic artist

Giuseppe Terragni (1904-1943) Italian architect and furniture designer

Robert Thompson (1876-1955) British furniture designer

Michael Thonet (1796-1971) German furniture designer

Nils Thorsson (1898-1975) Danish ceramic designer

Frank Thrower (1932-1987) British glass designer

Matteo Thun (1952-) Italian architect and furniture designer

Louis Comfort Tiffany (1848-1933) American glass designer

Sue Timney (1950-) British textile designer

Oliviero Toscani (1942-) Italian photographer

Ermanno Toso (1903-1973) Italian glass designer

Bernard Tschumi (1944-) Swiss architect and furniture designer based in America

Helena Tynell (1918-) Finnish glass designer

Masanori Umeda (1941-) Italian furniture designer

Chris Unterseher (1943-) American ceramic artist

Patricia Urquiola (1961-) Spanish architect and furniture designer

Sandro Vacchetti (1889-1976) Italian ceramic designer

William Van Allen (1883-1954) American architect

Artus Van Briggle (1869-1904) Dutch/American studio potter

Ludwig Mies van der Rohe (1886-1969) German architect and furniture designer

Henry Van de Velde (1863–1957) Belgian architect and interior designer

Theo van Doesburg (1883–1931) Dutch artist

Dirk van Erp (1859-1933) American metalware designer

Peter Vandenberge (1935-) American ceramic artist

Henry Varnum Poor (1888-1970) American artist and furniture maker

Victor Vasaérly (1906-1997) Hungarian-born painter and founder of the Op Art movement.

Paolo Venini (1895-1959) Italian glass designer

Robert Venturi (1925-) American architect and furniture designer

Bernard Villemot (1911-1989) French poster designer

František Vízner (1936-) Czech glass artist

Noi Volkov (1947-) Russian ceramic artist

Walter von Nessen (1889-1943) German/American lighting designer

Franz von Stuck (1863-1928) German artist, architect and sculptor

Peter Voulkos (1924-2002) American sculptor

C.F.A (Charles Frances Annesley) Voysey (1857-1941) British architect and furniture designer

Peter Waals (1870-1937) Dutch furniture designer

Wilhelm Wagenfeld (1900-1990) German glass and metalware designer

Otto Wagner (1841–1918) Austrian architect and designer

Amalric Walter (1870-1959) French glass artist

Marcel Wanders (1963-) Dutch designer

Ole Wanscher (1903–1985) Danish furniture designer

Andy Warhol (1928-1987) American artist

Sidney Biehler Waugh (1904-1963) American glass designer and sculptor

Philip Speakman Webb (1831-1915) British architect and furniture designer

Kem Weber (1889-1963) German furniture designer

Hans Wegner (1914–2007) Danish furniture designer

Wolfgang Weingart (1941-) German graphic designer

Robert Welch (1929-2000) British metalware designer

Jerk Werkmaster (1896 - 1978) Swedish ceramic designer

Bjorn Wiinblad (1918-2006) Danish ceramic artist

William Wilson (1905-1972) British glass designer

Tapio Wirkkala (1915-1985) Finnish glass designer

Philippe Wolfers (1858-1929) Belgian metalware designer

Beatrice Wood (1893-1998) American artist and studio potter

Betty Woodman (1930-) American sculptor

Edward J Wormley (1907-1995) American furniture designer

Frank Lloyd Wright (1867–1959) American architect and furniture designer

Russel Wright (1904-1976) American ceramic designer

Mina Wu (1976-2008) Taiwanese jewellery, product and textile designer

Karel Wünsch (1932-) Czech glass artist

Franz Würbel (1822-1900) Austrian poster designer

Kazumasa Yamashita (1937-) Japanese architect and ceramic designer

Sori Yanagi (1915–) Japanese furniture designer

Takeshi Yasuda (1943) British ceramic artist

Tadanori Yokoo (1936-) Japanese poster designer

Grace Young (1869-1947) American ceramic designer

Bruno Zach (1891-1935) German sculptor

Vladimír Žahour (1925-) Czech glass artist

Mario Zanini (1907-1971) Brazilian artist, furniture and glass designer

Marco Zanuso (1916–2001) Italian architect and furniture designer

Vittorio Zecchin (1878-1947) Italian artist and glass designer

Eva Zeisel (1906-) Hungarian-born American ceramic designer

Frantisek Zemek (1913-1960) Czech glass artist

Yan Zoritchak (1944-) Slovankian glass artist

Robert Zeppel-Sperl (1944-2005) Austrian glass artist

Toni Zuccheri (1937-) Italian glass artist

Mary Ann 'Toots' Zynsky (1951-) American glass artist

Index

Acknowledgements

Photographic Acknowledgements

Miller's would like to thank and acknowledge all the following collectors, dealers, designers, museums, shops and photographic agencies who have kindly provided images for use in this book.

Key: a above, b below, c centre, l left, r right

Akg-images Tony Vaccaro 70 a

Alamy Bildarchiv Monheim GmbH 10-11, 62 c, Danny Nebraska 244 r, Elizabeth Whiting & Associates 228 bl, Peter Horree 62 a, Tom Mackie 216

Alessi www.alessi.com: 251 a, 279 all

American Art Glass Works Inc 41 Wooster St, 1st floor, New York NY 10013, USA, www.americanartglassgallery.com: 270 cc

Michael Anastassiades www.michaelanastassiades.com: 272 a

Anderson & Garland Anderson House, Crispin court, Newbiggin Lane, Westerhope, Newcastle upon Tyne NE5 1BF, UK, www.andersonandgarland.com: 196 br © ADAGP, Paris and DACS, London 2009

Antique Gallery 8523 Germantown Avenue, Philadelphia, PA 19118, USA, www.antiquegal.com: 55

Ron Arad Associates www.ronarad.com, photo Paul Denton: 248 a,

Aram www.aram.co.uk: 74 a

Art Deco Etc 73 Upper Gloucester Road, Brighton, Sussex BN1 3LQ, UK: 114 ar

Ashmore and Burgess www.ashmoreandburgess.com: 121 br, 122 b, 123

Bauhaus Archiv, Berlin 66 br, 67

Below Stairs of Hungerford 103 High Street, Hungerford, Berks RG17 0NB, UK, www.belowstairs.co.uk: 242 bl

Auktionshaus Bergmann Möhrendorfer Strasse 4, 91056 Erlangen, Germany, www.auktion-bergmann.de: 21

Beverley Stand G023-25, Alfies Antique Market, 13 Church Street, Marylebone, London, NW8 8DT, UK: 9 a

The Big White House 220 a © DACS 2009, 222 b, 223 al, 225 cl, 227 ac, 229 b, 233 cr, 278

Joanna Bird Pottery Alexander Brattell/Joanna Bird Pottery/Fine Art Society 256 cl

Barbara Blau South Street Antiques Market, 615 South 6th Steet, Philadephia, PA 19147-2128, USA: 176 a

Bloomsbury Auctions New York 6 West 48th Street, New York, NY 100360-190, USA, www.nybloomsburyauctions.com: 83 © ARS, NY and DACS, London 2009 , 146 bl & br

Bonhams 101 New Bond Street, London W1S 1SR, UK, www.bonhams.com: 28 al © DACS 2009, 61 bl, 63 b & cr both © DACS 2009, 71 c, 73 ar © FLC/ADAGP, Paris and DACS, London 2009, 78 al & ar, 80 a, 214 cr, 238 bc

Bridgeman Art Library Wolfgang Neeb 228 c

Bukowskis Arsenalsgatan 4, Box 1754, 111 87 Stockholm, Sweden, www.bukowskis.se: 56 br, 77 cr, 189 © DACS 2009, 232 br, 236 bl © DACS 2009, 247 cb

Calderwood Gallery 1622 Spruce Street, Philadelphia, PA 19103, USA, www.calderwoodgallery.com: 95, 96 a & br, 97, 105 a © ADAGP, Paris and DACS, London 2009

Cappellini Design SpA www.cappellini.it: 234 a, 247 ca

Cassina SpA www.cassina.com: 19 bl

Centraal Museum, Utrecht 62 al

Chihuly Studio © Dave Chihuly 1998, photo Richard K Loesch 267 a, photo Stewart Charles Cohen 266 al

Chiswick Auctions 1-5 Colville Road, London W3 5BL, UK, www.chiswickauctions.co.uk: 114 al

Cloud Glass 43 Mountsfield Close, Newport Pagnell, Bucks MK16 0JE, UK, www.cloudglass.com: 64 a © DACS 2009, 212 br © ADAGP, Paris and DACS, London 2009, 286 br

Courtesy of **The Conservative Party** www.conservatives.com: 287 b

Contemporary Applied Arts 2 Percy Street, London W1T 1DD, UK, www.caa.org.uk: 53 bc

Contemporary Ceramics Somerset House, The Courtyard Room Strand, London WC2R 1LA, UK, www.cpaceramics.com: 52 c, 260 bc

Graham Cooley Collection 54 br, 182 cr, 188 br, 192 a & bl, 194 bl & br, 195, 196 al, 197 bcl, 198 bl & br

Corbis Angelo Hornak 58, Bettmann 38, 66 al, 68 a, 76 a, Christopher Felver 228 a, Hulton-Deutsch Collection 174 a, Paul Almasy 72 a, Paulo Fridman 250 a, Pete Souza/Obama Transition Team/Handout/CNP 221 br in timeline, Richard Bryant 27, Robert Maass 221 bl in timeline, Stephane Cardinale/People Avenue 246 a, Vanni Archive 66 ar

Matali Crasset photo Patrick Gries: 262 br

Lesley Craze Gallery 33-35a Clerkenwell Green, London EC1R 0DU, UK, www.lesleycrazegallery.co.uk: 272 cr

Deco Etc 122 West 25th Street, New York, NY 100001, USA, www.decoetc.net: 141 a & bcl, 142 b

Delorenzo 956 Madison Avenue, New York, NY 10021, USA, www.delorenzogallery.com: 91 c, 99 al, bl & br,

Decodame www.decodame.com: 6 a, 80 ac, 84 a & b, 88 a, 108 a © DACS 2009, 109, 130 cl, 131 cl & cr, 140 br, 148 bl

The Design Gallery 5 The Green, Westerham, Kent TN16 1AS, UK, www.designgallery.co.uk: 104 bl, 108 b

Dorotheum Dorotheergasse 17, 1010 Vienna, Austria, www.dorotheum.com: 12 l in timeline, 19 al, 25 bc, 74 bc, 113, 116 b, 132 a, 170 a & c, 201 bcr, 206 c, 238 br, 265

Dreweatts Donnington Priory Salerooms, Donnington, Newbury, Berks RG14 2JE, UK, www.dnfa.com: 92 br, 112 a, 128 br, 130 cl, 176 bl

Droog Design photo Gerard van Hees: 262 c

Dyson www.dyson.co.uk: 280 br

Edra www.edra.com: 251 cr

Elizabeth Whiting & Associates Tim Street-Porter 152-3

English Heritage 86

The End of History 548½ Hudson Street, New York, NY 10014, USA: 197 bcr

Etienne & Van den Doel De Lind 38, 5061 HX, Oisterwijk, Netherlands, www.etiennegalerie.nl: 268 bl, 270 bc © ADAGP, Paris and DACS, London 2009

Fieldings Auctioneers 12 Market Street, Stourbridge DY8 1AD, UK, www.fieldingsauctioneers.com: 49 bl, 118 b

The Fine Art Society 148 New Bond Street, London W1S 2JT, UK, www.faslondon.com: 12 b

Auktionshaus Dr Fischer Trappensee-Schößchen, D-74074 Heilbronn, Germany, www.auctions-fischer.de: 57, 185, 268 cr, 269

Fragile Design 14-5 The Custard Factory, Digbeth, Birmingham B9 4AA, UK, www.fragiledesign.com: 181 © DACS 2009, 190 bl

Freeman's 1808 Chestnut Street, Philadelphia, PA19103, USA, www.freemansauction.com: 29 a, 32 a, 36 a, 39 al, 72 b © FLC/ADAGP, Paris and DACS, London 2009, 131 b, 157 al, 164 a & bl, 165 © ARS, NY and DACS, London 2009, 205 a, 259 al

Barry Friedman Ltd 515 West 26th Street, New York, NY 10001, USA, www.barryfriedmanltd.com, courtesy Dr Frank Schneider, Nevada: 254 b

Gallery 1930 Susie Cooper 18 Church Street, London NW8 8EP, UK, www.susiecooperceramics.com: 91 ar, 277 al & cl

Gallery 532 142 Duane Street, New York, NY 10013, USA, www.gallery532.com: 33 bl

Monsieur Yves Gastou 12 rue Bonaparte, 75006 Paris, France, www.galerieyvesgastou.com: 100 bl, 101 br

Thos W M Gaze & Son Diss Auction Rooms, Roydon Road, Diss, Norfolk IP22 4LN, UK, www.twgaze.com: 156 r in timeline, 180a, 204 bl

Getty Images 281 & 221 c in timeline, Albin Guillot/Roger Viollet 98 a, Keystone 26

David Gilhooly www.davidgilhooly.com: 258 a, 259 bl

Gorringes 15 North Street, Lewes, East Sussex BN7 2PD, UK, www.gorringes.co.uk: 133 © ADAGP, Paris and DACS, London 2009, 135

Gary Grant www.choicepieces.co.uk: 183 bl

Adrian Grater Stand 26 Admiral Vernon Arcade, 141-149 Portobello Road, London W11, UK: 177

Jeanette Hayhurst Fine Glass 32a Kensington Church Street, London W8 4HA: 125 bl, 190 a

Jaime Hayon Studio www.hayonstudio.com: 262 ar, 272 bl

Heller Gallery photo Spencer Tsai: 268 a

Galerie Marianne Heller Friedrich-Ebert-Anlage 2, 69117 Heidelberg, Germany, www.galerie-heller.de: 260 cr

WG Herr Art & Auction House Friesenwall 35, 50672 Cologne, Germany, www.herr-auktionen.de: 218 a, 242 br © ADAGP, Paris and DACS, London 2009

Hi + Lo Modern www.hiandlomodern.com: 176 br © DACS 2009, 182 al, 194 a, 196 bc

Mark Hill Collection 54 bl, 116 a, 192 br, 193, 197 br

Holsten Galleries Elm Street, Stockbridge, Mass 01262, USA, www.holstengalleries.com: 266 bl, 270 cr, 271 bc & bl

Courtesy of The Huntington Library, Art Collections, and Botanical Gardens, San Marino, California 30-31

Huxtins www.huxtins.com: 156 c in timeline

In Kinsky Palais Kinsky, Freyung 4, A-1010 Wien, Austria, www.palais-kinsky.com: 13 bl in timeline, 20 a, 71 al & bl, 78 bl, 200 br

John Jesse 4 blb, 127, 130 a & cr, 140 ar, 150 al

Joel Australia 333 Malvern Rd, South Yarra, Victoria 3141, Australia, www.joelaustralia.com.au: 90 c

Auktionhaus Kaupp Schloss Sulzburg, Haupstrasse 62, 79295 Sulzburg, Germany, www.kaupp.de: 138a

Galerie Koller Hardturmstrasse 102, Postfach, 8031 Zürich, Switzerland, www.kollerauktionen.ch: 90 l in timeline

Mark Laino Mark of Time, 132 South 8th Street, Philadelphia, PA 19107, USA: 280 a

Danny Lane 19 Hythe Road, London, NW10 6RT, UK, www.dannylane.co.uk: 236 al, 243 br

Law Fine Art Ltd Ash Cottage, Ashmore Green Road, Thatcham, Berks RG18 9ER, UK, www.lawfineart.co.uk: 37 all

Lawrence's Fine Art Auctioneers The Linen Yard, South Street, Crewkerne, Somerset, TA18 8AB, UK, www.lawrences.co.uk: 90 c in timeline

Claude Lee at the Ginnel, The Ginnel Antiques Centre, off Parliament Street, Harrogate, North Yorkshire HG21 2RB, UK, www.redhouseyork.co.uk: 115 br

Lili Marleen Antiques www.lilimarleen.net: 64 bc, 96 bl, 100 br

Lyon & Turnbull Ltd 33 Broughton Place, Edinburgh EH1 3RR, UK, www.lyonandturnbull.com: 3 © ADAGP,

Paris and DACS, London 2009, 12 c in timeline, 14 a, 17 & 12 r in timeline, 32 br, 61 bc, 68 b © DACS 2009, 77 cl & b, 78 br, 89 © ADAGP, Paris and DACS, London 2009, 91 bl in timeline, 104 cl & bl, 115 a & bl, 134 br, 136 ac, 157 c, 162 b, 198 a, 204 br, 215, 238 c, 241 b

Made in Design www.madeindesign.co.uk: 280 bl

Magis Design www.magisdesign.com/www.konstantin-grcic.com: 237 bc

Mallet 141 New Bond Street, London W1S 2BS, UK, www.malletantiques.com: 125 bcl

Estudio Mariscal www.mariscal.com: 234 br © DACS 2009,

Francesca Martire F131-13, Alfies Antique Market, 13 Church Street, Marylebone, London NW8 8DT, UK: 175 ar

Mater Design www.materdesign.com: 272 cl

Galerie Maurer Kurfurstenstrasse 17, D-80799 Munich, Germany, www.galerie-objekte-maurer.de: 220 br, 222 a, 223 bl & br, 227 b, 228 br, 236 ar © DACS, London/VAGA, New York 2009, 242 al, cl & cr, 263 all, 273 a & bc

Memphis & Post www.memphis-milano.it: 226 b

Herman Miller Inc www.hermanmiller.com: 283 al

Moderne Gallery 111 North 3rd Street, Philadelphia, PA 19106, USA, www.modernegallery.com: 100 a © ADAGP, Paris and DACS, London 2009, 114 ac © ADAGP, Paris and DACS, London 2009, 140 bc, 141 bcr © ADAGP, Paris and DACS, London 2009, 148 a, 187 al

Courtesy of Moss, available at the Moss store and online at www.mossonline.com: 250 b

Alan Moss 436 Lafayette Street, New York, NY 10003, USA, www.alanmossny.com: 150 br

Lillian Nassau, LLC 220 East 57th Street, New York, NY 10022, USA, www.lilliannassau.com: 117

Marc Newson www.marc-mewson.com: 246 c, 247 ac

John Nicholsons The Auction Rooms, Longfield, Midhurst Rd, Fernhurst, Haslemere, Surrey GU27 3HA, UK, www.johnnicholsons.com: 49 cr, 134 bl, 167, 274 a

No Pink Carpet www.nopinkcarpet.com: 182 ac

Patrick Norguet www.patricknorguet.com: 273 bl

Octopus Publishing Group 94 bl, 121 a Courtesy of the Ohr-O'Keefe Museum of Art, Biloxi, MS 44, 45;

Onslows The Coach House, Manor Road, Stourpaine, Dorset DT11 8TQ, UK, www.onslows.co.uk: 34 a, 143 b, 145 b

Otford Antiques & Collectors Centre 26-28 High Street, Otford, Kent TN15 9DF, UK, www.otfordantiques.co.uk: 122 a © DACS 2009

Satyendra Pakhalé photo Schuurmans, info@corunum.com: 262 bl

Paley Studios Archive © 2006-2009 Paley Studios Ltd, photo Bruce Miller 284 a & b

Paola & Iaia Stand S057, Alfies Antiques Market, 13-25 Church Street, London NW8 8DT, UK: 182 bl

Gaetano Pesce www.gaetanopesce.com: 245 ar

Press Association Images AP 162 a

Puma www.puma.com: 223 al

Quittenbaum Theresienstrasse 60, D-80333 Munich, Germany, www.quiteenbaum.de: 6 b, 8 br, 16 c & br, 18 bc & c © DACS 2009, 19 br, 22 a, 24 bc, 25bl, 28 ac, ar, bl & bc © DACS 2009, 29 br, 33 br, 56 bl, 61 a © FLC/ADAGP, Paris and DACS, London 2009, 63 a © DACS 2009, 64 bl & br, 69 b © DACS 2009, 71 & br, 78 bl, 80 b & cbr, 101 bl, 154 a, 156 a, 170 b, 183 a, 187 ar, 196 ac, 197 a & bl, 200 acr & cr, 210 c, 211 bc, 223 ar, 225 cr & b, 227 ar, 236 ac, 237 bl & br, 239 a, 240 al, ac, bc, bl & br, 241 a, 242 al & ar, 243 bl, 249 al, ac & b, 251 cl, 264 bl & a, 267 br, 282 al & bc,

R20th Century 82 Franklin Street, New York, NY 10013, USA, www.r20thcentury.com: 168-169, 252-3, Garry Gear 230 a

David Rago Auctions 333 North Main Street, Lambertville, NJ 08530, USA, www.ragoarts.com: 5 a, 13 & 13 br in timeline, 14 bl & r, 15, 18 cl, 19 bc, 26 br and 27 b both © ARS, NY and DACS, London 2009, 32 bl, 34 bl, 35, 36 br, 39 c, 41 ar & br, 42 a, bc & br, 43, 44 all, 45 b, 50 ar & br, 51, 52 bl & ar © Jacqueline Poncelet. All rights reserved, DACS 2009, 53 al & bl, 88 b, 99 ar, 104 br, 106 b, 107, 110 a, 114 bl, 118 c, 119, 120 a, bc, bl & br all © ADAGP, Paris and DACS, London 2009, 121 bl © ADAGP, Paris and DACS, London 2009, 124 al, 125 a & br, 151 b, 166 a, 172 al, bl & cl, 200 c, 203 b, 208 l, 210 a, 211 a, 214 b, 219, 220 br in timeline, 224, 225 a, 226 a, 229 al, 230, 231 ar & b, 233 ar & b, 234 cr, 236 cr, 237a, 255 b, 256 bl & bc, 261 al & br, 264 c, 270 al & br, 282 ar & bl, 283 ac & br, 285 c & bl, 289 © Calder

Foundation, New York/DACS London 2009

R Duane Reed Gallery 4729 McPherson Ave, St Louis, MO 63108, USA, www.rduanereedgallery.com: 56 a, 257 bl & br

Rennies 47 The Old High Street, Folkestone, Kent CT20 1RN, UK, www.rennart.co.uk 213

Rex Features Jonathan Hordle 75 a, Sipa Press 232 a, Tony Larkin 276 a

Geoffrey Robinson Stand FO77-78 & GO91-2, Alfies Antiques Market, 13-25 Church Street, London NW8 8DT, UK: 180 br, 183 br

Rosebery's 74-76 Knight's Hill, West Norwood, London SE27 0JD, UK, www.roseberys.co.uk: 114 bc, 140 ac, 141 br, 273 br

Scala, Florence Digital image, The Museum of Modern Art, New York 251b, 276 b

The Silver Fund 472 Jackson Street, San Francisco, CA 94111, USA, www.thesilverfund.com: 81 all, 199, 200 a

Skinner 63 Park Plaza, Boston, MA 012116, USA, www.skinnerinc.com: 12 ar, 16 ar, 22 br, 29 bl © DACS 2009, 39 ar, 60 cl, 78 cr, 155, 173 b, 202 bl © Calder Foundation, New York/DACS London 2009, 239 bl, 240 cl, 261 bl

Sollo Rago Modern Auctions 333 North Main Street, Lambertville, NJ 08530, USA, www.ragoarts.com: 7, 8 a © DACS 2009, 9 bl © ADAGP, Paris and DACS, London 2009, 9 br, 19 ar, 20 br, 26 bl © ARS, NY and DACS, London 2009, 32 c, 33 a & bc, 34 br, 38, 39 bl & br, 40 a & b, 41 al, cl & cr & bl, 46 bl, 47, 49 cl, 50 bl, 52 al, cl, cr, & br; 53 ar & br, 60 br in timeline © DACS 2009, 62 b & 63 cl both © DACS 2009, 69 a & c both © DACS 2009, 70 b, 73 al, bl & br all © ADAGP, Paris and DACS, London 2009, 74 bla & br, 76 b, 77 a, 79 a & br, 84 c, 85, 92 bl, 94 b © ADAGP, Paris and DACS, London 2009, 102-103, 104 a & cr, 105 bl & br, 106 a & c, 126 a & b, 128 bl, 129 © ADAGP, Paris and DACS, London 2009, 130 br, 131 a, 138 bl & br, 140 l, 141 bl, 149, 150 a, 156 l in timeline, 157 b © ARS, NY and DACS, London 2009, 160-161, 163 all, 164 br, 166 b, 171, 172 ar & br, 173 a & cl, 174 b, 175 bl & br, 178 br & a © Succession Picasso/DACS 2009, 179, 184 b, 187 bl & bc, 201 a, bl, bcl & br, 202 a & br, 203 a © ARS, NY and DACS, London 2009, 206 a, bl & br © ADAGP, Paris and DACS, London 2009, 207, 208 a & r, 209 l & r, 210 cl, cr & b all, 211 bl & br, 214 cl, 220 bl, 221 a & b, 227 al & c, 229 ar, 231 al, cl & r, 233 cl, 234 cl, 235 ar & b, 236 cl, 237 a, 239 br, 240 ar, 243 a & bc, 244 b, 247 al, ar & b, 249 cl & cr, 255 al, ar, cl & cr, 256 al, ac, ar, br, cl & cr © Artists' Legacy Foundation/DACS, London/VAGA, New York 2009, 257 cl & bc, 259 ar, cl, cr, bl & br, 260 a, cl, bl & br, 261 ac & ar, 266 ar, 267 b, 268 br, 270 ac, 271 a & bl, 272 br, 274 bl, bc & br, 275, 282 ac, c & br, 283 bl, 285 al, ar, & br, 288 bl

Sotheby's London 34-35 New Bond Street, London W1A 2AA, UK, www.sothebys.com: 234 bl, 236 br, 246 b, 265 br

Sotheby's Paris Galerie Charpentier, 76 rue du Faubourg, Saint Honore, Paris 75008, France: 101 a © ADAGP, Paris and DACS, London 2009

Sotheby's New York 1334 York Avenue, New York, NY 10021, USA, www.sothebys.com: 5b © DACS 2009, 49 b, 60 cr, 80 bcl

Starck Network www.starck.com: 232 bl

Swann Galleries Image Library 104 East 25th Street, New York, NY 10010, USA, www.swanngalleries.com: 60a, 82 all, 90 r in timeline, 91 bc & r in timeline, 94 a, 142 a © ADAGP, Paris and DACS, London 2009, 143 a, 144 ar & b, 145 a, 146 ar © ADAGP, Paris and DACS, London 2009, 147, 157 r in timeline, 212 a & bl, 286 a & bl, 287 a

Kerry Taylor Auctions Unit 25C, Parkhall Road Trading Estate, 40 Martell Road, Dulwich, London, SE21 8EN, UK, www.kerrytalorauctions.com: 148 br

Tecta Sohnreystrasse 10, D-37697 Lauenförde, Germany, www.tecta.de: 60 bl in timeline, 66 bl © DACS 2009

Tendo Mokko 1-3-10 Midaregawa, Tendo, Yamagata, Japan, www.tendo-mokko.co.jp: 173 cr, 238 al

Tennants The Auction Centre, Leyburn, North Yorkshire DL8 5SG, UK, www.tennants.co.uk: 36 bl, 65, 75 b, 128 ar, 136 ar

These Old Jugs www.theseoldjugs.com: 42 bl

Timorous Beasties Image courtesy of www.timorousbeasties.com: 288 br

TioGruppen Image courtesy of 10-gruppen/Ten Swedish Designers AB: 288 a

Tom Dixon www.tomdixon.net: 277 ar, cr, bl & br

TopFoto Alinari 151 a, 224 a

Twentieth Century Marks Whitegates, Rectory Road, Little Burstead, Billericay Essex CM12 9TR, UK, www.20thcenturymarks.co.uk: 200 bl, 214 a

Undercurrents 28 Cowper Street, London EC2A 4AS, UK, www.undercurrents.biz: 124 br, 180 bl

V&A Images, Victoria and Albert Museum 98 b

Van Sabben Appelsteeg 1-B, Hoorn, 1621 BD, Netherlands, www.vansabbenauctions.nl: 91 ar
Vectis Auctions Ltd Fleck Way, Thornaby, Stockton-on-Tees, Tyneside TS17 9JZ, UK, www.vectis.co.uk: 157 c in timeline

Venini SpA www.venini.it: 186a

Victoria Miro Courtesy of the artist and Victoria Miro Gallery, © Grayson Perry, photo Stephen Brayne 257 ar

Vitra www.vitra.com: 235 al

Von Spaeth Wilhem-Diess-Weg 13, 81927 Munich, Germany, www.glasvonspaeth.com: 186

VON ZEZSCHWITZ Kunst und Design Friedrichstrasse 1a, 80801 Munich, Germany, www.von-zezschwitz.de: 1 © FLC/ADAGP, Paris and DACS, London 2009, 8 bl, 16 bl, 18 a, bl, br & br, 20 bl, 22 bl, 23, 24 al, ar & bl, 25 a & br, 28 br, 124 ar & bl, 132 b, 137 a, 144 al, 154 b, 156 b, 157 ar, 175 al, 184 a, 187 cr & br, 196 bl, 218 b, 236 bl, 240 cr, 242 bc, 248 b, 270 ar & bl

Courtesy of the **Voulkos & Co Catalogue Project** www.voulkos.com: 254 a

Richard Wallis Antiks www.richardwallisantiks.com: 182 br

Marcel Wanders www.marcelwanders.com: 262 al

Woolley & Wallis 51-61 Castle Street, Salisbury Wiltshire SP1 3SU, www.woolleyandwallis.co.uk: 4, 24 br © DACS 2009, 46 a & br, 48 a & b, 49a, 54 a, 61 br in timeline, 90 ar, 93, 110 b, 111, 112 b, 114 br, 118 a © DACS 2009, 125 bcr, 134 a & bc, 136 cl, bl & br, 137 b, cl & cr, 139, 178 bl, 182 ar, 188 bl, 191, 205 b

Zanotta www.zanotta.it: 79 bl, 157 bl in timeline, 164 c, 238 ar

Zeitgeist Interiors www.zeitgeist-i.com: 196

Glossary of Marks
Beverley Stand G023-25, Alfies Antique Market, 13 Church Street, Marylebone, London, NW8 8DT, UK; **Auktionshaus Bergmann** Möhrendorfer Strasse 4, 91056 Erlangen, Germany, www.auktion-bergmann.de; **Cheffins**, Clifton House, 1 & 2 Clifton Road, Cambridge CB1 7EA, UK, www.cheffins.co.uk; **Clevedon Salerooms**, The Auction Centre, Kenn Road, Kenn, Clevedon, Bristol, BS21 6TT, UK, www.clevedon-salerooms.com; **Delorenzo** 956 Madison Avenue, New York, NY 10021, USA, www.delorenzogallery.com; **Dorotheum** Dorotheergasse 17, 1010 Vienna, Austria, www.dorotheum.com; **David Rago Auctions** 333 North Main Street, Lambertville, NJ 08530, USA, www.ragoarts.com; **The End of History** 548½ Hudson Street, New York, NY 10014,

USA; **Fragile Design** 14-5 The Custard Factory, Digbeth, Birmingham B9 4AA, UK, www.fragiledesign.com; **Auktionshaus Dr Fischer** Trappensee-Schößchen, D-74074 Heilbronn, Germany, www.auctions-fischer.de; Thos **W M Gaze & Son** Diss Auction Rooms, Roydon Road, Diss, Norfolk IP22 4LN, UK, www.twgaze.com; **Geoffrey Diner Gallery**, 1730 21st Street NW, Washington, DC 20009, USA www.dinergallery.com; **Gary Grant** www.choicepieces.co.uk; **Gorringes** 15 North Street, Lewes, East Sussex BN7 2PD, UK, www.gorringes.co.uk; **Hi + Lo Modern** www.hiandlomodern.com; **Lyon & Turnbull Ltd** 33 Broughton Place, Edinburgh EH1 3RR, UK, www.lyonandturnbull.com; **Law Fine Art Ltd** Ash Cottage, Ashmore Green Road, Thatcham, Berks RG18 9ER, UK, www.lawfineart.co.uk; **mid20c** 530 Oxford Road, Reading RG30 1EG, UK, www.mid20c.co.uk; **Manic Attic**, Stand S48/49, Alfies Antiques Market, 13 Church Street, London NW8 8DT, UK; **Macklowe Gallery** 667 Madison Avenue, New York, NY 10021, USA 667 Madison Avenue, New York, NY 10021, USA; **Mark Hill Collection; Moderne Gallery**, 111 North 3rd Street, Philadelphia, PA 19106, USA, www.modernegallery.com; **Rosebery's** 74-76 Knight's Hill, West Norwood, London SE27 0JD, UK, www.roseberys co.uk; **Gallery 1930 Susie Cooper** 18 Church Street, Marylebone, London NW8 8EP, UK, www.susiecooperceramics.com; **Sollo Rago Modern Auctions** 333 North Main Street, Lambertville, NJ 08530, USA, www.ragoarts.com; **The Silver Fund** 472 Jackson Street, San Francisco, CA 94111, USA, www.thesilverfund.com; **Sotheby's** 34-35 New Bond Street, London W1A 2AA, UK, www.sothebys.com; *These Old Jugs*, 420 Adams Street, Annapolis, Maryland, 21403 USA www.theseoldjugs.com; **Undercurrents** 28 Cowper Street, London EC2A 4AS, UK, www.undercurrents.biz; **Woolley & Wallis** 51-61 Castle Street, Salisbury Wiltshire SP1 3SU, UK, www.woolleyandwallis.co.uk.

Publisher's Acknowledgements

We would like to thank the following people for the substantial contributions they have made to the production of this book.
The writers who contributed text: Marc Allum, Katy Armstrong, Jill Bace, Will Farmer, Chrissie Masters, Alycen Mitchell, and Anna Southgate.
The consultants who shared their expertise, especially: Keith Baker; Dr Graham Dry of VON ZEZSCHWITZ Kunst und Design, Munich; Mark Hill at Miller's Publications; David Rago of The Rago Arts and Auction Center, Lambertville, New Jersey; Nick Vinson, Special Projects Director, Wallpaper* magazine.
For their invaluable help, thanks also go to: Anthony Barnes at The Rago Arts and Auction Center, Lambertville, New Jersey;

Lily Kane at R 20th Century, New York; Jennifer Olshin at Friedman Benda Gallery, New York; photographer Graham Rae; and at Mitchell Beazley: Peter Hunt, Susan Meldrum, Pene Parker, Danielle Shaw and Tracey Smith.

Jacket images

Inside front: Charles and Ray Eames 'La Chaise', Dorotheum, Vienna.
Front jacket
Top row: Paul Evans sculpture, Rago Arts and Auction Center, Lambertville, NJ; Loetz Witwe coupe, by Maria Licarz, Rago Arts and Auction Center, Lambertville, NJ; Dennis Mitchell 'Sawanna' sculpture, John Nicholson's, Fernhurst, Surrey; George Nakashima walnut table, Freeman's, Philadelphia.
Second row: Howard Kottler 'Lemon Punch Pot', Rago Arts and Auction Center, Lambertville, NJ; Charles and Ray Eames 'DAW' chair, Quittenbaum, Munich; Dino Martens Aureliano Toso 'Oriente' vase, Quittenbaum, Munich; Paul Evans 'Sculptural Front' cabinet, Rago Arts and Auction Center, Lambertville, NJ; Sofa inspired by Salvador Dali's 'Mae West Lips' sofa, Rago Arts and Auction Center, Lambertville, NJ.
Third row: Arne Jacobsen 'Swan' chair, Skinner Inc, Boston; Flavio Poli vase designed for Seguso Vetri d'Arte, VON ZEZSCHWITZ Kunst and Design, Munich; Walter Dorwin Teague/Polaroid Corporation executive desk lamp, Rago Arts and Auction Center, Lambertville, NJ; pair of Frank Gehry wiggle chairs, Skinner Inc, Boston; Geoffrey Baxter for Whitefriars 'Banjo' vase, Graham Cooley Collection.
Fourth row: American chromed metal satellite table lamp, Skinner Inc, Boston; Charles and Ray Eames 'ESU 400' storage unit, Rago Arts and Auction Center, Lambertville, NJ; Ettore Sottsass 'Westside' chair, Bonhams, Edinburgh; Joseff Hoffman Wiener Werkstatte centerpiece, Rago Arts and Auction Center, Lambertville, NJ; Viktor Schreckengost for Cowan 'Jazz Bowl', Rago Arts and Auction Center, Lambertville, NJ;
Back jacket
Top row: Charles and Ray Eames 'DAW' chair, Quittenbaum, Munich; Dino Martens Aureliano Toso 'Oriente' vase, Quittenbaum, Munich; Paul Evans 'Sculptural Front' cabinet, Rago Arts and Auction Center, Lambertville, NJ; Sofa inspired by Salvador Dali's 'Mae West Lips' sofa, Rago Arts and Auction Center, Lambertville, NJ.
Bottom row: George Nakashima walnut lounge chair, Rago Arts and Auction Center, Lambertville, NJ; Michele de Lucchi prototype 'First' stool, Rago Arts and Auction Center, Lambertville, NJ.
Inside back: Alessandro Pianon glass and metal Pulcini Bird sculpture, for Vistosi Glassworks, Skinner Inc, Boston.